The Ideal Refugees

Gender, Culture, and Politics in the Middle East
miriam cooke, Suad Joseph, and Simona Sharoni, *Series Editors*

Other titles in Gender, Culture, and Politics in the Middle East

The Ideal Refugees

Gender, Islam, and the Sahrawi Politics of Survival

Elena Fiddian-Qasmiyeh

SYRACUSE UNIVERSITY PRESS

Library of Congress Cataloging-in-Publication Data
Available on request from publisher.

This book is dedicated with love to
Yousif M. Qasmiyeh and Bissan-Maria Fiddian-Qasmiyeh
and to my grandparents, Eric and Margery Fiddian.

Elena Fiddian-Qasmiyeh is Departmental Lecturer in Forced Migration at the Refugee Studies Centre, University of Oxford, and Junior Research Fellow in Refugee Studies at Lady Margaret Hall. Between 2010 and 2012, Elena was the Director of the International Summer School in Forced Migration at the University of Oxford.

Contents

Illustrations and Maps

Photographs and Images

Maps

Tables

Acknowledgments

THIS BOOK is the outcome of a multisited research effort funded by the Economic and Social Research Council (2005–9). My analysis has benefited from consultations with and feedback from various audiences, including during seminars and conferences at the Universities of Cambridge and Oxford, and the Council for British Research in the Levant. In particular, Dawn Chatty, Cathie Lloyd, and Michael Willis (all at the University of Oxford), in addition to Deniz Kandiyoti (School of Oriental and African Studies, University of London) provided helpful feedback on earlier versions of this book. I also thank my parents, Maria del Carmen Mendez Fernandez and Robin Fiddian, for reading all that I have presented before them. Emma Tobin, Bramble Coppins and Margaret Hauser provided invaluable editorial assistance, part of which was funded through an Oppenheimer Publication Grant awarded by the Oxford Department of International Development (University of Oxford). At Syracuse University Press, I am grateful to the series editors, Mary Selden Evans and Suzanne Guiod for supporting and commissioning this project; and to Marcia Hough, Lisa Renee Kuerbis, Victoria Lane, and Kay Steinmetz for all of their help over the past few years.

My most sincere gratitude is due to Yousif M. Qasmiyeh, for his patience, consistent support, and enduring friendship, especially in the wonderful months following Bissan-Maria's arrival. Neither this book nor I would be half of what we are today without his encouragement and constant demands that I strive to improve both my work and myself.

Acronyms and Abbreviations

Acronyms

AU	African Union
CEAS	Coordinadora Estatal de Asociaciones Solidarias con el Sahara (State Coordinator of Associations in Solidarity with the Sahara)
ECHO	European Community Humanitarian Office
FEDISSAH	Federación Estatal de Instituciones Solidarias con el Pueblo Saharaui (Spain's state federation of institutions, which are "in solidarity" with the Sahrawi people)
HRW	Human Rights Watch
INGO	international nongovernmental organization
MENA	Middle East and North Africa
MINURSO	UN Mission for the Referendum in the Western Sahara
NGO	nongovernmental organization
NUSW	National Union of Sahrawi Women
OAU	Organization of African Unity
Polisario Front	Popular Front for the Liberation of Saguiat el-Hamra and Río de Oro: the Sahrawi military and political liberation movement founded by students in 1973. Known in Spanish as the Frente Polisario
SADR	Sahrawi Arab Democratic Republic
SARC	Research Project: Children and Adolescents in Sahrawi and Afghani Refugee Households: Living with the Effects of Prolonged Armed Conflict and Forced Migration

SRC   Sahrawi Red Crescent
UJSARIO   Youth Union of Saguiat el-Hamra and Río de Oro;
               known by its Spanish acronym (Unión de Jóvenes de
               Saguiat el-Hamra y Río de Oro)
UN   United Nations
UNGA   United Nations General Assembly
UNHCR   United Nations High Commission for Refugees
VAW   Violence Against Women
WFP   World Food Programme

Abbreviations

fem. sing.   feminine singular
fem. pl.   feminine plural
m. sing.   masculine singular
m. pl.   masculine plural
n.d.   no date
n.a.   no author
undef.   undefined
def.   defined

The Ideal Refugees

Introduction

The "Ideal" Refugees

THE "UNIQUENESS" and social superiority of Sahrawi refugees over "other refugees" have been systematically proclaimed by Western academics and representatives of nongovernmental organizations (NGO) since the establishment of the Algerian-based Sahrawi refugee camps in 1975 and 1976. Based on her 15-day visit to the camps in 1981, Harrell-Bond's work on the Sahrawi (1981a/b, 1986, and 1999) has often been quoted and referenced in subsequent accounts of the camps. In *Imposing Aid* (1986), a seminal book that prompted a major shift in the way that refugees and refugee camps around the world are perceived and dealt with by aid providers and academics, she labels the Sahrawi camps a "success story" amid a failing humanitarian system that creates "dependency syndrome" among refugees (see also Voutira and Harrell-Bond 2000, 66). Further, under the heading "The 'ideal' refugee" in a 1999 chapter that relies on the same 1981 trip to the camps, Harrell-Bond writes:

> I proceeded to tell them [the Sudanese refugee committee] about *the "good" Saharawi* who lived under much worse conditions than they did, but who were reluctant to complain. (1999, 151; my emphasis)

The notions of "successful" camps and of "ideal" and "good" refugees have continued to dominate mainstream accounts of the Sahrawi refugee context, with Brazier referring to the Sahrawi camps as "the best run refugee camps in the world" (1997, 14). Lippert (1987) and San-Martín (2005) also both cite a Red Cross field representative who described the Sahrawi

1

in the 1980s as "the most unusual refugees" by virtue of their uncorrupt social organization, solidarity and coordination among themselves.

One major characteristic commonly invoked to substantiate claims that the Sahrawi are "the 'ideal' refugees" is their egalitarian approach to gender relations and the position of "Sahrawi women" in the camps. Hence, Harrell-Bond reports that Sahrawi refugees' political representatives, the Polisario Front, built "a twentieth-century democratic nation, women's equality being one of the strongest features of their social organization" (1999, 156), and that "[w]omen's equality was a most dominant theme of life in the Sahrawi camps" (quoted in Indra 1999a, 44). Equally, Oxfam's desk officer in the mid-1980s wrote that

> [p]erhaps the most impressive thing about Sahrawi society is that it is the most fundamentally balanced society I have ever come across in terms of the relationships between men and women. (Mowles 1986, 9)

This book examines the protracted Sahrawi refugee context (1975 to the present) through an analysis of the motivations behind and implications of such widespread representations of Sahrawi refugee women as "ideal," "free," "secular," and "unique." Specifically, I examine how and why Sahrawi refugee women are portrayed by their political representatives (the Polisario) and its associated National Union of Sahrawi Women (NUSW) to different audiences, how the identity of the audience relates to the nature of the representation unveiled, and what the implications are of these representations both for the terms of engagement between the Polisario and camp inhabitants with different audiences and for those living in the camps themselves.

In essence, I argue that gendered images and concepts have been strategically mobilized by the Polisario to secure the humanitarian and political support of Western state and nonstate actors that ensure the continued survival of the camps and their inhabitants. Indeed—while refugees and their representatives are habitually under the critical gaze of foreign visitors and funders and aid is often "conditional" or "tied" to certain provisos (such as "democratization" or the usage of funds for specified purposes)—the case under consideration demonstrates the extent to which such observations are multidirectional (cf. Foucault 1979, 203).

Hence, I propose that the Polisario has recognized the extent to which being perceived to be "ideal" refugees, directly associated with being "democratic," "secular," and "promoting women's equality" attracts the attention and support of Western academics, NGOs, and civil society and solidarity networks. They have in turn projected a specific image of the camps to ensure these actors' continued support, just as other aid recipients have done elsewhere (cf. Conklin 1997; Bob 2005). In this respect, the Polisario transcends its enforced status as the "observed" (i.e., under international scrutiny) and rather simultaneously becomes an "observer of its own observers" (i.e., the West or the Middle East), and of its own "observed" (the inhabitants of the refugee camps).

The creation and representation of Sahrawi women and men as the "ideal" refugees, and more specifically of Sahrawi society as "the most fundamentally balanced society . . . ever come across" (op. cit.), thus emerges as an indispensable part of the foundation upon which the international solidarity network that maintains the camps is based. This transcends Gandolfi's suggestion (1989) that the Polisario has internalized an image of Sahrawi women as strong and independent that is related more to a "desire" and "an ideal projection" than to something that existed during the colonial period (1884–1975) itself. More specifically, I hold that the hegemonic rhetoric vis-à-vis independent, strong, and secular Sahrawi women is part of the "politics of survival" developed by the Polisario and is indicative of power relations within and between different groups in the camps and other spheres.

Indeed, I maintain that the transnational political and humanitarian networks upon which the camps are based have a direct impact on the ways in which gendered identities and expectations are constructed and projected within the Sahrawi refugee camps and beyond. Specific representations of "Sahrawi women" developed and reproduced by the Polisario and non-Sahrawi observers thus reflect specific power dynamics between Sahrawi and non-Sahrawi men and women. In this sense, I aim to reveal the international nature of specific contemporary representations, idealizations, and manipulations of gender and imagined gender relations in the Sahrawi camps. Beyond local or "national" power dynamics and interplays between different groups in the camps, Sahrawi gender relations (both real and imagined) are also directly implicated in, affected by, and ensure the continuity of essential international solidarity and aid networks and power structures. In this way, Sahrawi gender relations are "constructed" not only in light of interactions between men and women within a specific refugee camp, but are also derived from social, political and humanitarian interactions on an international scale. Viewing the protracted Sahrawi refugee situation through a gendered lens therefore allows us both to situate the positions of Sahrawi men, women, and children in the camps and to identify the ways in which ideas about gender mediate connections on/between local and international levels.

Representations of Gender and Gendered Representations

Through their "role of bearers of cultural values, carriers of traditions, and symbols of the community," Moghadam argues that

> the representation of women assumes political significance, and certain images of women define and demarcate political groups, cultural projects, or ethnic communities. Women's behaviour and appearance . . . come to be defined by, and are frequently the subject of political or cultural objectives of political movements, states and leaderships. (1994, 2)

As Moghadam suggests, the representation of gendered identities or characteristics is based upon an "interpretive" process throughout which "[s]ome manipulation or transformation is unavoidable" (Bonner and Goodman 1992, 2). Far from reflecting "reality," the precise terms with which individuals and groups are described and portrayed will not only depend upon the interpretive processes of those who produce representations and purport to "speak for" Others but also on the identity of the particular audience(s) being addressed. Hence, the weakened, dependent, and victimized "womenandchildren" (Enloe 1990 and 1991) who populate mainstream accounts of complex emergencies and forced displacement (Malkki 1995a, 11; Nordstrom 1999, 65) are central to NGO campaigns designed to obtain political and humanitarian support from civil societies and states for different "causes" in contexts of complex emergencies (Ng 1997, 155; Nordstrom 1999, 65).

In the regional context of the Middle East and North Africa (MENA), the symbolic significance given to Muslim women in times of war and peace has in particular been explored by analysts in relation to a variety of colonial and postcolonial contexts. Indeed, Muslim women are habitually the most readily identifiable representatives of Arab Muslim communities, and their symbolic roles become increasingly politicized in periods of conflict and displacement (Afshar et al. 2005; Bahramitash 2005; Zine 2006). Building upon Fanon's work (in particular his seminal piece "Algeria Unveiled" (1965) first published in 1959) and Said's *Orientalism* (1979), gendered postcolonial studies of the MENA region concentrate on various forms of and motivations for interconnected representations of the national and gendered Self and Other (Yeğenoğlu 1998; Lewis 1995; Abu-Lughod 1998a/b, 2001, 2002). Much of this work explores and critiques "the metonymic association between the Orient and its women, or more precisely the *representation* of woman as tradition and as the essence of the Orient" (Yeğenoğlu 1998, 99; my emphasis).

Fanon's identification and analysis of French colonizers' "precise political doctrine" to "unveil" Algerian women as a means of conquering the colonized society (Fanon 1965, 37–38) has been the foundation of postcolonial work that has examined Orientalist representations of the veil[1] and the extent to which unveiling women has frequently become a "convenient instrument for signifying many issues at once, that is, the construction of modern [national] identity" (Yeğenoğlu 1998, 132). In certain historical contexts,[2] the veil has "carried connotations of Muslim backwardness" both in the eyes of Western Orientalists and MENA nationalists (ibid.). Indeed, as stressed by Kandiyoti (1991) and Yeğenoğlu (1998, 135) with reference to Atatürk's reforms in Turkey, processes of unveiling women as a means of demonstrating the "marginalization" or

1. Including Lewis 2003, El-Guindi 2003, and Woodhull 2003.

2. It is important to note that the character of nationalism, and the symbols used, change according to the context and the power dynamics underlying this (following Chaterjee, as discussed in Cole and Kandiyoti 2002, 189).

displacement of Islam have historically been central to the development of "secular" modern nationalist discourses.

While "secularism" is a much-debated concept and political project, it is crucial to note that "secularism is not an absence of religion" nor must it be "antagonistic to religion" (Warner 2007, 210). Rather, secularism is "a specific cultural formation in its own right" (ibid), with the processes of secularization altering the *position* of religious institutions and shifting the acceptable *spaces* available for religious practice and performance in a given sociopolitical landscape. Processes of secularization, understood here as the process of religion becoming and remaining a *private* matter (e.g., Asad 2001 and 2006, 494; also see Hann 2000), are often deeply intertwined with gendered representations and representations of gender that are in turn related to geopolitical dynamics. For instance, as international and national normative preferences for the development of a "good" and "progressive" Islam have been solidified throughout different periods of history, gender relations and symbols such as the veil have played a central role in defining the characteristics of "good" forms of "secular Islam" (see also Fiddian-Qasmiyeh 2011a). In addition to the aforementioned historical campaigns to unveil colonized Algerian women and Turkish women under Atatürk, contemporary cases, such as that of France, continue to reveal that

> the qualities of "secular Muslims" were equated with peace, justice, liberty, *laïcité*, freedom of conscience, freedom of speech, individual freedom, free will, the reform of Islam, *absolute equality in rights between men and women*, and inter-religious dialogue. (Mas 2006, 596; my emphasis)

The association of secularism with unveiling and the promotion of "absolute equality in rights between men and women" is arguably established and reproduced as a means of countering Orientalist constructions of Muslim cultures, in which "the harem, the veil and polygamy were highly charged symbols and they all functioned as synonyms of female oppression" (Yeğenoğlu 1998, 100). Indeed, Almond notes that,

> [a]mong Muslim female writers, the most frequently encountered objection against Western feminism is one of ethnocentrism: a number of

European and American theorists, it is alleged, simply devote their attention to chadors, polygamy and honour-crimes. (2007, 134)

Such objections parallel the challenges posed by Mohanty and Spivak, who have respectively demanded that Western feminist scholarship reject and deconstruct monolithic images of "third world women" (Mohanty 1988) and that white feminists challenge their own essentialist assumptions that "third world" women are, as a homogenized whole, subjugated, secluded, illiterate, and violated by their husbands and families (Spivak 1990, 1993b).[3] The body of work produced by postcolonial feminists has provided insights into the ways in which representations of women are connected to systems of domination and subordination on national and transnational levels (see Hyndman 2000 and Abu-Lughod 2002). For instance, Nzenza (quoting Alcoff) highlights one such element by stressing that "the practice of privileged people speaking for or on behalf of less privileged persons has actually 'resulted [in many cases] in increasing or reinforcing the oppression of the group spoken for'" (1997, 222).

The core of this book develops around a particular set of idealized claims regarding Sahrawi refugee women that I have identified as being repeatedly represented by the Polisario Front to specific non-Sahrawi audiences. In direct contrast to mainstream accounts—which habitually re/create "the refugee" as a generic and essentialized figure, either as *madonnalike* figures (Malkki 1992, 33, and 1996, 389) or as weakened, dependent, and victimized "womenandchildren" (Enloe 1990 and 1991)— Sahrawi women are presented by the Polisario to their Western observers as empowered and liberated women; they are primordial, almost omnipresent, in visual and textual representations of camp life not as victims but rather as key agents, who, to a large extent, appear to overshadow their male compatriots (Figure 1).

This representation of the Sahrawi case could be seen as both taking up the challenge posed by Mohanty and Spivak, and supporting material

---

3. While recognizing the limitations of the terms "West" and "Western," for ease of reference I use this term to refer primarily to Western Europe and North America.

1. Photograph taken during a "parade" held in Smara refugee camp, one of the four main Sahrawi refugee camps in southwest Algeria. The parade was organized for non-Sahrawis visiting the camps during the 2007 NUSW Conference (April 2007).

produced by feminist analysts determined to examine both the positive and the negative impacts of war and exile on gender relations (i.e., Indra 1999b, 16–21; Kumar 2001a, 21, and 2001b, 215ff.). It has been suggested that, since men may be involved in the military and may therefore be absent from civilian settlements, patriarchal structures are often eroded during conflict, and women thus adopt roles and responsibilities previously monopolized by men (see, for example, O'Barr 1985, 23–35; El-Bushra and Mukarubuga 1995; Byrne 1996; Sorensen 1998; Kumar 2001a, esp. 7 and 21).

Some of these analysts specifically call for aid provided during times of conflict to counter "not merely the harmful effects of conflict, but also to transform gender relations by seizing opportunities for women's advancement" (Kumar 2001b, 221). Indeed, as Moghadam and Kandiyoti remind us, gender equality and female participation are among the noneconomic "conditionalities" prioritized by Western NGOs and "mainstreamed" by the "new development agenda" (Moghadam 1997b, 36; Kandiyoti, in Hammami 2005, 1352; also Fiddian-Qasmiyeh, 2010d).

Rather than Sahrawi women being assigned secondary roles in accounts of this protracted refugee situation (as Massad 1995 indicates is the case in texts pertaining to Palestinian nationalism) or treating Sahrawi nationalism as a political movement that "fails women" (as Abu-Lughod 1998b, 17, stresses is often the case), common representations of the Sahrawi refugee camps emphasize and reemphasize women's significance as social and political actors (cf. Nzenza 1997, 218). Referring to women's visibility and centrality in social and political life in the camps (including that given to women in Article 41 of the 1999 Sahrawi Constitution),[4] this "positive" impact of the protracted refugee situation is one aspect that has acquired the status of conventional wisdom in the Sahrawi context both over time (from 1975 to the present) and over space (from the camps to audiences based in the West).

However, just as the politics and multiple motivations behind representations of victimized refugee "womenandchildren" discussed above have been challenged and critiqued, so too must the externally projected portrayal of Sahrawi women as ideal, empowered, and unique refugee women (also see Fiddian-Qasmiyeh 2009). Rather than taking the Sahrawi as an example that unequivocally supports the notion of refugee camps providing space for positive change, it is necessary to ask why this particular representation has been adopted and reproduced with such ease and precisely how and why it has been naturalized and become part of "the regime of the 'taken-for-granted'" (Hall 1985, 105 in Laffey and

---

4. This reads: *"L'État oeuvre à la promotion de la femme et à sa participation politique, économique, sociale et culturelle dans la construction de la société et le développement du pays."*

Weldes 2004, 28; also, Bourdieu 1985, 729). Indeed, as Abu-Lughod stresses regarding the Middle East,

> we have to remind ourselves that although negative images of women or gender relations in the region are certainly to be deplored, offering positive images or "nondistorted" images will not solve the basic problem . . . about the production of knowledge in and for the West. (2001, 105)

The way in which Sahrawi women have been placed in the "national" (i.e., Polisario) and international eye must therefore be examined in order to determine how and why the (primarily male) political representatives have developed what I term a *gynocentric* (i.e., female-centered) policy of international relations directed, specifically, to certain Western audiences.

The consistent repetition of a selected range of oral and written statements and specific visual images pertaining to "the situation of Sahrawi women in the camps" can be considered to be a coherent body that may be classified as a "discourse." I identify this particular discourse as an "archive" formed by accumulation and repetition (Foucault 1989, 25), which in this case may be viewed as embodying a source of "knowledge" to be consulted by and transmitted to both Sahrawis and non-Sahrawis. By discourse in this context, I refer to an interconnected body of specific meanings, concepts and images produced by social actors for specific audiences, for particular (often political) purposes. Indeed, Eagleton holds that discourse is "social action": while it may purport to describe the world in a specific way, its primary function is performative, as it uses language to bring about particular effects in the observer (1983, 118). The contexts in which discourses are produced and projected are therefore essential, with Ricoeur conceptualizing discourse as an "event" (1976), which is situated in a particular historical moment and location.

Given that discourses may be utilized to produce specific effects in specific audiences, audiences may not be aware of, or may not identify, the author(s)' intentions or motivations for creating or enacting a particular representation. Indeed the audience's interpretation of actions, statements, or processes may be distant from these original authorial intentions, and different audiences will rarely have a common interpretation of the same scenario. On other occasions, however, the distinction between observers and reproducers of a discourse may be blurred, as is the case of individuals and groups who "read" part of the discourse and then reproduce it themselves through written and oral statements. In this manner, it is possible to speak of a "traveling discourse" (a term derived from Said's (1983) notion of "traveling theory"), in the sense of a discourse "traveling" between individuals and groups both across time and space.[5]

That the content of a discourse should be reinscribed by separate authors and actors reflects just one aspect in which, beyond the linguistic or thematic components of this body of work, discourse is "both representational and *constitutive*" (Sunderland and Litosseliti 2002, 13; my emphasis). Thus, discourse transcends language per se, by not only transmitting messages to an audience, but also creating itself as both a subject and object of reproduction (Ricoeur 1976, 9), and of study (Sunderland and Litosseliti 2002). In this book, I therefore examine a coherent set of claims and images pertaining to Sahrawi gender relations as a historically and politically based form of representation, while simultaneously exploring the implications of discourses being "practices that systematically form the objects of which they speak" (Foucault 1972/2006, 54). Since discourses "create not only knowledge but also the very reality they appear to describe" (Said 1979, 94), I argue that this particular representation has played an essential role in "creating" Western "knowledge" about life in the Sahrawi refugee camps, in turn influencing the development of policies and programs implemented there.[6]

I use the term *official discourse* with regard to this particular representation, first, to illustrate that these terms and concepts are reproduced primarily by Sahrawi individuals in positions of authority within the Polisario and/or NUSW. To an extent, this official discourse can be

---

5. On traveling memories also see Fiddian-Qasmiyeh, 2011c and 2012a.

6. Such discourses evidently also interact with and constitute Sahrawi knowledge and action in different ways and in different sociopolitical spheres. The primary focus of this book is to explore the ways in which Sahrawi refugees encourage the development and reproduction of specific discourses for particular non-Sahrawi audiences, while recognizing the extent to which such discourses are in turn formative of Sahrawi experiences and understandings of their daily lives and future plans (as discussed in Chapters 4 and 5).

related to what Anderson refers to as the "official nationalism" developed by members of sociopolitical and military elites (1991, esp. 86) for political purposes. My conceptualization of a particular set of representations of Sahrawi refugee women as an official discourse is also in line with Kandiyoti's analysis of "a form of double-speak that upholds the principle of gender equality and social inclusiveness in *official* pronouncements, while marginalizing women in the allocation of development aid" (2007b, 513; my emphasis; also Mani 1989, 88–126, and Sunder Rajan 1993). We could thus reconceptualize this discourse as being intimately related to the aims and motivations of the dominant groups in the camps, and therefore as hegemonic, or "authoritative myths" (White 1987, x; also see Darby 1997, 3).

I consider that such discursive structures are often intimately related to the "politics of survival," since these are the

> stakes, par excellence, of political struggle, the inextricably theoretical and practical struggle for power to preserve or transform the social world by preserving or transforming the categories by which it is perceived. (Bourdieu 1985, 729)

By "politics of survival," I refer to the interconnected struggles fought by the Polisario and Sahrawi refugees to ensure that support is obtained from a range of non-Sahrawi state and nonstate actors. Such support both protects refugees' continued physical existence in the camps and the physical and political survival of the camps as a "national" project. A useful framework from which to consider the nature of these struggles can be derived from the Copenhagen School of International Relations, with Mälksoo proposing that the "politics of survival"

> not merely signif[ies] the seeking of physical survival for an entity in the international arena but also refer[s] to the quest for *meaningful survival*; indeed, for survival as a certain sort of being, and the quest to be recognized as such by the "significant other(s)."(2006, 278; emphasis in the original)

Combined with their underlying demand that the Sahrawi be given the right to self-determination, the Polisario face a "quest for *meaningful survival"* as a political and national entity in the broader international arena, a quest that is directly dependent upon being "recognized as such by the 'significant other(s).'"

I argue that the potential threats to the political survival of the Sahrawi as "a people" and of the Polisario as a representative body deserving international recognition, in addition to the precarious humanitarian situation that threatens the physical survival of many Sahrawi refugees, are tied in multiple ways to the recognition that gender too "is a project which has cultural survival as its end" (Butler 1988, 522). I would go further to claim that this case study demonstrates ways in which gender can be intimately related not only to "cultural survival" but also to "political survival." Of particular interest to this analysis, Butler posits (without specific reference to periods of conflict and refugeedom) that "the term *'strategy'* better suggests the situation of duress under which gender performance always and variously occurs" (ibid). In this book I argue that the official "performance" of gender, and more importantly, what I refer to as official *repress-entations* of gender, have been strategically mobilized to obtain and maintain the humanitarian and political support of particular "significant other(s)." These repress-entations purposefully centralize certain groups, identifiers, and dynamics, while simultaneously displacing and marginalizing those that challenge official accounts of the camps.[7]

In addition to underlining the hegemonic or authoritative nature of "official" representations, since "discourses exist in relation to other discourses" (Sunderland and Litosseliti 2002, 9), these may contradict or compete with each other, at times being examples of resistance to dominant portrayals and modes of being. Indeed, Scott identifies a hierarchy of forms of resistance, highlighting that, while "everyday forms of resistance make no headlines" (1985, xvii), it is necessary to document and recognize the significance of "petty" or informal acts of resistance, along with those more explicitly and formally confrontational acts that

---

7. In Fiddian-Qasmiyeh (2014a), I also explore histories of *repress-entation* and "footnoting of Islam" in accounts of Arab migration to Cuba.

do "make the headlines."[8] It is precisely due to this a priori acknowledgement of alternatives and the potential for resistance that we must examine the bases, motivations and implications of the privileged terms of engagement and representation that underlie this externally projected official discourse itself.

It is important to stress at this stage that I do not propose that the Polisario, Sahrawi refugees, or non-Sahrawi observers of the camps rely *solely* on gendered language, images, and concepts, nor do I intend to present my analysis as an overarching explanation of the protracted refugee situation. Rather, the discursive mechanisms that I explore and critique in the following chapters exist simultaneously and in parallel with other multiple, interrelated, and often paradoxical political and representational systems that underpin the refugee situation in local and international context (Fiddian-Qasmiyeh 2011a).

A final usage of the concept of representation which grounds the analysis presented in this book relates to the role of "performance" in social encounters as demonstrated, for instance, by Goffman in his landmark work *The Presentation of Self in Everyday Life* (1959/1971). In this sense, the existence of a number of (materially and politically) powerful external observers of/in the refugee camps directly impacts the representation of the Sahrawi self to diverse non-Sahrawi others. Dramaturgical analogies have numerous limitations (as Goffman himself noted in his 1959 preface), with Conquergood (1992, 92) recognizing that such analogies may re-create "simplistic divisions of social space into front-stage areas of masking and disguise (marked by presence of performance) and backstage areas of honesty and authenticity (marked by the absence of performance)." Despite these and other potential limitations, however, I find it useful to conceptualize the dynamics within and beyond the refugee camps as those between different groups of actors and actresses representing

8. In Chapters 3 and 4 I examine the role played by representations of ideal and alternative Sahrawi gender relations and voices in the Spanish media's portrayal of life in the refugee camps, with particular reference to the case of three Sahrawi girls whose desire to stay in Spain against their parents' wishes "made the headlines."

various scripts or discourses to a series of audiences. The primary audiences referred to in this book include members of Spanish civil society and the Algerian, Cuban, South African, and Syrian states.[9]

By drawing on insights from performance and performativity studies, the analysis presented in the following chapters rejects a "binary opposition between reality and appearance" (Conquergood 1992, 84). In order to explore the multiple roles that gender and Islam may play in protracted refugee situations, it is not my primary aim to identify and understand Sahrawi refugees' purportedly real "religious identity and practice," "religious belief," or understandings of "gender relations" per se or to ascertain what specific performances are "disguising." Rather, although I do ultimately contrast the Sahrawis' official representation of secularism to Western audiences onstage, with the "religious normality" expressed and performed offstage by diverse Sahrawi actors in the absence of Western observers (Chapter 4), the following chapters primarily explore the myriad ways through which gender and religion may variously reflect and condition refugees' interactions with diverse donor audiences.

Essentially, the naturalization of the script and its component parts (which are constitutive of "an archive of knowledge" vis-à-vis women in the camps) depends upon its reiteration, repetition, and ritualization (following Butler 1993, esp. 9–12). However, it is precisely the changing identity of the audience that allows, or in fact demands, the creation and presentation of different "selves" and the adoption of different "voices" in local, national, and international contexts. Further, the roles played by the social and political actors involved vary not only in relation to the identity of the audience and other observers but also in terms of the particular arena in which their representations occur. The norms (or scripts) to be followed by refugees in the family home, local camp, "national" spaces in the camps, or in different parts of the international sphere, vary accordingly, as does the visibility of the "directors" who, in this case, can

9. See Fiddian-Qasmiyeh 2011a for an analysis of Sahrawi representations of "religious tolerance" during interactions with American Evangelists in the camps and in the United States.

be identified as the male-run Polisario. In this context, I argue that these official "directors" do not only "direct" their populations but are also involved in "directing aid."[10] It is important to note that positing a drama-turgical analogy must be contextualized by recognizing that "the fictive character of this position does not mean that it is not real; on the contrary, it produces material effects by constituting the very bodies of the subjects that it subjects" (Yeğenoğlu 1998, 3).

As a final point, it must be noted that official statements made to different audiences, including Western parties from across the political spectrum, and a range of non-Sahrawi state and nonstate actors, con-firm that, whenever possible, the Polisario and NUSW orient themselves directly to the values espoused by their defined audience. A multiplic-ity of externally projected discourses therefore exists, depending on the observers' identity. Indeed, given the size and heterogeneity of the rel-evant humanitarian and political solidarity networks, engaging with dif-ferent constituent members will require the careful modification of the "public relations" discourse to secure their interest and support. None-theless, throughout the course of my research, it has become apparent that an overarching representational mechanism has been designed when addressing, not individual constituent members or separate groups but rather a "mass audience," including the Spanish solidarity network as a whole. Hence, a common selection of images arise in media interviews with Sahrawi officials, in the camp-based "parades" organized for non-Sahrawi visitors, or during conferences attended by hundreds of foreign visitors. It is this wide-reaching discursive framework that is the primary focus of this study.

Brief History of the Western Saharan Conflict

As shall become apparent in the following pages, the identity label used in the title of this book is a matter of great legal and political conten-tion. Although the term Ṣaḥrāwi in Arabic refers to any inhabitant of the desert (ṣaḥra'), it is most frequently used in the West as an umbrella term

---

10. The contrast with Harrell-Bond's *Imposing Aid* (1986) is purposeful.

to refer to those individuals who belong to specific tribes[11] that have traditionally lived in and moved throughout the territory currently defined as the Western Sahara. This usage is relatively recent, emerging toward the end of the Spanish colonial presence in the territory. In the 1970s, the term was increasingly mobilized (and arguably monopolized) by the Polisario as a political unifier and identifier for the multiple tribes that moved in and around the territory. It is, as a result, intimately related to this group's political struggles. Furthermore, given that tribal identification is the primary basis for the referendum for self-determination designed to resolve the conflict over the Western Sahara, precisely which tribes are defined as "Sahrawi" rather than "Moroccan" or "Mauritanian" is politically and legally highly significant.

Essentially, members of a tribe trace their origin back to either a common ancestor or a common point of origin, with Arabic-speaking tribes frequently being named "the sons of X" (*awlād* X, *banū* X or *abnā'* X) and Berber-speaking tribes referring to themselves as "the people of X" (*ait* X) (Abun-Nasr 1987, 12; Hart 2000, 10). With reference to the Rgaybat (arguably the most powerful and numerous of the "Sahrawi" tribes), Caratini indicates that, even though they define themselves through kinship, in reality only approximately one-third belong to the male descendants of the ancestor (Rgaybi).

The remaining members were at some point in history "adopted by the group" (1989a, 238; my translation), for instance, through incorporation via marriage. Tribal identity is always, and not solely in the case under consideration, based on a combination of both "real" and "fictive" kinship ties, and such ties can often be strategically invoked to confront political, military, and/or economic challenges, increasing the size of the tribal unit through incorporating more "common descendants" as necessary (ibid.). In this sense, I propose that it is possible to interpret the post-1970s claims of a unified "Sahrawi" supratribal identity as an extension of

11. A tribe is an organizational and identity group having social, political, and military functions and occupying a particular territory over which it has at least partial responsibility (Ahmed and Hart 1984, 1; Hart 2001, 1).

a "traditional" preexisting "politics of expansionism" and tribal "enlargement" to ensure the survival of the group(s) (ibid.).

Arab populations first arrived in northwest Africa toward the end of the seventh century AD, interacting with, and often conquering, the local Berber populations that had, in turn, arrived during the first millennium BC. Between the late fourteenth and late fifteenth centuries, a group of tribes known collectively as the *Banū Ḥassan* migrated from Yemen to the region (Norris 1962), enforcing the Arabization and Islamization of the area's Berber groups (Diego-Aguirre 1993, 104–107). These processes of migration and conquest were accompanied by intermarriage and alliances, giving rise, by the end of the seventeenth century, to "a new Arabic-speaking people, known to us today as the 'Moors,' a people of mixed ethnic origins" (Hodges 1983, 8–9). It is now widely recognized that the inhabitants of the territory of Saguiat el-Hamra y Río de Oro (now identified as the Western Sahara; see Map 1) shared "broad commonalities" with Berbers in southern Morocco and with *al-baydan* or *maures* in northern Mauritania, all of whom were camel-herding nomads with a selection of cultural practices in common and who often spoke Hassaniya Arabic (a name derived from *Banū Ḥassan*; Hodges 1987, 33).

The territory's Arab tribes were distributed among primarily nomadic groups that engaged in a range of livelihood strategies including pastoralism, agriculture, fishing, and trading. These groups would undertake seasonal movements along predetermined routes across the territory, stopping in small settlements throughout their migrations, as well as staying in the *bādiya* (the more remote desert areas) for extended periods of time. During their travels, individuals and groups would pass through or stay in areas currently designated as Morocco, Mauritania, Algeria, and Mali, confirming the porosity of the artificially created colonial borders and the socioeconomic and trading connections that existed between all of the neighboring countries.

Although a detailed analysis of the tribal system is beyond the scope of this book,[12] in Chapter 1 I present an overview of some of the principal

12. See Mulero-Clemente 1945; Flores-Morales 1946; Cola-Alberich 1962; Caratini 1989a/b/c; Gaudio 1993; Hart 1998; Cozza 2004.

Map 1: Map of the Western Sahara. Source: MINURSO deployment map, United Nations Map No. 3691 Rev. 70, January 2013; Department of Field Support Cartographic Section.

implications of the social system in place during different stages of the colonial era. Since Spain's colonial presence and infrastructure remained minimal from 1884 until the discovery of phosphates in 1947 (Marks 1976; Wirth and Balaguer 1976), in that chapter I argue that day-to-day life remained largely unaffected for the territory's population throughout the first five decades of Spanish control. As "notions of tribal fraction identity and loyalty had changed little even by the late 1950s from what they had been centuries earlier" (Hodges 1987, 32), many (although not all) of the features and processes discussed there are also relevant to contextualizing the social systems in place prior to the formal colonization of the territory in the mid-1880s.

At this stage, I briefly reflect on two key social characteristics regarding gender relations and Islamic practice that have systematically been attributed to tribes in the territory and the immediate region. While based on research conducted in the 1960s, Norris's conclusions regarding the position of nomadic women of the Sahara resonate with colonial ethnographers' accounts of conditions throughout the precolonial and early colonial periods:

> [She] has always enjoyed an honourable status compared with her sister in many Arab countries. She grows up and marries in a monogamous society, and although divorce is common, it is very often she who wishes it to further her own interests. The influence she plays in affairs openly and behind the scenes is quite remarkable, and . . . there is plenty of evidence to show that in days past her scholastic achievements were comparable with the men's. (1964, 10–11)

On the one hand, such an account clearly pertains to women from the higher levels of the tribal hierarchy (in particular those from scholarly tribes), and is not applicable to women from the lower levels (including slaves and "liberated slaves"). On the other hand, however, Tillion agrees that women in certain tribal societies across the Maghreb have historically been ascribed significant positions and rights within their social systems, while neighboring tribes have developed more restrictive interpretations of both pre-Islamic traditions and the Qur'an vis-à-vis women (2007, 155).

Unlike the limited rights accorded to women of the Greater and Lesser Kabyle, for instance, Tillion documents the freedoms accorded to nomadic and seminomadic women in Mauritania, where polygamy was not only exceptional, and repudiation infrequent, but where marriage contracts were designed to protect women from such occurrences (2007, 151). Along with agreeing with Norris's view that the nomadic women of the Sahara experienced great "freedom . . . within a warm environment" (ibid., 150), Tillion's account thus highlights the variety of interpretations and the selective application of Islam across nomadic, seminomadic, and sedentary populations in the Middle East and North Africa. This equation of Sahrawi women with freedom and an absence of polygamy and repudiation, along with the recognition that different sociopolitical groups may selectively, or strategically, interpret the Qur'an, are issues to which I return throughout this book.

Anticolonial Activism and the Birth of "the Exemplary Sahrawi People"

Following the discovery of phosphates in the late 1940s, Spanish interest and presence in the territory increased exponentially, and a formal and structured Spanish administration was finally established in the colony in 1963 (Damis 1983). This renewed interest was paralleled by both internal and international attempts to push Spain to decolonize the territory: the United Nations Decolonization Committee's first resolution on the Spanish Sahara was adopted in October 1964, while the territory experienced an increase in anticolonial sentiment and activism in the late 1960s.

The first major urban-based anticolonial movement, the Movement for the Liberation of Saguiat el-Hamra and Río de Oro, was established in 1968 by Mohamed Sid Brahim Bassir (also known as "Bassiri"), a member of the Rgaybat tribe who had studied in Casablanca, Cairo, and Damascus (Hodges 1987, 48–49). Influenced by the pan-Arabist and socialist ideas of the Baathists while studying journalism in Syria (Hodges 1984, 153), upon his return to the territory Bassiri taught the Qur'an and Arabic at Smara's mosque and started to recruit members for the liberation movement that was also known as the Muslim Party (*al-Ḥizb al-Muslim*; Hodges 1987, 49), advocating for "progressive independence through negotiation with the colonial administration" (San-Martín 2005, 589).

In June 1970, however, a peaceful demonstration organized by Bassiri's group in Zemla (Aaiun) eventually marked the birth of armed resistance and "Sahrawi nationalism," when the Spanish Foreign Legion killed over a dozen demonstrators, arresting others and leading to Bassiri's permanent "disappearance" (Pazzanita and Hodges 1994). A number of Bassiri's followers reportedly moved to Zouerate (Mauritania) following his disappearance and later participated in the foundation of the Polisario Front (Barbier 1982).

The following year, another member of the Rgaybat tribe who had also studied in Morocco visited France and Holland to identify international support for the anticolonial movement (Miské 1978). El-Ouali Mustafa Sayed (known as "Luali") had trained as a lawyer in Morocco and had reputedly read Fanon and Guevara in their first editions in Arabic (Damis 1983, 40) before emerging as the movement's new leader. In mid-1972 and early 1973, Luali undertook two visits to Algeria, Libya, and Mauritania to establish these countries' support for the movement (Barbier 1982; Miské 1978). Although Algeria was initially reluctant to offer its support (doing so only from late 1974 onward), Libya subsequently called for the liberation of the Spanish Sahara, announcing its intention to provide the movement with arms.[13]

In May 1973, Luali and other activists based in Zouerate (Barbier 1982) were among the founding members of the Popular Front for the Liberation of Saguiat El-Hamra y Río de Oro (known by its Spanish acronym Frente POLISARIO, henceforth Polisario). These men included graduates who, like Bassiri and Luali, had lived and studied in Morocco and/or Spain, such as Mohamed Lamine Ould Âhmed, who had studied law in Morocco and became the first prime minister of the Sahrawi Arab Democratic Republic (SADR) in February 1976; Mohamed Salem Ould Salek, who had studied political sciences and eventually become the minister of external affairs for the Sahrawi's state-in-exile, SADR, (see Chapter 2); Omar Hadrini, another Rgaybat who became a member of the SADR's

13. On Libyan-Sahrawi relations between 1976 and 2011, see Fiddian-Qasmiyeh 2011f, 2012, and unpublished.

Supreme Council of the Command for the Revolution (Hodges 1987, 61); and Bachir Mustafa Sayed (Luali's brother and therefore another Rgaybat) who became the Polisario's deputy secretary general in 1976 (Hodges 1984, 158).

As a result of their educational experiences, the movement was thus influenced by the anticolonial, socialist, and nonaligned theories, frameworks, and models that permeated the region at the time. While studying, these men had engaged with, and been impressed by, notions of pan-Arabism and the activities of African and Middle Eastern liberation movements, especially the Palestinian Resistance (Hodges 1984, 158). Although the Polisario's failure to secure active support from most Arab states (Libya and Algeria being the main exceptions) eventually led to increasing disillusionment with the Arab world (Hodges 1987, 53–54), in its early years the Polisario explicitly saw itself as an integral "part of the Arab revolution and of the world movement of national and democratic revolution" (ibid, 164).

A brief analysis of three intersecting issues is necessary at this stage: the ideological patterns underpinning the movement, the means through which the Polisario created a "national" identity, and the centrality accorded to women by "the revolutionary cause."

By 1970, the Spanish authorities had recognized that Bassiri's anticolonial organization was "seeking to destroy the tribal structure" in place throughout the territory (quoted in Hodges 1987, 49) in an attempt to promote a united front against the colonial power. Luali equally prioritized the unity of the territory's "Arab people" and denounced the divisiveness of the hierarchical tribal structure, which he declared had been accentuated and manipulated by Spain (quoted in San-Martín 2005). Defining itself primarily as a nonaligned, rather than socialist, movement, the Polisario demanded the abolition of tribal inequalities as a means of implementing the "strong reforming, egalitarian streak in the front's philosophy" (Hodges 1984, 164).

In order to create a unified "people" composed of equals, the Polisario "decided to eliminate 'tribalism' and to make 'the tribe,' as a sociopolitical unit, disappear" (Caratini 2000, 433; my translation; also see Fiddian-Qasmiyeh 2011c). Tribal lexicons, including references to the names of tribes, fractions or sub-fractions, were prohibited, and the term "comrade" (m. sing. *rfīq*)[14] introduced to the MENA region by Arab Marxists, replaced notions of "brothers," "sisters," and "cousins" (ibid., 439). Genealogical reference markers were replaced by a history of space and territory, with the Polisario declaring that the "Sahrawi people" were a "Sahrawi nation" with its own "national territory" demarcated by colonial borders (ibid.). The United Nations (UN) Mission of Inquiry to the territory in May 1975 prompted the first major pro-Polisario demonstration in the Spanish Sahara, leading the Mission to unambiguously declare that there was "overwhelming consensus [. . .] in favor of independence," and "support for one movement, the Frente Polisario" (UNGA 1975, 59). From 1973, and in particular following its Congress in Ain Bentili in 1975, the Polisario had successfully transformed the territory's pastoralist nomads "not only into a people, but into *an exemplary people*" (Caratini 2000, 433; my translation and emphasis; also see Firebrace 1987, 87; Caratini 2003a, 42;).

External analysts' perception of the Sahrawi's "exemplary" nature has in part arisen from the Polisario's "strong commitment to the principle of women's emancipation" in the 1970s (Hodges 1984, 164), which was a central concern within socialist and nonaligned movements at the time. Hence, the Polisario not only aimed to establish equality between the men of different tribes (including through the prohibition of slavery) but also between men and women of all tribes. Solidifying the abovementioned notion of the precolonial freedom of nomadic women, the Polisario stated that the Spanish had imposed artificial restrictions on Sahrawi women during the colonial era, and in its 1975 Program of Action declared that it would struggle "to reestablish the political and social rights of the woman and open up all perspectives to her" (quoted in Hodges 1984, 164; see Chapter 1). In addition to the ideological commitment to "reestablishing" the rights of women and promoting equality and unity between all men and women, these moves were also pragmatic in nature, since they automatically increased the potential membership base for the movement.

14. The classical Arabic term is *rafīq*.

This ideological and pragmatic rationale is identifiable in the following extract from the Polisario's official journal, published in 1974:

> It has become necessary for our struggle . . . that the Sahrawi woman
> bears all responsibilities and undertakes her duty in the national strug-
> gle by participating actively in the armed revolution like her sisters in
> the Palestinian, Algerian, and Guinea-Bissau revolutions. (quoted in
> Hodges 1984, 164)

While the erasure of tribal identities has been contested in the refugee
camps throughout the late 1980s and 1990s in particular (see below), the
centrality given to "Sahrawi women" has continued to be a central motif
of the Polisario's "cause." Although the movement's early political commitment to women's emancipation and activism may have been related
to its ideological position in the 1970s, in recent decades the Polisario's
motivations and modes of mobilizing Sahrawi women have shifted as a
result of a range of internal and international developments. One major
transformation that must be noted at this point pertains to the strategic
distance that has increasingly been created by the Polisario, during its
interactions with Western observers, from those whom it defined in the
1970s as the Sahrawis' Arab revolutionary "sisters."

Spanish Withdrawal and the "Green March"

In December 1974, as international and local pressure in favor of decolonization escalated, Spain conducted a census of the territory by means of
preparing for an eventual referendum for self-determination, registering
73,497 indigenous inhabitants from a selection of specified tribes (Barbier
1982).[15] Despite these "preparations," however, Spain's dictator (Franco)
was gravely ill, and the Spanish mainland was experiencing increasing

15. Pazzanita and Hodges (1994) suggest that "at least as many Sahrawi were in the
neighboring territories," including in Algeria's border zones, either as a result of refugee
movements fleeing from military unrest that engulfed the territory in 1958 or of processes
of sedentarization prompted by drought (see Chapter 1).

political instability due to violent threats from various political and military groups. These factors, and the related need for Spanish military and security forces to return to the mainland to "maintain the peace," are assumed to have influenced Spain's decision to withdraw without having formally decolonized the territory.

The International Court of Justice (ICJ) ruled on 16 October 1975 that neither Morocco nor Mauritania had legal claims to the territory that should impede the holding of a referendum for self-determination, but on the same day Morocco announced its "Green March" to "recover" what it still considers to be its "Southern Provinces." The first armed conflicts between Moroccan forces and the Polisario commenced on 31 October 1975, a week before the "Green March" crossed into the Spanish Sahara. On 6 November, 350,000 Moroccan civilians walked into the territory, reportedly accompanied and supported by delegations from Bahrain, Jordan, Kuwait, Oman, Saudi Arabia, and Qatar (Damis 1983; Chopra 1999; Julien 2003). While the Moroccan forces faced no Spanish resistance, on 6 November the United Nations passed Resolution 380 deploring the March and calling for its termination; this and subsequent UN Resolutions were ignored, with some 20,000 Moroccan soldiers joining their civilian compatriots in their "recovery" of the territory (Chopra 1999).

A week later, a Tripartite Interim Administration agreement was signed between Morocco, Mauritania, and Spain, only a week before Spain's General Franco died. Moroccan administration of the territory began shortly after, following the arrival of the Moroccan Deputy Governor of Aaiun on 25 November (Damis 1983) and the Spanish handover of Smara to Moroccan forces two days later (Algueró-Cuervo 2003). Moroccan troops arrived in Dakhla and Spanish troops withdrew from Aaiun in January 1976, while Mauritanian forces captured Ausserd from the Polisario in February 1976 (Pazzanita and Hodges 1994). The armed conflict between Morocco, Mauritania, and the Polisario intensified from the end of 1975 onward, and a mass exodus began, first being displaced to other parts of the territory and, later, following the bombardment of these first encampments with napalm and phosphate bombs (Mercer 1979a; Lippert 1987; Andrade 2003) to the nascent Algerian-based refugee camps near the territory's border with that country.

The Polisario: 1975 to Present

Although Morocco granted the border town of Tindouf to Algeria in the 1960s after a short war, it remains a sensitive bilateral issue. Following Algerian independence, the authorities had started to encourage the sedentarization of the Rgaybat tribes, whose traditional nomadic zone encompassed the area surrounding Tindouf (Gaudio 1978). Indeed, most of the 17,900 Rgaybat living in Algeria prior to 1975 were "essentially" based in and around Tindouf (Roussellier 2007, 64). Precisely why the Algerian government encouraged refugees fleeing the Spanish Sahara in 1975–76 to settle there (Hodges 1983, 132; Pazzanita and Hodges 1994, 405) rather than in Bechar or Oum el-Assel, both of which fell within the Rgaybat's traditional nomadic routes, ultimately remains unclear, although remaining close to the Algerian military base may have provided an increased sense of security. That the refugee camps should have been established in a location associated with the Rgaybat tribe by an organization led by Rgaybat men (despite the official eradication of tribal identification) is an issue to which I return briefly below.

As discussed in Chapter 2, as the Polisario founded the Sahrawi refugee camps in the vicinity of Tindouf, international humanitarian and political support strengthened for the organization and "its" refugees. The first Spanish and French "committees in support of the Sahrawi people" were created in October and November 1975 (Wirth and Balaguer 1976; Julien 2003), providing the foundation of a "solidarity movement" that has played an increasingly significant role in securing the political and physical survival of the camps and its inhabitants (see below). Soon after, the International Federation of the Red Cross and Red Crescent (IFRC) recognized the Sahrawi Red Crescent (Wirth and Balaguer 1976), and humanitarian supplies, including tents and medical items, were provided by the IFRC and the Algerian government. Indeed, Boumediene's regime promptly launched a "Sahara Solidarity Week" in Algeria to mobilize popular support for the Polisario's "cause," reinforcing its military bases along the Algerian/Moroccan border in the Bechar and Tindouf regions and providing the Polisario with arms (Damis 1983). The Algerian government also reportedly provided Algerian passports to the Polisario's elite to facilitate their diplomatic efforts in the international arena (Alguero-Cuervo 2003).

Spain finally withdrew from the Spanish Sahara, and unilaterally declared the end of its administration, on 26 February 1976. The following day the Polisario proclaimed the birth of its "state-in-exile." Given the extensive overlap of members of the Polisario Front and the representatives of the SADR (i.e., Mohamed Abdelaziz is currently both the Secretary General of the Polisario and the President of the SADR, also see Shelley 2004, 182), henceforth I shall refer to "the Polisario."

In March 1976, the Polisario continued to accrue international support for its "cause," with Algeria officially establishing diplomatic relations with the SADR that month, and Fidel Castro reportedly confirming Cuba's support for the Polisario during a visit to Algiers that month (Yara 2003, 68). Diplomatic efforts paralleled military confrontations on and around the territory, which in turn influenced the composition of the organization: the Polisario's first Secretary General, Luali, was killed during a Polisario attack on Nouakchott in June 1976 and the Polisario's Third Congress held in August that year led not only to the creation of the SADR's constitution but also to the formation of a new "government" headed by another member of the Rgaybat tribe: Mohamed Abdelaziz.

Political conflicts ensued between states that lobbied in favor of the Polisario's struggle for independence and those that did not.[16] Such conflicts were bilateral (between Algeria and Morocco, for instance) as well as multilateral, playing out in arenas such as the Organization of African Unity (OAU) and the Nonaligned Movement (Lynn Price 1981; Damis 1983; Saxena 1995).[17] As a result of intensive lobbying at the OAU in favor of the Polisario, Morocco eventually suspended its membership in 1982 and officially withdrew in 1984 after that organization recognized

16. Analyses of the legal dimension of the conflict include Naldi 1994; Rucz 1994; Bashir 1996; Scott 1996; Ramcharan 1998; Badía-Martí et al. 1999; Jacob et al. 2001; Ruíz-Miguel 2001; Soroeta-Licera 2001; Ferrer-Lloret 2002; Bhatia 2003; Nesiah 2003.

17. Also see Moha 1990; Mortimer 1993; Zoubir and Volman 1993; Chopra 1994, 1997, 1999; Pazzanita 1994; Layachi 1994; Von Hippel 1996; Zoubir 1996, 1998; Seddon 2000a and b; Mohamed 2001; Zunes and Mundy 2010.

the SADR. In addition to being recognized as a full member by the OAU and later the African Union, since 1976, more than seventy non-European countries have since established full diplomatic relations with the SADR (although a number of these countries have subsequently "cancelled" or "suspended" their recognition of the SADR, pending the referendum for self-determination).

Throughout the political negotiations to resolve the conflict in the 1980s, the military conflict continued between Polisario (reportedly with Algerian military support)[18] and Morocco.[19] The latter had French and U.S. support[20] but acted without Mauritania, which had signed a cease-fire with the Polisario on 12 July 1978, retracted its claims to (and soldiers from) the territory, and eventually recognized the SADR in 1984. Between 1980 and 1987, Morocco built six sand walls (with a length of more than 2000 km) with electronic detection networks and radar systems in place, to defend the areas of the territory under its control (including, in particular, phosphate-rich areas) and to keep Polisario guerrilla groups out. Despite the existence of the wall, armed hostilities continued until the OAU and UN brokered a ceasefire in 1988. The United Nations Mission for the Referendum in Western Sahara (MINURSO) was created in 1991 with a mandate to organize and hold a referendum for self-determination. Although the referendum has yet to be held, the ceasefire has been observed since then.

A combination of international events and the reported discovery of offshore oil reserves increased widespread geopolitical interest in the region and simultaneously decreased the likelihood of the referendum

18. Polisario and Algeria accept that the latter has offered political and humanitarian support, along with providing arms to Polisario. Algeria has officially refuted claims, however, that it was actively involved in military activities. Damis (1983) and Pazzanita and Hodges (1994) present evidence to the contrary.

19. The conflict between the Polisario and Morocco has often been reframed by analysts as reflecting hostilities between Algeria and Morocco, with many arguing that the Polisario was following Algerian commands.

20. See Mercer 1979; Lynn Price 1981; Pazzanita and Hodges 1994; Shelley 2004; Mundy 2007.

being held.[21] The unresolved nature of this conflict continues to affect regional and international politics, as evidenced in tense Algerian-Moroccan relations, Morocco's continued absence from key regional bodies (such as the African Union), the UN's attempts to promote peace talks between Morocco and the Polisario, and EU and UN debates regarding the legality of fishing agreements and oil contracts relating to the Western Sahara.

While strengthening its diplomatic position in the international arena throughout the 1980s and 1990s,[22] the Polisario faced numerous challenges and shifts during this period. The most notable of these, described as a "revolution within the revolution" (San-Martín 2005, 571–572; also García 2001, 256–308) took place in the late 1980s, when the Polisario's leadership was directly confronted by camp residents, in part on the basis of the Rgaybat's continued dominance over the movement and the camps (see Chapter 2). As documented by organizations such as Amnesty International (1996) and Human Rights Watch (2008, 116), the mass revolt known as "the 88" culminated in internal purges and major human rights violations. Indeed, a 54-year-old female SARC interviewee[23] reflected that "the events of 1988 changed a great deal in the ideological sphere and revolutionary platform of the Sahrawi struggle," changes that were paralleled by shifts in the Polisario/SADR's composition and structure. A year after the rebellion, the Polisario's Seventh Congress reduced the SADR's Ministerial core to eight men by "absorbing" the positions of the prime minister and the ministers of the interior and of justice (Serrano-Borrull 1999), while its Eighth Congress in June 1991 adopted a new constitution and "independent" legal system and led to the formation of a new Parliament and National Secretariat, following the abolition of the Political

21. For instance, it is argued that Pérez de Cuellar's efforts to resolve the crisis were aborted in 1990 as a result of the Iraqi invasion of Kuwait and the resulting Gulf War (Pazzanita and Hodges 1994).

22. At the same time, Libya declared in 1983 that it would no longer provide material or political support to the Polisario, signing a Moroccan-Libyan treaty in 1984 (Mace 1985; Pazzanita and Hodges 1994). Also see Fiddian-Qasmiyeh 2011f and unpublished.

23. The methodology underpinning this study is outlined below, including an outline of the SARC study which is the source of this quotation (also see Chatty 2010).

Bureau and the Polisario's Executive Committee (Pazzanita and Hodges 1994). However, despite these "radical" changes, the power of many of the Polisario's founding members was consolidated, including that of Mohamed Abdelaziz.

The year 1991 is also habitually perceived as a turning point in the camps' history, separating the first decades of active military engagement (characterized by humanitarian crises in the camps, total dependence on aid provided from outside of the camps, and the detrimental effect that the war had on civilians and soldiers alike) and the years following the ceasefire (commonly described by Sahrawi refugees and the Polisario as "neither peace nor war"). The gradual demobilization of soldiers from the front influenced the demography and division of labor in the camps, leading to a "normalization" of life therein (see Chapter 2), while MINURSO's attempts to organize a referendum for self-determination further challenged the Polisario's earlier proclamation of the end of "tribes." If "the 88" had revealed tensions within and between the movement's leadership and "its" refugee population, the significance of tribal identities was forcibly "revealed" and consolidated as a result of the UN identification program in the 1990s. Between 1993 and 1998 the SADR's "national" radio called daily for individuals, families, groups and tribes registered by the Spanish during the colonial era to identify themselves for the referendum (Abjean 2003, 106). Hence, although tribal identification had initially been considered by the Polisario to be a "crime against the [Sahrawi] nation," in the 1990s it "became the essential criterion for the construction of the nation" (Caratini 2000, 442–43; my translation; also Fiddian-Qasmiyeh 2011c).

Although the protracted voter identification process was eventually abandoned and the referendum has never been held, rather than dividing the "Sahrawi nation," preliminary studies of Sahrawi nationalism in the refugee camps have argued that the shifts prompted by the ceasefire have both strengthened the Polisario's "state" control over the camps, and the population's nationalist determination to continue struggling for the creation of an independent state (i.e., San-Martín 2005, 572; Mundy 2007). The source and nature of political and humanitarian support offered to the Polisario after the ceasefire also changed both as a result of a reduction of Algeria's support for the Polisario (due to its internal crises), and following a dramatic increase in European (especially Spanish) projects and investments in the camps. While Algeria and numerous international organizations continue to provide substantial aid to refugees, in this book I argue that since the early 1990s the Polisario and the camps' inhabitants have recognized the extent to which European "solidarity" movements are able to lobby politically in favor of "the Sahrawi people's right to self-determination" in the international arena, as well as the significance of their direct financial and material contributions.

The main support network which I refer to in this book is formed by Spanish NGOs that consider themselves to be "Friends of the Sahrawi People" (*Amigos del Pueblo Saharaui*) and "in solidarity" with the Sahrawi. Solidarity is a concept that is often drawn upon in the social and political sciences to refer to a form of integration and empathy that binds individuals together in a broader society and/or social system (i.e., social solidarity or, in anthropology, agnatic solidarity). In this context, however, I use the term as it is employed in Spanish (*solidaridad*), to mean the "humanitarian" act of offering moral, political and/or material support to individuals and collectivities that are conceptualized as being "in need" of and deserving such support.[24] Individuals who support and "care" for others in need are referred to in Spanish as *solidarios* (sing. *solidario*), which is a more precise meaning than that encompassed by the English term "solidary" (more broadly defined (Brown, 1993) as "characterized by or having solidarity or coincidence of interests").

Solidarity can be defined as being underpinned by "the feeling" of "sympathy and responsibility" for others (Wilde 2007, 171), in this case primarily between members of Spanish civil society (the former colonial power) and the Sahrawi refugee population. "As such," Wilde reminds us, solidarity "has subjective and emotional elements" (ibid), partly based in the case of Spanish *solidarios* on their sense of "shame" (*vergüenza*) that the Spanish government "abandoned" the Sahrawi to their fate in 1975 (see Fiddian-Qasmiyeh 2011b). Based on these "feelings," solidarity

---

24. The first meaning of the adjective *solidario* in the Collins Spanish-English Dictionary (Butterfield 2003) is "(= *humanitario*) caring."

movements offer moral support, political engagement and lobbying, along with financing and implementing humanitarian projects and maintaining cooperation networks.

However, while solidarity is often viewed in relation to notions of fraternity (ibid, 173; Martín-Márquez 2006) or, as I argue, "sorority," this term hides the imbalanced power dynamics that often underlie "solidary relations." Rather than "solidarity" being offered between equals, there is frequently a clear imbalance between those who provide solidarity, and those who are conceptualized as the "recipients" of support. This is especially the case in a refugee context, with "refugees being expected to *conform* to the values of their sponsors" (Harrell-Bond 1999, 145 emphasis in the original). Indeed, as Bob stresses, "the development and retention of support are best conceived not as philanthropic gestures but as exchanges based on the relative power of each party to the transaction" (2005, 5). At times these could be characterized as founded upon paternalism, while Butler uses the terms "exclusionary" and "coercive" to define the foundations of solidarity movements (1990, 14–15).

Last, therefore, analysts are increasingly documenting how multiple forms of dependence on externally provided aid and support have directly impacted the ways in which the "recipients" of solidarity represent or "market" (Bob 2005, passim) themselves to their "solidarity providers." Since NGOs and other solidarity groups habitually differentiate between groups that are or are not worthy of support, their continued engagement with a "cause" often depends on their being convinced as to the cultural "authenticity" of the recipient (Conklin 1997; also MacCannell 1973), or the usage of particular political discourses and methods by recipients (Jasper 1997; Jean-Klein 1997; Bob 2005). In this way, "broader political contexts" often influence the particular identity that is presented by social and political movements (Jasper 1997, 329–330), and "movements must often alter key characteristics to meet the expectations of patrons" (Bob 2005, 5). Such "patrons" often act as "auditors" (Jean-Klein 1997) observing both the implementation of their projects, and what we may call the "justifiability" of their engagement.

It is within this framework that I suggest that the Polisario has constructed a particular strategy of "international public relations" to secure

Spaniards' solidary support for "the cause." In the remainder of this book I examine how, why and to what effect the Polisario has mobilized an image of "free," "secular" and "active" Sahrawi women drawing on historical, political and pragmatic justifications for their prominence in the camps to demonstrate the ideal nature of the Sahrawi refugee camps and their "national cause."

Methodological Note

My analysis draws on observations and interviews that I conducted in Arabic, English, French and Spanish[25] with over 100 Sahrawi youth and adults in the Algerian-based Sahrawi refugee camps (2001, 2002, 2007), Cuba (2006), Syria (2006), Spain (2000, 2005–2009) and South Africa (2007). My decision to conduct research in a range of locations was influenced by my earliest visits to the refugee camps in 2001 and 2002.[26] These visits led me to simultaneously recognize that official permission to conduct research in the camps is easily revoked and access denied, and that the camps are dependent upon a number of highly significant transnational networks.

While "interested" non-Sahrawis have been welcome to visit the refugee camps for short periods between the 1980s and the 2010s (usually up to two weeks), few researchers to date have been able to complete long-term investigations there. This is in part because of a tradition of practice-oriented, rather than research-oriented, visits to the camps (Chatty 2010). It also appears to be related to official (Polisario) suspicions regarding the presence of foreigners in the camps for longer periods of time. Since the camps are based on Algerian soil and the Polisario has no independent visa system, these are issued by the Algerian authorities. When applying to travel to Tindouf's military zone one must present an official Polisario

25. All translations from Spanish and French are my own, while Arabic language interview transcripts and documents have been translated with the assistance of Yousif M. Qasmiyeh to ensure accuracy.

26. I undertook two separate visits to the Sahrawi camps with a humanitarian group in March and April 2001, returning as a "foreign guest" invited to the Fourth Conference of the National Union of Sahrawi Women (NUSW) in April 2002.

invitation letter to the Algerian authorities, who will grant the visa once they *and* the Polisario are content that the visitors' intention is to support "the cause." Throughout the 1990s and 2000s, NGO workers, academics, and journalists have been permitted to visit the camps for a maximum of three months at a time (although the vast majority of visitors stay between two and 14 days), with the possibility of applying for a new three-month visa once they have left Algerian territory.[27] While there are several NGO workers and some American Evangelists (Fiddian-Qasmiyeh 2011a) who have reportedly spent up to a total of two years in the camps on consecutive three-month visas, some researchers have been refused entry visas upon their first application to visit the camps (i.e., Caratini 2003a, 9), while several researchers have been asked to leave the camps before their intended departure dates, and others still have been refused re-entry after leaving the camps (i.e., Cozza 2004, 13). Although I did not personally face such difficulties when I conducted fieldwork in the camps, it was partly for these reasons that I had identified alternative or supplementary research sites, as "Plan B" or "Plan C" scenarios if my access to the camps had been denied or revoked.

The second reason for developing a multisited research strategy is related to the range of highly significant transnational networks that ensure the political and physical survival of the camps and their inhabitants. A useful definition of "transnationalism" in this context is "a nexus of social and material relationships that blur the centrality of borders" and equally decenter "the state" as the main actor to be examined in analyses of social and political relations (Hyndman and Walton-Roberts 2000, 246);

27. Most authors have undertaken short research visits, with Firebrace having visited the camps from 9–17 April 1985 and Mowles from 16–21 June 1986. San-Martín has more recently spent a relatively longer period of fieldwork in the camps, but his work had previously been based solely on short visits (2010, 10). Cuban voluntary doctors are an exception to this rule, working in the camps for up to two years at a time. Based in a special complex at Rabouni's National Hospital, they are regularly granted permission to visit Tindouf for "shopping and relaxation" (interviews with Cuban doctors, Rabouni, April 2007; interview with Dr Kenia Serrano, Cuban Government's *Comité Central* Coordinator for Africa and the Middle East, Havana, November 2006).

in the context of this study, I extend this nexus to also include political and politicized ones. That the Sahrawi refugee camps are deeply dependent upon a number of international and transnational networks and systems is therefore simultaneously a conclusion I have reached throughout my research, and the foundation of the methodology adopted for this thesis (see also Horst 2006b, esp. 12).

In addition to the research that I have conducted in and about the camps, I also refer to an innovative and significant interview data-set resulting from an Andrew Mellon Foundation–funded research project entitled *Children and Adolescents in Sahrawi and Afghani Refugee Households: Living with the Effects of Prolonged Armed Conflict and Forced Migration,* known as "SARC."[28] As part of this investigation into the experiences of Sahrawi refugee children and youth, interviews were conducted with fifty refugee households by local Sahrawi teams in the refugee camps between 2002 and 2003, and with fifty Sahrawi children by myself and Gina Crivello in Spain in 2005. In particular, I draw upon the SARC household-based research data as a means of exploring male and female Sahrawi adults' accounts of the Spanish colonial era (see Chapter 1). This data has allowed me to document transformations in social and gendered realities throughout different stages of the colonial era (1884–1975), which has in turn enriched my analysis of the refugee period (1975/1976 to the present).

Complementing the interviews conducted in these locations, I also draw upon materials produced and published in English, Spanish, French and Arabic by a number of Polisario/SADR Ministries and/ or representatives,[29] as well as Arabic and Spanish language NUSW

28. I am grateful to Dawn Chatty for granting me access to this data-set. Acknowledgements are also due to the team leaders in each research site. For a detailed methodology see Chatty 2010 and Chatty, Fiddian-Qasmiyeh and Crivello 2010.

29. With regard to my analysis of newspaper extracts and journalistic interviews with SADR officials, Korteweg and Yurdakul stress that this is a useful strategy not "because they [newspaper extracts] give an unmediated reflection of general public debate, but because they are one of the loci from which discursive strategies that influence such debate are drawn" (2008, 6).

documents and conference proceedings.[30] Further, I refer to a range of university theses written by Sahrawi students formerly based in Cuba and Syria. These dissertations were supervised by Cuban or Syrian university professors, as well as diplomatic members of the SADR Embassy in Havana or the Polisario representative in Damascus. These students thus rely heavily upon historical documents, references, and anecdotes provided by Sahrawi officials. By drawing on Polisario influenced and/ or (re)produced material, I have developed a more nuanced interpretation of the connections between what I refer to as "official" texts and statements, and non-Sahrawi materials concerning sociopolitical dynamics in the camps.

Among the Arabic language texts I refer to is a trilogy written by the Polisario/SADR representative to the Middle East (Kuttab), whose account of the early colonial era provides a unique approach to a history of the Sahrawi conflict.[31] Given the extent to which Kuttab's trilogy is largely based on, and supported by, historically validated facts, I propose that it is possible to use his trilogy as an official (Polisario) historiography of the conflict. Indeed, during several of our meetings in Damascus, including on the day that he presented me with a copy of his books, Kuttab stressed that he had started to write a conventional history of the period but had decided that the format of a novel would be more appropriate. Despite the change in style, his aim remained the same: to document the colonial period and indicate the specificities of the Sahrawi colonial experience.

Essentially, Kuttab's texts and other Sahrawi sources do not only present insights into the historical periods being discussed but also "authorial intention" (Darby 1997, 16ff) emerges as a central concern to be examined, in particular when considering Polisario/SADR officials' accounts of the refugee situation. It is precisely the politics underlying the creation and

30. I have translated all French and Spanish documents myself, while written and audio sources have been translated from Arabic to English by Yousif M. Qasmiyeh and are duly indicated upon first occurrence.

31. It is worth noting that certain sources have been privileged over others in different disciplines. Hence, Darby suggests that International Relations scholars have tended to neglect Said's *Orientalism* precisely due to "a disciplinary distaste for his sources" (1997, 6).

re/presentation of specific images and interpretations of the history and present of the refugee context (while sidelining or silencing others/Others) that demands analysis. Simultaneously, Darby reminds us that such sources are, "of course," invaluable, since they "themselves are part of the process of international exchange, and the critical debate that they engender represents a new form of enquiry into the relationship between different peoples" (ibid, 8).

In addition to these multisited interviews with Sahrawi refugees, and my analysis of documents produced by Polisario representatives and Sahrawi students, I also I draw on interviews and informal conversations with more than fifty Spanish NGO workers both in the camps and in Spain and questionnaires administered electronically to forty Spaniards who lived in the Spanish Sahara during the colonial era.[32] Combined with my interviews and group discussions with Spanish Friends of the Sahara and academics in Spain (primarily in Madrid, Tenerife, and Gran Canaria), the interviews and informal conversations that I held between 2002 and 2007 with Spanish NGO workers while I was conducting fieldwork in the camps and when I attended the Fourth and Fifth NUSW Conferences provided me with a wide range of Spanish informants. In turn, the abovementioned questionnaires aimed to fill a major gap in the literature pertaining to the colonial period; responses were obtained by establishing contact with a selection of Internet-based groups composed of Spanish men who completed their obligatory military service in the Spanish Sahara. Drawing on Spaniards' recollections of the colonial period provides another vantage point from which to explore the nature of interactions between Sahrawis and Spaniards throughout the colonial period. In so doing, it also helps us further contextualize the significance of the Polisario/SADR's official discourse concerning the colonial era and the refugee camps, including reference to the nature of Spanish civil society's solidarity with the Sahrawi people since 1975.

A final set of interviews were conducted with a dozen Cuban and a dozen South African civilians, students, academics and politicians in

---

32. On Spanish soldiers' accounts of the colonial period see Fiddian-Qasmiyeh 2011b.

Havana and Santiago de Cuba (October–December 2006), and in Pretoria and Johannesburg (May 2007), respectively. While in Cuba I also interviewed ten non-Sahrawi Muslim students from the Middle East (Palestinians, Syrians and Yemenis) on their perspectives regarding the Western Sahara. In the UK I interviewed Moroccan, Egyptian, Palestinian, Sudanese, and Libyan academics and nonacademics (2007 and 2008). These additional interviews have provided perspectives from beyond the camps and/or Spain, which have until now been the primary focus of research on the Western Saharan conflict.

My own and the SARC interview transcripts, my research notes, and diverse documents including official publications, theses, and newspaper articles were all imported into NVIVO, an analytical software program which has facilitated the identification of relevant themes emerging in the interviewees' accounts and additional documentation. The thematic coding of these interviews and documents in turn provided the foundations for the detailed multilingual discourse analysis presented throughout the remainder of this study.

My interpretation of this wide array of materials has been directly influenced by my having worked and conducted research in a variety of Middle Eastern locations, and having interviewed over a hundred non-Sahrawi Middle Eastern and North African (MENA) asylum seekers, refugees, and citizens in a number of contexts since 2001 (i.e., see Fiddian 2006b; Fiddian-Qasmiyeh 2010a, 2011f, 2013; Fiddian-Qasmiyeh and Qasmiyeh 2010). During such encounters, my critical understanding of the geopolitical, socioreligious, and gendered frameworks characterizing the MENA region developed considerably, permitting a more nuanced observation of life in, and descriptions of, the Sahrawi refugee camps. This has been particularly important given the extent to which accounts of the camps depend upon claims of Sahrawi women's uniqueness and difference from other Middle Eastern and North African women.

Ethics

All social encounters, including research encounters, are characterized by power inequalities of different types. In the case of research populations formed entirely by refugees, the inequality of these interactions may be particularly accentuated. Nonetheless, this research is not based on an a priori understanding of Sahrawi refugees as "vulnerable individuals." Rather, in the following chapters I argue that Sahrawi refugees are acutely aware of the power imbalances that characterize their interactions with non-Sahrawi individuals and agencies and have developed specific mechanisms to address them. Refugees in the camps, however, have habitually assumed that non-Sahrawis undertaking research there would eventually provide services or develop projects for inhabitants. As a result, the separation between "academic research" and policy development has been a complex one that I have discussed in detail with my interviewees.

With reference to participants' agency to give consent or decline to participate in research, the particularities of the Sahrawi camps, characterized by relatively high levels of self-management and local participation on many levels of social and political life, must be borne in mind. I have ensured that informed consent has been continuously negotiated throughout the research process, explaining the broad aims of my research to participants and stressing participants' right at any stage of the research to ask not to be interviewed or quoted in publications. In all instances, interviewees' confidentiality and anonymity has been maintained, including through modifying certain details (such as age, subject of study, or profession) to ensure that participants could not be identified. Several individuals provided information "off the record," and I have respected their request while writing this book. In other cases I have decided not to draw on material provided by individuals who clearly did not identify me as a "researcher" but rather, for instance, as an "eldest daughter" (*ibna kabīra*), as occurred with the members of the family with whom I lived in 27 February Camp.

A main issue arising in the small 27 February refugee camp where I conducted much of my research was ensuring that interviews were conducted and recorded in a confidential fashion. Given the social fluidity of life in the camps, people move in and out of each other's *khiyām* (tents) with great frequency, and there is only a limited amount of "private" space. Interviews were generally conducted in "public spaces," in particular within the confines of the 27 February Women's School and in a number of Rabouni-based institutions. Due to the nature of the topic under consideration (gender relations in the camps), I do not believe that respondents felt uncomfortable speaking in such contexts (an exception being discussions of violence against women, as in Chapter 5), although interviewees were as a whole either unable or unwilling to challenge the official political rhetoric proposed by the Polisario/SADR.

My primary concern when planning and conducting research was my ethical responsibility to my respondents and other Sahrawi refugees, being aware of the ways in which data collected, analyzed, and written about, has in the past been, and could in the future potentially be, used against camp residents. Following discussions with a selection of academics and NGO workers on the topic of ethical responsibilities toward a people who are still struggling for self-determination and are almost entirely dependent on humanitarian aid, it is apparent that there is widespread concern that the Moroccan government might use academic or NGO reports to undermine the basis of the Sahrawi struggle.

The visible vulnerability and dependence of the refugee population has led to a recognition, or rather a powerful assumption, that public statements can threaten the humanitarian system that ensures the physical survival of refugees: fears that studies on corruption or smuggling could result in a reduction of food aid, for instance, have been taken seriously by many of the researchers I interviewed. Indeed, those who have decided to tackle such "sensitive" issues have often found their visas revoked and future visits to the camps curtailed, and their studies have subsequently been negatively evaluated by those "solidary" academics and nonacademics who agree that critical statements by necessity undermine the "cause,"[33] and should in essence be kept "private."

In this sense, just as a distinction has been made between "good" or "ideal," and "bad" refugees (Harrell-Bond 1999), in the Sahrawi context an equally strict distinction has habitually been made by Sahrawi refugees, the Polisario/SADR, and much of Spanish civil society between "good" and "bad" researchers. "Good" researchers could be understood

33. Researchers habitually face, and develop different responses to, the dilemma of how to "do no harm" to the population being researched (Jacobsen and Landau 2003, 4).

as those who align themselves with solidarity movements or inclinations and support the Sahrawi "cause." One way in which "good" researchers can be seen to support "the cause" is through repetition: by reproducing the claims that have been previously made, "solidary" researchers have solidified an "archive of knowledge" (following Foucault) about the camps. "Bad" researchers, conversely, include those who publicly question the Sahrawi's right to self-determination, or present the official Moroccan perspective vis-à-vis the conflict, but also those labeled by others as "anti-Sahrawi" and, consequently, "pro-Moroccan." Such labels arise if researchers criticize the Polisario/SADR, for instance through references to corruption, or, I would suggest, if she or he questions any of the bases of the Sahrawi "national project."

In the following chapters, however, I argue that the resulting silences that have arisen vis-à-vis potentially disruptive topics are neither ethical nor morally defendable.[34] Many of these silences have had serious policy implications with detrimental effects on camp inhabitants, and I hold it is therefore unethical to perpetuate systems of selective representation and "solidary" research.[35] Throughout my investigations it has therefore become my aim to represent the complex nature of social realities in the camps in a critical manner, including a selection of issues that have until now been displaced from view.

Structure

In the following chapter I analyze the gendered nature and impacts of different stages of the colonial encounter (1884–1975), drawing on primary research conducted with first generation refugees and with Spaniards who were formerly resident in the Spanish Sahara. The chapter is divided into three main parts. I firstly outline the nomadic and pastoralist livelihood strategies that characterized the early colonial period

---

34. On self-censorship during research also see Hale (1996, 8ff), Kandiyoti (quoted in Hammami 2005, 1348), and Keddie (2007, 227).

35. I use the term *solidary* in line with my focus on solidarity networks, while recognizing that the concept of "advocacy research" is commonly used in similar contexts (e.g., Jacobsen and Landau 2003, 2).

(approximately 1884–1947), documenting the ways in which gender, generation and family background influenced the opportunities and responsibilities assigned to girls and boys as they grew up. I also highlight the privileges and power that the members of particular social groups have historically held over others. In the second part I examine the impacts of the increasing Spanish colonial presence that followed the discovery of phosphates in 1947. In particular, I focus on the processes of sedentarization and urbanization that were fomented by the colonial administration, asking how girls and boys, women and men were affected by their greater proximity with, and dependence upon, the colonizers. Finally, I examine the terms of engagement between different groups of Spanish and Sahrawi residents throughout the later colonial period. A discussion of accounts relayed by first-generation refugees and by Spaniards who were formerly resident in the colony is particularly pertinent, given the widely made assertions regarding Spanish "fraternity" with "the Sahrawi people" and given that the presence and dependence on Spaniards in the refugee camps continues to be both a reality and a necessity. I conclude by highlighting the prevalence and nature of tension between the colonized population and the Spanish colonial power. This chapter thus provides a vantage point from which to explore the dynamics upon which the Sahrawi refugee camps are currently based and thus the motivations for the projection of specific representations to non-Sahrawi audiences.

In Chapter 2 I provide a detailed overview of the Sahrawi refugee camps. I start by complementing an outline of the organizational structure of the camps with a brief examination of the ways in which the Polisario/SADR has projected these as "democratic" and "gender egalitarian" spaces to non-Sahrawi observers. I then highlight the camps' political and physical dependence upon a range of international and transnational networks. While a multiplicity of such networks exists, I maintain that the Spanish solidarity network has been prioritized by the Polisario/SADR and many refugees alike. I outline the characteristics and activities of this network and highlight the palpable connection that exists between Sahrawi refugees and Spanish *solidarios*. I then submit that beyond "general" support for the "Sahrawi national cause," many Spaniards explicitly connect their solidarity with the projected image of gender equality and the importance of Sahrawi women in the camps. With reference to the NUSW, I demonstrate the extent of support that is channeled by solidary Spaniards specifically to Sahrawi women. I conclude the chapter by contrasting the gendered basis of the Spanish solidarity system with the Polisario/SADR's relationship with two non-Western states (Cuba and South Africa) that offer significant humanitarian and political support to the Sahrawi "cause." This analysis demonstrates the extent to which the Polisario/SADR orients itself to the particular audience being addressed, emphasizing specific aspects and characteristics according to its perceptions of what will ensure the continued support of different state and nonstate actors. It is precisely the existence of alternative discourses in these two non-Western contexts that leads me to propose the necessity of analyzing the mainstream representations of Sahrawi women as "free" and "unique" specifically vis-à-vis the Polisario/SADR's connection with, and dependence on, the Spanish solidarity system.

I draw upon my multisited interviews with Polisario/SADR officials and Sahrawi students to identify and explore a core of themes and images that repeatedly arise in mainstream accounts of the Sahrawi refugee camps in Chapter 3. The four principal sections of this chapter respectively explore common representations of Sahrawi women in relation to veiling, freedom of movement and participation in the public sphere, *mahr*[36] and marriage, and divorce and the "divorce party." I consider these four core elements to be a set of mutually reinforcing images and conceptualizations that re/create Sahrawi women as uniquely unveiled, liberal, secular, and empowered refugee women for particular political purposes. Importantly, this mainstream representation is founded upon the separation and distinctiveness of Sahrawi women from Other Muslim Arab women, with a particular reliance on creating and maintaining a distance from Islam and religious identity for strategic reasons. In summary, if Sahrawi refugee women are represented as "free," "empowered,"

---

36. *Mahr* is the "bridal money given by the husband to his wife at the time of marriage" (sura 2:237).

and "democratic," MENA women are represented in the Polisario/SADR official discourse as brutally oppressed and violated.

In Chapter 4 I argue that the mainstream portrayal of Sahrawi women is a highly politicized part of the Polisario/SADR's broader "politics of survival." I start by contending that images of "empowered" and "secular" Sahrawi women have been discursively mobilized by the Polisario/SADR to reinforce ties between Sahrawis and their Western observers. This is achieved both by explicitly accentuating commonalities and a shared sense of "sisterhood" between "secular" Sahrawi women and their Western counterparts, and through a purposeful re/creation of "Arab Muslim women" as the Sahrawis' and Spaniards' common Other. While these interconnected images are projected to the West, however, my fieldwork in the Sahrawi refugee camps reveals that this mainstream representation hides both the heterogeneity and the diverse priorities of Sahrawi refugees. Nonetheless, despite recognizing that the official discourse misrepresents the camps on numerous levels, the Polisario/SADR and many refugees are acutely aware that aid may be withdrawn if certain conditions are not met: in this case, the existence of secular, liberal, and modern gender equality. I conclude the chapter by examining a case study that illustrates both the strain that often typifies Sahrawi-Spanish relations and what I refer to as the "conditional" dimension of Spanish public support for "the cause." Examining the essentially Orientalist imagery that was successfully mobilized by Spanish civil society to "liberate" three young Sahrawi women ostensibly "abducted" by their families in the camps demonstrates the dangers that may arise when differences between Spaniards and Sahrawis are strategically accentuated through reference to gender and Islam. Indeed, many Spaniards threatened to withdraw their support for the camps and to cut solidary ties unless the girls were "saved" from what was broadly depicted as the enactment of "barbaric" Muslim traditions. This case study ultimately proves why the Polisario/SADR is so determined, in its interactions with Western audiences, to separate the Sahrawi Self from the Muslim Arab world, and why it depicts the MENA region as a space of female oppression rather than challenging such Orientalist perspectives.

I examine the constitutive impact of the Polisario/SADR's official discourse projected to Western audiences in Chapter 5. I draw together the discussions presented in the preceding chapters to argue that the official discourse that has "created" ideal and idealized Sahrawi women has directly affected policies developed by non-Sahrawis and has simultaneously been strengthened by the same. I first submit that despite a multiplicity of projects run in the camps, the majority of residents' voices and needs have been marginalized through this discursive idealization and homogenization. If "ideal" women are hypervisible in the official discourse, I identify three groups of refugees ("nonideal" Sahrawi women who do not embody the characteristics prioritized by the Polisario/SADR; refugee girls; and adult and young refugee men) who have been rendered invisible by the Polisario/SADR and who have, in turn, been marginalized by Western-sponsored projects. In addition to this process of discursive marginalization, both the Polisario/SADR and certain non-Sahrawi audiences have designated a number of "issues" as "private" and therefore beyond the scope of Western attention. The policy implications of an emphasis on "Sahrawi women" and what I conceptualize as Western individuals' and agencies' "self-censorship" regarding cases that unsettle the key foundations of the official discourse, are therefore addressed in the final part of the chapter with particular reference to the silenced reality of violence against women in the camps.

Finally I summarize the key arguments presented in this study, highlight its main contributions to existing academic debates, and present a range of recommendations to policy-makers and practitioners alike; I conclude by identifying a number of areas that require further research, both with particular reference to the Sahrawi refugee camps and the politics of representation more broadly.

— 1 —

Engendering the Colonial Encounter

REPORTS OF THE SAHRAWI REFUGEE CONTEXT habitually claim that Sahrawi women are, and always have been, "free," "equal," and "active participants" in all areas of refugee camp life due to their historically "equal" role in "Sahrawi society" both before and during much of the colonial era. References to the historical basis of Sahrawi women's "equality" include *Africa Confidential* (which refers to "Women's Lib in the Sahara," 1997), Hamdi (1993), Juliano (1998) and Pineda (1991). By subtitling her book on Sahrawi women "we were always so free" (1998; my translation), Juliano immediately indicates to the (actual/potential) reader that Sahrawi refugee women's present "freedom" is intimately connected to their "freedom" in the past.

Polisario/SADR and non-Sahrawi analysts also explain Sahrawi refugee women's current significance by stating that, while Sahrawi women have "always" enjoyed a powerful social position, their movements and roles were artificially limited by the Spanish administration during the colonial era.[1] They continue by explaining that the camps have therefore been specially designed by the "socially progressive" and "liberal" Polisario/SADR to reverse these unnatural restrictions, and return women to their preexisting high levels of social power and sociopolitical participation (e.g. Fernández-Aceytuno 1996, 65; Es-Sweyih 2001, 36). Sah-

---

1. Shoemaker uses the term "declension narratives" to refer to broadly made claims "that colonised women had status and power which they lost under the white patriarchal rule of colonists" (in Bulbeck 1998, 19).

rawi refugee women's current significance is thus represented as being historically rooted and simultaneously as politically and pragmatically necessary in line with the Polisario/SADR's (early) socialist orientation and men's absence from the camps throughout the first two decades of the conflict.

It is widely acknowledged that colonial projects impacted upon gender relations in multiple ways, usually empowering certain groups of colonial and colonized men to the disadvantage of both other men and the majority of women (i.e., Ahmed 1992; Badran 1995; McClintock 1995; Alexander and Mohanty 1997; Barnes 1999; Young 2001, 360–382). Colonialism (like other periods of accelerated and enforced change) is thus recognized to have been a process that "profoundly transformed the everyday lives and discursive terms of the colonized" (Abu-Lughod 1998b, 17). However, to date the Spanish Sahara has largely been marginalized by academics influenced by postcolonial studies, and few analyses have thus been developed vis-à-vis the impact of the colonial administration on social and gendered relations throughout the eight decades that Spain colonized the territory (1884–1975; cf. Fiddian-Qasmiyeh 2011b). Since contemporary accounts of sociopolitical dynamics in the Sahrawi refugee camps frequently draw on historically based claims, this chapter examines how the Sahrawi-Spanish colonial encounter was experienced by different groups of women and men in the territory.

Although many of the dynamics and policies that characterize the colonial period of the Western Sahara parallel those experienced by other colonized populations, this chapter does not compare the Sahrawi colonial experience with that of other peoples. Rather, drawing on primary research conducted with first generation refugees in the camps[2] and with Spaniards who lived and worked in the colony between the 1950s and 1970s,[3] I present a focused analysis of the different "colonial encounters"

2. Unless otherwise specified, all interviews with Sahrawis referred to throughout this chapter are derived from the SARC dataset.

3. This chapter draws on the testimonies of thirty-four former Spanish soldiers who completed their obligatory military service in the Spanish Sahara during the colonial period, along with those of three professional soldiers, one Spanish woman, and three

that diverse groups of individuals faced in light of the increasing Spanish presence in the territory.

I start by addressing a range of gendered themes that have emerged in first generation Sahrawi refugees' recollections of their experiences of the early colonial period (until the late 1940s), when the limited numerical and infrastructural Spanish presence in the colony during the first six decades of colonialism meant that day-to-day life for the majority of the territory's inhabitants was little affected by the colonizers. I then examine the gendered impacts of the increasing Spanish colonial presence that followed the discovery of phosphates in 1947, exploring a range of changes in livelihood strategies and differential access to spaces and services (according to gender, age, and family background) that characterized the processes of sedentarization and urbanization fomented by the colonial administration. Responses to the increasing colonial presence also varied according to the nature and extent of contact, with some individuals benefiting from emerging employment options, while others actively resisted colonialism in different ways. In the final section I therefore examine the terms of engagement between different groups of Spanish and Sahrawi residents throughout the later colonial period. Beyond analyzing the military resistance to the Spanish colonial power, this has remained a highly marginalized issue in the existing academic literature (one notable exception is Gandolfi 1989). A discussion of Spanish and Sahrawi refugees' accounts of the colonial encounter is particularly pertinent, given that widespread assertions are currently made regarding Spanish "fraternity" with "the Sahrawi people" and given that the presence of and dependence on Spaniards in the refugee camps continues to be both a reality and a necessity.

The Early Colonial Era

During (and indeed before) the early colonial era, tribes living in and around the Spanish Sahara were primarily nomadic groups that engaged

---

Spanish men who were born and raised there. All translations from Spanish are my own. For a detailed analysis of these Spanish informants' memories and accounts of the colonial encounter, see Fiddian-Qasmiyeh 2011b.

in a range of livelihood strategies including pastoralism, agriculture, fishing, and trading. All first generation refugees interviewed by the SARC team in the camps stressed the significance of movement and mobility in their lives prior to leaving the Spanish Sahara and of the particular social structure of the nomadic groups (sing. *frīg*, pl. *firgān*)[4] in which they lived as children and young adults. Each *frīg* was composed of a number of *khiyām* (tents, sing. *khayma*), which in turn were normally each run by a married couple and their children and sometimes included members of their extended family.

Throughout their periods of movement and settlement, different members of the *firgān* completed a range of activities and tasks according to their gender, age, and tribe. Girls and women, on the one hand, were traditionally in charge of the *khayma* and completed domestic jobs/tasks in or close to their home. Boys and men, on the other hand, undertook a wider variety of socioeconomic and political roles, including being a Qur'anic *mrābeṭ* (teacher), a *shaykh* (an old, knowledgeable, and respected man in the tribe), a trader, or a herdsman. Such roles can be placed in a clear social hierarchy, with both the *mrābeṭ* and the *shaykh* being central figures in each *frīg*, with higher levels of economic, social, and political power than other members of their nomadic group.[5] While the *mrābeṭ*'s power could be conceptualized as having been concentrated within the *frīg* in which he worked, by virtue of belonging to a scholarly religious tribe, his power transcended the *frīg* (El-Hamel 1999, 66),[6] just as the *shaykh*'s power transcended his tribe to greater or lesser degrees (especially if he was a representative at the tribal confederation, the *Ait Arbein*).[7]

Both male and female interviewees indicated that they had started studying the Qur'an at the age of approximately seven with a *mrābeṭ* who

---

4. The classical Arabic term is *farīq*, and refers broadly to "gatherings."

5. Bonte stresses that the majority of Sahrawi tribal groups are characterized by "strong differences of ranks within the tribe" (2006, 100).

6. A *mrābeṭ* could also be considered to be a *shaykh* (El-Hamel 1999, 66, 70).

7. Commonly referred to in English as "the Council of Forty," the *Ait Arbein* was the "Tribe of Forty Tribes" or, in essence, the "Tribe of Tribes."

worked within the *frīg*, providing a mobile religious education to the children of the group.[8]

> The neighbors also collectively contracted the *mrābeṭ* so that he could teach their children. They offered him a place, which would represent a mosque-like location. Children arrived carrying lots of wood; they used coal and a special mixture to write with. Children also brought money and many other things with them to give to the *mrābeṭ*. Children listened to and respected the *mrābeṭ*. (52-year-old man)

Remarking on the spatial division of girls and boys in the *mrābeṭ's khayma*, a 51-year-old woman observed that "all the children of the *frīg* studied with the *mrābeṭ*, the girls on one side and the boys on the other side of the tent." While both were able to study together due to this particular gendered division of space, equal access to education did not exist at the time. One of the most frequently mentioned reasons was that offered by a 72-year-old woman: "I was the eldest, and I was not given the opportunity to study Qur'anic school, although I knew enough to know my prayers and how to pray." As the eldest daughter, this woman would have been responsible for assisting her mother in all domestic tasks, taking on many or most of her mother's responsibilities as she grew older. As such, her access to an education would have been highly limited precisely due to her gender and sibling order.

Access to education at this time was also determined by the child's tribal background: girls from scholarly tribes were more likely to know how to read and write than other girls (El-Hamel 1999, 75), and only a small number of male adolescents from particular tribes were able to attend sedentary Qur'anic schools (known in the region as *maḥāḍir*)[9] in

8. Teachers also established sedentary schools; however, given the predominance of nomadism throughout the precolonial and colonial eras, mobile schooling was the norm. On Islamic education in Moorish society see El-Hamel 1999.

9. Deriving from the Arabic verb *ḥaḍara* ("to attend"), this term (sing. *maḥaḍra*, pl. *maḥāḍir*) does not exist in its present form as a noun in Arabic itself. *Maḥāḍir* are widely found in Mauritania (Hamel 1999) as well as in the Western Sahara, and are sedentary or nomadic educational institutions dedicated primarily to Islamic instruction.

the city of Smara or farther afield in Mauritania or Morocco (Perregaux 1987; El-Hamel 1999). This, in turn, meant that only young men from certain tribes were able to become teachers in the future, ensuring not only a continued "monopoly" of scholastic/religious knowledge, but the superiority of the scholastic group over others (ibid., 66).

Another major difference between boys and girls relates to social and familial expectations for their respective futures, and the processes by which they respectively entered the realm of adulthood. Male interviewees indicated that they were encouraged from an early age to help their fathers or uncles to tend to livestock close to the *khayma* and later at greater distances. After adolescence, they traveled with others to trading posts or cities in the region, with such travels continuing after marriage and parenthood. The routes to manhood were therefore many and varied, ranging from tending to herds, becoming a warrior, a fisherman, a scholar, or a tradesman.

Women's accounts of their childhoods and early adolescence, on the other hand, revolved around their preparation to leave *al-khayma al-kabīra* ("the big tent," i.e., their parents' tent) to establish *al-khayma al-ṣaghīra* ("the small tent"), which would at first house a newly-wed bride and her husband, and eventually her growing family. As her life cycle continued, and her family increased, a new *khayma kabīra* would thereafter be born. In essence, women's narratives tended to be united around the notion that, "some girls were married at a young age, others not, but the future of all girls was believed to be a woman's tent and her own family. Your future is your tent" (59-year-old woman). Notably, although the husband would also move to a new *khayma* and create a new family, men did not make reference to this change, or to either *al-khayma al-ṣaghīra* or *al-kabīra*. As such, this is a female-centered discourse, which was not shared or reproduced by men. If a woman's future was her tent, a man's future was much more widely dispersed, located, and conceptualized.

In the years before marriage, when boys were learning to complete their fathers' or uncles' roles, women reported undergoing a variety of steps to become ready for their new life in *al-khayma al-ṣaghīra*. These steps included the practical issues of learning to complete the tasks performed by their mothers and other members of their mothers' generation:

When we came back from the *lemrabet*, we tended to the small goats and sheep. We also helped our mothers to fetch wood, ignited the fire and made butter from milk using *al-shakwa*. When still young, we learned from the older women all the tasks around the tent, so that when we got married, we would be able to take care of our own tents. (45-year-old woman)

Further steps to growing up included donning the *milḥafa* (a long piece of fabric worn by women over an existing layer of clothing and loosely wrapped around their bodies and head), which, despite its usage among varied groups of Muslim women throughout the Arab world,[10] continues to be one of the main identifiers, a *sine qua non*, of "Sahrawi womanhood" (see Chapter 3). All girls eventually wore the *milḥafa*, and certainly did so before marriage, which in turn was perhaps the clearest marker of adulthood.[11] Several interviewees associated adopting the *milḥafa* with the age at which a girl's religious practice expanded to fasting during Ramadan[12] and therefore also to praying while wearing a veil (in this case the *milḥafa* itself). This view therefore intimately links the *milḥafa* to both womanhood and Islam and not solely to national or cultural identifiers.[13]

10. See Fernández-Puertas 1994, 379; Stillman 2003, xxv, 14, and 149; Rouse 2004, 230; Harvey 2005, 72; Taylor 2005, 10 and 32.

11. Female interviewees reported having been married between the ages of 14 and 17 during the colonial era, with parents having chosen the groom from among their (usually older) "cousins." Male interviewees also frequently made reference to the process by which they had married, sometimes indicating that they, unlike the women, had chosen their own spouse, but usually indicating that their parents had also chosen their marriage partner for them.

12. There is no fixed age at which children start to fast. Physical maturity, along with the child's family background, influence the age at which s/he fasts on a regular basis. I would suggest that girls become especially aware of their religious responsibilities as puberty advances, and their approaches to fasting change accordingly.

13. Challenging this connection is the recognition that girls started to wear the *milḥafa* at a diversity of ages. A woman brought up in Mauritania during the colonial era indicated that "there you have to wear the *milḥafa* much earlier" (49-year-old woman). She stated that she had started to wear the *milḥafa* at the age of around 14 or 15, suggesting that other girls would have started "much later."

An additional practice associated with girls becoming women during the colonial era was that of "fattening up," precisely in order to expedite "growing up." Explicitly connecting food, growth and adulthood, a 72-year-old woman recalled that: "I was given a special diet, *bluh*, to grow up quickly and become a girl [*sic*], and ready for the time I would have my own tent." In this context, womanhood is reached when a girl is ready to set up her own *khayma ṣaghīra* (with a husband), as confirmed by a third interviewee who clearly indicates the connection between eating, fattening up, and marriage:

> We were given a lot of food, especially milk, when we were in the tent. We were made to drink a lot and gain weight to make us healthy and beautiful. We drank many litres of milk, night and day . . . so we can grow up healthy and full to prepare us young girls for marriage, and for husbands, and to be able to manage a family and our own tent. (59-year-old woman)

Analyzing the food term *"bluh"* helps us better understand this connection. Cheikh claims that this term refers to "dates which are cut and exposed to the sun to make them mature more quickly" (quoted in Popenoe 2004). However, the Arabic root of the word (correctly transliterated as *bulūgh*), is the verb *balagha*, which means, along with "to mature" in general, more specifically "to attain puberty," or "to become marriageable, pubescent." Bearing out the etymology of the term, *bulūgh*'s physical purpose was to expedite the onset of puberty, to transform girls into women ("feeding their bodies to plump womanliness"; ibid., 44), and, most important, thus enable them to marry at a younger age.[14]

Beyond making a girl "healthy and beautiful," the material significance of such fattening is clearly presented by Harter (with reference to contemporary Northern Mauritania), who indicates that a girl's early

---

14. On the continued existence and rationale behind "fattening practices" and "force-feeding" in the region see Popenoe 2004; Rguibi and Belahsen 2006; Harter 2007; Al-Jazeera 2008. Importantly, fattening was/is not only encouraged among young girls to ensure their marriageability, but rather was/is a practice which is seen as favorable for women of all ages.

marriage thereby increases "her chances of securing a wealthy man, benefiting her whole family" (Harter 2007). In this sense, a "fattened" girl's increased *desirability* to men was both preceded and paralleled by her family's desire that she obtain the highest possible *mahr* (bridal payment) from a "wealthy man."[15]

Changing Contexts: Contact with the Colonizers

The discovery of phosphates in 1947 led to a major shift in colonial (economic) interest in the territory paralleled by a mass influx of Spanish civilians and soldiers. Spanish approaches to the territory altered considerably, if slowly at first, with the territory becoming a Spanish province in 1958 and officially forming part of the country of Spain from that date. From a Spanish civilian population of 1,220 in 1950, numbers increased to 5,304 by 1960 (Damis 1983) and 20,126 in 1974 (Barbier 1982). The determination to exploit the territory's natural resources and the need to control emerging anticolonial movements also caused the Spanish military presence to soar from 700 Spanish troops in 1925 to some 10,000 Spanish soldiers in 1966 and approximately 15,000 in 1970 (Damis 1983). This increased civilian and military presence significantly altered the characteristics of the Spanish population and the size and structure of urban settings where a large proportion of Spaniards lived and worked. The ever-expanding number of Spanish civilians and soldiers was accompanied by the settlement of many members of the until-then primarily nomadic tribes, who gradually moved (especially from the 1960s onward) to live around the territory's growing urban centers.

The colonial government estimated that 82% of the "native" population (more than 60,000 people) was sedentarized by 1974, if not urbanized (in Gonzálvez-Pérez 1994, 48). Of the fifty refugee households interviewed for the SARC project in the camps, eighteen reported having lived in cities during the late colonial period. This process of sedentarization and

15. Plumpness was also a clear sign of the girl's family's wealth and socioeconomic security. Although *mahr* is commonly conceptualized as "bridal money," this can be substituted or complemented with other material gifts, such as jewelry, furniture, or animals.

urbanization was partly due to the severe periods of drought which affected the territory between 1949 and 1974. Gaudio calculates that the droughts of 1959 led to the death of 50% of the territory's 60,000 camels, while all 40,000 sheep were slaughtered by their owners due to the desperate nature of their situation (1978). Other sources estimate that 60% of all livestock died between 1959 and 1963 (Pazzanita and Hodges 1994) in a drought that affected the MENA region more broadly. Several interviewees indicated that individuals, groups, and families started to move toward the urban centers to find alternative livelihood strategies directly as a result of the droughts and the subsequent death of their livestock.

This explanation, however, is insufficient when we note that serious droughts had affected the territory sporadically throughout the preceding centuries, and the population had developed strategies to survive such periods. One 59-year-old woman reflected that "previous generations tell us of times when they confronted drought and harsh weather, which forced them to live and eat plants they had not been used to." Other interviewees consistently referred to droughts that characterized their childhoods and adolescence and outlined how their families and other *frīg* members ensured the continued survival of the group: they moved closer to wells and waterholes; traveled in search of rainfall; exchanged animals for grains and clothes; or stored ground barley in special containers under the sand precisely for usage during times of drought. Given that even the "severe drought" of 1946 to 1950 (Pazzanita and Hodges 1994) was managed through "traditional" means, rather than via an increased reliance on the colonial power, we must ask what was particular about the late colonial era (from the 1950s and 1960s onward) which led to people approaching the urban areas rather than continuing to engage with their longer-standing strategies.

While conducting research in Cuba in 2006, I located a range of written Sahrawi sources which explicitly describe the process of urbanization and sedentarization as having been both forced and violent in character.[16]

---

16. Such responses to pastoral livelihood strategies, by means of "civilizing" nomads, are not restricted to the Spanish colonial administration of the territory, with similar

These sources include official SADR documents, which state that forced sedentarization and the extermination of livestock were symptomatic of the consolidation of Spain's colonial presence in the territory (SADR 1980, 28). A second group of sources are university theses written by Sahrawi students who completed their education in Cuba during the 1980s,[17] including B. A. Mahamoud (then studying history) who refers to the "intense campaign designed to push for the forced sedentarization of the nomadic population around the cities" (1986, 51; my translation). He further asserts that, especially after the anticolonial activities of 1957–1958, pasturelands were burnt and waterholes poisoned by the Spanish in order to destroy the only means of subsistence available until then: nomadism and pastoralism (ibid., 49). Claims concerning the colonial destruction of livestock are independently supported by three female SARC interviewees aged 51, 65, and 74.

On an official level, such pressure to sedentarize was often presented by the Spanish as a means of improving local living conditions. A more functionalist rationale can be found for enforcing urbanization, however: Wirth and Balaguer (1976) argue that a need for more fixed and Spanish-speaking workers for the phosphate mines and other nascent industries prompted the construction of over 5,000 houses for Spain's colonial subjects between 1960 and 1970.[18] The same authors claim that the increased number of Sahrawis able to access primary and secondary educations, although still limited, was equally related to this need. They accede that this was only possible in practical terms because of the parallel necessity

---

policies having been imposed by French, British and Italian powers in their respective colonies (e.g. Chatty and Colchester 2002, 5–6; Campbell 2004, 15).

17. While these Cuban-educated Sahrawi youth present the colonial experience as a highly negative and violent one, similar comments on the colonial period made in Spain and in the camps focus on the extremely negative and violent Moroccan occupation, and emphasize the "fraternal" connections which exist with Spain. I return to this point in the following chapters in relation to the impact of the audience on official representations of the colonial and refugee eras.

18. Wirth and Balaguer do not specify the number of houses built; this figure is taken from Barbier 1982.

of opening more schools for the children of Spaniards living and working in the territory.

A second student, M. A. Cisse, who graduated in law in the mid-1980s, equally identifies this connection between sedentarization and the mining industry:

> The nomads who constitute the majority of the population begin a process of sedentarization and urbanization due to the destruction of the traditional subsistence economy (which were agriculture and commerce between *saharianos*) and the necessity of being able to access workers for the mining centres. At that point a process of expropriation and exploitation of the emergent working class begins. (1985, 25; my translation)

The Spanish need for more workers, combined with the Sahrawi need to diversify livelihood strategies to support their families, therefore further help us to explain the trend toward sedentarization at this particular period.

Before turning to the impact of sedentarization on different inhabitants of the Spanish Sahara, it is essential to note that the colonized subjects' preference for greater or lesser degrees of movement could not be disrupted, despite the Spanish administration's sedentarist bias and its attempts to encourage the settlement of the nomadic population through housing schemes and the provision of food aid. As studies of periods of enforced change (including drought and colonization, as well as processes of forced migration and refugeedom) demonstrate, individuals and groups often prioritize "saving a way of life" over "saving a life" (Allen and Turton 1996), attempting to ensure the survival of the social group's customs, traditions, and norms despite the major shifts taking place around them.

Clearly indicating a preference for pastoralism over sedentarization, one 59-year-old woman reflected that "some people worked [in the cities] until they were able to save money and buy animals again and returned to their traditional lives."[19] Affirming the relevance of Salzman's concep-

---

19. As argued elsewhere, mobility continues to play a central role in social life in the Western Sahara and in the refugee camps today (Chatty, Fiddian-Qasmiyeh and Crivello 2010; Crivello and Fiddian-Qasmiyeh 2010).

tualization of processes of sedentarization as being based on a fluid continuum (1980, 10ff), another 51-year-old woman noted that

> [w]ith Spanish colonialism, people began to move to towns and cities and lived there during the summer. In the autumn they returned to the countryside to their camels and goats, but returned to the city during the hot season in the summer . . . I remember that we lived in the city in the summer and went back to the camels and goats in the *bādiya* during the winter.

Even those who lived in the city returned to the *bādiya*[20] on a seasonal basis, thereby indicating the enduring significance of both movement and nonurban living throughout the colonial period.

In addition to the seasons, a new form of dividing the years also emerged:

> My father got a place [in the city] through his own hard work and he used to take us there during the school year, and during the holidays we used to go to the *bādiya*. (33-year-old woman)

While the nomadic education system required the *mrābeṭ* to move with the *frīg*, in an urban context the seasons and work or school commitments influenced individuals' and families' movements between the city and the *bādiya*. Moving to a village/town during school term time and "having an address," while continuing to implement nomadic livelihood strategies, would leave nomads less visible in official figures (Lancaster and Lancaster 1998, 34), solidifying an image of "successful" sedentarization and urbanization.

Despite many people's continued determination to practice a nomadic or "traditional" lifestyle, a multitude of major changes nonetheless clearly *were* prompted by the colonial administration, and often simply due to

---

20. *Al-bādiya* is described as being a cooler and healthier place to live than the refugee camps, with many refugee families moving there in the summer months or sporadically throughout the year. It is estimated that several thousand Sahrawi nomads may live there permanently, herding their camels and goats in the area. It is a densely landmined territory, leading to frequent, and often fatal, landmine accidents.

contact with Spanish soldiers and civilians. While men, women, and youth in the *bādiya* continued to complete many of the activities prevalent in the early colonial period, a broad scope of new employment possibilities characterized by contact with the colonial powers became available for men in the territory.

The Spanish administration calculated that 13,000 Sahrawis had worked in the public and private sectors in 1974, of which 8,000 worked in construction and public works, 2,500 were "specialized workers" and 800 were civil servants (in Gonzálvez-Pérez 1994). The census data clearly indicates that while agriculturalists and herdsmen were "older" men, those employed by construction agencies and public works, different members of the military, and drivers were all "young" men: 46% of Sahrawi working in the police and military corps, and 56% of drivers, were men aged 20–29 (ibid.). Individuals clearly will have been prompted to move to the growing cities for different reasons according, among other factors, to their age and gender. While I discuss the impact of sedentarization and the colonial period on different groups of women below, according to Kuttab (2002) and SARC interviewees, masculinity and its ramifications and representations emerge as multiply related to working for and/or with the Spanish in urban locations. Hence, some men may have approached the city to maintain their families while others may have been simultaneously driven by the need to *prove* their ability to maintain their families (in order to demonstrate and enact their effective masculinity). A further number might have traveled to fulfill a "dream" (Kuttab 2002, 74) or to follow other male friends or relatives. However, city visits could have also led to a rejection of the colonial system, thereby demonstrating the ambiguous nature of the city (see below).

The nature of engagement between the Sahrawi and Spanish populations is particularly pertinent, given the claims that are habitually made in the refugee context about Spanish-Sahrawi "fraternity" during and after the colonial era. Despite current claims of proximity and mutual understanding, the majority of Spanish soldiers and civilians who participated in my research indicated that their interaction with the civilian Sahrawi population was limited to work or school relationships and that there were few "friendships" or social encounters between the "natives" and Spaniards (also see Fiddian-Qasmiyeh 2011b). Eight former soldiers described their exchanges with the civilian Sahrawi population as "scarce" or "minimal," and eighteen admitted that all or most of their encounters with the "natives" were either as a result of interactions with street vendors or employees in shops, tea houses, or restaurants or through working alongside local soldiers in the military Nomadic Troops (first created in 1923) or Territorial Police. Although I return to the limited nature of Spanish-Sahrawi contact below, a considerable number of Sahrawis continued to have independent jobs or occupations that required little contact with the colonizers, such as agriculturalists, herdsmen, traders, and fishermen.

While maintaining this distance may have been a matter of choice, gaining access to urban locations became increasingly difficult for both young and older men alike. From 1970 onward, movement to the cities was limited to those who had registered with the Spanish authorities and applied for a Spanish identity card (Diego-Aguirre 1988, 611; also SARC-A39 and Kuttab 2002, 31). The registration process was not automatic and was complicated both by the nomadic nature of the population[21] and the need to obtain support from a *shaykh* (as head of tribe) who would validate one's tribal identity (Kuttab 2002, 32). While creating difficulties and limitations for some Sahrawis, as in other colonial contexts this process simultaneously strengthened the power of others, including those *shaykh*s who worked with or alongside the colonizers.

Indeed, as several SARC interviewees remind us, while the *Ait Arbein* tribal confederate system existed well before the 1960s, in 1967, Spain

> established a special tribal system. It appointed a Sheikh for each tribe, who would be responsible for registering the members of his tribe. The Sheikh would also look after the interests and affairs of his tribe. (70-year-old man)

21. While questioning the reliability of the statistics, it is claimed that by 1974 only 30,271 out of a total registered Sahrawi population of 73,497 had obtained *carnés* (17,957 men and 12,334 women). Although this amounts to less than half of the population, Diego-Aguirre stresses that, since only individuals aged 15 or over were eligible, 75% of the eligible population held identity cards (1988).

The name of the new confederation was the *jamā'a* (the "group"), and the new *shaykhs'* tasks expanded to include distributing food provided by the Spanish and collecting taxes from members of his tribe.

Spain's interest in engaging with tribal leaders and increasing the Spanish-speaking labor pool drew communicative issues to the fore, since almost no Sahrawis had access to formal education throughout the preceding decades. Table 1 provides an overview of Sahrawi students' access to a formal education in the territory from 1948 to the end of the colonial era, documenting the number of children enrolled in colonial educational institutions along with changes in the number of these institutions per se.

From only one primary school with ninety-one Sahrawi students in 1948, by the end of the colonial era 6,059 children were enrolled alongside Spanish primary level students across the territory.[22] Access to a colonial education was almost entirely restricted to the children of urbanized families, with only a few (sixteen by 1967) rural or mobile schools (*escuelas nómadas*) being sponsored by the Spanish (Barona-Castañeda 2004, 249), specifically to "favor the adaptation of the nomad" to "la vie de tous" (Gaudio 1978, 186).

The majority of these children were not only privileged by virtue of being among the relatively few families living in cities at the time but also tended to be the children of high-ranking Sahrawis, including *shaykhs* who assisted the colonial administration and others already employed by Spain.

While the Spanish men who were born in the territory described their childhood contact with Sahrawis as "normal, like with any European," or "universally friendly . . . we were all at school together," only five SARC interviewees reported having attended Spanish colonial schools. Indeed, while the majority of interviewees stressed the Polisario/SADR's prioritization of education, a lack of access to a formal colonial education emerges as a noticeable theme in these interviews, with nine interviewees directly

---

22. By point of comparison, censual literacy in Spain was 73% in 1930 and 86% in 1960 (Tortella 1996, 192).

TABLE 1. Overview of students' access to education in the Spanish Sahara from 1948 to 1975

Date	Type of school
1948	One primary school (91 students).
1960	Rural schools and mobile schools opened for nomadic children.
1963	First secondary schools opened (23 secondary level students by 1964).
1965	850 students in primary schools.
1967	Two professional training centers (Aaiun and Villa Cisneros).
1968	General government orders that all students completing *Bachillerato* in Villa Cisneros forfeit further study to join the colonial administration.
1968	Male students first allowed access to Spanish and other universities.
1974	6,059 students in primary (incl. 909 girls) and 111 in secondary schools (incl. three girls); 124 boys and 70 girls in professional training.
1975	Population of 73,497, including 35,161 girls. Literacy rate under 5%. 75 students in Spain, 52 of these in Spanish universities.

Sources: Based on Barbier 1982; Gaudio 1975 and 1978; Pazzanita and Hodges 1994; Perregaux 1987; and Wirth and Balaguer 1976.

equating the colonial period not only with an absence but an explicit denial of formal education.[23]

Paralleling the gendered nature of access to a Qur'anic education, most children who had access to a colonial education were boys, with only 909 girls enrolled in primary schools and three in secondary schools in 1974 (Barbier 1982). This trend is reflected in the SARC interviews: while several men indicated that they had studied in Spanish schools, only one female informant had done so (a 39-year-old woman). Two other women

23. This equation is present in comments such as "the colonial presence was repressive, they did not build us schools" (49-year-old woman), "illiteracy was the result of Spanish colonialism" (32-year-old woman), and "we lived under colonialism which hindered us from acquiring an education" (38-year-old woman). More explicitly, one 40-year-old woman describes the colonial system as implementing "a policy of keeping the people ignorant and backward."

specified that the males in their family had attended school while the girls had been unable to. In one of these cases, the interviewee stated (with reference to her own children) that "the boys were educated, at least the primary school and technical training, and the girls were married at an early age, and had their own families" (72-year-old woman).

The only female interviewee who had studied at a Spanish school is worth brief consideration, since her case reflects a more general trend. Having studied with a *mrābeṭ* in the *bādiya* from the age of six, she first attended a Spanish school when she and her family moved to a town. The reason why she, unlike the daughters of the previously quoted woman who also lived in a city, was able to study at a Spanish school is directly related to her family background: her father, according to his own account, "was chosen as the *Shaykh* of a tribe" in 1966 and was appointed by the Spanish to be a member of the *jamā'a* (74-year-old man). He is the only SARC interviewee who can be considered to be a member of the elite upper social and administrative echelon, having "occupied numerous positions" during the colonial era, including being a representative before the UN Decolonization Committee. It appears clear that it was by virtue of her father's connections and associations with the Spanish that this woman was able to access a colonial education as a child.

While so few girls were enrolled in primary and secondary schools at the time, however, it is necessary to briefly analyze the nature of female education during the colonial era. This is particularly important since "studying at Spanish schools" is one of only two opportunities identified by informants as allowing girls or young women to have contact with Spaniards during the later colonial period.[24]

Beyond reproducing the gendered trends of primarily providing a Qur'anic education to small groups of boys from specific tribes, the education system also reproduced Francoist notions of education for boys and girls. Those girls who were educated in the colony were primarily taught by members of the Sección Femenina (Women's Section, henceforth

---

24. Although educational statistics during the colonial era have been presented in several studies, the content and aims of the curriculum have not received academic attention.

Sección), which was the female branch of the Spanish Falangist Party. Both followed and encouraged specific notions of femininity and womanhood in the Spanish Sahara.[25]

Spain's Falangist Party was founded by José-Antonio Primo de Rivera, and his sister Pilar headed the Party's Women's Section from June 1934. Given the nature of the Francoist regime at the time, the Sección promoted a form of Catholic traditionalism that appeared repressive and incongruous to many Spanish women. Nonetheless, while associating womanhood with motherhood, and prohibiting female employment following marriage, Bowen suggests that the Sección simultaneously offered Spanish girls and young women "a measure of autonomy" (2006, 9), providing "an arena for young girls and unmarried women to learn, teach and even participate in the political life of the nation" (ibid., 170). As such it allowed women who supported the regime to be part of the otherwise male-only institution, and simultaneously provided less politically-motivated women a degree of choice regarding their social and professional activities (the latter, only if they remained unmarried).

In the Spanish Sahara, the Sección was active in several ways, including providing a social network for Spanish military leaders' wives and daughters (Fiddian-Qasmiyeh 2011b), and, more important, in this context, providing an education to a small number of privileged Sahrawi girls and young women. The educational component of the Sección's work was based primarily in a boarding school in Aaiun, which housed students from all over the territory and from as far afield as Villa Cisneros/Dakhla. A number of other schools also provided a small group of young women with vocational training in line with the Francoist preferences of the time.

In Aaiun, all of the Sección's teachers were unmarried Spanish women who lived in the boarding school with their Sahrawi students, teaching both girls and young women:

25. Given the absence of literature on the Sección in the Spanish Sahara, the following paragraphs are based on information provided by two of the Spanish soldiers who responded to my electronic questionnaires, in addition to research conducted with a Spanish woman who taught with the Sección in Aaiun throughout the last five years of the colonial era.

> The work carried out by the Sección . . . was very complete . . . the edu-
> cational directives of the time were followed, and they [girls] were also
> offered extracurricular activities like theatre, music, or dancing . . . The
> women received literacy classes, and training in dressmaking, handicrafts,
> childcare, sewing, etc. (Former Spanish female teacher, January 2006)

While all of these activities are intimately associated with specific notions
of femininity and womanhood, especially with reference to both wifehood
and motherhood, this is not exclusively the case. Consequently, this teacher
states that she is still in touch with some of her former students, who have
gone on to play significant roles in the Algerian-based refugee camps:

> It gives me great pride to know that nowadays several of the girls/
> women [sic] who studied with me are working in the Tindouf camps as
> nurses, teachers, doctors, etc.

She thereby considers that she provided her students with essential training not only to become mothers, but also much more: nurses, teachers and
doctors.

Despite the wholly positive account of female schooling offered by this
former teacher, Kuttab (2002, 143ff) emphatically dismisses the colonial
education system (which he himself attended as a child) as simply preparing girls and young women to become mothers, challenging the broader
system as being colonialist and failing to address the local population's
(linguistic and other) needs. Indeed, his rejection of the way in which the
education system was run is echoed in various interviews conducted in
the camps, as well as by one of the Spanish soldiers contacted. As the
latter stresses, female schooling was not only limited to a miniscule elite
in the territory, but offered these young women what he terms "una for-
mación político-social" (politico-social training) from the perspective of the
Falangist Sección. Nevertheless, he notes that this system failed to provide
students with any interactions with the broader female European population, beyond the teachers themselves.

As was the case in other colonies at the time, in this soldier's view
the girls studying at the Sección's schools belonged to the richest families
at the top of the social hierarchy, including those involved in commerce

and business and who were "more or less collaborationists with the Spanish Administration." He suggests that these families' main rationale for sending "their women" to European-style schools was that the families would thus be able to establish further associations with Europeans, thereby facilitating applications for licenses (including to open shops) and other privileges. Indeed, just as both exogamous and endogamous marriage practices have been conceptualized as means of establishing and/or strengthening social or political ties between families and social classes, in this sense a colonial education, not marriage, is presented as a social bridge allowing for the further social mobility of the girls' families, rather than solely for the girls themselves.

Thus, the official motivation of these schools was to transform these elite girls and young women into "proper" wives and mothers, while simultaneously offering a yet smaller number of them the opportunity to tentatively enter certain professions designated as "feminine" during the colonial era, such as professional nursing and child care. Although studying at colonial schools was mentioned as one of only two "roles" that allowed girls and young women to have contact with the colonizers, in interviews conducted in the camps, and in Kuttab's discussion of the colonial period, a number of additional female jobs have emerged from this brief discussion. Being taught by Spanish teachers also provided these young Sahrawi women with Spanish role models who reinforced some of the notions of femininity and womanhood pervading the curriculum, while simultaneously offering them the direct example of relatively independent, unmarried professional women. This particular form of contact and exposure would have affected these young Sahrawi women's expectations and opportunities for the future, providing them with an additional level of both familial and personal power and leverage.

Although the Spanish colonial education system had a direct impact on a small number of elite female students in many ways, one overarching explanation offered by many commentators for broader changes in women's movements and roles during the colonial era is that it was as a direct result of sedentarization. Gaudio stresses that "nomadic life left them free, as the keepers [maîtresses] of their tent. Sedentarized, they became secondary and secluded" (1978, 142–143; my translation). With reference to the impact of sedentarization on Maure women more widely, Chassey indicates that "there followed, in the cities in particular, a degradation of the status of women: secluded, veiled, reduced to domestic tasks and a condition of subjugation" (1977, 79; my translation). Indeed, according to my own research and the testimonies analyzed by Gandolfi (1989), the vast majority of accounts offered by Spanish civilians and members of the military who resided in the territory during the colonial era tend to support this depiction of sedentarized Sahrawi women as subjugated and weak, which is in direct contrast to the "powerful" and "free" women who populate contemporary mainstream accounts of Sahrawi gender relations. Gandolfi indicates that, unlike nomadic women, urban Sahrawi women were described by her Spanish informants as "typical Arab women, kept in private spaces, subjected to the law of the husband, without the right to speak and without culture" (ibid.; my translation).

Such accounts are substantiated by a wide range of ethnographic studies of nomadic populations and hunter-gatherers, including those conducted by feminist anthropologists such as Draper (1975) and Moore (1988). The roots of the debate on women's statuses in nomadic and sedentary societies reach as far back as Ibn Khaldun's *Al-Muqaddimah* (1967; originally published in 1311) or Engels' *The Origin of the Family, Private Property, and the State* (1902; first published in 1884). Further, given the recognition that an increase in violence against women tends to occur within private walled spaces (Pain 1997), Gaudio and Chassey's conclusions are far from unique.

Beyond the general impact of sedentarization, however, Gandolfi (1989) offers further reasons for the apparent discrepancy between "free and strong" women before and after the colonial era and the "weak and subjugated" women of the colonial cities. She suggests that Spanish testimonies might reflect the effects of the machismo espoused by the Spanish administration and its members in the colony. My discussion of the Sección Femenina above could be taken as partial support for this view of the introduction of Spanish *machista* policies and perspectives vis-à-vis female education strategies and general Falangist preferences.

Alternatively, Gandolfi proposes, changes in gender relations could have arisen as a result of the city-based Sahrawi population "mimicking"

either the Spaniards they were in contact with or other sedentary populations surrounding them. While rejecting Gandolfi's claim that a unidirec-
tional form of "mimicry" or straightforward and uncritical adoption of
Spanish or sedentary practices could have taken place, I would suggest
that the reality of observing a range of Spanish family, social, and professional relations would have all affected the ways in which Sahrawis, both
male and female, viewed the Spanish, and, in turn, their own family and
social systems. Such observations could in some cases have led to tangible
changes in gender relations.

Keenan's analysis of the Algerian Tuareg confirms the impact of sedentarization by claiming that sedentary Tuareg women "became reduced
more to the status of 'domestic workers'" (2004a, 139) due to the new location of these tasks ("'indoors,' rather than in the open"), and the general
move toward the greater seclusion of women (ibid., 139). However, he also
directly associates the increase in Tuareg women's domesticity with their
reduced reliance on "their *tiklatin*," their slave women (ibid. and 2006,
926–927), therefore highlighting that sedentarization will have affected
women differently depending on their legal, social, and/or ethnic/racial
identity. Although one may lament the increased domesticity of urbanized free women, the impact on their slaves would be worthy of further
examination (see HRW 2008 for preliminary accounts of the legacy of
slavery in the Sahrawi refugee camps).

The Colonial Encounter: Spanish and Sahrawi Views

Other than tracing the emergence of armed resistance against the
colonial power, Spanish accounts written during and after the colonial
era have tended to ignore the tension and anticolonial sentiment felt by
the territory's inhabitants toward the colonizers. Equally, Spanish soldiers
and civilians who lived in the then-Spanish Sahara appear to have failed
to understand why the Sahrawi population rejected Spanish colonialism.
Discussing the emergence of the anticolonial Polisario Front in the 1970s,
one soldier characteristically stated to me that "I was very disappointed by
the Sahrawi population, we behaved extraordinarily with them and with
sublime respect." Another concluded, as many Spaniards still do today,
that the Sahrawi should not have pushed for the Spanish withdrawal,

since the colonial presence would always have been preferable to their exodus to Algeria as a result of the Moroccan and Mauritanian invasions in 1975. The essence of this complaint is that, if the Sahrawi had accepted Spanish rule, they would have continued to live peacefully in their land, even if under Spanish social, political, economic, and legal control.

The following quotation by a high-ranking member of the Spanish military summarizes his understanding of life in the Spanish Sahara:

> They had the highest "per capita" income in Africa . . . they were practically sedentary . . . all families received a part of a salary and the food aid which was provided . . . The ambiance . . . had traditionally been good since Spain respected their ethnic, cultural and religious particularities . . . there was great religious freedom. Spain even built them a mosque.

Despite this, and other official governmental accounts of the positive and harmonious nature of the colonial experience, the majority of interviews conducted with refugees who lived through the colonial era reveal otherwise. So too do the accounts offered by a small number of Spanish soldiers and a few of the limited (due to Spanish censorship) news reports that commented on living conditions. Outlining the nature of the newly urbanized population's living quarters, and directly in contrast with the preceding quotation, the following extract from a Canary Islands newspaper published in 1974 states that,

> although the per capita income is [high], there is much visible poverty in many sectors. A large part of the Sahrawi population live in *khaimas* and tin huts, forming great belts around El-Aaiun or spread out in areas of the desert that have not yet died due to the drought. One sees terrible cases of poverty and of the natives subsisting in scandalously poor living conditions. (in Algueró-Cuervo 2003; my translation)

Indeed, one soldier's account is diametrically opposed to the military superior quoted above, indicating clearly that "Spain provided nothing toward the development of that territory" and concluding that "we didn't even know why we were there."

Only two soldiers identified the reasons for their being stationed in the Spanish colony. The first simply noted "we were an Army Unit, with a military mission in a colonial territory and we only had contact with the natives when it was entirely necessary," thereby indicating the major separation that existed between the Spanish military and the Sahrawi civilian population. A second soldier was the single informant who indicated an awareness, and understanding, of why the "natives" would have rejected colonization:

> due to my ideology, I was against the obligatory military service and on top of that I considered myself to be an "occupying" force. I thought that the Sahara was for the Sahrawis, just like Palestine . . . If I considered myself to be an occupying force, just imagine [how they perceived me].

This leads us to ask, indeed, what did the Sahrawi consider the Spanish "to be," and how do refugees today describe the colonial encounter?

Despite the majority of Spanish soldiers holding the Polisario responsible for instigating anti-Spanish sentiment, and although many Sahrawis collaborated with and supported the Spanish administration of the territory, anticolonial activities existed in the territory well before the UN called for the decolonization of the then-Spanish Sahara. Armed resistance was enacted against the French in the 1930s (along with Moroccans) and, more significantly, against the French and Spanish in the 1957 Ifni War (referred to by interviewees as *'am al-hajma*, "year of the attack"). By the 1970s, such sentiments were magnifying, influenced by a combination of the harsh physical conditions in the territory and the population's increased awareness, through diverse means, of the possibility of resisting occupation and demanding independence.

Racism, unequal treatment of Sahrawis, multiple forms of mistreatment, the increasing presence of Spanish soldiers in the territory, and the realization that Spanish interest was due to a desire to exploit natural resources for financial gain are all divulged by interviewees as factors prompting the colonized population to reject Spanish colonialism (cf. Sayeh 1998). As discussed earlier, such a rejection was fomented in particular by young men who had studied in Morocco and Spain, many of whom were eventually the founding members of the Polisario.

While several interviewees suggested that the Spanish did not "really" colonize them (contrasted with the Algerian or Mauritanian colonial experience), and one 71-year-old woman even proposed that "under Spain we did not feel the oppression," members from fourteen households interviewed in the camps explicitly reflected on their own or their family's direct involvement in a range of anticolonial activities. Four male interviewees indicated that they had been members of the Polisario from its birth, having fought against the Spanish in the late colonial period. Women's involvement in nonmilitary activities is stressed by six interviewees (both male and female) and is unsurprising insofar as a breadth of literature has successfully highlighted the multiple ways in which women from around the world have been involved in innumerable anticolonial and liberation movements (e.g., Enloe 1989; Pettman 1996).

In addition to a relatively miniscule number of women who were reportedly militarily involved (79-year-old woman cited above), some of the female interviewees were themselves active in anti-Spanish demonstrations, and many others supported their brothers', husbands' and fathers' political and military actions in a number of ways. Indeed, it was during the later colonial period that women and older girls gained access to a greater range of roles and activities outside of the family home.

While not wishing to undermine the significance of the anticolonial sentiments and activities of those women who were involved at that time—and while there can be no doubt that women were active agents throughout the later colonial period (just as they had been in earlier historical periods)—it is equally clear that these activities would have depended on a range of intersecting factors, including women's social, tribal, educational, marital, and parental statuses.[26] According to these interviews, women's involvement appears to have taken place within the context of, and according to, their parental or marital family's political and/or military activism. What seems essential is not to refute women's involvement but rather to explore why there is such a strong contemporary focus, as directed by the Polisario/SADR, on women's high level of involvement in

26. These are but a small selection of key identity markers and statuses that are significant to the opportunities available to different individuals and social groups; other factors which are beyond the scope of this thesis include sexuality and disability status.

the anticolonial struggle, and why, for instance, claims such as "the Sahrawi, *especially women*, were very active" (54-year-old man; my emphasis), are repeatedly made when discussing this period. I return to this core question throughout the remainder of the book.

When discussing women's participation in the anticolonial movement, it is worth noting that, according to several interviewees, in the 1970s and certainly before, there had been, as a whole, a "lack of political consciousness among the Sahrawi, especially women" (50-year-old woman). This lack of political awareness appears to have been particularly common among the nomadic population, which is one of the reasons why other interviewees highlight the significance of providing "political education" to members of the nomadic and urban communities. Based on the SARC interviews, we can infer that those women who were involved in anticolonial activities were those based in the larger urban settings such as Aaiun, rather than girls and women living in the *bādiya*. These city contexts were characterized by social and political interactions with other urbanites, individuals who in turn had increasingly regular contact with the colonizers in what emerges as a key locus of contestation.

One female interviewee reflected on the period following the 1970 Zemla incident (in Aaiun), when the Spanish Legion fired against anticolonial demonstrators, killing several dozen of them:

> My husband began to tell me about the real situation and what was to be expected in the future political horizon . . . The revolutionaries began to raise awareness among people regarding the necessity of the revolution to liberate the homeland. They instilled nationalist sentiments among the Sahrawis and spread political consciousness. Although for the Sahrawis these ideas were new, many of them responded and agreed with them. (54-year-old woman)

In this sense, while there had been some engagement in anticolonial activities throughout the colonial period, it was not until the late 1960s and early 1970s that this became a more widespread exercise. Beyond the emergence and intensification of a range of explicit activities designed to unsettle and/or overthrow the colonial occupation, I shall now briefly explore the nature of specific labels used by interviewees to describe colonial Spaniards. Given that some of these terms continue to be used in the contemporary refugee context, the following overview will enable us to contextualize the nature of Spanish-Sahrawi relations in the camps, which I argue has led to certain characteristics being highlighted, while others are silenced.

Naṣārā: The Religious Dimension

Throughout my research in the refugee camps and in South Africa, as well as in the SARC interview transcripts and Arabic-language texts consulted, the word *Naṣrāni* (m. pl.) has emerged as a pivotal descriptive term used to refer to Spaniards. It is interesting to note that this term has remained entirely unexamined in any of the literature on the Western Sahara, and broader research indicates that this lexical idiom has received only limited academic attention (in English) by a few theologians, notably Muhibbu-Din (2000) and Steenbrink (2002).

Kuttab (2002) and SARC interviewees' usage of this word is of particular interest, and yet, simultaneously, it is important to note that while *Naṣārā* is a Qur'anic term that means "Christian" and is habitually used to refer to the People of the Book (*Ahl al-Kitab*), it has misleadingly been translated by the Sahrawi SARC researchers as meaning "Europeans." This leads us not only to ask why Kuttab and SARC interviewees decided to use this particular term to refer to the colonizers but also why SARC researchers should have mistranslated the label, hiding its exclusively religious meaning.

Since the present discussion focuses on the colonial era, in this section I draw upon examples derived from the SARC interviews and Kuttab's historiography, while in Chapter 4 I contextualize the usage of this term in the refugee camp setting. The following extracts are copied directly from the SARC transcripts, with the translation or explanation appearing as in the original:[27]

27. The interview transcripts analyzed had been translated from Hassaniya into English when I gained access to them; in light of the frequency with which Sahrawi refugees used the term during my fieldwork in the refugee camps, this descriptor was probably used by SARC interviewees more frequently than currently appears in the transcripts.

and they fought with the *Naṣārā* (Europeans) . . . (71-year-old woman)

They sold it to the Europeans (*Naṣārā*) as well as to Muslims. (74-year-old woman)

It is my conclusion that these are incorrect translations following an analysis of the relevant Qur'anic references and Al-Jaberi's in-depth overview of Christian and Muslim scholars' diverse interpretations of this term, which reflects the complexity of the concept in theological and historical senses (2006, 37–39), along with in-depth consultation with several experts in the Arabic language and with Arabic-language speakers from across the MENA region (Sudan, Libya, Palestine, Egypt and Morocco). Noting that the term *Naṣrānī* was first cited in 1583, according to the *Oxford English Dictionary*, taken to mean a "Christian" (Cannon and Méndez-Egle 1979), my research confirms that this term should solely be translated as Christians and that it is intrinsically imbued with religious significance. Indeed, my sources stressed that by describing people as *Naṣārā* one is in essence indicating their religious "otherness."[28] This observation is supported by Steenbrink, who states in a resentful account of the usage of the term *Naṣārā* in "Qur'anic readings," that the word "underlines the 'otherness' of the Christians . . . otherness is clearly dominating" (2002, 201).

This brief discussion suggests some reasons why Sahrawi translators might have distanced themselves from the literal translation of the term *Naṣārā*, purposely presenting it as meaning "Europeans," which is considerably less value laden. I present an additional reason for this mistranslation (or semantic dilution) in subsequent chapters, suggesting that within the context of the refugee camps and the refugees' dependence on the (primarily Spanish/European) humanitarian and broader solidarity system, the question of external relations, and therefore how one presents one's impressions regarding the Other, becomes a matter of the Sahrawi's "politics of survival."

---

28. A Libyan and a Palestinian/Egyptian academic indicated that they would use the words *ajnabī* or *ajnabiyya* (m. and f. sing.), *Inglīzi* (Englishman), and *mesīhi* or *mesihiyya* (m. and f. sing.) to refer respectively to a foreigner, someone's country of origin, or a Christian person's religion.

Returning to the interviewees' discussions of the colonial era, in the second example quoted above it appears clear that by contrasting the term *Naṣārā* with the latter term, "Muslims," the speaker's intention was to use the word as a religious marker, rather than simply referring to the people's origin (from Europe). References made in Kuttab's account highlight the religious significance of the term, mentioning the debate of whether it was haram or halal (Islamically forbidden or permitted, respectively) to make the pilgrimage to Mecca relying on *mal an-Naṣārā* ("the Christians' money;" 2002, 185), and including references to the *Naṣārā* in relation to the existence of brothels and bars in Aaiun (ibid., 158).

A second term to be considered in this context is *rūm*, which the Sahrawi SARC researchers translate in the following transcript as "westerners":

> The colonial presence was repressive (Spain), they did not build us schools, and we used to say that studying with the *"roum"* (meaning westerners), is difficult and we do not like it. (49-year-old woman)

While the term *rūm* can indeed refer to "westerners," I would suggest that in this context the second meaning offered by the *Munjid* Arabic dictionary ("a Christian denomination") is the more appropriate definition. As such, the frequency with which these terms appear in narratives pertaining to the colonial era indicates the extent to which the colonial encounter was a religious one and that the colonized population was resentful of their Christian occupiers who are presented as religious Others and as holders and transmitters of Islamically forbidden goods and services.

Until now, both the religious dimensions of the colonial encounter and the general animosity toward the Spanish colonial presence in the territory have been marginalized in popular Spanish and Sahrawi histories of the colonial era, for reasons I explore later. Despite this major silence in the literature, and beyond the terminological matters raised above, religion emerges as a central feature throughout the SARC interviews, my own interviews in the camps and elsewhere, and Kuttab's historiography. This is also the case in the responses provided by former Spanish soldiers, many of whom refer to the colonized population as *"los árabes," "moros," "mojamés"* [sic], and *"musulmanes"* ("the Arabs," "moors,"

"Mohammedans," and "Muslims," respectively), all of which carry (pejorative) religious meanings.[29] Multiple references are made to "Muslim men's" innate machismo and to other exploitative and violent practices that are directly related by these Spanish respondents to Islam and Islamic practice (also see Fiddian-Qasmiyeh 2011b).

While one interviewee quoted above suggested that Spain was respectful and tolerant of their colonial subjects' beliefs since "Spain even built them a mosque," some interviewees indicated that the religious divide was not only a key concern for them but could also be understood as a motivating factor for rejecting the colonial presence. With reference to the birth of the armed anticolonial movement, a 70-year-old former *mrābeṭ* states:

> We, the teachers of the Qur'an were the first ones to be informed and we welcomed the resistance for the liberation of *this country of Islam* from the Spaniards. (my emphasis)

Building upon this preliminary analysis, in subsequent chapters I explore the continued reality of tension between Spaniards and Sahrawi refugees despite official claims to "fraternity" and "friendship." In part I will do so by specifically asking how and why mainstream accounts of the Sahrawi refugee camps consistently marginalize the significance of religious identity and practice through declaring the secular nature of the "Sahrawi people" in highly gendered terms.

Conclusion

Social relations altered in a multiplicity of ways and for a variety of reasons throughout the colonial era, as social environments changed and both contact and dependence upon Spaniards increased. Although some changes may have been voluntary in nature, others were forced as a result

---

29. Labels like *moro* (which has a strongly negative connotation in Spanish) parallel the demeaning descriptions of "native" ways of life offered by a number of soldiers. Pejorative terms offered in the Spanish soldiers' responses indicate the extent to which racism continues, in the 2000s, to play a central part in how they conceptualize the colonial encounter and Sahrawi "natives."

of the increasingly unequal power dynamics at play between different groups and sociopolitical structures. Building upon this recognition, in the following chapters I will continue to examine the impact that political and material dependence on non-Sahrawis has had on different social, organizational, and representational structures in and underpinning the refugee camps. Although major organizational and social changes have continued to take place under the Polisario/SADR's leadership since 1975–1976, in particular I identify and examine the differences that may exist between official claims regarding women's freedom and activism in the camps and many refugees' determination to prioritize certain identities and practices (including religiously motivated ones) that are strategically marginalized by their representatives.

It is important to document the extent to which individuals' and groups' experiences of the colonial era were mediated by intersecting factors such as gender, generation, and family and tribal background; doing so confirms that "it is not easy to draw a sufficiently clear picture of the Saharawi woman prior to the colonial period," precisely because there was no readily identifiable homogenized "Saharawi society" in the precolonial or early colonial eras (Amoretti 1987, 188). Having refuted the validity of widespread claims that "Sahrawi women" as a unified whole have "always been so free" (Juliano *op. cit.*) thereby leads us to ask why and through which discursive mechanisms such claims have been re/produced since the camps' creation in 1975–1976. A related matter to be explored is the impact of hiding this heterogeneity and the continued reality of hierarchical structures in the refugee camps.

— 2 —

The Sahrawi Refugee Camps

International and Solidarity Networks

UNLIKE REFUGEE CAMPS that are run and controlled by international organizations such as the United Nations High Commission for Refugees (UNHCR), the Sahrawi refugee camps have been "managed" since their creation by the Polisario Front, which proclaimed the birth of the camp-based SADR in February 1976. Malkki argues that refugee camps provide the potential for "managers" to control medical and sanitary matters, observe and limit socioeconomic dynamics, "regularize" refugees' status, and "normalize" their lives (Malkki 1995a, 112). At the same time, as a device of power that contains and encloses groups, refugee camps enable both the production of their own "fixed and objectified" objects and domains of knowledge ("the refugees") and simultaneously provide a space for continual subversion and transformation (ibid., 237). Camps act as "controlling institutions"[1] and "technologies of power" (Malkki 1995b, 498) and therefore potentially both enable and inhibit action and discourses, allowing for social and political invention and change. In the case under consideration, the Sahrawi refugee camps have habitually been presented by the Polisario/SADR and many Western observers alike as a location for an experiment in "social democracy" and participatory aid management. Most important for this study, the Sahrawi refugee camps

1. Hitchcox quoted in Callamard 1999, 203.

79

can be identified as a space for the re/production of particular representations of gender.[2]

Although this book primarily explores the "ideal" representation of "secular gender equality" in/from the camps, this is only one element of a broader strategy of international public relations designed by the Polisario/SADR to secure international support. In the first part of this chapter, I briefly examine the ways in which the Polisario/SADR has successfully projected the camps as a "democratic" and "egalitarian" space to non-Sahrawi visitors and external observers. I then provide an overview of the history and structure of the camps, with particular reference to their organization and demography and to educational and employment systems in place there. In the second part of this chapter, I highlight the extent to which the camps are ultimately politically and physically dependent upon a range of international and transnational networks.

Indeed, Appadurai has stressed that "every major refugee camp . . . is a translocality" (2003, 339), hinting at the multiple ways in which refugees may be implicated in international or transnational networks, including the presence of international NGOs and the role of remittances and transnational livelihood strategies (Hyndman and Walton-Roberts 2000; Jacobsen 2002; Crisp 2003). The Sahrawi refugee context is characterized by these and other transnational dynamics, in particular a specific dependence on a range of non-Sahrawi state and nonstate actors that offer the Polisario/SADR different forms of humanitarian and political support. I argue that this dependency has led to the development of particular strategies designed to ensure the continuation of support that keeps the camps, their inhabitants, and the Sahrawi "cause" alive. While a multiplicity of such networks exists,[3] I will focus primarily on the solidarity network formed by members of Western civil society and especially those of the former colonial power, Spain.

2. Malkki's focus is on the re/creation of "mythico-histories" (1995a, 237).

3. See Fiddian-Qasmiyeh 2011a and 2011g for analyses of solidarity networks based around Evangelical-humanitarians.

The Sahrawi Refugee Camps

The vast majority of the earliest reports written on the camps in the 1980s stressed the Polisario/SADR's extraordinary "participatory ideology" and "democratic" organization of the camps (e.g., Harrell-Bond 1981a, 1–4; Black 1984, 1–2; Mowles 1986, 8–9). These further highlighted that the camps are "models of efficient local government" (Brazier 1997, 14), whose members are elected in "state" elections during National Conferences, which are held every five years.

However, while Zunes notes a "high degree of economic and social democracy" since the camps' creation, he points to the fact that "actual political democracy for most of [the 1980s] was limited" (1999, 44). Indeed, he acknowledges with reference to an earlier article that he published in 1988 entitled "Participatory Democracy in the Sahara: A Study of Polisario Self-Governance," "that in hindsight, parts of my analysis dealing with the actual level of political democracy at that time appear to have been premature in light of subsequent events" (1999, 50; also Shelley 2004, 176).

Outlining the characteristics of the period he is referring to (the 1980s), which led to a major camp-based rebellion against the Polisario and subsequent human rights abuses in 1988, he writes:

> Many Sahrawis felt there was too much domination by one element of the Polisario [i.e., members of the Rgaybat tribe] and *serious discrepancies* between the movement's *egalitarian line and the political reality*. On the political level, the Polisario's executive committee made all the real decisions despite the *façade of participatory democracy*. (1999, 50; my emphasis)

His frank acknowledgment that things had not been quite as they appeared at the time of his short (10 day) visit highlights both the extent to which the authors of earlier pieces accepted and reproduced what he retrospectively describes as a *"façade* of participatory democracy," and simultaneously the extent to which Polisario/SADR had successfully projected this image to its observers *as* a "reality" to be transmitted to a broader audience in their articles and reports.

Despite recognizing the ways in which Polisario/SADR successfully "conditioned" external perceptions of the camps in the past, Zunes claims that "radical reforms" have followed the 1991 Polisario Conference and that "there is now a new and more democratic constitution and an independent human rights commission" (1999, 44). Recently he has once again declared, using the same terms that he conceded he had "prematurely" employed in 1988, that "the self-governing structures within the refugee camps are among the most impressive examples of participatory democracy in the world," describing them as a uniquely "progressive and democratic model" (quoted in Mundy and Zunes 2002).

Although reforms have undoubtedly led toward a "more" democratic system in the camps[4] and the terms "participation" and "democracy" are themselves open to multiple interpretation in this context (Wilson 2010), major discrepancies continue to exist between the Polisario/SADR's representation of the camps as an ideal space characterized by participatory democracy and egalitarianism (what we can call the official "façade"), and the complex sociopolitical realities of life in the camps. One of the main questions that I address in this book is one that Zunes has marginalized from view: precisely *why* certain façades (including those of participatory democracy but more precisely in the context of the current study, gender equality) should have been created by the Polisario/SADR and projected to specific external audiences.

The role played by academics and other commentators who have repeated and reinscribed this script, and have therefore "shifted from the role of consumer [or audience] to that of producer" (Eagleton 1983, 119), cannot be overemphasized in this case:

> A great deal of power and social control is exercised not by brutal force or even by economic coercion, but by the activities of "experts" who are licensed to define, describe and classify things and people. (Cameron 2001, 16, in Sunderland and Litosseliti 2002, 30)

---

4. Abdelaziz was reelected SADR president in 2003, receiving an "incredible" 92% of the vote (Mundy 2007, 283).

In the case under consideration the Polisario/SADR, academics and practitioners alike have idealized and heralded a particular image of refugee women, whilst silencing both "ordinary" Sahrawi women and other
women in the process. Having rejected what Hyndman refers to as "the
charity script of the needy *and* grateful" (2000, 156; emphasis in original),
the Polisario/SADR has developed an alternative script oriented to the
international aid system, with "liberated" and "empowered" women as
its key protagonists. In this manner, it is possible to discern that the refugee camps are reformulated, for reasons and with implications explored
throughout this book, as what we may label a "secular, liberating and
empowering space," which is a direct antithesis of Kristeva's conceptualization of the Islamic world as a "space of repression" (Kristeva 2000, 28;
on Kristeva and Islam, see Almond 2007, 131–155).

Camp Structures

Although the number, location, and composition of the camps have
changed since their establishment in 1975 due to epidemics and floods,[5]
there are currently four major established refugee camps run by the
Polisario/SADR. They are named after the main cities/towns of the
Western Sahara: Aaiun, Ausserd, Smara, and Dakhla. The first three are
respectively approximately 65, 40, and 50 km from the nearest Algerian
city, Tindouf (WFP 2002, 7), and a 22, 40, and 19 km drive from Rabouni
(ECHO 2001:13), which is the administrative center of the camps and
where the SADR's camp-based Ministries are found. Dakhla is the far-
thermost camp, being over 180 km from Tindouf, 150 km from Rabouni,
and very close to the Algerian-Mauritanian border.[6] A fifth, smaller camp

5. A number of smaller camps were abandoned early on due to measles epidemics
(SARC-L08), while Ausserd was only built in 1985. Ausserd's low-lying tents were destroyed
by torrential rains in 1986, leading to a substantial relocation of part of the camp (Firebrace
1987). Later, Aaiun suffered greatly during the 1995 floods (Abjean 2003), with all camps
being hard-hit by the 2006 rains, resulting in many families leaving Dakhla and moving to
other camps.

6. Such distances must be evaluated in relation to the absence of regular transport
and of asphalted roads in most cases.

has developed around the National Women's School, called 27 February School/Camp, and was the location of the majority of my research in the camps (see Map 2). A number of "national" SADR institutions, such as the National Parliament and National Council, National Hospital and Pharmaceutical Laboratory, the National War Hospital and the Landmine Victims' Centre, are all located close to the administrative capital, which, in turn, is approximately 25 km from Tindouf and its military airport.

In addition to managing these well-established spaces, the Polisario/ SADR has recently decided to assert its "national" "authority" or "sovereignty" 280 km to the southwest of the camps, proclaiming that the settlement of Tifariti (see Map 1) will be the SADR's new "capital" (SPS 2005; Cembrero 2008). Tifariti will reportedly be the new base for the existing National Council and Parliament and an expansion of projects and infrastructure supported by major foreign investment (including South Africa and Spanish regional authorities) aim to encourage the relocation of current camp residents (ibid.). It is unclear how such a change would impact upon the delivery of aid provided by the World Food Programme (WFP), UNHCR and the European Community Humanitarian Office (ECHO), or indeed the definition of Sahrawis as "refugees," given that relocating to Tifariti would entail reentering the territory of the Western Sahara, thereby rendering the Sahrawi "internally displaced" (also see Fiddian-Qasmiyeh 2011d).

Upon the camps' establishment, "refugees were originally grouped in their psychologically reassuring preexodus social patterns," but by 1979 the Polisario/SADR had redistributed refugees "in order to break down tribalism" (Mercer 1979, 19; Caratini 2000, 442) and to create allegiances to the Polisario/SADR's newly defined "Sahrawi nation" (Hacene-Djaballah 1985; Caratini 2000). The Polisario/SADR prohibited the usage of tribal identifiers (Caratini 2000, 433) and displaced the power of traditional tribal elders by asserting control over its "refugee-citizens" through the development of its own constitution, camp-based police force (and prisons), army, and parallel state and religious legal systems[7] (the latter

---

7. Such a strategy is not unique to the Polisario: Kandiyoti, for instance, notes that Roy (2004) "also contends that the Taliban undermined the legitimacy of traditional tribal elders and of established ulama and explicitly rejected customary tribal law" (in Kandiyoti 2007b, 517).

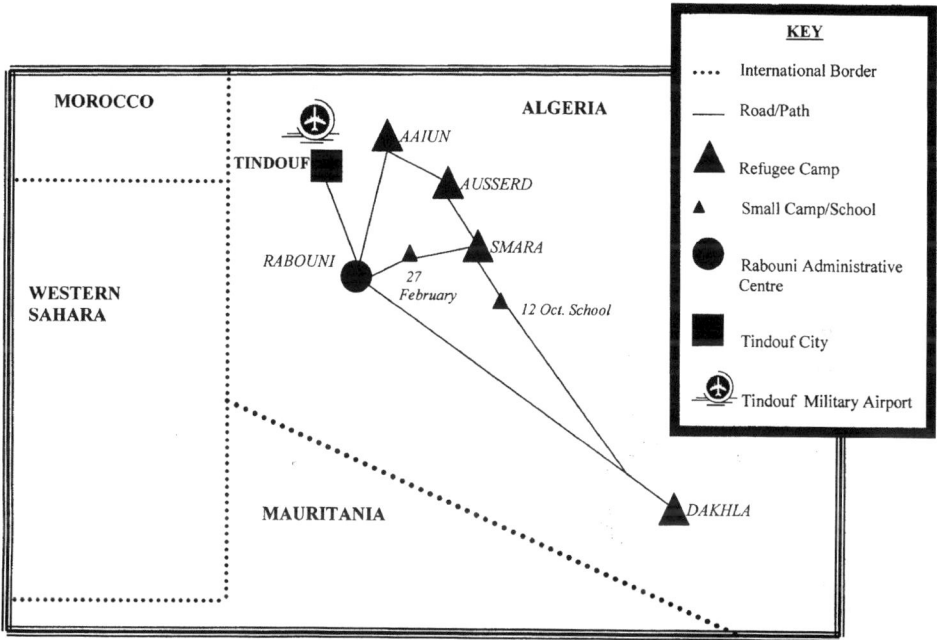

Map 2: Map of the distribution of the Sahrawi refugee camps (*not to scale*). Author's own elaboration based on aerial view of refugee camps from Googleearth (2008) and from a map in ECHO (2001).

implements a Maliki interpretation of Islam).[8] Since the camps' birth, the Polisario/SADR has been "the only authority with which camp residents have regular contact," with the Algerian government having "ceded de facto administration" to the Polisario/SADR (HRW 2008, 9).

8. Four main Sunni *madhāhib* (pl. legal schools of interpretation of Islam) exist. The Maliki *madhhab* (sing.) predominates throughout North Africa, although individuals are free to follow a different school. Despite much in common, the four *madhāhib* provide their respective followers with particular interpretations of the Qur'an, Sunna, Hadith and the juridical practice of Medina, which directly influence the community's social and religious legal frameworks. Given the complexities of Islamic jurisprudence, throughout the following chapters I will limit myself to contextualizing specific Sahrawi marriage and divorce practices (including custody issues) with reference to the Maliki tradition followed in the region. On family law, or personal status law, in the Middle East, see Joseph (2000, 20–22) and Esposito with DeLong-Bas (2001).

The four main camps (*wilayāt*)[9] are headed by a *wāli* (governor) who is appointed by the "head of state" (Shelley 2004, 183), with administrative and managerial functions completed by camp residents employed by the Polisario/SADR. Each camp (sing. *wilāya*) is divided into a number of districts (*dawā'ir*, sing. *dā'ira*), and each district is subdivided into neighborhoods (*aḥya'a*, sing. *ḥay*). 27 February Camp, however, is managed not by a *wāli* or *wāliya* (fem. sing.) but by the director of the National Women's School. This camp's relatively small population (estimated at approximately 2,000–2,500) is shared between four neighborhoods: three on one side of a recently paved road running through the camp, and the fourth on the other side, where the Women's and Primary Schools, the headquarters of the National Union of Sahrawi Women (NUSW), local hospital, state court building, and National Museum, are all located (Figures 2–4).

By 2008, Rabouni and nearby 27 February Camp had established stable electricity supplies, while inhabitants in the remaining camps continue to rely on electricity provided by solar panels and, especially in the case of hospitals and dispensary units, on small generators. Permanent electricity—along with the proximity to the National Hospital and the Algerian military town of Tindouf—have all acted as incentives for certain families to move from other camps to these expanding locations. This and other developments have led to considerable and ongoing demographic shifts within and between the camps between 1975 and the present.

Demography

From the mid-1970s until the early to mid-1990s, the vast majority of young and adult Sahrawi men were stationed at the military front, and women were therefore in charge not only of their families but also of camp structures as a whole. However, the demobilization and return of soldiers to the camps after the 1991 ceasefire coincided with the arrival of the first

---

9. This Arabic word means "province," but in the Sahrawi refugee camp setting coincides with the administrative division of the population into self-contained refugee camps.

2. View of 27 February Camp, home to approximately 2,000 Sahrawi refugees in southwest Algeria (2007).

generation of graduates educated abroad, and both the camps' demography and the camp-based division of labor, shifted considerably.

Despite the contradictory nature of census data pertaining to the camps, in 1999 a preliminary registration concluded that at least 107,000 camp-based refugees (potential voters and their immediate families) would wish to return to the Western Sahara under the auspices of a UNHCR repatriation program if a referendum for self-determination is conducted (WFP 1999, 4; UNHCR 2000b, 187). The total camp population, including "nonvoters" living in the camps, is thus now calculated by UNHCR and WFP as being over 155,000 (also see Fiddian-Qasmiyeh 2011d).

Recent WFP population estimates based on random samples suggest that roughly 60% of the current resident population are women and girls and that the average household size was between 6.7 and 5.2 in 2000 and 2002 respectively (WFP, 2000 and 2002). It is important to note, however,

3. View of 27 February Camp, southwest Algeria (2007).

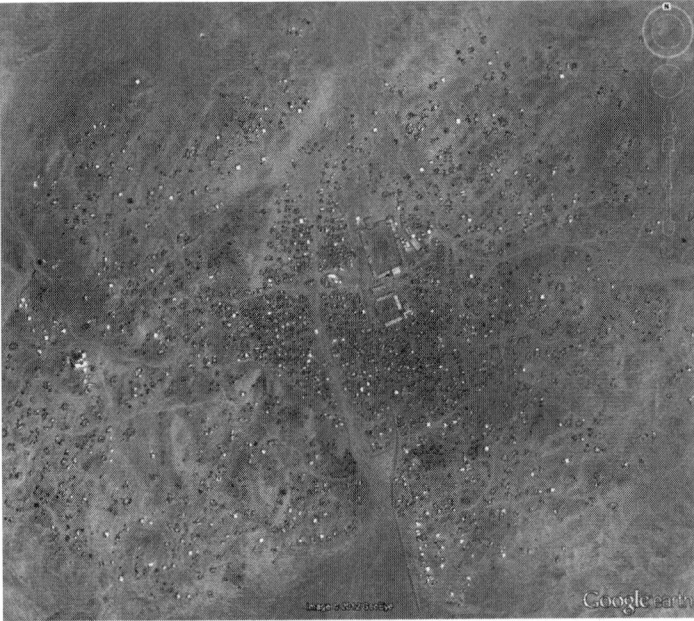

4. Aerial image of 27 February Camp showing the distribution of Sahrawi refugees' tents across four neighborhoods (southwest Algeria). © 2011 Google.

TABLE 2. Total camp population distributed by age group

Age group	%
0 to 4	19
5 to 17	37
18 to 59	31
60+	13

Source: UNHCR 2004b.

that these statistics fail to reflect the fluidity of household structures, many of whose members continue to be highly mobile, traveling between the camps, to the *bādiya* or abroad to visit family, to complete their schooling, or for employment purposes. Despite these limitations, the number of dependents per household is high, especially given that the overall camp population is young, with a large proportion of inhabitants having been born in the camps between 1975 and today. The UNHCR estimated in 2004 that 59% of the refugee camp population was under the age of 18 (2004b; see Table 2).

ECHO's figures for 1999, however, calculate that 57% of the population in the five camps (but excluding the boarding secondary schools and the National Hospital) was under the age of 12 (83,602 children out of its estimated total population of 147,474—note the discrepancy with WFP figures for the same year). These statistics suggest that well over 59% of the population would have been under the age of 18 five years later, as UNHCR propose (ECHO 2001).

Immigrant Labor

As a brief aside, it is important to stress that in addition to Sahrawi refugees, individuals from Mauritania (who may or may not define themselves as "Sahrawi") also live in the camps (personal observations; also Gimeno-Martín and Laman 2005, 24 and 76).[10] While the existence of the

10. There are also an uncounted number of women who arrived in the camps from Mauritania and Algeria following their marriage to Sahrawi men.

trade networks between the camps and Mauritania has been documented (Cozza 2004), Mauritania's precarious socioeconomic situation[11] has led many Hassaniya-speaking Mauritanians (in particular men) to work and live in the refugee camps. They are employed, for instance, as servants and builders, in addition to working as imams (trained in Mauritania) in the local camp-based mosques who therefore bring alternative perspectives on Islam in the camps.[12] These immigrants often send remittances to Mauritania with the intention of returning there after a few years (interview with Mauritanian camp residents, 27 February Camp, 2007), while some may intend to travel to Spain once they have obtained a Sahrawi identity card.[13] Along with this (uncounted) number of Mauritanians, Algerian men from nearby Tindouf are also reportedly (illegally) working in the camps, primarily in the booming construction business (personal observations, April 2007).

The existence of immigration *to* the camps from Mauritania and Tindouf parallels the emigration of (mainly) youth and adult men who leave the camps to work abroad (especially in Spain) and send remittances to their families (see Chapter 5). While the phenomenon of remittances to refugee camp "stayees" has received much academic attention in numerous contexts (i.e., Crisp 2003; Jacobsen 2005), the emerging trend of immigration *to* the Sahrawi refugee camps not only highlights the socioeconomic discrepancies that exist between the refugee camps and their immediate and broader environment but also the ever-growing socioeconomic differentiation within the camps themselves. Hence, some refugee

11. Mauritania was ranked 159 out of 187 countries in the 2011 Human Development Index (UNDP 2011).

12. For instance, the increased number of prepubescent girls wearing the hijab (qua Islamic veil) in the camps is attributed by San-Martín to the arrival of Mauritanians therein (cited in Crivello, Fiddian, and Chatty 2005). I discuss the role of religion in the camps in Chapters 3 and 4.

13. This claim was made by a number of my interviewees and parallel Gimeno-Martín and Laman's conclusions regarding the intentions of Sahrawis arriving to the camps from Morocco and the Western Sahara (2005, 79).

families are able to employ Mauritanian servants or pay Algerian builders to extend or renovate existing buildings (often using remittances sent
from abroad) or may rent (or own) air-conditioned apartments in Tindouf
where increasing numbers of Sahrawis spend the hot summer months.
However, others remain entirely dependent on externally provided aid,
and chronic health problems remain high, with 35% of children under the
age of five suffering from chronic malnutrition (WFP 2006).

Food Aid

Of the total camp population, in 2008 some 125,000 refugees received food
aid from international organizations. However, the number of WFP food
aid recipients since 1993 has ranged from a minimum of 49,000 "most vulnerable" refugees in the first half of 1998, to a maximum of 155,430 in 2002
(Table 3).

Although the majority of aid is brought in from outside of the camps,
it is usually distributed by Sahrawi refugees themselves, rather than by
foreign humanitarian workers. Indeed, in line with the Polisario/SADR's
determination to ensure the "self-sufficiency" of the camps, Sahrawi refugees have often informed visitors that "we do not want 'experts' in our
camps" (Harrell-Bond 1999, 156). International agencies and bodies wishing to implement or fund projects in the camps must all obtain permission from the Polisario/SADR to access the camps (visas are dependent
upon this).

The Sahrawi Red Crescent (SRC) thus collects and distributes aid from
Rabouni's central warehouses (WFP 2000, 1), with camp-based assistants
(typically women) at the local neighborhood level being in charge of allo-
cating food rations to each household's head (also women). In 2002 there
were 3,108 neighborhood "groups of 50 beneficiaries each, among whom
29,830 women receive household rations" (WFP 2002, 8). Six years later
WFP indicated that each female group leader was distributing rations to
a group of 150 people (WFP 2008, 8). Food delivered by the WFP is supplemented by a small amount of vegetables (mainly potatoes, onions, and
carrots) grown in camp-based allotments, eggs produced in one of three
air-conditioned henhouses (EU 2004), and milk, dairy products, and meat

TABLE 3. WFP estimates of the camp population (UNHCR estimates marked *
where different) and numbers for whom food aid was provided in given years

Year	Total WFP beneficiaries	Number and definition of "vulnerable population"	Total population estimate
1993	80,000		165,000*
1994	80,000		165,000*
1995	80,000		
1996	80,000		165,000*
1997	80,000		144,000 (165,000*)
1998 (Jan–June)	49,000	49,000 = "the most vulnerable population"	122,000
1998 (July–Dec)	80,000	80,000 = "the full number of vulnerable refugees"	
1999	80,000	61,000 "vulnerable people" + 11,000 anaemic women and 8,000 severely malnourished children	155,000
2000	155,000		
2001			
2002	155,430	Include 4,000 children and 2,380 women suffering from various degrees of malnutrition + supplementary feeding of 6,380 children and "vulnerable women"	
2003			146,925*
2004	125,000	125,000 = "the most vulnerable refugees"	158,000 (170,000*)
2006	90,484*	UNHCR provide "international protection and multisectoral assistance to the 90,000 most vulnerable refugees in the camps"	
2007			125,000
2008	90,000*		125,000

TABLE 3. *(cont.)*

Year	Total WFP beneficiaries	Number and definition of "vulnerable population"	Total population estimate
2009		"90,000 of the most vulnerable refugees," with additional supplements for 35,000	125,000
2010	125,000	"Pending a registration exercise, UNHCR's assistance programme continues to be based on a planning figure of 90,000 vulnerable refugees in the camps. Since November 2007, UNHCR and WFP have been distributing 125,000 food rations in an effort to improve the refugees' nutritional status in the camps"	

Compiled from WFP reports (1997–2010) and UNHCR Statistical Yearbooks (1994–2009). Different sections of the UNHCR provide widely divergent statistics regarding the total camp population and those receiving (or requiring) food aid: directly contradicting the WFP and UNHCR statistics included in Table 2, a UNHCR EXCOM report drawing on UNHCR statistics indicates that the population was 165,000 between 1998 and 2004, decreasing to 90,000 in 2005 and 2006 (Feb 2008).

from goats, sheep, and camels kept by individual families. Such supplements are essential given that in 2002 the WFP warned that refugees received only 11% of their daily nutritional requirements through food aid (WFP 2002), with chronic infant and maternal malnutrition continuing to be common in the camps (UNHCR/WFP/INRAN 2005). WFP has more recently estimated that "[a]lmost 95 percent of refugee households have no alternative means of fulfilling their food requirements or procuring fresh food" (2004, 3), while the Italian NGO CISP estimated that in 1997 only 10% of households in the camps could afford to buy fresh food (WFP 1999, 7).

Education and Training

Although many changes have taken place since the camps' creation, the education system currently in place is broadly similar to that developed upon their inception, and continues to be invoked as demonstrating the Polisario/SADR's commitment to educating the camp-based population to ensure national self-sufficiency. When the Sahrawi Ministry of Education, Health and Social Affairs was created in 1976, its main aims included not only creating and organizing primary and secondary schools in the camps but also, given infrastructural limitations, requesting that friendly countries welcome as many Sahrawi children and youth as possible to educate them abroad (Velloso de Santisteban 1993).

Replacing both the precolonial religious education system and its powerful teachers, and compensating for the almost total absence of the colonial education system (see Chapter 1), in 1975–1976 the Polisario/SADR established a mixed, universal, obligatory, and "secular education system" in the camps, in order, according to Gimeno-Martín and Laman, to "constitute a modern society" (2005, 23) led by educated men and women who could ensure the self-sufficiency of "the Sahrawi nation." While the Polisario/SADR had initially relied upon externally provided materials (primarily from Algeria), by 1984 a national syllabus had been developed by the Polisario/SADR (Perregaux 1990b). Indeed, as indicated by Cole and Kandiyoti, "nations" can be created in many ways, "including by setting up national school systems that impose a single linguistic standard and a cobbled-together 'national' history" (2002, 195–196; also see Kandiyoti 2007a, 172).

The camp's children currently attend twenty-nine primary schools and twenty-five preschool centers in the camps (UNHCR 2006b, 6), with some students eventually moving to a "national" boarding school to complete their secondary studies. A smaller cohort, as indicated earlier, has annually left the camps to complete their secondary and tertiary educations abroad, primarily in Algeria, Cuba, and Libya but also Syria and more recently in Qatar.[14]

14. The impact of the so-called Arab Spring on the Libyan and Syrian pan-Arabist scholarship systems remains to be determined (see Fiddian-Qasmiyeh 2011f).

Although two boarding schools existed in the camps until recently, only the 12 October Secondary School has been functioning since the major floods of 2006 destroyed the 9 June School. The destruction of the 9 June School has dramatically limited the number of students able to attend secondary school in the camps; according to UNHCR (2006b), the Spanish government's Cooperation Unit (AECI) in Tindouf has offered to complement the UN agency's role in the education sector by "putting in place a secondary education system, entirely funded by the Spanish government, within refugee sites" (ibid.). While it is unclear how long such a project might take to be implemented, the need is considerably clearer.[15]

It is important to note that, while families and immediate social environments often provide the strongest forms of guidance during childhood, the structural reality of the camps and the Polisario/SADR's struggle for "national" independence led to a major shift in supervisory roles from families to "the Sahrawi state."[16] As a result of, or perhaps in order to achieve, this shift, children were separated from their families and home camps at an early age (often leaving the camps as young as 7), with such separations continuing throughout children's formative years and often extending beyond adolescence. While one of the reasons for this separation was to provide children with an education in an otherwise hostile environment, withdrawing children from their families also strengthened the power of the Polisario/SADR over the younger generation(s), creating an ideal space from which to teach children and youth about the significance of the war against Morocco, of the particularities of Sahrawi

15. More recently, the Spanish Coordinator of Associations in Solidarity with the Sahara (see below), partner universities from across Spain, Algeria and Cuba, and the South African government have declared their support for an international campaign to establish a Sahrawi University in Tifariti. As discussed in Fiddian-Qasmiyeh 2011d, this project reflects the broader identification of this area as an alternative to the refugee camps in Algeria.

16. We could conceptualize this shift in responsibility for children's socialization from their *um* (mother) to their *umma* (nation). I thank Yousif M. Qasmiyeh for his insights regarding this transition.

history and "national identity," and of their role in the future of the state (see Chapter 3 and Fiddian-Qasmiyeh 2012a).

Beyond primary and secondary schooling, a wide range of national centers also offer professional training to young and adult refugees in the camps, once more "demonstrating" the Polisario/SADR's commitment to self-sufficiency. These include the male-dominated Gazwane (near Rabouni) that mainly provides computer, vocational, and technical training courses; a nursing college; and a number of additional Women's schools and centers that have been opened throughout the camps via foreign funding, primarily from the Euskadi (Basque Country) and other regional Spanish governments. The 27 February National Women's School continues to be the largest of these centers, with boarding possibilities for women from all camps to be trained in a range of subjects such as computing, driving, weaving, and languages (in association with the Italian NGO, CRIC).

The successful development of these educational structures in the camps has frequently been heralded by external observers, supported by claims made by the Polisario/SADR, *solidarios* and even WFP that "school attendance level is almost 100 percent among refugee children" (WFP 2004, 6). Such claims were also reproduced by a number of my interviewees, including a student who informed me: "If you compare the literacy of Bedouins in Asia and Africa, we are better. They don't study at all. *Alhamdulillah*, it's good that we study. Compared to other people's situations, we're much better" (history student, Damascus, July 2006). Nonetheless, Table 4 indicates the percentage and number of children who were not enrolled in camp-based schools (excluding 27 February Camp) according to UNHCR statistics for 2003.

These data, which are not referred to in reports on the camps, reveal an alarming trend that directly refutes commonly made claims that the camps have "the highest literacy rates in Africa" (Mundy 2007, 287).[17]

17. It is unclear whether it may be younger children who are not attending primary school, or older children who are unable to enroll in the camp-based boarding schools due, perhaps, to insufficient school places, infrastructural limitations and poor conditions (as suggested in ECHO 2005).

TABLE 4. Percentage and number of children enrolled/not enrolled in each main camp's schools, not including 27 February Camp

Camp	Total Population	% population aged 5–17 enrolled in school	No. children aged 5–17 NOT enrolled in camp school
Smara	39,466	57.6%	6,210
Dakhla	38,180	43.3%	8,030
Aaiun	36,675	60.1%	5,440
Ausserd	32,624	61.2%	4,690
TOTAL	146,945	Average: 55.5%	24,370

Source: UNHCR 2004a

Further, the relevant UNHCR figures fail to document the reality of gender disparities in school attendance (see Chatty, Fiddian-Qasmiyeh, and Crivello 2010), which are nonetheless recognized by the WFP. This organization states that it is "only" at the upper primary level that "household chores and lack of women's sanitary materials compel older girls to drop out or to attend school irregularly" (2004, 6–7). Given the official importance given to female education by the Polisario/SADR and non-Sahrawi observers alike, I discuss girls' early withdrawal from school in Chapter 5.

Employment and Unpaid Activities

Although the Polisario/SADR claims that the camps are entirely dependent upon externally provided aid—as there are "no economic activities [in the camps] and unemployment is 100%" (SADR 2007 document on file with author; my translation)—a small market economy emerged for the first time in the camps following the 1991 ceasefire. At this stage, Sahrawi men gradually returned from the military front and Spain started to pay some of its former colonial employees a pension. With the introduction of a cash economy, those who could afford it supplemented their food rations with products purchased in the camps themselves. The new circulation of money also affected NGO–refugee relationships, with NGOs running projects in the camps having to consider for the first time whether to pay their Sahrawi employees (Abjean 2003, 96–97). The creation of paid employment has led to significant changes in the formerly unpaid social systems and networks that had initially been established and managed by the Polisario/SADR without external intervention.

Clear socioeconomic differentiation in the camps has thus intensified and broadened since the early 1990s, with male and female refugees currently completing a wide range of activities, jobs, and tasks, including work associated with the ministries and organizations outlined above. Recent projects in the camps include the establishment of *hammams*, "Internet teas" (rather than Internet cafés), hairdressers, and taxi services run with externally provided microcredits (NUSW document on file with author; Elizondo et al. 2008).

Women in the Camps

An extensive number of reports are almost entirely dedicated to examining women's roles and positions in the refugee camps, including Amoretti (1987), Perregaux (1990), Pineda (1991), Ayat (1993), Balac (1993), Chinkin (1993), Hamdi (1993), Juliano (1998), Serrano-Borrull (1999), La Ventana (2002), Caratini (2003a), Daha (2004) and Tortajada Orriols (2004). The active roles of women as distributors of aid, nurses, teachers, builders, in the singular case of Senia Ahmed Marhba as the *wāliya* of Smara camp from 1985, as members of the NUSW and SADR, and as individuals who received military training are all stressed throughout Polisario and non-Polisario articles, reports, and solidarity events.[18] One such event is the "parade" that was held in Smara camp for non-Sahrawis visiting the camps during the 2007 NUSW Conference (see Figures 5–7), and that portrayed Sahrawi women as central, active nodes that keep the tightly structured camps in full working order.

18. For instance, between 800 and 900 women are reported to have marched in military uniform during the Polisario/SADR's Twentieth Anniversary celebrations in 1993 (Chopra 1994). Reports sometimes underscore that women were trained to protect the camps if they came under attack, but were not soldiers at the front (i.e., Firebrace 1987, 181; Caratini 2000, 443).

5. Female Sahrawi refugee doctors and nurses participating in a "parade" held in Smara refugee camp for non-Sahrawi visitors during the 2007 NUSW Conference (southwest Algeria, April 2007).

The visibility of Sahrawi women in key institutions is understood by many as directly symbolizing and embodying the significance of Sahrawi women in "Sahrawi society" (Perregaux 1990a, 45). Drawing on "historical" explanations, the reader/observer is thus informed in these accounts that since "all" Sahrawi men were "at the front" during the war (1975–1991), it fell upon Sahrawi women (as is common in many war and nationalist contexts) to establish, run, and maintain the camps and their emerging structures, including schools and hospitals in particular.

Indeed, female and male Sahrawis of all ages systematically reiterate these features of life in the camps during their interactions with non-Sahrawi visitors and researchers, with one 74-year-old woman who arrived in the refugee camps in March 1976 recalling in her SARC interview that

> [w]e [the women] took care of the organization of life in the refugee camps, while the army took care of the war of resistance. We started building our schools

6. Sahrawi women participating in a "parade" held in Smara refugee camp (southwest Algeria), being represented as producers of Sahrawi cultural artifacts and
"bearers of Sahrawi culture" (April 2007).

and tents. Children went to Algeria, Cuba and Libya for schooling. The
other tents were used as classrooms. Literacy campaigns were launched,
and *women were the basis of this construction, and despite the suffering of families since 1976 until now, women have been contributing to the state and their
families.* (emphasis added)

Such accounts of the gendered and generational distribution of the Sahrawi
refugee population across different spaces (the military front, the refugee
camps, and educational hosting contexts) and of the distinctive but com-
plementary areas of male and female responsibility and agency, are also
paralleled by the NUSW's Embarca Hamudi's more recent declaration that
"given our situation, we could say that we [Sahrawi women] are the State
and they [Sahrawi men] are the Army" (in Hevio 1995, 43; my translation).

Because of the minimal presence of men in the camps throughout
the first decades of the conflict, Sahrawi refugees publically celebrate the

7. Sahrawi woman leading female "military parade" as part of a "parade" held in Smara refugee camp for non-Sahrawi visitors attending the 2007 NUSW Conference (southwest Algeria, April 2007).

determination and resourcefulness of Sahrawi women as they managed the harsh camp conditions despite suffering as mothers, wives, sisters, and daughters:

> *One could not see men around here,* maybe you would find one man in each *dā'ira.* The men were fighting at the battlefronts, and women did not know whether they would be called to be told that a husband or brother was martyred. Despite all this, women worked with enthusiasm and conviction. (38-year-old woman; emphasis added)

Further reflecting the transgenerational nature of these female-centered historical accounts, a 14-year-old girl born and raised in the camps also indicated in her SARC interview that the Sahrawi woman "is *the most important* [in the camps]. She built the tents, and provides the food, organizes the municipalities, *and in all the refugee camps, they are active.* During the war, *the men were not in the camps,* otherwise they would have helped" (emphasis added).

Indeed, Sahrawi men themselves equally centralize women's presence, achievements and roles in the camps, with a 47-year-old man who enrolled in the Sahrawi army in 1975 asserting that

> we must not forget the role of women at that time, *women contributed even more than men*, they participated in popular campaigns. The slogan at that time was that the army was a people's army. Each individual worked in their own capacity and location. (emphasis added)

This national division of labor is thus presented by Sahrawi refugees and their political representatives alike as demonstrating both Sahrawi women's capacity and simultaneously their past, current, and future importance in the national struggle (e.g., Lippert 1992).

However, such depictions of the camps as female-dominated and female-run spaces simultaneously elide the heterogeneity of the female camp population and the extent to which women's spheres of action and access to resources depended on age, tribal background, education, and marital status (amongst other factors);[19] equally, they fail to recognize the presence of certain cohorts of men in the camps throughout the 1970s, 1980s, and early 1990s. Without dismissing the importance of Sahrawi women's roles since the refugee camps' creation, it is important to note that the above-cited claims that "one could not see men around here, maybe you would find one man in each *dā'ira*" and that "the men were not in the camps," do not recognize the presence or activities of older/elderly men who lived in the camps or the extent to which the camps' political structures have in fact consistently been managed by elite men since the 1970s. Given that only one woman has ever acted as a camp governor (see above), it is clear that throughout the 1970s and 1980s, men held the most powerful positions in the political administration of the individual camps,

---

19. This study focuses primarily on exploring the intersections between gender, age, tribal identity and political background, within a broader study of the significance of gender and religion in representations of Sahrawi refugees; it is unfortunately beyond the scope of the study to integrate other key factors such as sexuality or disability status within this analysis. These deserve further exploration in future research.

districts, and neighborhoods and also systematically controlled Rabouni, the camps' male-dominated "capital" and structural core.

Nonetheless—in spite of the clear population shifts that took place following the 1991 ceasefire and the male monopoly over key politico-administrative positions from the 1970s to the present—discourses that represent (and in turn constitute) the camps as feminized spaces inhabited by active women and children continue to render inequalities between women, and both men and male-run structures invisible to date. Such discursive representations have wide-ranging effects, as explored throughout the remainder of this study.

Reproducing the mainstream depictions of life in the camps, in its overview of conditions there in 2002, the World Food Programme state that Sahrawi women "are known to be assertive and to participate in all aspects of camp life" (WFP 2002), indicating that in the years 2000, 2002, and 2004 Sahrawi women (always) constituted 80% of the health workers in twenty-nine health centers in the camps, and 60% of both medical and paramedical staff and camp teachers (WFP 2000, 2002, 2004). The organization's description of Sahrawi women's participation in the camps was substantially magnified in 2004, when the organization ingenuously claimed, with no supporting references or consideration of the complexities of the terms invoked, that "Saharan society is primarily *matriarchal* and the women are *totally empowered*" (WFP 2004, 8; my emphasis). In addition to such reports by WFP, Maima Mahmud Nayem (director of the Dakhla Women's School since its creation in 1999 and that camp's representative of the Secretary of Social Affairs and Emancipation of Sahrawi Women) has also proclaimed that "this is a matriarchal society," justifying her claim by stating "here you will never see even one tent being pitched by a man" (Portinari 2007; my translation).[20]

20. Connecting female ownership of the tent with matriarchy is misleading on many fronts: the tent is habitually conceptualized as a female space among Bedouin groups, and reflects a particular gendered division of space, with men being "in control" of other arenas and areas of sociopolitical and economic interaction.

Such a resolute representation of Sahrawi women's participation and agency is simultaneously reminiscent of Mowles' declaration almost 20 years earlier that Sahrawi society "is the most fundamentally balanced society I have ever come across in terms of the relationships between men and women" (1986, 9; quoted in the Introduction), and yet in direct contrast with the more frequently reproduced image of women as helpless victims of war and forced displacement (Malkki 1995a/b; also see Fiddian-Qasmiyeh 2009). It is important to note that Malkki has highlighted the existence and repetition of conceptualizations of "normal" or "generic" refugees against whom "ordinary" others can be compared (Shami 1996, 6). The tendency to compare refugee groups and evaluate them accordingly is confirmed by many "generic" accounts of the Sahrawi refugee camps, including a recent report by the Norwegian Refugee Council, which explicitly indicates that the Sahrawi camps are "unique" by virtue of their difference from "other" camps (NRC 2008, 7). In the words of Voutira and Harrell-Bond, the Sahrawi camps are an "exception" to "what has become the norm" (2000, 68), while Williams claims that Sahrawi women are "unique" and a "positive example" specifically through comparing their position with the "usual" position of generic refugee women in generic refugee camps (2005, 22).

The images of active and empowered Sahrawi women outlined above are thus particularly powerful precisely because they are "unexpected" when compared with the "standardized" and "generic images" that have become the norm when discussing refugee camps (Fisk 1995, 15, in Shami 1996, 9). In essence, the camps portrayed by the Polisario/SADR and Western observers alike are the antithesis of what refugee camps "are meant to look like":[21] democratic, safe for women, and "empowering" (also see Caratini 2000, 444). These "generic images" are particularly important to the development of mainstream accounts of the Sahrawi refugee camps, since commentators and authors have only rarely undertaken research

---

21. This was an exclamation of surprise made by a visitor to a Tanzanian refugee camp (quoted in Malkki 1995a, 40), and indicates the extent to which observers have come to accept the "generic" representations of both refugee camps and refugees themselves.

with other refugee groups in situ. Although international NGO workers may have visited other refugee contexts, only one of the Spanish solidarios I met throughout the course of my research had done so. Amongst academic visitors, Chatty, Farah, and Harrell-Bond are major exceptions.

Without dismissing the importance of Sahrawi women's roles since the refugee camps' creation, this leads us to ask why these specific "ideal" images of Sahrawi refugee women should have been emphasized by the Polisario/SADR, and to whom. While I address the first part of this question throughout the following chapters, at this stage I shall outline a range of humanitarian and political international networks that the camps are dependent upon. This is especially necessary in relation to the official "façade" of female empowerment that has been developed to ensure the continued (and indispensable) support of specific actors in the international sphere.

International Camps

As suggested above, the Sahrawi refugee camps are highly dependent upon a wide range of networks that are economic, humanitarian, solidary, and political in nature. Quantitatively, one of the most influential connections with the outside world is through official humanitarian networks that provide food, clothes and shelter. Despite the Polisario/SADR's claims to administrative and political self-sufficiency, until recently, refugees were entirely reliant upon humanitarian assistance provided by a range of international donors. These include, in particular, the Algerian state (that has granted the Polisario/SADR control of the desert where the camps are based and sends regular supplies of gas and water), ECHO (the major donor), the WFP, and UNHCR. Refugees were assisted predominantly by the government of Algeria between 1975 and 1984, after which point Algiers explicitly "requested the international community to assume responsibility for their care and maintenance" (WFP 2008, 2). UNHCR provided limited assistance to the camps from 1975 to 1980 via a "special emergency fund" exempt from UNHCR's normal eligibility process and directed personally by the UN High Commissioner. In 1980 the camps were finally allocated funds from the UNHCR's General Fund (Firebrace 1987, 173), in 1986 WFP started providing food aid to the camps (www.wfp.org), and UNHCR opened its first sub-office in Tindouf in 1996 (UNHCR 2006b, 2).

In many respects, however, these major international organizations are invisible in the camps, other than through the widespread presence of their logos on everything ranging from tins of sardines and powdered milk and bottles of shampoo. Almost all of my interviewees in the camps dismissed organizations like the UNHCR, perhaps due to their disappointment that they had been unable and/or unwilling to hold the referendum for self-determination but also because they were generally seen as ineffective and insincere bodies. It is also worth noting that, since the Polisario/SADR is directly implicated in the delivery and distribution of food aid in the camps, these international organizations could be overshadowed by the visibility and presence of the Polisario/SADR, reinforcing families' and individuals' perceptions of these INGOs as insignificant and marginal to their daily experiences. That one of the Sahrawi Red Cresent's (SRC) former presidents (Bellahi Sid) should have held both the position of SADR Minister of Health and Minister of the Interior (elected in 2007) demonstrates the interconnection between SRC and the SADR (also see San-Martín 2005, 590).

Unlike these "absent" or "invisible" organizations, and despite the fact that most aid is quantitatively brought to the camps through such projects, during my fieldwork in the camps individuals and families repeatedly reiterated their gratitude and support for other actors implicated in alternative networks active in the camps and beyond. Just as families prioritize the significance of these networks for their own and their children's futures, in the following chapters I will also focus on these actors and networks, rather than on the role of Algeria, the larger UN bodies, or regional organizations such as ECHO.

Solidarity Networks

WFP notes in a recent report that "[t]he resources from UNHCR do not cover all needs: they are complemented by inputs from the Government of Algeria, *solidarity groups*, and a number of NGOs" (2008, 9; my emphasis). "Solidarity groups" in this respect refer to the organized mobilization of members of civil society who define themselves as being "in solidarity with" or "friends of" the Sahrawi people and the Sahrawi cause for self-determination. While multiple solidarity actors are engaged in working to support the camps and the cause, in this section I focus on the largest and most active network: the Spanish solidarity movement.

Before providing an overview of this network, it is worth noting a parallel between the implications of the 1991 ceasefire and the changes that took place between the early and later colonial periods. Just as contact with the Spanish colonial administration was minimal throughout the early colonial period (1884 to the mid-twentieth century), the period of direct military action between 1975 and 1991 is equally characterized by an almost total absence of non-Sahrawis in the camps. The 1991 ceasefire, however, marked a turning point both within the refugee camps and abroad, with refugees witnessing a dramatic increase in the presence of foreigners in the camps, as happened in the colonial period following the discovery of phosphates in the territory. Also paralleling the colonial era, the majority of this contact has been with Spaniards, with Spanish solidarity workers, campaigners, and Friends of the Sahara replacing the civilians and members of the military who were posted in the then-Spanish colony.

Of interest is that the UN-brokered ceasefire also coincided with escalating violence in Algeria. Although Sahrawi students continued to study in Algerian cities throughout this time, international visitors were recommended to travel directly to Tindouf rather than stay in Algiers, which was increasingly unstable. The realities of Algeria's civil war (see Zoubir 2002) also point to that country's decreasing ability to sustain the camps. This in turn led to a shift toward Sahrawis' economic and material dependence upon aid sent by NGOs and Western *solidarios*. This has consequently heightened the significance of securing the continued support of these Western individuals and organizations through a variety of mechanisms.

From the mid-1990s onward in particular, Western NGO projects as well as individuals and groups visiting the camps for solidarity, academic, and journalistic purposes increased to such an extent that Tindouf airport (which is otherwise simply a military base in the southwesternmost point of Algeria) is now one of the airports in Algeria that reportedly receives the largest number of "tourists" per annum. While one could characterize these visits to the camps as part of a broader phenomenon of "disaster tourism," this is in fact a two-way phenomenon: an ever-increasing number of Sahrawi refugees temporarily leave the camps to participate in "hosting" programs, or for educational purposes or medical treatment. These movements in people have resulted in material goods arriving both en masse and piecemeal to the camps, either through major collective "solidarity" convoys of food, clothes, medicine, and toys or individual Sahrawi children's suitcases packed with "presents" from Spanish host families (see below).

Although older Sahrawi interviewees in the camps stressed their anticolonial sentiment and activities when recalling their experiences and contact with Spaniards during the colonial era, contemporary discussions of the colonial period tend to be overshadowed by the recognition that Spanish civil society provides highly significant humanitarian and political support to the Polisario/SADR and to individual families.[22] Whilst criticizing the Spanish government for having "abandoned" the Sahara, and unequivocally demonizing the "violent Moroccan occupation" of the then-Spanish Sahara, the constant public reiteration of ties with Spanish civil society lead to the presentation of an image of "fraternity" with, and the overwhelming sympathy of, the Spanish nation (Martin-Márquez 2006; Martín-Corrales 2004, 43). Connections between Spain and the Sahrawi are strongly emphasized by the Polisario/SADR in this context, ranging from claims that it is thanks to Spanish civil society that people eat in the camps and that Felipe González won the Spanish elections in 1982 explicitly due to his promise to back the independence of the Western Sahara,[23] to heartfelt references to the support provided through the Friends of the Saharawi People associations that abound in Spain.[24]

22. It is not uncommon for Western states and civil societies to continue engaging with and "supporting" their former colonies in different ways.

23. These claims were made by the Havana-based SADR Cultural Attaché during a Cuban solidarity meeting held in the University of Havana (verbatim proceedings, December 2006).

24. See, for instance, Mariem Salek's accounts at the time that she was the SADR Minister of Culture and Sport, as quoted by Íñiguez (2000).

Along with official gratitude for Spanish solidarity, youth interviewed in Cuba, Syria, Spain, and in the camps all indicated the magnitude of Spanish civil society's support, either through the Holidays in Peace (Vacaciones en Paz) summer hosting program, through mass "solidarity" visits to Tindouf, or NGO projects run in the camps. Although some of these interviewees expressed concerns that young children traveling to Spain every summer might be exposed to "things" they should not experience when they were not yet adults, it was only when conducting interviews in Cuba that both students and SADR representatives alike openly presented a more critical perspective vis-à-vis Spanish-Sahrawi relations during the colonial period and spoke vehemently about the violence that had characterized the colonial encounter.

Rather than blaming the Moroccan side and their "violent occupation" for "all of the negative things" that have affected the refugee population (as one is repeatedly informed in interviews, articles, and discussions on the protracted refugee situation), it was only in Cuba that I heard Sahrawis explicitly assigning blame to Spanish colonialism. One of only three female Sahrawi students in the island at the time of my fieldwork there explained that

> all of the negative things, all of the difficulties and hardships that myself and the other students have experienced [in Cuba and elsewhere] are due to colonialism. The Sahara was occupied by the British and the Portuguese, and, well, you know about Spanish colonialism . . . We are in this situation because of colonialism. Full stop. (Havana, November 2006)

The critical approach expressed by this interviewee appears to be intimately related to the fact that she had spent almost her entire adult life living and studying in Cuba; I believe that such comments would be unthinkable either in the presence of members of Spanish civil society or in Spain itself, where the solidarity network is based on remedying the failures and shortages of the present rather than critically reflecting on the nature of the colonial period itself. Amongst Spanish civil society, colonial guilt appears to exist primarily in so far as some *solidarios* (and former soldiers) feel ashamed (*avergonzados*) at Spain's withdrawal from the territory; a commonly expressed sentiment is nonetheless that "the Sahrawi would have been better off if they hadn't complained about us [the Spanish] during the 1970s. It's their own fault" (Spanish solidarity worker, 27 February Camp, April 2007).

Spanish Friends

In Spain, the Coordinadora Estatal de Asociaciones Solidarias con el Sahara (CEAS: "State Coordinator of Associations in Solidarity with the Sahara")[25] organizes the activities of over 200 associations that support the Sahrawi people through humanitarian, development, and political means. Over 300 groups of Amigos del Pueblo Saharaui (Friends of the Sahrawi People) exist throughout Spain (Crivello, Fiddian and Chatty, 2005), and not all pro-Sahrawi organizations are coordinated by CEAS. For instance, the Federación Estatal de Instituciones Solidarias con el Pueblo Saharaui (FEDISSAH) is a federation of Spanish state institutions that are "in solidarity" with the Sahrawi people, with over 140 Spanish state institutions including municipal and city councils attending the second state conference of institutions "twinned" with the Sahrawi camps and in solidarity with the Sahrawi people. Indeed, reflecting a high level of institutional support, it is noteworthy that in the Basque Country alone, 71% of all cooperation and development projects financed and managed by Guipúzcoa's twenty-seven municipal councils were related to the Sahrawi people in 2007–2008 (M.O. 2008). The importance of Spanish NGO aid is so great that the SADR has established ministerial "coordination offices" across Spain (San-Martín 2005, 590).

On a less institutional level than FEDISSAH, CEAS estimates that these groups have a total of over 14,700 active members, with CEAS itself being supported by over 5,000 volunteers, the majority of whom are reportedly women aged 35 to 50, men aged 40 to 55, and young people aged 18 to 30. *Solidarios* include men and women from across Spain's autonomous communities and regions and from all points of the political spectrum. To this I would add—based on my observations of numerous meetings held by local solidarity groups in a number of localities in Spain

---

25. Information accessed at http://www.saharaindependiente.org/ceas/ceas.htm.

and having visited Sahrawi children in their host families' homes as part of the SARC project—that individuals from all walks of life are members of these groups, although a large proportion of these appear to have what we could label "modest" incomes. Of 8,600 children participating in the Vacaciones en Paz program in 2005, nearly one-third were hosted by families in Andalucía, one of Spain's poorest regions (Crivello, Fiddian, and Chatty 2005).

The main activities that CEAS and its members undertake or supervise include awareness-raising projects in Spain, humanitarian work (especially collecting and sending food aid to the camps), designing and funding health and educational projects for the camps, and helping to coordinate the annual Holidays in Peace program. A brief overview of this last program helps situate the significance of the Spanish solidarity network.

The Vacaciones en Paz summer hosting program has been analyzed in detail for the first time by Crivello and myself (2010), based on research conducted in Spain and in the camps as part of the SARC project. Having started in the late 1980s and being coordinated by over 300 Spanish NGOs and the Polisario's Youth Union (the UJSARIO), this annual project currently transports up to 10,000 Sahrawi children aged between 8 and 12 to Spain during the summer months (usually in July and August), thereby allowing them to avoid the hottest periods in the camps. The connections that are built between Sahrawi and Spanish host families during these two-month-long visits are perceived by camp residents as being essential for their short-term and longer-term prospects, allowing children to benefit directly during the summer itself and to return to the camps bearing gifts, money, medical supplies, and food for their immediate and extended families.

Charter planes are organized to allow Spanish host families to visit "their" children in the camps at least twice a year, with several thousand Spaniards arriving *en masse* during the Spanish Easter and Christmas vacations. During these visits, Spanish visitors bring commodities and cash to "their" Sahrawi families, in addition to having the opportunity to see living conditions *in situ*. The material significance of such connections should not be understated: WFP identifies "the very vulnerable households" as those that "had not built any contacts with the civil societies of Spain and of other countries that provide support to refugee *families*" (2008, 3; my emphasis).

It is this palpable connection and physical proximity to the people who provide them with much needed material and financial assistance, along with social capital, which leads many Sahrawi families to recognize the significance of the solidarity network, in contrast with the less visible and more taken-for-granted humanitarian projects, which are, according to my research, marginalized in both the popular and the "national" imagination. Following Betteridge's work on formal and personal gift exchange in Iran (1985), we could conceptualize this as a perceived distinction between invisible and anonymous "official aid" and hypervisible and personally granted "intimate aid."

"Special" Friends

Beyond "general" support for the "Sahrawi national cause," many Spaniards directly relate their solidarity to the "special" nature of Sahrawi women in the camps, with an "International Platform of Solidarity with Saharawi Women" having been created in Barcelona in 1998. Indeed, one of the primary aims granted by the SADR Constitution (art. 137) to "mass organizations" and "unions" such as the NUSW is precisely to *"help widen the field of solidarity* with the Sahrawi people and to draw attention to its national cause" (my translation and emphasis; also stressed by Es-Sweyih 2001, 62). The NUSW itself states that one of the organization's international objectives is to "enlarge the solidarity and support base for our people's struggle for self-determination and independence" (NUSW pamphlet on file with the author; my translation).

As such, the NUSW

calls for all women across the world to express their moral and political solidarity with the legitimate struggle of the Sahrawi people . . . We consider that solidarity between all women . . . is highly important because that solidarity constitutes an essential pillar in the interwoven relations of cooperation, solidarity and friendship and exchange of experiences and thus constitutes an essential factor in the search for solutions for the innumerable problems that women encounter in their struggle for the freedom and dignity of women [*sic*].[26]

A brief overview of the non-Sahrawi delegates invited to or involved in the preparation of the Fifth NUSW Conference (2007) demonstrates the extent and multifaceted nature of Spanish support for the Sahrawi, and its gendered orientation. The terminology used by the vast majority of these non-Sahrawi organizations both during the Conference and on their respective websites reflects that their commitment and involvement in the camps is based on "solidarity" (*solidaridad*) and "friendship" (*amistad*) with the Sahrawi refugee community, and with Sahrawi women more exactly, rather than a more general aim to fund development projects per se.

The Fifth NUSW Conference

The NUSW's Fifth Conference (*al-mu'tamar al-khāmis*) was held in the 27 February Camp in early April 2007, with each main refugee camp being represented by between eighty and eighty-five women (NUSW document on file with author).[27] These women had previously been elected at a range of colloquia held around the camps in March 2007, when all of the camps' women were invited to discuss issues of concern (see Figures 8 and 9). Following these preliminary discussions, the Conference provided a forum for the NUSW's policy agenda for the next five years (2007–2012) to be debated and set. On the last day of the Conference, the executive members of the NUSW were elected (or in most cases, as I discuss in later chapters, reelected).

The Fifth Conference was attended by international bodies including UNHCR and the Federation of African Women, as well as state and non-state representatives from Algeria (over 20), Botswana (2), Cuba (1), France (1), Italy (1), Mexico (1), Namibia (3), Slovenia (1), and South Africa (4). The distinct absence of women from the MENA region (other than Algerian women) is notable and should be borne in mind throughout the remainder of this book.

26. NUSW statement accessed at http://www.arso.org/UNMS-1.htm; my translation.
27. An abridged version of this discussion has appeared in Fiddian-Qasmiyeh 2010d.

8. The Fifth NUSW Conference's plenary session in the 27 February Camp, south-west Algeria (April 2007).

Despite this relatively modest international turnout, the vast majority of participants and funders were Spanish, with over 150 Spaniards (almost all women) having traveled to the camps to attend the conference, living with families in the 27 February Camp during their time there. Among those attending or funding the event were Spain's National, Basque, and Canary Islands Institutos de la Mujer (Women's Institutes), representatives from Spain's national socialist, conservative, and left-wing political parties (including PSOE, Partido Popular, and Izquierda Unida, respectively) and trade unions, and over ten national-level NGOs (including ACSUR-Las Segovias, AIETI, Caritas-Spain, CANAE, Spanish Cruz Roja (Red Cross), and Médicos del Mundo). Major regional development organizations were primarily from the Basque Country, including Euskal Fondoa, HEGOA, and the Basque Government's Development Fund. Twenty Municipal Councils were represented from around Spain (half of these were from the Basque Country), as were at least twenty-three groups of

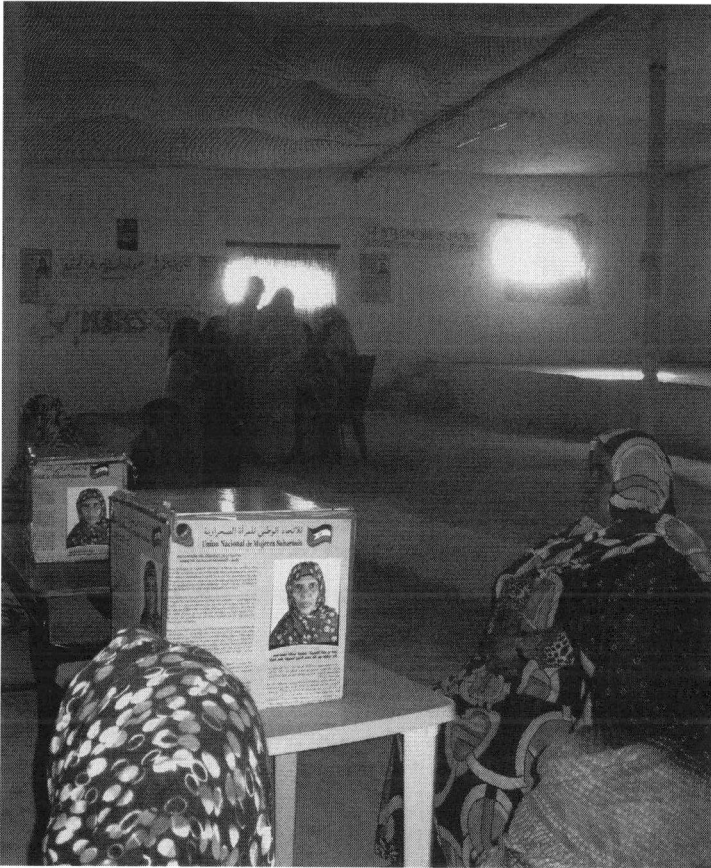

9. Sahrawi women preparing for the elections during the Fifth NUSW Conference in the 27 February Camp, southwest Algeria (April 2007).

"Friends of the Sahrawi People." A further sixteen regional or local Spanish women's organizations were present, in addition to the Spanish Support Network for the NUSW and the Basque Support Network for the NUSW, which were significant funders for the Fifth Conference [see Figure 10].

We could denominate many of the organizations and parties present in the conference as "general" Friends of the Sahara (i.e., supportive of "the cause" as a whole), while others could be more precisely defined by virtue of their particular interest in supporting Sahrawi women through

10. NUSW Conference poster reading "The Fifth Conference of the National Union of Sahrawi Women, 5, 6, 7 of
April 2007." The Arabic text states that the conference
will be held in the "Western Sahara"; the Spanish version
indicates that its location is the "Sahara."

the NUSW. Even "general" Friends often use the NUSW as their implementing partner along with the SRC and a range of SADR Ministries,
including those of Health, Education, and "Social Affairs and the Promotion of Women." This list therefore demonstrates the strong and active
support that the NUSW and Polisario/SADR enjoy from a variety of both
high-profile and local-level organizations in Spain, all of which provide

the NUSW and SADR Ministries with essential financial support. For the preparation of the Fifth NUSW Congress, the Basque government alone offered the NUSW 40,000 euros through an agreement signed between the NUSW and EMAKUNDE (the Basque Country's Women's Institute).

It is worth noting that, despite claims of the NUSW's political and financial independence from the Polisario/SADR, the SADR Constitution indicates that the Polisario's National Secretariat supervises the activities of the Sahrawi unions (of which the NUSW is one), which are in turn the "pillars" of the Polisario (Es-Sweyih 2001, 61 and 62). Further, not only is the Secretary General of the NUSW automatically granted a position in the SADR's National Secretariat but one of its main executive members (and former secretary general) is President Abdelaziz's wife, Khadija Hamdi. Indeed, Hamdi is both a key figure in the NUSW and the SADR Minister for Culture and Sport (elected in 2007 and 2011, having replaced Mariem Salek in 2007, who in turn became the Minister for Education). Another key example of the connection between the NUSW and the Polisario/SADR and of the "recyclable" nature of power[28] is that of Senia Ahmed Marhba, who was a member of the SADR Political Bureau (from 1982) and the National Secretariat (1985), *wāliya* of Smara camp (from 1985), Polisario/SADR representative for Switzerland (2003–2004) and was more recently elected as the Ambassador to Libya (2007). She was also the NUSW's Secretary General between 1990 and 1995 and the director of the 27 February Camp and National Women's School from 1990 (Lippert 1992; ARSO 2004; Mundos de Mujeres 2008).

As such, the connection between the NUSW and SADR is tangible, and funds designated to the NUSW may therefore have always been part of the resources potentially available to the Polisario/SADR. Remarks made by members of several Spanish women's groups during our interviews indicated that they had more confidence in financial contributions not "going astray" when given to the NUSW, in contrast with their awareness of the regularly made charges of corruption and mismanagement of funds in the camps, as reported, for instance, by Cozza (2004) and García (2001).

---

28. Thanks are due to Yousif M. Qasmiyeh for sharing this conceptualization with me.

It could be posited that the political post of Secretary of State Responsible for Social Assistance and the Promotion/Empowerment of Women (created in 2002 and first held by Mahfouda Mohamed Rahal) is connected to the recognition that "women's issues" attract considerable investment from Spanish and other Western NGOs. While the NUSW and its Basque Support Network claim that the new SADR position allows the Union to focus more specifically on working on "politically essential women's issues,"[29] rather than dealing with social assistance as it had often done in the past (Fiddian 2002), it is equally the case that this new position has diverted funds and institutional capacity from the Union directly to a growing SADR Ministry. The potential of this gynocentric and female-directed economy and aid industry in the camps suggests that the NUSW and Polisario/SADR may increasingly compete to obtain funds and political support from Spanish and Western NGOs that are particularly dedicated to solidarity with Sahrawi women. As such, the official rhetoric regarding women's roles and identity in the camps emerges as a prerequisite ensuring continued investment in these agencies, that could be defined as one way in which the representation is strategically related to the survival of these bodies.

Spanish feminist and "gender equality" groups (including those referred to above) have offered "Sahrawi women" support via the NUSW on the basis of "shared sisterhood" and a "shared" goal of female empowerment (see Chapter 4; cf. Moghadam 1997b, 36), a relationship that has been actively fostered by the NUSW's Departments for External Relations and Cooperation, on the one hand, and Spanish women's groups, on the other. The "promotion of women" has increasingly become a central political and social concern in Spain: the last Spanish government (2004–2011) invested considerably in addressing ever-increasing rates of violence against women (Morán 2008), and more visibly, in April 2008 the then–prime minister Rodríguez-Zapatero created not only an Equality Ministry but also a female-led cabinet (including, for the first time in Spanish

29. NUSW documents on file with the author; my translation.

history, a female Minister of Defense).[30] These and other shifts toward gender parity and female "empowerment" in Spanish governmental institutions (Lafuente 2008) have been paralleled by an increasing commitment by NGOs and Spanish regional and municipal authorities to fund female-centered projects in Spain and abroad.

In addition to the strengthening of NUSW ties with Spanish women's groups, declarations made by representatives of the Friends of the Sahara also explicitly connect the solidarity network with the projected image of gender equality and the importance of women in the camps. In a letter to the Director of *El País* in 2002, Vallbé-Bach (from Barcelona's Municipal Council) refers to the basis of such groups' solidarity with the SADR as follows:

> those of us who have always defended the legitimacy of the Sahrawi cause in their fight for their legitimate independence . . . [do so] *because* we have always defended the democratic basis upon which the SADR's constitution is founded and *upon the values of equality between all Sahrawi men and women.* (my emphasis)

This extract clearly indicates that support for "the Sahrawi cause" in general is both justifiable and necessary when the camps are simultaneously perceived to be a location for "democracy" and gender equality. This parallels the claim reached by Voutira and Harrell-Bond that the Sahrawi's unique "success" has come to be "measured by the extent to which they . . . promote their longer-term democratic goals, which include the equality of women" (2000, 68).

As I discuss in Chapters 4 and 5, the international incident that instigated Vallbé-Bach's letter demonstrates that cases that contradict the internationally transmitted script about Sahrawi women's position in the camps have the potential to undermine not only its veracity but also the entire solidarity framework upon which the camps and the "national

---

30. In 2010, the Equality Ministry was merged with the Ministry of Health and Social Services, and a Secretary of State for Equality was established.

project" are dependent. The unequal power dynamics underlying the Spanish-Sahrawi "solidarity" movements are therefore brought to the fore, since threats are frequently both explicitly and implicitly made that support will be withdrawn if certain key conditions are not met.

Cuban and South African Solidarity

While claims regarding Sahrawi women's independence, secularism, and modernity play a prominent role in acquiring and maintaining the support of Spanish civil society, alternative trends emerge in the Cuban and South African solidarity systems. The following brief discussion aims to demonstrate the extent to which the Polisario/SADR orients the Sahrawi self to the audience being addressed, emphasizing specific aspects and characteristics according to the Polisario/SADR's perceptions of what will capture and ensure the continued support of different non-Sahrawi state and nonstate actors. It is precisely the existence of alternative discourses in these contexts that leads me to propose the necessity of analyzing the mainstream representations of Sahrawi women specifically vis-à-vis the Polisario/SADR's connection with, and dependence on, the Spanish solidarity system.

Cuba and South Africa officially recognized the SADR as a state in 1980 and 2004, respectively. These countries house SADR embassies, and their connection with the Polisario/SADR thus emerges as an institutional one. These governments' support for the Sahrawi "cause" has been guaranteed, in direct opposition to the situation in Spain, where the Polisario/SADR mobilizes a civil society-driven movement that opposes its state's failure to recognize the SADR or to push for the Sahrawi's right for self-determination. As such, the need to engage with the broader public in Cuba or South Africa is less urgent than in Europe and especially Spain, where it is civil society that keeps the matter of the Western Sahara on national and regional political agendas.

The terms of engagement between the Polisario/SADR and these solidary states are therefore not dependent upon the same set of representations as those that capture the attention of Western/Spanish civil society audiences, with alternative terms and experiences being summoned to encourage these states' continued "solidarity" for "the cause." If the Spanish solidarity system is founded (and even dependent) upon certain notions of Sahrawi "democracy" and "female empowerment," these representations are revealed as irrelevant and thus absent from Polisario/ SADR's diplomatic relations with many non-Spanish audiences, including Cuba and South Africa.

Cuba

It is perhaps unsurprising that anticolonial sentiment should have been openly expressed primarily by Cuban-educated students once we recognize that the longstanding Cuban-Polisario solidarity framework largely draws upon parallels between the Sahrawi's colonial history and Cuban experiences of Spanish colonialism and exploitation (i.e., Castro in Amuchastegui-Alvarez 1988, 261; Almeida-Bosque[31] 1997, 13–14). During a seminar given to a group of solidary Cuban students from the University of Havana in December 2006, the terms in that the history of the conflict was presented were particularly poignant: references to the struggle for independence from a colonial power emerged as the primary mode of relating to the audience, with the SADR representative dedicating an entire hour to the history of the conflict and only mentioning the refugee camps in passing (verbatim proceedings).

When I asked why he had not addressed conditions in the camps, the same Sahrawi official indicated that, unlike Spaniards, Cubans would not be motivated by references to a socioeconomic crisis there since Cubans "live like that themselves" (i.e., hungry, poor, and isolated) due to the U.S.-led embargo (also see Fiddian-Qasmiyeh 2010a). While particular representations of the camps play a—if not *the*—central role in activating solidarity in Spain, the strategy implemented by the Cuban-based SADR representative appears to have been in line with the ideological frameworks that inform the mainstream Cuban understanding of international relations and solidarity with the developing world (Almeida-Bosque 1997, 8ff). Despite

31. This Cuban "Revolutionary Commander" visited the Sahrawi camps in the 1990s.

the significance of the Cuban education system that has been developed to ensure Sahrawi self-sufficiency within the camps—and to provide a professional cadre for the future—it is the Spanish solidarity system that directs the official discourse in the Western sphere. I posit that while Cuba may educate Sahrawi youth and therefore provide for the future, Spain feeds not only the population but also the viability of the "national" political project and is prioritized accordingly by the Polisario/SADR.

South Africa

An alternative basis for supporting the Sahrawi "cause" emerged throughout my interviews, and my participation in and observations of events held during the Week of Solidarity with the Sahrawi People held in Pretoria and Johannesburg (May 2007). Reflecting the strong state and institutional support that the Polisario/SADR enjoys from South Africa, this week of events was held at the invitation of the African National Congress, African National Conference Youth League, South African Communist Party, Conference of South African Trade Unions, South African National NGO Coalition and the South African Students' Coalition. On 24 May 2007, these bodies signed and presented a Memorandum to the Moroccan Embassy in Pretoria, demanding the immediate end of the occupation of the Western Sahara. Indeed, since recognizing the SADR in 2004, South Africa has been officially, politically, and financially committed to supporting "stabilization efforts in Western Sahara" (Republic of South Africa 2008; also Department of Foreign Affairs 2007 and 2008). Given South Africa's role as the major southern African power (politically and economically speaking, for instance through the African Union and the Southern African Development Community), its potential position in the United Nations,[32] and the substantial increase in South African-sponsored projects run in the Sahrawi refugee camps and in the Polisario-controlled areas of the Western

---

32. Along with its role at the General Assembly, South Africa was an elected member of the UN Security Council in 2008. Pretoria's representative at the UN has criticized the weak terms included in UNSC Resolutions on the Western Sahara.

Sahara,[33] Polisario/SADR is determined to further strengthen its relationship with the government.

Throughout all of my meetings with South African politicians, international diplomats, trade unionists, academics, and journalists, references to the shared histories of South Africa and the SADR were paramount: apartheid, colonialism, oppression, and violation of human rights were all key terms emerging in the official South African position on the matter of the Western Sahara, mirroring the language used by Polisario/SADR Embassy staff. Hence, the chief director of South Africa's Department of Foreign Affairs' North Africa Directorate and representative at the UNSC during 2007, Ambassador Ebrahim Saley, recalled in a seminar at the Institute for Global Justice that "President Mbeki, at the opening of the Pan-African Parliament . . . drew the parallel between the Sahrawi cause and the South African struggle" (verbatim proceedings, Johannesburg, 30 May 2007), indicating that "countries that have fought wars of liberation are the countries that are the strongest supporters of the Polisario and of the Sahrawis." He then reiterated that South Africa is "duty-bound to keep on supporting the Sahrawis to exercise their right to self-determination" through its "principled foreign policy." Also representing the DFA's North Africa Directorate, Lara Swart declared at a presentation offered at the South African Human Rights Committee that "As we [South Africans] fought for our freedom, and as we were supported to fight for our freedom, we [the government of South Africa] will continue to fight for the freedom of the people of Western Sahara" (verbatim proceedings, Johannesburg, 25 May 2007).

Conclusion

Created by the Polisario in the mid-1970s with Algerian support, the Sahrawi refugee camps are now home to approximately 155,000 refugees living in spaces administered by the Polisario/SADR with substantial

33. Including funding demining campaigns, leisure/sports programs for camp-based youth, and investments in Tifariti (verbatim proceedings of speech offered by Ambassador Saley at the Institute of Global Justice, 30 May 2007).

support from international state and nonstate actors. For the past three decades, the Polisario/SADR has officially demonstrated its capacity to organize the camps internally, developing political, educational, health, and social structures and services to attend to the needs of its refugee-citizens. Over time, however, conditions in the camps have changed considerably with the emergence of major socioeconomic differences among residents, influenced by money arriving in the form of remittances, pensions from the Spanish government, employment by NGOs, and gifts from solidary Spanish families who host Sahrawi children each year.

Without dismissing the achievements of the Polisario/SADR, NUSW and individual refugees since the camps' creation, despite claims of self-sufficiency and the reality of well-managed camps, Sahrawi refugees, families, camps, and the Polisario/SADR political project are highly dependent upon the provision of humanitarian aid and political support via specific solidarity networks. The visibility of and dependence on support provided by Spanish families and solidarity groups since the 1990s in particular, rather than the quantitatively greater aid provided by international organizations such as ECHO, WFP and UNHCR since the mid- to late 1980s, has in turn influenced the development and reproduction of a precise representation of the camps as democratic and egalitarian spaces during interactions with Western audiences.

In this chapter I have highlighted the Polisario/SADR's capacity to successfully transmit specific images, concepts, and claims relating to the camps to non-Sahrawi observers, arguing that mainstream accounts directed to Western, and especially Spanish, audiences are different from those invoked during encounters with other, non-Western solidary actors, such as Cuba and South Africa. In these cases, support is summoned with reference to common experiences of colonial oppression and racism, factors that are explicitly absent(ed) from encounters with Spanish solidarios, as members of the former colonial power.

As stressed by Harrell-Bond, "most refugees are able to infer" that in order to be "successful in obtaining aid" and gaining "the approval of the helper," one of "the most effective survival strategies" is to "ingratiate themselves" with aid providers (1999, 151). Equally, following Horst, we must accept that refugees have "the power and choice to create knowledge about and give meaning to their own situation" (2006a, 25). In the following chapters I argue that the Polisario/SADR has identified which claims and images may best "ingratiate" them with different audiences and has strategically mobilized these claims accordingly.

While Allen and Turton argue that refugees often prioritize "saving a way of life" over "saving a life" (1996, 1–21), in this case I suggest that a major concern has been to develop a system that will enable a combination of physical, material, and political survival in and of the camps and in the broader international arena. As indicated in the Introduction, I consider that this system is a central part of the Polisario/SADR's "politics of survival," and I propose that it has been characterized by the re/creation of the camps as democratic, secular, and gender-equal spaces that are worth being saved. Indeed, as we saw in the Introduction, we could identify that the Polisario/SADR faces multiple "quests" "for *meaningful survival*," including their demand that the Sahrawi people should enjoy their right to self-determination; to ensure that "significant other(s)" continue to recognize them (i.e., the Polisario/SADR) as the Sahrawi people's legitimate representatives; and to guarantee that these "significant other(s)" support its "cause" and continue to provide essential humanitarian and political support.

In the following pages, I examine the "way of life" that is presented to specific, non-Sahrawi audiences by the Polisario/SADR and NUSW, with special emphasis on the mainstream representation of Sahrawi women's position in the refugee camps. According to my research, the identity of, and terms of relationship with, the Western (or, more exclusively, Spanish) audience have significantly determined both the motivations for and content of what I term here as "inter/nationally scripted Sahrawi gender relations." Such a script reveals that contemporary representations, idealizations, and manipulations of gender and imagined gender relations in the camps are profoundly international in nature. Hence, in addition to local or national power dynamics and interplays between different groups of men, women, and children in the camps, Sahrawi gender relations (both real and imagined) have come to be directly implicated in, affected by and invoked to ensure the continuity of solidarity and aid networks and power structures.

3

Emerging Discourse

Concealing Islam

ALTHOUGH ALTERNATIVE, and sometimes competing, descriptions emerge in many reports and articles on the Sahrawi refugee camps, the frequency with which the same terms and conceptualizations of Sahrawi women arose during my multisited interviews demands careful examination. After presenting a range of extracts taken from interviews with Sahrawi political figures and youth, the four principal sections of this chapter explore common representations of Sahrawi women in relation to veiling, freedom of movement and participation in the public sphere, *mahr* and marriage, and divorce and the "divorce party." I consider these four core elements to be a set of mutually reinforcing images and conceptualizations that re/create Sahrawi women as uniquely liberal, secular, and empowered refugee women for particular political purposes.

In the case under consideration, the mainstream representation of Sahrawi refugee women's position and identity in the camps is founded upon the separation of Sahrawi women from Other Arab Muslim women, with a particular reliance on creating and maintaining a distance from Islam and religious identity for strategic reasons. The portrayal of Sahrawi women explored in this chapter therefore emerges as a highly politicized one that I consider to be part of the Polisario/Sahrawi's broader "politics of survival." It is through analyzing the component parts of the official discourse that it will become possible in later chapters to examine and critique the Polisario/SADR's motivations behind such a representation of life in the camps. I will subsequently explore which social groups (including "nonideal" women, girls, and men) have been absent(ed) from mainstream accounts of the camps via this discursive strategy and to what effect.

Identifying the Official Discourse

The views portrayed in the following extract from my interview with an SADR representative in the Middle East is paralleled by a wide range of publications that make reference to the Polisario/SADR conceptualization of "Sahrawi women's position" in Sahrawi society (including Navarrio-Asín n.d.; Kuttab 2002; Feo 2003; AFP 2004):

> There are many differences between Sahrawi and Syrian societies . . . Sahrawi women have *more freedom* . . . Unlike in Jordan, where honor killings and sexual abuse prevail, and in Spain, where violence against women is common, *women do not suffer from domestic violence in the camps*—she would be able to *divorce him* [her husband] immediately if he did, and a Sahrawi man would be unable to remarry if he hit his wife or abused her in any way; his reputation would be destroyed . . . Sahrawi women *do not accept polygamy*, for there is a "law of never before or after," and the woman can demand a divorce, which is common. (Damascus, July 2006; my emphasis[1])

Further reflecting on the distance projected by SADR spokespeople between Sahrawi women and Other Arab women, the then-SADR Minister of Culture and Sport, Mariem Salek, is quoted in Mexico City's leading newspaper as follows:

> I sometimes ask myself . . . *if Arab women exist.* In the Arab world, the [form of] *feminism* which has developed up until now lacks depth; there is nothing serious. If they wanted to recognize us, they would have to admit that what we have achieved is a treasure [*una joya*]. (Petrich 2005; my emphasis)

Similarly comparing Sahrawi women with "the rest of the Arab and Muslim world," Es-Sweyih, former Polisario Representative to France and the

1. All translations from Spanish and French are my own, unless noted otherwise.

UK, and former Permanent SADR Representative at the UN, wrote that Sahrawi "women are not marginalized," continuing:

> There is space for everyone, and *especially* for women, for whom the values and traditions of the *bidhan* (maure) society in general and Sahrawi society in particular, give a *privileged* place, clearly different from the position of their *sisters* in the rest of the Arab and Muslim world. *In contrast with what you find in other Arab and African societies,* the Sahrawi woman plays an important role, in both the productive-economic sector and in the political and administrative structures of the SADR. (2001, 36; my emphasis)

Further, the thrice-elected (2002, 2007 and 2011) Secretary General of the NUSW, Fatma Mehdi, has indicated that "for us, religion is not an obstacle as far as going out to work or socializing is concerned, *as happens in other Arab countries such as Algeria,* for example" (in Esteso 2006; my translation and emphasis).

In all of these extracts, which express sentiments commonly reproduced in Polisario/SADR documents, along with being transmitted orally to visitors to the camps and individuals attending solidarity events in Spain and elsewhere, Sahrawi women's positions and roles in the camps are explicitly compared with those of Other Arab women. Hence, we are informed that Sahrawi women are *not* forced into polygamous marriages and are *not* restricted by religion in matters of employment and interacting with others. At the same time, they *are* able to demand and obtain divorce, *do* play an important role in economic, political and administrative areas, and *have* developed a "serious" and "deep" form of "feminism" ("a treasure" in the Sahara). The explicit message is that Other Arab and Muslim women as a homogenized and essentialized whole embody the opposite of these virtues and successes. In such examples, Sahrawi informants consistently use the terms "Arab" and "Muslim" interchangeably, as synonyms that fail to recognize both·the religious and ethnic heterogeneity of the Arab world and the marked differences that exist between Muslim women both in and outside of the Arab world (cf. Salhi 2008, 296).

Below and in the following chapters, I examine the nature and implications of, and reasons for, such emblematic statements vis-à-vis Sahrawi women and Other Arab and Muslim women. First, however, I draw on a range of interviews conducted with young Sahrawi refugees in Syria, Cuba, and the 27 February Camp in Algeria as a means of stressing the extent to which this particular representation is made and underscoring the precise terms in which it is expressed. Given the geopolitical diversity of these interview locations and the fact that most of these interviewees had spent their adolescent and postadolescent years outside of the camps, the proximity of their responses to those offered by the SADR/Polisario officers is notable and requires careful consideration. The following extracts correspond closely to the answers that I was provided with in over 100 separate interviews conducted with Sahrawi men and women in these various locations.

Sahrawi Refugee Youth

During my fieldwork in Syria (July–August 2006), a History student who had spent eight years living in Damascus stated that "Sahrawi women are like Sahrawi men. There is freedom. Men never insult or hit women." Contrasting Sahrawi women's situation to that of women in the West, he continued:

> In the Sahrawi society, *women have a very special status* . . . In Spain, Britain, and France, women are being beaten, but it's *impossible for a Sahrawi woman who is Bedouin to be beaten.* Women in the Sahrawi camps live a very ordinary life. (my emphasis, Qasmiyeh's translation)

Revealing his impressions of Sahrawi women's experiences vis-à-vis those of Arab, rather than Western, women he indicated that

> [w]omen in other Arab and Muslim countries lead a very unexciting life; they hardly leave their houses. In general, Arab society is closed, but in the Sahrawi society the position of women is nearly the same as men's . . . to a large extent Sahrawi women have full freedom to move from one place to another. Other Arab women are always in their houses or indoors, and it's impossible for them to leave their houses without permission. But in the desert, women are completely different; they can go from one place to another freely. They can do whatever they want to do. (Qasmiyeh's translation)

Supporting this individual student's views, during a group interview with five male Sahrawi students in Damascus I was repeatedly informed, as a response to my question about Sahrawi women's situation in the camps, that "it's hard, but it's the best in the Arab world." When I asked why this might be the case, one of them repeated that it was due to what they classified as their Bedouin nature. When I asked whether there are similarities between Sahrawi women and Bedouin women living in Syria and the Middle East generally, one of the young men responded: "Yes, of course, but Sahrawi women are *unique*—their importance is not reflected in other countries" (my emphasis). These students continued by stressing the "difference" and "uniqueness" of Sahrawi women, not only through comparing their situation with that of Bedouin or Arab women, or of Western women but in fact in universal terms:

> The Mauritanian and Sahrawi tradition is the only one that celebrates divorce as well as marriage. Unlike the rest of the world, there is no violence against women among the Sahrawi or Mauritanians.

In a completely different socioreligious setting, and after 18 years living outside of the camps, in Cuba a 29-year-old Biology MA student responded as follows to a similarly worded question about Sahrawi women's situation in the camps:

> The two most different nations in the Arab world are the Mauritanian and the Sahrawi societies, which are the only nations where women do not cover their faces or hands. In other places in the Arab world, you can only see the woman's eyes, but the Sahrawi women wear the *milḥafa*, and people ask them their opinions and listen to them. (Havana, November 2006; my translation)

Another Cuban-based student in his early 30s (who has been on the island since 1988) told me that he was writing his sociology master's thesis on the position of Sahrawi women in the camps, both in terms of the changes that have taken place since the camps were created and in relation to their differences from "other Arab and Muslim women." After showing me Juliano's book on Sahrawi women (1998), he explained his rationale behind choosing this topic:

> I am proud to know that, *despite the Sahrawi being Muslim,* and despite the
> limited conditions in the camps, Sahrawi women have made so many
> advancements since the camps were created. They are *free, unlike other
> Muslim and Arab women.* (Havana, December 2006; my emphasis)

While I shall return to the "bases" of these students' views of "Muslim
and Arab" gender relations, it should be apparent at this stage that these
Cuban- and Syrian-educated students reproduced very similar images of
Sahrawi women when interviewed.

Notably, in the camps, two young men who currently work as aides
for two separate SADR ministries after having completed their studies
in Libya and Algeria, also shared their views on Sahrawi women with
me (Rabouni, April 2007). While the first presented a view similar to the
official representations outlined above, he suggested that it would be
"impossible to compare the situation of Mauritanian and Sahrawi women,
because the Sahrawi are not yet in a democratic, stable situation." Nonetheless, he continued by stressing that "Sahrawi women can have a pass-
port and can travel without permission from their menfolk, *unlike in other
Arab countries,*" and that "the woman has the right to request a *unilateral
divorce,* unlike in most places in the world" (my emphasis). The second
informed me that "in contrast with the Arab world in general, I can talk
with any Sahrawi woman *about any topic.* I can greet *all women* in the street,
which is not the case in Algeria, Morocco, Tunisia, Libya" (my emphasis).

As is clear from this range of quotations, and those of the male and
female SADR officials included above, these young men's claims regarding Sahrawi women are not only based on a particular understanding of
life in the camps per se (even if the interviewees in question had not lived
there for an extended period of time) but also of the situation of "Other
women" with whom the Sahrawi are compared (see Table 5). In these
accounts, the Sahrawi woman is presented as unique, and exceptional—
not only is she an example to be followed by other Arab women, according to Sahrawi women and Western analysts alike, but she is also to be
admired for having achieved what the Spanish have not: to live without
a fear of violence against women (VAW), which officially claimed sixty-
eight women's lives in Spain in 2006 and seventy-four in 2007 (Belaza

TABLE 5. Summary of claims made about Sahrawi, Western, and "Other Muslim and Arab" women as expressed by interviewees and the Polisario/ SADR literature reviewed

Topic	Sahrawi Women	Western Women	Other Muslim and Arab Women
Veiling	Unveiled; or "accept the veil with love" (Petrich 2005)	Unveiled	Forcibly veiled
Freedom of movement	Total	Total	None, seclusion
Participation in public sphere	Very active, "a treasure" in the Sahara (Petrich 2005)	Very active	Subjugated and "bored" at home
Right to divorce	Free to divorce	Free to divorce, but may become victim of VAW	Unable to divorce

2008). These are dynamics that I explore in greater detail in the current and following chapters.

When addressing the question of Sahrawi women's situation in the camps, the same examples demonstrating their freedom recur: "not being veiled," having freedom of movement, and not only being able to divorce freely and "unilaterally," but even celebrating this event via a "divorce party." Given the centrality of these examples in these interviews and extracts, which are characteristic of the interviews I conducted in all of my research locations, as well as in the materials reviewed in English, Spanish, French, and Arabic (especially Kuttab's 2002 historiography and NUSW reports from 2007), I shall address each of these in turn. In so doing, I question some of the bases of these representations (often pointing to the difference between descriptions of the camps and my observations of the same), while providing the foundations from which I will later develop a nuanced examination of the terms of engagement between the Polisario/SADR and particular non-Sahrawi audiences.

Embodying the Official Discourse: Summoning Sahrawi Women

Veiling and "Veiling" the Milḥafa

The veil has so frequently been centrally positioned in Western analyses (and historically, in Western colonial projects) that it is unsurprising that descriptions of Sahrawi women, *qua* Muslim women, should also include references to veiling. Fanon's identification and analysis of French colonizers' "precise political doctrine" to "unveil" Algerian women as a means of conquering the colonized society (Fanon 1965, 37–38) have been the foundation of much feminist postcolonial work that has examined Orientalist representations of both the veil (i.e., El-Guindi 2003; Lewis 2003; and Woodhull 2003) and the extent to which unveiling women has frequently become a "convenient instrument for signifying many issues at once, i.e., the construction of modern [national] identity" (Yeğenoğlu 1998, 132). In certain historical contexts, we are reminded, the veil has "carried connotations of Muslim backwardness" both in the eyes of Western Orientalists and MENA nationalists (ibid.). Indeed, as stressed by Kandiyoti (1991) and Yeğenoğlu (1998, 135) with reference to Atatürk's reforms in Turkey, processes of unveiling women as a means of demonstrating the "marginalization" or displacement of Islam have historically been central to the development of "secular" modern nationalist discourses.

Contemporary popular and political debates concerning the place of veiling in "secular" European states have emerged as a result of Muslim girls and women, as well as their families and broader communities, demanding that Muslim women should have the *right* to wear the veil (be this the hijab, chador, or niqab) in schools—both as students and as teachers—and other public places. Major disputes have taken place since the late 1980s in European countries including France,[2] Spain,[3] and the United Kingdom.[4] The veil in the aforementioned analyses has often been identified as being the most visible (or public) sign of difference between Muslim

2. Blank 1999; Abu-Rabia 2006; Hamdan 2007; Scott 2007.
3. EFE 2007; Vargas-Llosa 2007.
4. Sturcke 2006; Tempest 2006.

and Western societies, with such "difference" being negatively evaluated by Western audiences, who have directly equated the veil with the oppression of women, and often claimed that (neo)colonial intervention has been *necessary* to save "brown women from brown men" (Spivak 1993a, 93).[5] In more recent popular debates in Western and non-Western states, Muslim women and men have framed "veiling" within a discourse of rights, arguing that the veil can enable and empower women rather than unequivocally "oppress" them (Hoodfar 1991; Zuhur 1992). In these and other historical and contemporary cases, veiling has often become a symbol of personal, communal, and national resistance and identity, directly opposing ethnocentric and Orientalist assumptions, stereotypes, and "unveiling" desires. It is important to note that the personal, religious, social, and political significance of the veil for Muslim women and their communities has not been denied or rejected, but rather emphasized, by those who argue that girls and women should have the right to veil, if they so wish.

In a radically divergent approach to the direct confrontation to and rejection of essentialist (mis)understandings of the veil, the mainstream discourse projected by the Polisario/SADR to Western observers with regard to Sahrawi women is permeated with claims that, unlike other Arab/Muslim women, they "did not veil" either during, before, or after the colonial era. Hence, Kuttab, discussing Sahrawi women during the colonial era, states that "she does not veil" (2002, 63; *"hiya la tatahajjab,"* where *hajaba* is the Arabic root of the verb "to conceal" or "to veil," Qasmiyeh's translation). Equally, like other visitors to the camps, Harrell-Bond was told by informants during her visit that "[o]ur women were never veiled and they always worked" (1999, 156), and, following an interview with Zahra Ramdan (executive member of the NUSW and its Spanish-based International Relations representative), Feo also indicates that "the Sahrawi woman is not obliged to veil" (2003; my translation). Such accounts of Sahrawi women "not veiling" either in the past or in the present appear to be largely incongruous when considered along with my

5. On "saving" Afghan women from the burqa, see Abu-Lughod 2002; Hirschkind and Mahmood 2002; Rutter 2004; Stabile and Kumar 2005, 766ff; Kandiyoti 2007b.

analysis of the relationship between girls' entry into womanhood and the *milḥafa* in the colonial era, where I related the *milḥafa* to both physical and religious maturation.

While there is no fixed age at which girls start to wear the *milḥafa* (Crivello, Fiddian and Chatty 2005, 14), it is "unthinkable" for a Sahrawi woman not to wear the *milḥafa* in the camps, as young women returning from studying in Cuba have encountered upon their arrival (Fiddian 2002). During their studies in Algeria, in contrast, young Sahrawi women tend to wear headscarves, rather than the *milḥafa*, as demonstrated in photographs shown by many female informants in the camps. Further, although many Sahrawi women living in the Canary Islands and other parts of Spain continue to wear the *milḥafa*, others decide to either wear headscarves or leave their heads uncovered (personal observations, 2001–2013). In contrast, in the refugee camps all women wear the *milḥafa*, although the way in which it is worn varies throughout women's life cycles, with older women veiling less strictly than younger, fertile, and supposedly more attractive women (also see Mernissi 2003b, 493). The *milḥafa* is therefore directly related to curtailing the risk of *fitna* (temptation or its related chaos), with older women seen as being less "tempting" to men than their younger counterparts. This move toward "looser" or more "relaxed" veiling with age is in line with sura 24:60, which indicates that women who are "past the age of bearing children" and "have no hope of marriage" may even "take off their outer garments," although they should remain modestly clothed and "not display their charms."

Clear confirmation that the *milḥafa* should be considered to be a veil is derived from my research visit to the camps in 2007. Given that all Sahrawi women wear the *milḥafa* in the camps, upon my arrival I was clearly dressed in a different fashion to the majority of women there, but I still considered myself to be "modestly covered," since I was wearing a headscarf and loose-fitting long-sleeved shirts and trousers. While living, working, and conducting research in other countries with majority Muslim populations, this had even been sufficient to enter mosques that required non-Muslims to observe/respect veiling requirements (such as the Al-Azhar mosque in Cairo). Many women and girls in the camps, however, clearly did not consider me to be "covered," with adolescent girls in particular repeatedly asking me "Why aren't you *muḥajjaba*?" (veiled, f. sing.). On several occasions during my first weeks in the camps I was confronted quite aggressively by three women in their late 50s and early 60s on this matter. While they, like many older (usually postmenopausal) women in the camps, wore relatively loose-fitting and "revealing" *malāḥif* (pl. of *milḥafa*), frequently with only a "skimpy" top underneath that allowed their arms and shoulders to be seen, they were adamant that I, like all other young women in the camps, should be *muḥajjaba*.

After a short time in the camps, I eventually decided to wear the *milḥafa* rather than a headscarf, resulting in older women immediately ceasing to challenge me on this matter. Equally, the young girls (who I believe were expressing more widely held views) instantly stopped asking me why I was not *muḥajjaba*. This direct cessation of daily confrontations demonstrated that, for these women and girls alike, the *milḥafa* is clearly a form of hijab, or veil, and, further, that in their opinion women *should* be *muḥajjabāt* (veiled, f. pl.).

While it may appear self-evident that the *milḥafa* is a traditional item that fulfills common interpretations of the Qur'anic requirements of veiling/covering, and therefore should be understood as a "veil," conventional Sahrawi representations of this item of clothing to Westerners purport to distance the *milḥafa* from religious obligations or connotations, even overtly declaring that Sahrawi women "do not veil."

Western observers are often informed by Sahrawi men and women that the *milḥafa* is a traditional or national item of clothing, rather than a religiously motivated one. This is reflected in the response offered by Khira Mohamed, a young Spanish-educated Sahrawi doctor, when asked by a journalist at Spain's leading national newspaper, *El País*, if she had ever worn the veil:

I am Muslim, a believer, but I do not wear it [the veil]. There is no obligation to wear it. In the camps I do wear the traditional Sahrawi clothes and the *melfa* [*sic*], which is a long scarf, different from that which other Arab women wear.

(Mohamed cited in Alberola 2003; my translation)

The ways in which journalists writing for *El País* from the 1980s onward have defined the *milḥafa* (variously written *melhfa, melhhfa,* or *melfa*) to their readers is of note here: in 1985, Martín refers to " . . . the traditional *melfa* (women's clothing);" in 1997, Sanz describes an encounter with "a woman covered in the traditional *melhhfa* (tunic);" and in 2001, Velázquez-Gaztelu met with a woman who was "wearing a *melhfa,* the traditional clothing of Sahrawi women" (my translations).

In all of these descriptions, which are based on visits to the camps and interviews with Spanish-speaking Sahrawis there, the *milḥafa* appears as a traditional dress,[6] making no reference to which parts of the body it covers and, in Sanz's case, vaguely describing it to the reader as a "tunic." In other cases, Sahrawi women are described as being "wrapped in colored *saris*" (AFP, 2004; my emphasis). Such an understanding of the *milḥafa* clearly makes no connection to any possible religious motivations or requirements, with references to Sahrawi women's Muslim identity either being entirely absent or marginal in these pieces. This representation fails, for instance, to recognize that Sahrawi women who attend the mosque on Fridays ideally wear a newly washed *milḥafa* when they do so, and all women carefully adjust their *malāḥif* before praying to ensure that their heads and hair are covered accordingly (personal observations, 27 February Camp, March–May 2007). Indeed, not only do Sahrawi refugee women "veil," but the typical assumption in the camps is that all Muslim women are *Islamically obliged* to wear some sort of veil (despite Khira Mohamed's declaration to the contrary)[7] and that if they are Sahrawi women, they should

6. It appears probable that Khira Mohamed does not personally consider the *milḥafa* to be a religious item, since, while she may wear "traditional" clothes *in the refugee camps,* she does not wear the *milḥafa* while in Spain, nor (given the journalist's question) does she wear the hijab. Veiling has been common among Christian, Jewish, and Muslim women in the Arab world (El-Guindi 2003, 595) and elsewhere (Küng 2007, 620–621), thereby highlighting the cultural and religious significance of the veil beyond Islam.

7. Both before and after donning the *milḥafa* I discussed different forms of veiling practices and interpretations of the Qur'an with the women and girls who were determined that I should veil. Referring to my experiences of working in Egypt and Syria, I indicated that some Muslim women and men in the Middle East and Europe believe that, while

specifically wear the *milḥafa*. Although we shall return to the ways in which the official discourse creates and maintains a distance from Islam, what is of interest in this section is the separation that is created, for a Western audience, between "the veil" and the *milḥafa*.

The identifiers "veil," "veiling," and "unveiling" are omnipresent throughout analyses of women in the Middle East, and yet these terms' meanings often remain unexplored or undefined, despite authors referring to the heterogeneity of practice and significance given to veiling by women themselves and by the communities they live in.[8] Lewis and Mills' anthology (2003) contains a section specifically dedicated to the "Harem and the Veil," composed of six articles by Mernissi, Graham-Brown, Lewis, Yeğenoğlu, Woodhull, and El-Guindi. In this collection it is only El-Guindi who explicitly differentiates between "veiling in two feminisms" (referring to the experiences and politics of Sha'rawi and Nasif), thereby exploring alternative forms of both veiling and unveiling. In the remaining pieces, the authors all make reference to "the veil," "veiling," and/or "unveiling" without defining precisely what it is that they are describing. In so doing, it appears that the authors assume that their readers will a priori know what "the veil" is, understand its multifaceted purposes, interpretations, justifications, and regulations, as well as its physical nature, including what it covers or leaves exposed. The Sahrawi claims that "they do not veil" while wearing the *milḥafa* lead us to explore precisely these questions in greater detail.

The same suras (24:30, 31 and 33:53 and 59) and examples from the Hadith are habitually drawn upon by members of contemporary Islamic movements when they defend the Islamic bases for specific dress and behavioral codes (El-Guindi 2003, 588–589; Küng 2007, 621ff) and yet the religious requirement to veil remains a debated issue within Muslim

---

Muslim women should dress modestly, they were under no obligation to wear the veil. The response to my proposal was categorical: I was told that all Muslim women *are obliged* to veil, and that it is *haram* not to do so.

8. Lindisfarne-Tapper and Ingham provide a detailed examination of the diversity of clothing and veiling in the Middle East (1997).

communities, in part explaining the variety of veiling practices around the world. In the Qur'an, the terms *ḥijāb* (mentioned seven times), *jilbāb* (33:59), and *khimār* (24:31), respectively, refer to an item/piece of cloth that broadly conceals or separates (in this case) women from men; "an outer garment" used by decent women "[when in public];" and, last, a long head covering (Küng 2007, 621ff). While not included specifically in the Qur'an, many other types of veils are worn by Muslim women, including the burqa, chador, haïk, and niqab, all of which cover different parts of women's heads (including their necks and faces) and are worn in combination with modest clothing, often with gloves and socks (El-Guindi 2003).

Only one of the Qur'anic terms, *khimār*, specifies that the woman's head in particular should be covered, since hijab was initially used to refer to a curtain or barrier separating men's from women's spaces (Küng 2007, 622). Indeed, it is perhaps this notion of spatial segregation from men, rather than covering women's heads and faces, that travelers such as (the fourteenth century) Ibn Batuta may have referred to when stating that "Maure" women in North West Africa "[did] not veil themselves" at the time (in El-Hamel 1999, 74). The reflexive nature of this term ("veiling themselves" rather than "veiling") could lead to such a reading. It was only later that the hijab became associated with a woman's head-covering more specifically (Küng 2007, 622), and in some accounts both the hijab and "the headscarf, which covers head and neck," are now in practice used interchangeably as synonyms for "the veil" (such as Heng 1997; Küng 2007, 622; Scott 2007). When Khira Mohamed indicated that she has never worn "it," with specific reference to "the veil," while admitting that she does wear the traditional *milḥafa*, it appears clear that she is directly equating the hijab or headscarf with "the veil."[9] In the five articles mentioned above, by simply using the term "veil" rather than explaining whether the author is referring to a chador, niqab, jilbab or hijab, not only are the various

9. In the Spanish context, the term *"velo"* is commonly used to refer to both "the veil" in abstract, and the hijab *qua* veil more specifically. Hence, Vargas-Llosa directly equates the hijab with what he refers to as the "Islamic veil" (2007).

types of "veils" worn by different Muslim women elided, but so too is the significance of the terms "veiled" and "unveiled."

El-Guindi's discussion of the significance of the veil in two case studies of Muslim feminism is particularly relevant at this point. With reference to a "public political feminist act" in which Sha'rawi "unveiled ceremonially," El-Guindi reminds us that

> The phrase used in the discourse surrounding the context of lifting the 'veil' was *raf' al-higab* (the lifting of the *hijab*). Ironically, what secular feminists lifted was the traditional face veil (*burqu'*), which is rooted in cultural tradition and history rather than Islamic sources, not the *hijab* ... When Huda Sha'rawi dramatically cast off the veil in 1923, it was the face veil she removed, not the *hijab*. (2003, 596)

As this case clearly demonstrates, it is possible to "remove the veil" and yet "remain veiled," since there are different degrees and forms of veiling that Muslim women may don. Such insights appear to be absent from Graham-Brown's usage of the term "unveiled" in the caption that accompanies a late-nineteenth-century photograph of three women in Egypt:

> *The unveiled woman* in the foreground, gazing directly at the camera, is contrasted with the *two veiled women* in the background . . . However, *she draws her head-veil slightly across her face* in the presence of the man behind the camera. (2003, 507; my emphasis)

As indicated in the caption itself, "the unveiled woman" is in fact wearing a "head-veil," and the briefest examination of the photograph demonstrates that the term "unveiled" refers solely to the absence of a face veil, since the three women are all wearing loose cloths that cover their bodies, necks, heads, and foreheads.

It is thus precisely through recognizing the different ways in which "veiling" and "unveiling" can be conceptualized, and by asking who and what Sahrawi women and the *milḥafa* are being *compared* with when analysts declare that they "did not [or do not] veil," that we can best understand the mainstream representation regarding veiling in the camps. Hence, if *compared* with those Bedouin women who wear face veils or Muslim women who wear the niqab or burqa (who are *munaqqabāt*;

El-Guindi 1999, 144), it might be valid to note that Sahrawi women did not, and do not, cover their faces (major exceptions being when women protect their faces from the sun or the sand). Such an understanding is offered by the Cuban-based master's student quoted above, who claimed that the only Arab women who "do not cover their faces or hands" are Mauritanian and Sahrawi women who wear the *milḥafa*. He continues by (equally unfoundedly) stating that "in other places in the Arab world, you can only see the woman's eyes," leading us to recognize that, if one considers face-veiling to be "veiling" per se, one might in fact reach the conclusion that Sahrawi women "did not veil" in the past or "do not veil" in the present.

The above discussion does not purport to claim that all analysts or visitors to the camps consider Sahrawi women to be "unveiled." Yet many observers who accept that Sahrawi women "use the veil as ordered in the Qur'an" often rely on interviews with women who report that even if they do veil, they do so "with a great deal of tenderness" and as a sign "of identity and pride" (Petrich 2005; my translation). Claims to this effect were made during several of my interviews with Spanish solidarity workers and visitors in the camps. By including these quotations and references, the Western observer is immediately led to contrast the Sahrawi *milḥafa* with the ways other Muslim women veil: if Sahrawi women unequivocally embrace their identity-enforcing veil with "tenderness," we are led to understand that non-Sahrawi Muslim women are violently *forced* to wear the veil against their will.[10] Accordingly, Other Muslim women must experience this practice as a violent curtailment of their rights and have their identity and pride subjugated as a result.

In conclusion, while the *milḥafa* may, as a matter of fact, be a traditional item of clothing, and while it is admittedly neither a hijab (*qua* headscarf) nor a niqab or burqa, the *milḥafa* is nevertheless a "veil" in religious terms. As discussed earlier, nationalist movements have often promoted

---

10. Any recognition of (for instance) Tunisian laws passed since 1981 against Muslim women wearing the veil in public institutions (including universities) is absent from the official discourse.

the "unveiling" of women in an attempt to both distance themselves from Islam and to create a "secular" (and therefore "modern") national identity. This leads us to question the determination with which Polisario/SADR spokespeople have distanced themselves from the veil as a visible sign of Muslim identity in their portrayals of Sahrawi womanhood. In the following chapter I suggest that by doing so, the official discourse not only fails to confront ethnocentric understandings of both the veil and Islam, but is rather simultaneously based on, and in fact reproduces and solidifies such rhetoric.

Gendering Mobility and Social Participation

The initial usage of the term *hijab* to refer to a barrier separating men's from women's spaces (Küng 2007, 622) reflects concerns about direct contact between the sexes. In addition to veiling, therefore, Muslim women in a wide range of contexts have often been encouraged to minimize their exposure to men from outside of their kinship groups, which has, in turn, often led to limitations on the places and spaces they could (or ideally should) access (see Hoodfar 1991; Badran 1995). In this section, I address a second group of "official" claims vis-à-vis Sahrawi women's movement outside of the *khayma* and their participation in the "public" sphere. As emerged from my interviews and observations of life in the camps, the official discourse indicates that Sahrawi women "have full freedom to move from one place to another . . . they can go from one place to another freely" and are more active than Other Muslim Arab women.

Indeed, since the establishment of the refugee camps, thousands of Sahrawi women have left their families' camp to either study abroad[11] or move to the 27 February Camp to attend the National Women's School, which has a small boarding arrangement for women who do not have their own *khayma* in the camp itself. Although new locally based women's schools have opened across the camps in the past few years, young women continue to travel to the 27 February Camp to participate in

11. On Sahrawi girls' participation in the transnational educational network, see Fiddian-Qasmiyeh 2009.

activities there. During the Fifth Women's Conference, for instance, over 300 women left their home camps and spent between three and seven days in the 27 February Camp,[12] often leaving small children in the care of other female relatives.

Some other women, including second-generation refugees who have completed their secondary and tertiary educations abroad, have full-time positions in Rabouni or the national headquarters of the NUSW based in the 27 February Camp. Although their employment could be considered to demonstrate their "freedom of movement," many of the women I interviewed nonetheless indicated that they preferred to commute to and from the nearer camps (Ausserd, Aaiun, and Smara) on a daily basis rather than sleep in the 27 February Camp. On a practical level, it must be noted that traveling in these conditions is difficult for all residents, since no regular transport network exists, and most people must rely on "hitching a lift" on trucks or jeeps making the journey. Small taxi cooperatives have appeared in the camps, and there is a driving school for women in the 27 February Camp, which hopes to allow more women to start driving and, further, to enable the establishment of a female-run and female-oriented taxi service. However, women's decisions to commute often transcend such practical issues. Hence, one Cuban-educated woman in her early 30s who works in the NUSW offices lives in another camp, where she continues to look after her younger siblings. She explained to me that to stay away from her home camp, even if she were to stay with friends or family, would inevitably lead to people "gossiping" about her, since, she concluded "this society is a bit difficult" (27 February Camp, May 2007).

Like other Cuban-educated women, having lived in Havana this young woman found that her family and broader community are often prone to evaluate women's movements between camps negatively, and she has thus acceded to commuting everyday rather than live in the room

---

12. According to the NUSW's meeting with Spanish delegates, ten women were elected to represent each *dā'ira* (district), resulting in eighty to ninety women representing each *wilāya* (camp) at the National Congress. They had previously discussed the issues debated in the National Congress on both neighborhood and camp levels.

provided by the NUSW. Another young female interviewee had also studied in Cuba and was on sick leave from her job in one of the ministries in
Rabouni (some 15 km from the 27 February Camp, and a 10 to 15 minute
drive away) at the time of our interview. She admitted that she was considering not returning to her ministerial position, but rather wanted to
look for a job in her own camp, since her family thought that it was "not
a good idea" for her to work so far away from home (27 February Camp,
April 2007). In addition to revealing the discrepancy between the official
discourse and women's lived experiences in the camps, one key differ-
entiator that arises (as is the case among many Muslim and non-Muslim
women) is the question of precisely which "places" Sahrawi women are
free to move between and when.

Sahrawi refugee women are undoubtedly as a whole able to move
around the camp itself "freely" to visit friends and relatives, to attend
school, to go to work, or to complete household-related tasks. Being outside
of the house is particularly acceptable for women when this is considered
necessary or productive for the immediate family or broader community,
for instance when women participate in an NGO project or local committee or fulfill tasks that are traditionally associated with women (such
as tending small livestock, collecting water, etc.). Such activities are even
acceptable after dark, as long as they are justifiable for familial or community reasons (again, the prime example being bringing in the sheep
and goats after dusk). These activities thus often take place in spaces that
are considered to be related to a woman's family (such as the areas where
animals are kept) and where women's movement can be monitored by
family members.

On the local level, despite widely made claims that neither spatial nor
conversational limits exist in the camps, these elements are nonetheless
directly linked, since speaking with men to whom they are not related
in public may still be perceived by young women as potentially damaging their reputations, as became evident during my interviews with
young women in the camp and while walking with them outdoors. Some
young women were particularly anxious not to be seen speaking with
kinsmen where their fathers or brothers could see them, even when they
worked outside of the *khayma* on a daily basis and often alongside men.

Such concerns reflect not only concerns about *fitna*—reputation and marriageability—but also codes of behavior that are designed to demonstrate
younger individuals' respect for their elders (and especially for elder men)
and that are still strongly followed in the camps by young men and women
alike. Hence, communication between unrelated men and women is seen
as acceptable in arenas where older family members are generally absent,
such as within the precinct of the Women's School and in the NUSW headquarters. Communication outside of these spaces (that are associated with
NGO projects, education, and employment) leaves speakers increasingly
open to scrutiny by male and female members of the community, and
both women and men will be more guarded in their interactions with the
opposite sex.

My interviews and observations indicate that the acceptability of
women's movements appears to be greatest in and around the house, in the
family's immediate neighborhood, district, and the home camp (*wilāya*),
although some spaces within the *wilāya* appear to be more feminized than
others. As I argue below with reference to changes in *mahr* (brideswealth),
leaving the house and/or one's own camp at night are considered to be the
most threatening forms of movement for women, potentially resulting in
the spread of rumors that could damage their reputations and marriage
prospects. Indeed, difficulties begin to emerge when young women wish
to travel between camps, and this is also the case for some girls, as I wit-
nessed clearly during a Spanish NGO's recruitment drive for children to
participate in a three-day trip (*riḥla*) for an "activity camp" to be held in
the dunes located between the refugee camps.

The Spanish women expressed their shock and disapproval when
mothers were reluctant to allow their daughters, but not their sons, to
spend a few days away from home "having fun." The mothers wanted to
know (understandably I believe) where the girls would sleep, what sort of
contact they would have with the boys, exactly who would be responsible
for them (i.e., Spanish or Sahrawi, female or male instructors), and when
they would be back home. While several girls did eventually go to the
dunes, it was clear that not only gender, but also sibling-order and age
can affect girls' movements in the camps: while a younger daughter (aged
8) was rapidly granted permission to go on the *riḥla*, the eldest daughter

(13) of a woman with six children aged 10 and under was unable to leave the 27 February Camp since her mother needed her to help with child care and domestic work. The Spanish NGO workers were so happy to have "gotten another girl" that they made no attempt to understand the reasons why the eldest daughter should have been unable to participate in the trip. The eldest daughter's physical maturity must be noted at this point, since this will inevitably have influenced her mother's interpretation of the suggestion that she spend the night away from home in close contact with boys and men.

Even more substantial concerns arise if girls and women are to leave the camps without their families. Although girls have always participated in the Vacaciones en Paz program (Crivello, Fiddian and Chatty 2005; Crivello and Fiddian-Qasmiyeh 2010), and many traveled in the 1980s and 1990s to study in Cuba and elsewhere,[13] changes in the study-abroad program parallel this continued preference for girls and women to stay nearer to home, with girls increasingly being sent to study in locations that are both geographically and culturally closer to the camps (Chatty, Fiddian-Qasmiyeh and Crivello 2010; Fiddian-Qasmiyeh 2009). In addition to lower female participation rates in a range of study-abroad programs, Sahrawi women also continue to be underrepresented as Polisario/SADR delegates and "diplomats" at international levels, with women holding only 7% of diplomatic positions in 2007 (NUSW document on file with the author).

Indeed, concerns that the Polisario/SADR remains an androcentric and male-run institution were raised by Spanish women during the post-Conference meeting held by the NUSW in April 2007. Responding to the Spanish demand that the NUSW should pressure the Polisario to ensure that more women represent "the cause" in Spain and elsewhere, Fatma Mehdi indicated that it was not the Polisario that was stopping

---

13. Since the late 1970s, Sahrawi girls have studied in Algeria, Cuba, Libya, Spain, and the former USSR. They have not, however, participated in the Syrian educational program, which is solely for young men attending university, nor, to the best of my knowledge, in the more recently established Qatari program.

women from going, but the women themselves (verbatim proceedings, 27 February Camp, April 2007). She explained that only recently she had asked for two or three women to be the SADR's envoys at the African Parliament (where the SADR has full membership) and that the Polisario had agreed to this request. She had spent over a week looking for possible candidates but eventually resorted to "those women whom I already know" (i.e., women who already work for the NUSW), since no other women were reportedly willing to take up the position, which would entail traveling abroad several times a year. Family commitments, difficulties traveling alone, and language barriers were all offered as reasons for women not participating in the male-dominated international sphere, although other issues, such as those explained above with reference to obstacles to working in another camp, must also influence such decisions.

This example also raises several matters vis-à-vis the nature of female participation in the camps that deserve brief examination. One main factor influencing women's movements and activism outside of the *khayma* is their age. It is the older generation of women (primarily first-generation refugee women, many of whom are now postmenopausal) who continue to dominate the political, economic, and social spheres in the camps, despite the younger generation's having been educated to higher levels in numerous locations around the world.[14] The limited visibility (and inaudibility) of younger women in the NUSW and other institutions and organizations based in the camps has been noted by the NUSW, who have ostensibly created programs and "new spaces" to combat this marginalization and increase their participation.[15] New spaces solely accessible to young women have been designed to allow them to "speak out" during meetings, since they are otherwise habitually overshadowed by older women. Such

14. The predominance of older women in social and political activities outside of the *khayma* is common in Bedouin groups. It is also in line with the above-mentioned tendency to allow for less-strict veiling of menopausal or postmenopausal women.

15. Verbatim proceedings, NUSW meeting with Spanish delegates, 27 February Camp (April 2007).

dynamics were evident when I attended both the pre-Conference and post-Conference meetings held in the 27 February Camp in 2007, where older women (especially those aged over 50) were vocal and outspoken about their concerns and priorities for the Conference and the future of women in the camps, while the younger women remained silent throughout.[16]

Fatma Mehdi's election as secretary general at the Fourth NUSW Conference was particularly celebrated in 2002, since she was the first member of the "younger" generation (in her late 30s at the time) to be elected to such a prominent role. The presence of Cuban-educated young women in the NUSW offices in the 27 February Camp is also notable, as is their participation as employees in projects established and run jointly with non-Sahrawi NGOs, such as the CRIC-initiated anthropology group and sewing cooperative. This is not to say that only those young women who studied in Cuba have obtained roles in the NUSW, since Mehdi, for instance, was educated in Libya, and I met several female employees who had trained in Algeria. At the same time, I suggest that the presence of Cuban-educated young women in ministries and Union organizations is particularly important to the way in which the official discourse is received and evaluated by visitors to the camps.

These women play central roles within the camps' administrative and services structures, working as nurses and doctors, while their male counterparts have tended to migrate to Spain where a need for qualified doctors guarantees them full-time (and fully paid) jobs (Fiddian-Qasmiyeh 2011e). The majority of young women stay in the camps for a range of reasons, including supporting their mothers and younger siblings, and due to both family and societal pressure that continues to encourage women to stay close to home. Beyond these direct contributions to running the camps and interacting with NGO projects, Cuban-educated young women's roles

---

16. I would argue that older women often have a greater level of security than younger women, allowing them to be vocal or to "experiment" with their views and voices without undermining their marriage prospects, for instance, as could be the case (or a fear) for younger women.

as "guides" for Spanish visitors to the camps for practical, linguistic reasons are significant in many ways. Hence, their visibility to Spaniards can largely be understood as literally embodying (for a non-Sahrawi audience) the official principles of female "freedom of movement" for education and employment, claims pertaining to women's "secularism" and "liberalism," and their political participation in the camps. By acting not only as guides, but also as bridges between Spanish civil society and the camp administration, these young women are perfectly situated to "demonstrate" to their visitors the centrality of women in running the camps and ensuring their survival. In many respects, in their interactions with Western visitors to the camps these young women personify the official discourse and the roles that women represent therein.[17]

However, although these young women may be ideal agents of representation to a Western audience, and despite their visibility to Spaniards, and therefore their greater access to both material and social capital and networks, during the Fifth NUSW Conference the Cuban-educated women were nevertheless restricted to fulfilling their assigned roles as "guides" and "interpreters," rather than being able to participate as delegates as many of them would have wished (personal observations, 27 February Camp, April 2007). While enjoying more "freedom of movement" around the camps, and accompanying NGOs and journalists during their tours of the entire refugee setting, many of these young women are, for instance, unable to join these representational structures, which continue as a whole to be run by the same women who are repeatedly reelected to executive positions.

Even those young Cuban-educated women who do work in the NUSW encounter major difficulties in traveling to and from work and find that their activities are judged by family members and neighbors alike. These are contradictions that challenge the Polisario/SADR's official and "idealized" image of life in the camps and yet rarely reach the Western audience.

---

17. On Moroccan, Polisario, and Spanish representations of Cuban-educated Sahrawi women see Fiddian-Qasmiyeh 2009.

Movement, Mahr, and Marriage

The "liberal" nature of marriage practices among Sahrawi refugees was referred to both indirectly and directly throughout my research. Indeed, shortly after the camps' creation, the Polisario/SADR developed a legal framework declaring that both the future bride and groom should consent to marriage[18] and that (since tribal markers and references had officially been erased) individuals should freely choose their partners rather than marrying first cousins as had historically been the case. The Polisario/SADR has since then declared that marriage practices have been radically altered by these legislative changes and that such changes demonstrate the equality of women and men in the camps. In this section I explore the official claims that marriage is entered into "freely" by young women, building upon my discussion of issues pertaining to movement and participation outside of the *khayma*.

Socioeconomic conditions in the refugee camps have undergone substantial change since their establishment, with these changes affecting gender relations in numerous ways. During the late 1970s and 1980s, the war period and total dependence on humanitarian aid allowed for a certain degree of equality between camp inhabitants, as emphasized by a Cuban-educated male based in the SADR National Hospital:

> In the early days . . . socially there was equality. You eat couscous, I eat couscous . . . The difference of [access to and consumption of] meat does not exist; differences between a good house and a good car do not exist; we are all the same. Everyone was defending a cause, all for one cause. The men were at war and the women in the camps. There was no money, nothing was circulating. (Rabouni, April 2007)

Since the 1990s, conversely, "with the social and political change, with the end of the war, social difference started to emerge" (ibid.). At this time (post-1991), a market economy began to develop in the camps, with increasing numbers of families supplementing their food aid through

18. Common readings of the Qur'an do in fact call for a bride's approval for the marriage (Joseph and Najmabadi 2003, 65).

products bought from (now ubiquitous) little shops. As such, families with working-husbands (either in the camps or abroad), with husbands who have received Spanish pensions since the early 1990s (former colonial employees) or with children who are able to travel to Spain on the summer fostering program, have considerably more stable financial, material, and nutritional situations than those without these income options. Those households that neither receive regular remittances from family members living abroad nor have children who travel to Spain during the summer months are therefore among the most vulnerable families in the camps (also see WFP 2008, 3, quoted in Chapter 2). My research in the camps indicated that these socioeconomic inequalities—and a parallel increase in consumerism in the camps as some families' wealth has increased—have led to major changes in the basis of marriages.

In the Sahrawi camps, the traditional notion that "fat is beautiful" (see Chapter 1) has been threatened by widespread scarcity and uncertainty of food provision and also by the Polisario/SADR's public campaigns (based on medical reasoning) against obesity and force-feeding in the camps. However, although controlling girls' bodies via fattening practices may no longer be the norm in the camps (Cozza 2010), and while legal structures have affected marriage practices by introducing a minimum age of marriage and the requirement of mutual consent, young Sahrawi refugee women face new forms of familial and social pressure to marry young in order to maximize the payment of *mahr*. I have identified two interrelated factors affecting young women as they contemplate marriage.

The first, with reference to changes in *mahr*, was discussed by delegates at the Fourth NUSW Conference held in the 27 February Camp in 2002.[19] Humanitarian agency reports suggest that *mahr* had disappeared,[20] or been replaced by a small symbolic payment by the 1980s (Firebrace 1985, 32 and 1987, 182; Lippert 1987, 162), but it appears that the emergence

19. An earlier version of this discussion was presented in Fiddian 2002.

20. Similar changes have taken place throughout many Arab countries (with the exception of the Arab Gulf), even without the severe material restrictions which characterize this context. Such changes aim to facilitate marriage procedures for young men who might otherwise be unable to gather the necessary *mahr*.

of a camp economy following the ceasefire has influenced marriage practices. During the Workshop on Social Affairs held in the 2002 Conference,
female delegates discussed the implications of increasing *mahr*, rejecting the practice as dangerous for young women. Counteracting the legal
reforms requiring full female consent to marriage, they strongly believed
that the increase in *mahr* could lead to older, wealthier men being able to
"select" young brides—who are perhaps viewed as more compliant and
whose sexual integrity can be more easily assured—who might, in turn,
be pressured by their families to marry for money.

While *mahr* can be conceptualized as a means of providing brides
with a degree of economic independence and security in case of divorce, it
must always be evaluated according to its context—in this case, in a refugee camp where a considerable proportion of the population continues to
be almost entirely dependent on humanitarian assistance. For vulnerable
families, *mahr* thus potentially becomes increasingly important in order to
supplement rations by purchasing foodstuffs in the camps.

Even if families do not explicitly force girls to marry richer, older men,
girls whose families do not benefit from remittances or from employment in the camp economy may find it very difficult to enact any form
of "free choice" in terms of the selection of a marriage partner when they
are approached by men who offer them a large *mahr*.[21] If their family's
health is in their hands, exercising their legal right to choose their spouse
in such a situation may be a luxury that many girls cannot enjoy. In such
circumstances, girls may relinquish their right to "choose" their marriage
partner, in order to access the benefits that may be immediately accrued
from the *mahr*. In these cases, the *mahr* will no longer necessarily offer the
bride long-term security, as it will often be spent to ensure the family's
short-term survival.[22]

21. A higher *mahr* can in some contexts be understood as providing the bride with
greater security, as a decrease in *mahr* could lead to men divorcing their spouses and finding new wives more easily (and at less expense) than in a situation where *mahr* is expected
to be high (see Kumar 2001a, 14).

22. Such a short-term approach to *mahr* is not limited to the Sahrawi camps. The common practice of giving a bride only a part of her *mahr* at the time of the marriage (*muqaddam*),

A second transformation in marriage practices is also connected to socioeconomic differentiation but is more directly related to the increasing impact of consumerism in the camps. When I visited Dakhla camp in 2007, I held an interview with a Cuban-educated Sahrawi woman who had acted as an interpreter and "guide" for Spanish delegates attending the Fifth NUSW Conference. I asked her if women's lives were different in Dakhla and in the 27 February Camp: her answer was yes, given Dakhla's distance from Tindouf and the other camps, there is "less influence from outside"[23] so it is therefore a "more traditional camp."[24]

In part, I was told, this continued "traditionalism" is due to Dakhla's geographical location (circa 150 km from Rabouni) and the absence of permanent electricity supplies, which have made it unfeasible to create the types of markets that have flourished through buying products in Tindouf and selling them in the nearby camps. Transporting goods from Tindouf to Dakhla is expensive and time-consuming, and, without refrigerators, fresh products in Dakhla do not last as long as in the other camps. As a result of the water supplied by Dakhla's oasis, many families have small plots where they grow their own limited supplies of vegetables and fruit to supplement their rations. The camp layout is also different, being much more widely spread out (around the oasis) than the other camps, which are more concentrated around a common politico-administrative point: with more space between each compound, people in Dakhla are able to have a wider range of animals near their tents,[25] and they are therefore still largely dependent upon their own livestock and small vegetable plots, rather than on little shops as in the other camps.

---

leaving the remaining payment to be made in case of divorce (*mu'akhkhar*), does, in this respect, ensure that a woman has financial means at her disposal at the end of her marriage. Such an approach, as I outline below, however, first depends on the husband granting her a divorce and, second, on his actually paying the *mahr* that is still owed to her.

23. These claims apparently referred to connections with both Algerians and Spaniards due to the other camps' proximity to Tindouf airport.

24. On the "uniqueness" of Dakhla, also see Cozza 2004, 143.

25. Unlike in the other camps, camels and donkeys are seen throughout Dakhla, not just goats and sheep.

At the same time, according to the same interviewee, women can "stay outside until later than in the other camps," they can "stay out after dark unlike in the 27 February [Camp], where their families expect them to be at home early." When I asked her why this should be the case, she indicated that

> in the camps, they are obsessed with marriage and girls get a bad reputation if they are out late. There is a materialistic interest in marriage in the camps now, but not so much in Dakhla. Before, women could stay out late, but now there's the issue of reputation, and this can influence *mahr* . . . (April 2007)

While matters of "reputation" will have always been a greater or lesser concern for women, this "materialistic interest in marriage" is not simply related to what could be called "vulnerable" families' necessity-driven desire for a high *mahr*. Families and young women are aware of the benefits of marrying a rich man, and the most visible expensive goods in the camps are greatly coveted by the younger generations in particular: expensive cars bought in Spain, satellite dishes, air-conditioning units, the most recent mobile telephones and music systems are only a few of the consumer items that young men and women are interested in obtaining in the camps. While some of these items may be achieved through work and contacts with foreign visitors to the camps, others may be in closer reach through marriage.

With the increased visibility of valuable goods (both in financial and status terms) in the camps since the mid-1990s, young women, as well as their families, may become more concerned about obtaining a suitable (i.e., rich) marriage partner. At such a time, this interviewee pointed out, the notion of "reputation" had taken on a new meaning, with girls' movements being more closely observed and controlled by both men and women as a result. While women were encouraged to go home early to protect their reputation in other camps, the lesser impact of consumerist drives in Dakhla meant that young women's movements, in this interviewee's opinion, were "freer," and would not impact negatively on their marriage prospects.

The "Divorce Party": Celebrating the "Unique"

The prime example that is used to demonstrate the "liberal" nature of Sahrawi marriage practices is their "unique" approach to ending marriages. The centrality of divorce to the Polisario/SADR's official discourse (as evidenced by the extracts included above) is directly related to the analogous significance given to marriage practices that are interpreted as abusive (including polygamy and unilateral divorce) in ethnocentric and Orientalist discussions of Arab gender relations (Yeğenoğlu 1998, 100; Almond 2007, 134; Keddie 2007, 57).

Divorce in Muslim contexts is commonly perceived in the West as being unilaterally initiated and monopolized by men who leave their ex-wives to face lives of emotional and material hardship after taking their children away from them (e.g., Joseph and Najmabadi 2003, 141; Menski 2006, 376). In the situation under consideration, however, divorce plays a pivotal role in accounts of Sahrawi women's freedom both during the colonial era and in the camps and is frequently extolled as "empowering women" rather than oppressing them. While young women (virgins) may have been expected to accept an arranged marriage during the colonial era, divorced women "had the freedom to choose" (Gaudio 1978, 200; my translation; also Keenan 2006, 931), that is unequivocally presented by contemporary Sahrawi and both colonial and contemporary Western sources alike as a "positive" reality. Divorce, in these accounts, is conceptualized as a means of escaping from abusive relationships or as empowering women to marry for love rather than as a result of parental encouragement or pressure. For analysts considering the tribal system in place during/before the colonial era, such examples are presented as evidence of the power of Sahrawi women, the extent of their choice regarding marriage partners (after the initial arranged marriage), their centrality in the social system, and their particular difference from the women of other neighboring countries (Gaudio 1978; Harter 2003 and 2004).

Although no reliable divorce statistics exist in/for the camps, throughout the course of my interviews and in the literature reviewed, Polisario/ SADR politicians and youth extolled the frequency with which divorce occurs. One interviewee in Damascus, for instance, reflected that his female cousin had been divorced six times, a fact that was reiterated by the Polisario/SADR envoy there, and presented as a positive feature of women's lives in the camps. In such accounts, the extent to which women initiate divorce proceedings ("unilaterally"), and, most interestingly, the celebratory nature of the "divorce party" or *al-iḥtifāl wa it'arqība* are consistently highlighted (الإحتفال و اتعرقيبة, Kuttab 2002; the latter term is also spelled تعركيبة—*t'arkība*[26]—by El-Fethi 2007).[27]

Based on her interviews with high-ranking members of the NUSW and the female Minister of Culture during her visit to the camps, Petrich came to a conclusion that has become common among visitors to the camps:

> [Sahrawi women] hold a party when they divorce and it is not unusual for one to have gone through two or more marriages . . . and in thirty years of life in exile, there has only been one case of polygamy in the camps . . . In legal terms, *all women enjoy all rights* in the broadest sense of the term: social, political, [and] cultural. *They have the Arab world's most advanced laws regarding divorce, separation of goods, custody of children, and inheritance.* (2005; my translation and emphasis)

26. The translation of *al-iḥtifāl* is "the celebration." The meaning of the second part of the term is open to debate given that there are separate roots for the words *t'arqība* or *t'arkība*. The Arabic verb *raqaba* (with a Q) means "to watch over," "to honor," or "to take care of." Alternatively, the verb *rakaba* (with a K) can be translated as "to ride," "to mount," "to seat oneself" or "to embark" (in the latter case, on a journey/means of transport, for instance). The "divorce party" could therefore arguably refer to either a celebration which is either characterized by members of the community watching over the divorcée and/or supporting her (as is often claimed by Sahrawis—see below) or by a woman sitting (high) on the "special platform" referred to by interviewees and written sources (see below) and/or embarking on a new stage of her life. I thank Yousif M. Qasmiyeh for his insights into these terms, in addition to A. Boubekeur for her helpful interpretation of the word *it'arkība*. A third interpretation of this term is included below.

27. This term is examined and reconceptualized sociolinguistically, along with other Arabic-language constructs central to this case study, in Fiddian-Qasmiyeh and Qasmiyeh (unpublished paper on file with authors).

Petrich's account of divorce and marriage practices in the camps is clearly based on her interviews with Spanish-speaking Sahrawi functionaries there, and I have been offered similar summaries of the situation by numerous Spanish solidarity workers. Like Petrich, they agree that the Sahrawi are more liberal and "advanced" than other Muslim societies and that their approaches to marriage and divorce are uniquely progressive.[28]

While conducting research in Syria, Kuttab informed me that in his trilogy he draws his readers' attention to the Sahrawi divorce party explicitly as a way of differentiating Sahrawi women from Other Arab women, including, in particular, those from Morocco (Damascus, July 2006; also Kuttab 2002, 63). This image is reproduced to considerably wider audiences through popular national and international media, including *BBC World* (Harter 2003 and 2004). This emphasis on the exceptionality of Sahrawi gender relations must be viewed in relation to the documented tendency for boundaries between cultural or national groups to be embodied in representations of women's cultural authenticity or integrity as discussed earlier.

In the ways outlined above, Sahrawi divorce practices, and the "divorce party" more precisely, can be perceived as defining and determining the *uniqueness* of the "nation" and of Sahrawi gender relations, as was reiterated in my interviews with many students in a range of locations. Given that the Polisario's claim to self-determination depends upon the international community recognizing the Sahrawi as a "people," representations of Sahrawi women's uniqueness and difference *from* Other Arab women could be seen as "brightening" the separation between the Sahrawi and Moroccan "nations." Indeed, Farah indicates that "when asked to distinguish a Sahrawi culture [as distinct from a Moroccan identity], refugees point to such factors as . . . their mode of livelihood; food, dress, songs

28. In contrast, Kandiyoti stresses that in Afghanistan "the personal status law passed in 1959 was recognized to give women some of the broadest rights in the Middle East" (2007b, 507), while Grami states that "the [Tunisian 1956] Code of Personal Status is widely credited with making Tunisian women among the most liberal in the Muslim world" (2008, 354).

and *the status of Sahrawi women*" (2006, n.p.; my emphasis). Sahrawi women's "uniqueness" can thus be understood as providing "a position from which they [the Sahrawi] may begin to assert themselves both externally and internally as a 'people' in modern terms" (Amoretti 1987, 188).

In terms of the exceptionality of the Sahrawi "divorce party," I located only one other documented example of a Muslim (or even non-Muslim) society that actively celebrates divorce.[29] Hence, in her book on MENA women (1988), Shaaban's chapter on Algeria includes an account of her encounter with Tarqui women in the south of the country, where she is told that divorce is celebrated as lavishly as marriage: "On that date [chosen by her mother], the divorcée wears her best clothes and silver and make up and is the star of the Tendi party, a party as good as her wedding party" (1988, 231).[30] Concluding her review of Shaaban's book two years after its publication, Afshar remarks that

> [it] ends with a delightful visit to Tarqui women in the Southern Sahara
> . . . there is also a party *tendis* to celebrate divorce, which is conducted by
> women in the presence of four witnesses—as against the usual Muslim
> practice which allows only men to do so in the presence of two witness-
> es.[31] (1990, 79–80)

Afshar quotes Shaaban at this point as stating that "(o)nce the Tarqui woman gets her first divorce . . . she is free to marry whoever she likes without consulting anyone" (cited in Afshar 1990, 79), before concluding that

29. There have recently been instances of individual women and/or couples celebrating the end of unsuccessful marriages (on the Netherlands see Ferrer 2008). Such cases, however, are exceptions within the former couple's cultural environment rather than the norm, as in the Sahrawi context.

30. It is plausible to suggest that the second part of the term *al-ihtifāl wa it'arqība* could be related to the Tarqui people amongst whom divorce parties are also held. While the Tarqui refer to these celebrations as *tendis*, the connection between the words *t'arqība* and *tarqui* is notable.

31. Afshar's contrast between four witnesses and two witnesses does not specify the gender of these. In the case of "the usual Muslim practice," it is in fact not necessary for a witness to be present when the divorce takes place, let alone when a divorce is "celebrated."

> Thus divorce becomes part of the ritual of growing up rather than the social and economic disaster that it often is for urban-dwelling Muslim women. (ibid., 80)

For Afshar and observers of the Sahrawi refugee camps, the divorce party is perceived as epitomizing the difference between those fortunate and empowered women who celebrate divorce (the Tarqui and the Sahrawi) and those who live it as a major disaster (as is "often" the case for "urban-dwelling Muslim women"[32] or, more sweepingly, for "other Arab women," as I was informed in interviews).

Before turning more concretely to how and why divorce proceedings have been portrayed to and by Westerners, I now explore what is presented as the most "liberal" and "modern" feature of divorce proceedings in the Sahrawi arena: the divorce party. I shall then, drawing on research conducted in the camps, ask whether divorce is as "liberating" and "empowering" as its proponents lead visitors to believe.

Kuttab, like many others in the camps and beyond, explains that after a divorce has been proclaimed, the divorcée is celebrated by her friends, who give her honorable gifts and express "their solidarity with her" (2002, 63). The "party," where the woman is seated "on a platform" with her belongings (including furniture) behind her, is presented by Kuttab and others as providing the newly divorced woman with moral support, so that she does not feel "alone" or "sad" after having ended her marriage (ibid.).[33] One Sahrawi woman is quoted by Harter as stating that "The party is meant to pay homage to the divorced woman, so that she doesn't feel weak or ashamed" (2004). Such accounts are reproduced almost verbatim in a blog entry posted on a "pro-Sahara" website:

> After the divorce, once the time period established by the Sharia has passed, the woman's family organizes a party with music and dances

---

32. With reference to Mauritanian cities, Bonte also notes that "a woman who has been courted, married, and divorced on numerous occasions is not socially excluded, as in other Muslim societies, but often the subject of greater male interest" (2006, 103).

33. Such accounts frequently represent the divorce as resulting directly from the woman's decision, rather than the man's.

that lasts the entire night. [At the party], the divorcée, surrounded by her friends and dressed in her best clothing, sits on a special platform, where she receives all of the men who are interested in her, who inundate her with presents. These parties are designed to demonstrate to the divorcee that she has not lost her social value, but rather has the support of all of those around her.[34]

While still comparing Sahrawi women with other MENA women (we still understand that "other" women *do* lose their social value following divorce), during discussions and interviews with Spanish *solidarios* between 2001 and 2008 many of them remarked that the Sahrawi have a "better" approach to divorce than in Spain; these *solidarios* inevitably state this as they lament the violent deaths of sixty or seventy Spanish women at the hands of their ex-husbands or ex-partners each year. In these accounts, Sahrawi women are not only "more advanced" than "other Arab countries" but are even "more advanced" than Western ones. It is this "unique" and "advanced" nature, I argue, that has captured Western observers' attention, allowing (or in fact *requiring*) it to play a significant role in the development and maintenance of the solidarity movements that support Sahrawi women's rights in the camps via the NUSW, or the broader Polisario/SADR aim of self-determination and independence from Morocco.

In addition to reflecting the way in that these post-divorce activities are often viewed by Westerners (supportive and festive), the preceding extract indicates an awareness of the particular legal framework that underpins the divorce itself: Shari'a. Rarely does one encounter formal Polisario/SADR accounts that refer to the *'idda*, the obligatory time (three menstrual periods) that must pass according to the Qur'an from the declaration of the divorce until a woman may remarry (sura 2:228). There is no such period for men. One such reference is made by Embarca Hamudi of the NUSW in her account of marriage and divorce in the Sahrawi context, where she explains to the Spanish reader the rationale behind such an interval (to establish whether the divorcée is pregnant, and, if so, to clearly

---

34. www.saharafito.blogspot.com/2007/06, entry dated 04/06/2007; my translation.

ascertain the paternity of the child; n.d.).[35] She continues by differentiating between divorce practices in "Muslim societies" and those in the Sahrawi case, indicating that, in the latter,

> [d]ivorce occurs by following what is stated in the Shari'a, after having passed *"el ed-da"* [*sic*] the woman, with her male and female friends, celebrate a party where all of her supporters can participate, also, if anyone is interested in her he can declare himself on this occasion. It is important to highlight that in customary terms, married women have more freedom to announce their engagement than those who have never been married. (my translation)

The *'idda*'s almost total absence from public statements on divorce largely explains its absence from popular accounts of life in the camps by non-Sahrawis who are, as a whole, unfamiliar with Islamic jurisprudence. Such an absence of references to the *'idda*, overshadowed by the presentation of the divorce party, and combined with most visitors' nonexistent or limited knowledge of Islam, allow visitors to be convinced by the official discourse that claims, as quoted above, that the Sahrawi "have the Arab world's most advanced laws regarding divorce, separation of goods, custody of children, and inheritance."

Relying on the information provided by their Sahrawi guides in the camps, Spanish and other Western visitors fail to recognize that such laws are ultimately regulated by a Maliki interpretation (prevalent throughout North Africa) of the Qur'an and Hadith, which are in turn the common basis of other Muslim countries' legal frameworks.[36] Hence, despite mainstream representations to the contrary, divorce proceedings in the camps are conducted under the auspices of the *qāḍi* (Islamic judge), rather than in the secular state court, and have a great deal in common with many other Arab countries. One element that is presented as demonstrating the Sahrawi's

35. A pregnant woman is prohibited from entering a new marriage until her child has been born (sura 65:4).

36. On similarities and differences between personal status laws in the Maghreb region, see Ennaji 2008, esp. 341; Grami 2008, esp. 349; Sadiqi 2008, esp. 329ff. On divorce laws "in Islamic history," see Sonbol's 1996 edited collection.

progressive marriage practices (the so-called "law of never before or after" to impede polygamous marriages) is in fact frequently included as a legal stipulation before a marriage takes place in many other locations (including Algeria, Egypt, Jordan, and Morocco; see Ennaji 2008, 341 and USDOS 2007; Karam 1998, 145–146; Welchman 1988; Sadiqi 2008, 336, respectively). Divorce is officially presented to non-Sahrawi observers as a means of freeing women from oppressive conditions, and yet we must ask how divorce is perceived and experienced by women in the camps themselves.[37] In order to evaluate this matter, I draw on my observations of and interviews held in the camps, as well as on the proceedings of and Arabic-language documents relating to the Fourth and Fifth Conferences of the NUSW that took place in the 27 February Camp in 2002 and 2007 respectively.

First, although the divorce party is commonly portrayed as an event that celebrates the end of an unsuccessful marriage by supporting the divorcée, upon closer examination it appears clear that it ideally sets the scene to enable the celebration of a new marriage. That the divorce party should be held after the entire 'idda period has passed, that the woman should be presented to wider society surrounded by her belongings (in a sense, reflecting her material value), and that interested men should take this opportunity to express their intention to marry the divorcée, all indicate this vividly. This is equally the case among the Tarqui, as stated by one of Shaaban's interviewees, herself a divorcée:

> Most presents come from the men who would like to get married and who are glad to have another potential wife among the women of their tribe . . . It is usually at this party that the divorcée is approached by one of the men who later on will propose to her. (1988, 231)

Even in a context where divorce may be accepted as a part of "growing up," it is primarily perceived as a stage through that women pass before

---

37. By projecting Sahrawi women as being free to marry and divorce, Sahrawi men are arguably reduced to being those from which Sahrawi women unilaterally *demand* a divorce, and those who would be *shunned* were they to mistreat their wives (also Salek in AFP 2004). I address men's invisibility in the official discourse in Chapter 5.

entering a new marriage—remaining a divorcée, rather than eventually becoming a new wife, is highly challenging in both material and social terms in the camps. Indeed, one SARC interviewee reflected: "The older generations had a saying, 'May God not leave a woman without a man.' This is because a woman by herself cannot take care of the family and it is important to have a man with her" (38-year-old woman). While her lamentation was instigated by the death of her husband, it equally reflects the hardships faced by many divorcées: a male income is essential in a context where interviewees confirm that "what the humanitarian organizations distribute is not enough" (41-year-old woman). More broadly, as Mernissi (2003a, 59) stresses, abstinence and celibacy are commonly interpreted as being discouraged in Islam (suras 24:32 and 24:33), and Keddie indicates that marriage is "virtually universal for women" in the Arab Middle East (2007, 35). This preference for women and men to remarry rather than remain unmarried is intimately related to concerns about *fitna* and its potential consequences.

During my second visit to the camps in 2002, I stayed in the tent of a divorcée in her mid-40s who reflected on the great hardships she had experienced since her husband had abandoned her a few years before. While divorced women may have been able to maintain their children and themselves reasonably well during "the early years" (1976–1991), without a male income to supplement the meager rations received in the camps, her only means to feed her children and buy them clothes, was to "welcome Spaniards" during their visits. On that occasion in 2002 she had physically moved her tent from Smara to the Rabouni reception area (circa 20 km) to be closer to the "tourists" or "guests," since she knew that doing so would guarantee a form of income and possibly longer-term connections with Europeans who could improve her family's social capital (also Crivello and Fiddian-Qasmiyeh 2010). Her situation was among the worst I saw during my visits to the camps (her *khayma* was badly in need of repair, her children were clearly malnourished and needed new clothes, and she herself was seriously ill), and this financial crisis had, according to her, been created largely due to her status as a woman who had been unable to remarry.

Two main issues thus immediately problematize the "romanticized" and idealized notions of divorce and the divorce party. Firstly, as in the case outlined above, not all divorcées are able to remarry, leading to serious material implications. Although *some* women may have greater "choice" when marrying a new husband following divorce, as is claimed by most Sahrawi men and women and non-Sahrawi writers alike, we must ask at what point in their life cycle women may no longer be able to remarry with ease: while divorce and remarriage are intimately related, it may become increasingly difficult as women approach menopause. Indeed, Mernissi claims that the *'idda* "constitutes a rather harsh penalty . . . in particular for menopausal women who have the further disadvantage of being middle-aged in a society in which youth is avidly prized" (2003a:63). Equally, Keddie stresses that remarriage has often been easy for *premenopausal* divorced women in the Middle East (2007, 37), suggesting that women beyond child-bearing age may encounter difficulties in finding a new husband.

Wealth is an additional factor that may influence a woman's "desirability" for a second or third marriage, as suggested by the prominence given to her belongings during the "divorce party" and substantiated by my interviews in the camps. A balance may therefore be reached whereby an older woman might continue to be considered attractive to prospective husbands due to her demonstrable wealth. This therefore leads us to recognize that women who neither have such belongings nor, indeed, a large party of friends and family to "celebrate" with and support her may find remarriage complicated, if not impossible.

A further factor affecting remarriage may be the presence of children from a woman's ex-husband(s): five of my interviewees in Spain, Syria, and in the camps separately indicated that their respective mothers had remarried, but that the new husbands had "encouraged" the younger children to move to their maternal grandparents' *khayma* (see Caratini 2000 on matrilocality following divorce). In a context where children tend to remain with their mother and maternal grandparents until early adolescence following divorce (see Gimeno-Martín and Laman 2005, 17), this could be recognized as affecting women's opportunities to remarry more than men's. The Maliki *madhhab* to which the Sahrawi belong, grants mothers the custody of their young children for longer than other schools

(Keddie 2007, 38).[38] Within this *madhhab*, it is commonly accepted that children should stay with their mother until puberty in the case of boys, and until the consummation of marriage in the case of daughters (Heyneman 2004, 77). Of the children interviewed by Crivello and Fiddian-Qasmiyeh for the SARC project, all six girls (ages 8 to 11) who reported having divorced parents were living with their mothers at the time of meeting.

Second, as the example drawn from my visit to the camps in 2002 indicates, women who are repudiated by their husbands clearly do not necessarily benefit from the ease with which divorce takes place. With reference to the increasing frequency of divorce in Mauritania, Bonte equally remarks that this is not "idyllic," as "growing numbers of women have become solely responsible for their family" (30% of domestic groups in a 2001 study). Regarding the impact on children, Bonte reports that 15% of these are "raised outside the domestic group (without a father and mother)," while 27% "are exclusively raised by the mother." He stresses that this has also led to "a marked pauperization of women" (2006, 103). This reality is undeniably a grave concern for the NUSW, who have focused in at least two of their five Conferences (2002 and 2007) on the implications of what they refer to in Arabic-language documents related to the Fifth Conference (2007) as "chaotic divorcing" (*at-ṭalāq al-fawḍawī*) in the camps. Such debates (and labels) do not reach the Western audience since they are not only inconsistent but directly in conflict with the official discourse pertaining to divorce and marriage in the camps. According to my research, when the NUSW discuss such problems (either orally or in written formats), this occurs in Hassaniya Arabic, thereby ensuring that the deliberations remain "private" even in the presence of Spaniards and other non-Arabic speakers (English, Spanish, French, and Arabic language NUSW documents on file with the author). In the case of the

---

38. By point of comparison, in Algeria, divorcées are able to retain the family home until children reach 18 years of age (USDOS 2007), whilst in Syria (under the Personal Status Law modified in October 2003), "a divorced mother loses the right to physical custody of her sons when they reach the age of 13 and of her daughters at age 15" (USDOS 2008a). On developments in custody rights in the Maghreb, see the articles by Sadiqi, Ennaji, and Grami (all 2008).

Fifth NUSW Conference, non-Sahrawi "guests" were removed from the 27 February Camp on the day that workshops were scheduled (they were taken to "visit" other camps where celebratory marches and demonstrations had been organized), guaranteeing that no conflicting debates could reach the non-Sahrawi audience.

Among the issues raised and discussed in Hassaniya by the Sahrawi delegates who attended the Fifth NUSW Conference in 2007 are the increase in the number of divorce cases in the camps, "one-sided" male-initiated divorces,[39] and the implications of men refusing to provide material support for their wife and child(ren) following divorce, despite this support (*nafaqa*) being stipulated in sura 2: 241 (verbatim proceedings and Arabic language documents on file with the author). Indeed, five of the Sahrawi children who reported having divorced parents during interviews in Madrid as part of the SARC project indicated that their fathers had not contributed any money since divorcing their mothers and had visited them only rarely, if at all. While diametrically opposed to the mainstream references included above concerning female initiated "unilateral" divorces and the "divorce party," such a characterization of divorce as a negative phenomenon is broadly in keeping with similar accounts of women being "at risk of divorce" throughout the Muslim world (i.e., Yusuf 2005).

In the Sahrawi case, I was offered one relevant reason to explain the relative infrequency of polygamy in the camps (beyond the influence of limited material resources). One of the Spanish former soldiers who participated in my research on the colonial era suggested that the low incidence of polygamy among the Sahrawi during the colonial era had been due to the high incidence of repudiation/divorce and subsequent remarriage. Rather than concurrently having more than one spouse (polygamy), serial divorcing allows for serial monogamy (on "staggered polygamy" see Modood 2001, 250), with second and third marriages being common

39. In comparison, unilateral repudiation has been abolished in Tunisia (Grami 2008, 352).

rather than an exception in the camps, as indicated by the following 41-year-old woman interviewed by the SARC team:

[after the death of my first husband] I married another man, and had a daughter with him . . . Then we divorced and I had with me the children, two from my first husband who was martyred, and my daughter from the second husband . . . I married another time and had a second son with him while the other was still nursing.

While polygamy may not be widespread in this context, such practices nonetheless appear to unsettle the "law of never before or after," which has originally been understood as preventing husbands from marrying additional wives. Indeed, Kuttab, speaking of a "first marriage" indicates that "it might succeed and develop into a family forever, or fail and end in divorce" (2002, 63)—marriage in this respect is entered into with a relatively strong expectation that there will, indeed, be "someone after."

Another major "chronic" legal problem is termed by the NUSW as the status of *la 'alāqa*, which translates as "not a relationship" and refers to women who can neither be considered to be married nor divorced, but who are rather "suspended in-between" statuses, since their husbands have not officially granted them the divorce that they have requested (NUSW document on file with author).[40] Without either the presence of a husband or the payments due to divorcées and their children,[41] these women's and children's situations remain in limbo, as the divorcée does not have the possibility to remarry, with particularly serious implications in the context of a refugee camp.

The status of being neither married nor divorced reveals that, although a woman may request a divorce (an abstract concept), she can by no means "unilaterally divorce her husband" (a concrete act) as claimed by the interviewees quoted above. A woman's request for divorce is embodied in the

40. This parallels the popular Arabic saying "*lā mu'allaqa wa lā muṭallaqa*": "neither attached nor detached" or "neither married nor divorced."

41. Refusing to divorce a wife may be a way of avoiding such financial responsibilities.

tamlīk, which in essence transforms the man's repudiation formula (*'isma*) of "I divorce thee," to "I divorce thee whenever thou decides it" (Mernissi 2003a, 61).[42] When a woman asks for a divorce, it is ultimately a matter for the husband and/or the *qāḍi* to make the divorce a reality, with no possibility of holding a divorce party until one of these men has declared an end to the relationship.

Although I was informed in the camps that the *qāḍi* may receive counsel from a small group of women who support the female petitioner (also see Lippert 1992, 645), it is ultimately his decision if the husband contests his wife's request for a divorce. This, in addition to the high incidence of "one-sided" divorces initiated by men, and men's reluctance or inability to pay child support is a major concern for many women in the camps, who do not support the divorce system in place as unequivocally as the Polisario/SADR sources would lead us to believe:

> It is very difficult raising them up alone and it is important to have some-
> one to help, especially when they are sick. To be honest, since their father
> left, and even before he left, he was not helping much . . . Sometimes [he]
> stops by as a matter of formality and does not worry about their needs
> or what they want, their problems, never. (30-year-old female SARC
> interviewee)

In order to remedy some of these "problems," some Sahrawi women are reportedly calling for the development of a new Family Code, as discussed at the Fifth NUSW Conference.

After the end of the three-day NUSW Conference, the newly (re)elected NUSW leadership met with some of the foreign (mainly Spanish) Conference delegates, by means of summarizing the proceedings and providing additional information about how the Conference had been organized. The Union's leaders provided an overview of the main issues which had been

---

42. On the implementation of an alternative mode of divorce recognized in Islam (*khul'*) in Egypt, see Tucker 1985, 53ff; Joseph and Najmabadi 2003, 99–100; Nazir and Tomp-pert 2005, 73–74.

discussed by local delegates, including the possibility of developing a family code:

> In the following years, we need to work on the bases of the Family Code, bearing in mind that, in a situation like ours, husbands' salaries do not exist. . . . What can a father provide to his children if he does not have a salary? How can we demand that he maintain his children? Certain things must wait until we are free, including the Family Code. We have norms, and they work like a Family Code. This is helped by the solidarity which forms a part of our culture, which is that our children are always with their mothers, with their grandparents . . . here [in the camps] we do not have the extremely serious problem of violence: women are not killed, mistreated or beaten here, this helps us. (verbatim proceedings, 8 April 2007, 27 February Camp)

Although the Qur'an specifically makes reference to the payment of maintenance in cases of economic hardship (sura 65:7), this extract indicates that the Family Code "must wait until we are free," along with claiming that internal solidarity has enabled Sahrawi women to negotiate the marriage and divorce systems in place. Significantly, it ends with a strong reminder to the Spanish audience that *even if* there were a problem with divorce and child-support, it would be minor compared with the "extremely serious problem" of violence against women (VAW) that, according to the official discourse, does not exist in the camps. I return to the nature of and reasons for the repeated public declarations of the absence of VAW in the camps by both Sahrawi and Spanish sources in Chapter 5, by means of exploring the terms of engagement between Spanish *solidarios* and the "objects" of their solidarity.

Conclusion

This chapter has identified and analyzed a number of intersecting themes and images that have, for several decades, been directed to (and further reproduced by) Western visitors to the camps via the spoken, visual and written repetition of Polisario/SADR and NUSW accounts of life there. The common thread uniting each of the four elements examined is that of constituting Sahrawi women in the popular Western imagination as "free" from a number of practices which have commonly been identified as being "inherently oppressive" for women.[43] Fundamentally, the idealized Sahrawi women who are constituted in this discursive mechanism are re/created for the audience as "free" specifically through distancing them from (specific understandings of) Muslim identities and practices. Beyond asserting the "uniqueness" of Sahrawi women through comparing them with Other Arab women (and at times with Western women), the association that is thus strategically re/created is a synecdochic relationship between the liberal, "free" and "secular" nature of Sahrawi women and the liberal and "secular" nature of the Sahrawi "nation."

This discussion thus raises three key issues to be explored throughout the remainder of the book. Firstly, mainstream representations of the refugee camps are based upon and reproduce specific processes of centralization and marginalization, of amplification and silencing, highlighting not only a number of idealized and essentialized characteristics while concealing others, but also focusing on specific "constituents" while sidelining others. In turn, it is essential to examine the reasons for, and impacts of, not only comparing Sahrawi women with Other Arab women by means of demonstrating the former's uniqueness, but in effect marginalizing and silencing the complex experiences of those camp inhabitants who are absent (or, I posit, *absented*) from the official discourse.

While deconstructing the mainstream idealized image of "Sahrawi women" in the preceding pages, I have already pointed to the heterogeneity of women's experiences in the camps, with reference to various impacts of age, generation, the stage of a woman's life cycle, wealth and poverty, educational background, and political engagement. Additional factors that affect women's experiences in and of the camps will be explored in subsequent chapters, where I also examine the implications of constituting Sahrawi women as the "ideal" refugees, while marginalizing "non-ideal" women, girls and both adult and young males in the process.

---

43. Yeğenoğlu indicates that "the veil is taken as the sign of the inherently oppressive and unfree nature of the entire tradition of Islam and Oriental cultures and by extension it is used as a proof of oppression of women in these societies" (1998, 99).

A related point is the recognition that, although the mainstream representation dominates Sahrawi and Western accounts of the camps, careful analysis reveals multiple contradictions and discontinuities on a variety of fronts. Through exploring each of these representational components, I have highlighted a range of contradictions that exists between descriptions of the camps and observations and conclusions reached during my multisited research. We must ask how and why such a high degree of correspondence exists between the statements made by Polisario/SADR and NUSW officials and refugee youth who have studied in a wide variety of locations. However, I shall continue to focus on the inconsistencies that exist between what is said to Westerners, what is said *about* Westerners, and how individuals, families, and organizations negotiate the social, political, and material complexities of life in the camps. Such an analysis will reveal a number of strategies developed by individuals in the camps, reflecting instances of complicity and complacency along with resistance and disengagement from different authority structures that affect refugees' lives.

A final matter to be addressed is precisely what the official discourse reveals about the terms of engagement and power dynamics between Sahrawi refugees, their political representatives, and a range of non-Sahrawi actors in the international arena. In particular, I argue that exploring the politics of gendered representations provides unique insights into the Polisario/SADR's strategy of "international public relations" that draws in and captivates its "significant other(s)" (Mälksso 2006, 278) while, indeed, dismissing others as insignificant.

4

Secular Sisters, Muslim Others, and the Politics of Survival

DURING THEIR INTERACTIONS with Western aid providers, the Polisario/SADR has engaged in a process of what Yeğenoğlu refers to as "the historical inscription of a particular identity" (1998, 3) by emphasizing certain characteristics while silencing others for strategic reasons. The Polisario/SADR seem to have identified these self-designated descriptors to ensure the continued attention and/or cooperation of Western NGOs, civil societies, and solidarity networks for the Sahrawi "cause." Concretely, I argue here that the camps are dependent not on "unconditional solidarity" but rather on "conditional solidarity networks" that risk being undermined when certain central conditions are not met: in this case the existence of secular, liberal, and modern gender equality. This conditionality visibly demonstrates the unequal power dynamics that underpin both the solidarity network that maintains the refugee camps and the official discourse to which it is inextricably linked.

As indicated earlier, boundaries between cultural or national groups have historically been embodied in representations of women's cultural authenticity or integrity (Abu-Lughod 1998b, 3; Yeğenoğlu 1998, 136; Kandiyoti 2000, 491). Indeed, building upon Alba's notions of "bright-vs.-blurred boundaries" (2005), Korteweg and Yurdakul (2008) indicate that "processes of boundary formation" between Muslim and Western communities are frequently informed not through dominant understandings of Islam "in general" but rather through gender inequalities attributed to Islam. They continue by suggesting that discourses that

emphasize similarities between Muslim and Western groups' understandings of gender relations "contain elements of boundary blurring"
(2008, 3ff), while reinforcing differences is a means of solidifying separations between groups.

With this framework in mind, in the following pages I argue that
images of "empowered" and "secular" Sahrawi women have been discursively mobilized by the Polisario/SADR to create what we may label
"bright bonds" between Sahrawis and their Western observers. This is
achieved both by explicitly accentuating commonalities and a shared
sense of "sisterhood" between "secular" Sahrawi women and their Western counterparts and through a purposeful re/creation of Arab Muslim
women as the Sahrawis' and Spaniards' common Other. This chapter
explores the reasons behind Sahrawi women's "hypervisibility" in mainstream accounts of the camps. In the following chapter, I discuss the ways
in which Sahrawi girls, youth, and men have in essence been absent(ed)
by the official discourse.

Indeed, while the official discourse is projected to the West, my
research in the Sahrawi refugee camps reveals that this official portrayal
hides both the heterogeneity and the diverse priorities of Sahrawi refugees in the camps. Thus, I continue the chapter by arguing that despite
claims of "sisterhood" with the West, refugees have an ambivalent relationship toward those *solidarios* upon whom they are physically and
politically dependent. An analysis of the terminology used by Sahrawi
refugees in Arabic to refer to *solidarios* in the latter's absence highlights an
element of tension with the West, as well as the extent to which the official
discourse is designed for "external consumption," with local discourses
being strictly for "internal consumption" (cf. San-Martín 2005, 577).

Despite recognizing that the official discourse misrepresents the heterogeneous priorities of its inhabitants, the Polisario/SADR and many refugees are acutely aware that aid may be withdrawn if certain conditions
are not met. Through a case study I illustrate the strain that often typifies
Sahrawi-Spanish relations and what I have referred to as the "conditional"
dimension of Spanish public support for "the cause." Examining the
essentially Orientalist imagery that was successfully mobilized by Spaniards to "liberate" three young Sahrawi women ostensibly "abducted" by

their families in the camps demonstrates the dangers that may arise when boundaries are strategically brightened and solidified through reference to gendered and religious difference. Much of Spanish civil society threatened to withdraw its support for the camps unless the Polisario/SADR "saved" the girls from what they depicted as oppressive camps characterized by "atavistic" traditions. This case study in turn proves why the Polisario/SADR is so determined, in its interactions with Western audiences, to separate the Sahrawi Self from the Muslim Arab world, and why it depicts the Middle East as a space of female oppression.

As a preface to this chapter I must reiterate that the identity of the audience directly influences the terms and images projected by the Polisario/SADR. I am acutely aware that it was precisely my identity as a female Western researcher that prompted my interviewees to consistently describe Sahrawi women as "unique," "empowered," and "secular." Indeed, although the vast majority of my interviewees were either unable or unwilling to critique what I term the official discourse, two male SADR ministerial aides educated in Algeria and Libya conceded in the last of our three interviews that "the Polisario sells an image to the West that isn't necessarily the Sahrawi's own vision of themselves" (Rabouni, April 2007). Without explaining how or why the Polisario/SADR "sells" this image, they indicated that this process of selective representation exists precisely because the Polisario/SADR is "in dialogue with the West." This suggests that the Polisario/SADR has invested in its engagement with Western observers and is aware that the latter's interest in "the cause" can be "encouraged" via certain claims about life in the refugee camps.

None of my other Sahrawi interviewees openly reflected on the ways in which the Polisario/SADR represents women to Western audiences,[1] highlighting some of the methodological difficulties that characterize conducting research in the Sahrawi refugee camps. Despite these limitations,

---

1. The Polisario/SADR's orientation toward the West was recognized as a tendency by a number of non-Sahrawi MENA interviewees. These included a Palestinian academic who attended meetings with proponents of self-determination for the Western Sahara while studying in Poland in the mid-1970s (Oxford, July 2007).

however, a female Sahrawi Internet blogger has commented directly on this matter.[2] Discussing the NUSW's activities in Spain, she presents her disappointment and anger toward Union officials for "shamefully" misrepresenting and thus revealing "a lack of respect for Sahrawi women in general."

Going beyond the neutral tone of the aides' recognition of the relationship between Polisario/SADR discourse and the Western audience, the blogger, whose pseudonym in Wurud, laments that the NUSW have

> create[d] and adorn[ed] a wall, a false façade and a frequently nauseating rhetoric of openness, freedom and emancipation, thus selling a completely twisted image of the real situation of our women.

She decries a process through which the NUSW "have brought the same discourse [to Spain], they have once again sold the same image of us [Sahrawi women] and they have returned [to the camps] with the same compliments from their Western 'friends.'" The image that is portrayed by Sahrawi officials, she reiterates, is an "ideal image of free, educated women who have fully equal rights" that, it is important to note, she stresses "our friends in the West are so enchanted by." Wurud thus highlights a range of images that are projected by Sahrawi politicians specifically to obtain the interest and enthusiasm of Western observers and stresses that this discursive construction is a misrepresentation of Sahrawi women. Neither she nor the aides quoted above, however, ask why Polisario/SADR and NUSW officials should do this—or precisely how. In the following pages, I explore why certain characteristics are accentuated as what Wurud refers to as "part of the makeup that they paint us with when the Westerners ask."

Mobilizing Sahrawi Refugee Women and the Politics of Survival

Al-mara' as-ṣaḥrāwiyya mujannada *min ajli-l-istiqlāl al-waṭanī, [wa] al-binā' wa-at-taqaddum*

---

2. All extracts are taken from http://wurudsahrablogspotcom-wurud.blogspot.com. All translations are my own.

Sahrawi women: a *mobilized* force for national independence and progress.[3]

In the NUSW slogan quoted above, the Arabic term *mujannada* (f. sing.) is translated by the NUSW as "mobilized" in English and *"mobilizada"* in Spanish and yet can also literally be translated as "recruited," "enlisted," "drafted," "conscripted," "employed," and "used." The military connotations of the term—and suggesting that women could have been drafted or conscripted to fulfill a national service—lends credence to the idea that Sahrawi women were considered necessary to defend the "nation" and ensure its continued survival and that power imbalances may exist between those "ideal women" being mobilized, the (principally male) elites directing the national project, and the Western audience being addressed. I argue that the images of Sahrawi women analyzed in the preceding chapter have been "mobilized" for the goals of "national independence and progress" in ways that are intimately related to the international solidarity networks that sustain the viability of the refugee camps.

As indicated earlier, a multitude of feminist/gendered studies of nationalist and refugee movements have documented the extent to which representations of women have been politicized and strategically utilized to mobilize local, national, and international solidarity during times of war and conflict. In many instances, this strategic idealization of women builds upon a widespread and longstanding tendency throughout Arab countries in particular to emphasize the centrality of women to family and social life, as evidenced, for instance, in numerous suras (including 4:1 and 17:23) and Hadith. Cultural and national boundaries have thus frequently been re/created by invoking images of women, with Abu-Lughod pointing to the dual nature of nationalism as a political movement and "also as a cultural or discursive project in which ideals of womanhood and notions of the modern" are "key elements" (1998b, 17). As a means

3. Arabic and English language NUSW documents on file with author, my emphasis. The Arabic version above reads: "The Sahrawi woman, mobilized for national independence, construction and progress."

of "idealizing" both the nation and "its women," such discursive projects depend upon structured processes of Othering that create the "positive" Self through the projection of the Other as (the nation's) "negative" (Cole and Kandiyoti 2002, 189).

Edward Said and others have exposed the basis and vested importance of the system of Orientalism, by which the Orient is reproduced as the ultimate negative Other to the positive West (Said 1979; also Fanon 1963). The gendered dynamics of Orientalism have been explored by analysts such as Yeğenoğlu, who examines the ways in which women are represented as embodying the tradition and "essence of the Orient" (1998, 99; also Lewis 1995; Abu-Lughod 2001, 2002). She stresses that the "absolute and systematic difference between the West and the Orient . . . is repeated (and evidenced) in the respective positions of their women" (1998, 104).

The multisited field observations I refer to in the following pages lead me to argue that the Polisario/SADR ultimately presents an equally stagnant, homogenizing, and ultimately unfounded form of Othering via the official discourse. Rather than presenting Sahrawi Muslim women's "Other" as "non-Muslim" Westerners, the Other is rather a group with whom Sahrawi women share their religious values and language. This could be conceptualized as an example of the "rule of gendered difference" (Abu-Lughod quoting Chaterjee 1998b, 17), where difference does not only exist between (and re/creates) "the genders" (male and female) but also essentially between women of a particular background and those with different religious, cultural, linguistic, and other characteristics.

Hence, through claims designed to demonstrate the absolute difference between Sahrawi and Muslim MENA women, the Middle East is re/constituted by the Polisario/SADR as the antithesis of the Sahrawi and Western "way of life." In this framework, the Sahrawi's identifiable "common selves," or "sisters," are revealed to be, not Arab women, but Western women. Rather than being an example of "East-vs.-West" (Abu-Lughod 1998b, 5), embodied as Polisario/SADR=East-vs.-Spain=West, in this context the relationship is rather represented as Polisario/SADR= West-vs.-MENA=East.

Blurring Boundaries and Brightening Bonds:
Sahrawi and Spanish "Sisters"

The discursive alignment of the Sahrawi with Spanish *solidarios* is directly evidenced in the contemporary terminology that "blurs boundaries" between the two groups. The significance of the Polisario/SADR's strategic usage of the notion of "fraternity" between the Spanish and Sahrawi to elicit support has been explored by Martin-Márquez (2006). In this context, however, I explore the more specific notion of a shared "sisterhood" that is mobilized by Sahrawi officials in the NUSW's Conferences and in their frequent meetings, agreements, and contracts with Western NGOs and Women's Institutes.

The concepts of "feminist sisterhood" and "international female solidarity" are based on women's common experience of oppression and exploitation (Steans 2006, 119). Despite the fundamental limits of this term (Simons 1979; Steans 2006), the equation between "sisters" and "feminism" has reached the *Oxford English Dictionary*, which defines a "sister" as "a fellow woman seen in relation to feminist issues" (2005). In this context, Sahrawi officials' claims to sisterhood and overarching commonalities immediately enables them to call for more involvement (and investment) by Western women to help Sahrawi women continue to struggle for self-determination on individual, group (as women) and "national" levels (as Sahrawis struggling against Moroccan occupation), both in the camps and in the international arena. It is Sahrawi women's oppression by Morocco that is explicitly referred to in such accounts, rather than "patriarchal" oppression by Sahrawi men: the existence of the latter in the camps is resolutely denied through describing Sahrawi society as "matriarchal" and claiming that there is a total absence of violence against women in the camps.

Sororidad (sisterhood) was explicitly evoked by Fatma Mehdi during and after the 2007 NUSW conference (verbatim proceedings and quoted in Peralta 2007), just as similar claims have been made during smaller encounters with "solidary women." Celebrating the participation of a group of socialist Swedish women in a camp-based conference about the rights of Sahrawi women and children, for instance, Mehdi declared that these Western women "have come to exchange ideas with their socialist *sisters* [i.e., Sahrawi women] and to manifest their solidarity and support for Sahrawi women's struggle for freedom and independence." She reflected that the conference would provide Sahrawi women with an opportunity to "familiarize themselves with the experiences and struggle of their [non-Sahrawi] *sisters* around the world" (quoted in SPS 2004; my translation and emphasis). The description of Sahrawi women as the Swedish visitors' "socialist sisters" demonstrates the extent to which the Polisario/SADR and NUSW orient themselves to the specific priorities of the precise audience being addressed (in this case, socialist Swedish women), highlighting their political commonalities through such adjectives.

Broader claims to common gendered interests and goals simultaneously create ties with Western women's groups while/by reflecting the importance assigned by the new development agenda to "the mantras of gender mainstreaming and gender equality" (Kandiyoti in Hammami 2005, 1352; Moghadam 1997b, 36). Hence, when addressing the primarily Spanish and overwhelmingly female non-Sahrawi delegates after the Fifth NUSW Conference, the newly reelected secretary general concluded: "we need your intervention, courses on leadership, on gender politics, empowerment, education regarding human rights and women's rights" (verbatim proceedings, 8 April 2007). NUSW representatives' declarations,[4] along with documents produced for the Fifth NUSW Conference, and agreements signed by the NUSW and Spanish feminist groups, are all widely infused with strategic Spanish feminist terms such as *empoderamiento* (empowerment), *emancipación* (emancipation), *liderazgo* (leadership), *educación feminista* (feminist education), and *feminismo* (feminism).[5]

4. Abu-Lughod reminds us that "[o]ne must also be careful not to accept uncritically the terms of the upper-middle and middle-class women involved in most feminist projects—the notions of 'awakening,' 'women's rights,' and 'empowerment' that are part of the narratives of progress and enlightenment that still have currency among secular progressives in the Middle East today" (1998b, 25). Nonetheless, such terms are not "irrelevant to other classes," especially since these are diffused, for instance, through mass educational systems (ibid., 31, footnote 70).

5. Abu-Lughod discusses the usage of the term *feminism* in the MENA context (1998b, esp. 22–23). Also see Kandiyoti 1996.

Key examples include the invitation letter for the Fifth NUSW Conference (written in Spanish), which refers to this event as a space that will enable the NUSW to continue working toward the "emancipation of women" (on file with author); claims that the creation of the NUSW Statutes has "contributed to the dissemination of feminist thought" (on file with author); the title of a presentation offered by Mehdi in Madrid in 2006: "Sahrawi women as an example of empowerment"; and Hamdi's declaration that "despite social, cultural, and political differences, the feminist cause is the same in any corner of the world" (in Tendeiro-Parrilla 2007; all my translations).

It could be argued that by repeatedly pinpointing claims to "sisterhood" and a commonality of "feminist" values during their interactions with Western audiences, Polisario/SADR and NUSW officials re/create Sahrawi women according to Spanish preferences. This is reminiscent of the creation of "ideal" Sahrawi women via the Francoist education program enacted in the Spanish Sahara during the colonial era (see Chapter 1).

However, "sisterhood" can be interpreted in a second way within the remit of a "politics of classification" (Callaway 1986, 221). This term also relates to the (currently) less prevalent and yet significant references to Other Arab Muslim women as the Sahrawi's sisters.[6] Combined with a feminist understanding of sisterhood, an alternative usage of the term is evidenced in the Egyptian Muslim Sisterhood (Talhami 2001, 262) or the Malaysian Sisters in Islam women's group (Ong 2003, 404–405). Muslim women are often referred to by other Muslims via this identifier, which reflects a female community of believers (what Bartkowski and Ghazal Read call a "feminized *ummah*" 2003, 84–97) with shared core beliefs (ibid.). However, even though such a term might evoke notions of empathy, connectedness, and respect, in the present case the connotations appear rather different.

As quoted earlier, the former Polisario/SADR representative, Es-Sweyih, wrote that Sahrawi women's position is "clearly different from the position of their *sisters* in the rest of the Arab and Muslim world" (2001,

6. I thank Yousif M. Qasmiyeh for drawing my attention to this point.

36; my translation and emphasis). Although the Sahrawi and Other Arab women do in a factual sense share a set of religious beliefs and a language, the official distancing from their Arab and Muslim "sisters" increasingly prevails in the non-Sahrawi realm, with Mariem Salek (in Petrich 2005) going as far as to tell the international audience that she sometimes asks herself "if Arab women exist." I propose that the official dissociation from their Muslim "sisters" may in part be *possible* due to their utilization of the concept of "sisterhood." By associating themselves with this concept, Sahrawi women and men can be seen as demonstrating to the Western audience their authority to criticize and reject the fate of "Muslim Arab women," even in the light, to quote Said, of an absence of substantiated "supporting arguments or modulating qualifications" (1997, xviii). In this context, the term *sister* is primarily used to validate an argument presented by a group that *knows* what is "inside" of the matter and yet prefers to occupy the "outside." This is evidently significant given the primarily comparative nature of the Sahrawi official discourse concerning gender relations in the camps.

Indeed, in the above conceptualization of the Spanish "sister" aligned to the Sahrawi Self, Arab/Muslim women play a key function as the Other. By sharing Arab/Muslim women as their respective Other, the imagined alignment between the Sahrawi and the Spanish Selves can become clearer, forming a "bond" that is "bright" in *solidarios'* eyes. In the Sahrawi processes of ipseity and alterity embodied in the externally projected official discourse, the Sahrawi Self is aligned closely to the West, while distanced officially from the Arab world as a whole.

Brightening Boundaries with Other Arab "Sisters"

As Arab/Muslim women are constructed in the Sahrawi official discourse as subjugated victims of domestic violence who are veiled and forced into oppressive marriages against their will, they play a pivotal role in mediating the Polisario's relations with Western observers. Indeed, without relying upon "generic images" of MENA women, the significance of the official discourse collapses. Such "generic images," however, cannot be mobilized in all contexts, as recognized by the SADR representative to the Middle East.

In our interview, the MENA representative recognized that the gendered concepts that are evoked when addressing the West cannot be used during interactions with MENA audiences (Damascus, July 2006). He stated that, "although Sahrawi women's importance in the camps is received in a positive light in Europe, it is more complicated in the Middle East." He also asserted that, much as some individual Muslim women might "like" or "approve" of the importance of Sahrawi refugee women, it would be difficult to approach this issue in MENA societies. He gave three interconnected reasons for this difficulty.

First, he indicated that, unlike in Spain, the Sahrawi issue is "not well known" in the region and would therefore be of little interest to Arab civil society or politicians. Indeed, this conclusion was confirmed by all of the non-Sahrawi MENA students interviewed in Cuba in 2006, who indicated that they had heard for the first time about "the Sahrawi" while in Havana. Second, he explained that in the MENA region it is not possible to speak openly about Sahrawi women's high level of participation in the public sphere and of the virtues of democracy, since these factors "do not exist in the region" itself.[7] By contrast, he asserted that these are common factors uniting the Spanish and Sahrawi people. The third, and intimately related reason, is that, if one were to speak of women's activism and activities in the same terms as they are discussed in Spain, such a representation would, according to him, be perceived as "licentiousness" (*libertinaje*). He expanded by claiming that a MENA audience would reject such an image as proving that "your women are not women, but whores" and that Sahrawi women's "free" position in the camps is a result of "Western influence."

7. Despite denouncing the absence of "democracy" in the MENA region, the SADR's representational presence in the Middle East has historically generally been tolerated. Although the SADR MENA representative informed me in 2006 that it had been difficult for him to enter into discussions promoting the independence of the Western Sahara with Syrian, Lebanese, or Jordanian politicians, he had nonetheless lived in Syria for several years and appeared to have little or no difficulties traveling in and out of MENA countries (Damascus, August 2006).

The MENA representative's responses reflect the way in which Arab Muslim women are conceptualized by Polisario/SADR representatives, when they are addressing Western observers, as distinctly unlike Sahrawi women. Of particular significance is the way that all of my Sahrawi interviewees, including those students and officials who have lived in the Middle East for several years, describe the region's social systems in a highly essentialist and homogenizing fashion, in effect reproducing key tenets of Orientalist views of Arab societies. While consistently drawing a clear boundary between MENA and Western ways of life with specific reference to the position of women in the MENA region, none of my interviewees offered any recognition of religious, political, ethnic, or social diversity in the Middle East (cf. Salhi 2008, 296).[8]

Hence, the claim that one could not discuss the "high participation" of Sahrawi women in the public sphere because such participation does not exist in the Middle East appears unfounded in countries like Algeria, Egypt, Lebanon, or Syria, where large numbers of veiled and unveiled Muslim women have habitually been very active outside of their homes. Indeed, diametrically opposed to the view outlined above, a Palestinian academic and former member of the Palestine Liberation Organization stated in our interview that

> women, as viewed from the Middle East, are essential for social and economic life. As viewed from the West, they are veiled women who ride camels. If Westerners visit the Middle East, however, they will see that this is not the case, and that women work and participate in social and economic life very actively. (Oxford, July 2006)

Like the Sahrawi students I interviewed in Syria, Cuba, and the camps (many of whom had studied in Algeria), the SADR's MENA representative appears to either ignore, or not know about, female employment rates in many Arab countries (see Khoury and Moghadam 1995; Moghadam 2003,

---

8. Ayotte and Husain note the "ethnocentrism" of "a discursive commitment to the religious and geographic homogeneity of Islam in the language of a 'Muslim world'" (2005, 120).

33–78).[9] Indeed, the "imagined" Middle East projected by the Polisario/ SADR official discourse seems to be more closely aligned to "the basically conservative" Gulf countries and Saudi Arabia (Chatty 2000, 241), where more extreme forms of veiling and segregation prevail than in the countries of the Levant or Maghreb.

While female employment rates in the Middle East are lower than in other regions worldwide,[10] over 30% of the public service was female in the 1990s in Kuwait (39% in 1994), Morocco (31% in 1991), Syria (27% in 1992), and Turkey (35% in 1994; Moghadam 2003, 53). In contrast and despite the absence of reliable statistics about employment and participation in the Sahrawi refugee camps, in 2007 the NUSW claimed that, since 2002, 11% of government positions had been held by women, 24% in parliament, and 7% in diplomatic positions (NUSW document on file with author). Following the introduction of a revised quota system for the 2007 parliamentary elections, female representation in parliament reportedly reached 34% (www.upes.com). Such figures, if correct, do not demonstrate a greatly higher degree of participation in the Sahrawi refugee camps than when compared with the figures provided by UNDP.

Further, such official statements disregard the intensity and significance of Muslim women's roles in MENA liberation struggles and womanist movements. Indeed, the NUSW's international relations officer, Zahra Ramdan, currently presents no recognition of Muslim women's historical involvement in nationalist movements, stating that

> [u]nlike that which happens in the rest of the Muslim world, Sahrawi women have stood out since the colonial period for their active protagonism in their people's struggle. (2005; my translation)

9. Such claims also fail to recognize the historical shifts in women's rights and public roles which have taken place in different parts of the Middle East, as documented with reference to Afghanistan, for instance, by Stabile and Kumar (2005, 768) and Kandiyoti (2007a).

10. In the MENA region as a whole, 26% of the formal labor force was female in 2009 versus 34.6% in South Asia and 62.9% in Sub-Saharan Africa (UNDP 2011, 142).

In direct contrast with the Polisario's early attempts to encourage Sahrawi women to participate "actively in the armed revolution *like her sisters* in the Palestinian [and] Algerian . . . revolutions" (cited in the Introduction; my emphasis), this approach publically dismisses the centrality of Palestinian refugee women in creating the Palestinian refugee camps in Lebanon, which was so prominent that "Ain el-Helwe camp came to be known in Europe as *jumhuriyyat an-nissa'* [the Republic of Women]" (Suleiman, Oxford, July 2006; also see Sadiqi 2008).[11]

When Muslim women's involvement in nationalist struggles *is* currently recognized by Polisario/SADR officials, this is nonetheless presented as a means of demonstrating Sahrawi women's uniqueness. "Algerian women" in particular are often used as reference points in this context. Hence, the MENA representative submitted to me that Algerian women's situation had "worsened" after the end of the Algerian revolution because they had in/voluntarily returned to the roles and identities that had existed "before." There had therefore been a reversion to the *status quo ante*. However, he claimed that, "unlike them," Sahrawi women's future centrality in the SADR is "guaranteed" since Sahrawi women have "always" been important and free, and there is therefore little difference between "now and before" (Damascus, August 2006). Such a historical account of Sahrawi women "always having been so free" evidently fails to engage with the heterogeneity of women's positions during and before the colonial era.

Despite creating a distance between the Sahrawi and Algerian Selves in such contexts, Sahrawis' direct interactions with Algerians reveal the extent to which the notions of "fraternity" and "sorority" may be mobilized to

---

11. Palestinian women's activism and activities have been carefully documented by Palestinians and non-Palestinians (including Jammal 1985; Peteet 1991; Holt 1996; Kawar 1996; Sayigh 1998). What is of note is that Palestinian women are not a critical core of political discourses developed to obtain or maintain solidarity for the Palestinian cause, as I claim Sahrawi women are. Further, research which explores the roles of Palestinian women habitually evaluates this in historical terms, tracing changes in women's organizations over time, rather than in relation to other Arab or Western women.

obtain support from different audiences. Hence, an Algerian woman who had worked with UNICEF in Algiers asked me if I too had found it surprising that Sahrawi children and youth energetically described themselves as "Algerians" and as the "brothers and sisters" of the Algerian people (personal communication, London, June 2008). Such descriptions are evidently incompatible with the official discourse presented to European audiences. My observations prior to and during the Fifth NUSW Conference also indicate that Sahrawi families were often reluctant to welcome Algerian guests, although they were enthusiastic to house Spanish visitors. The primary motivation for this rejection may be financial: Spaniards habitually leave considerable sums of money and goods for their host families in the camps, while *individual* Algerians are unable to do the same. The way in which Algerian and Spanish civil societies' solidarity for the "cause" is conceptualized when both groups are present in the camps is, I believe, directly related to the visibility and tangibility of the aid and/or political support they can offer in such situations. In this sense, the solidarity offered by Algerian civil society can never be as profitable as that offered by members of Spanish civil society, although ties with Algeria's civil society and state may be strategically brightened through diverse claims, including the invocation of "sisterhood," when Spanish solidarios are absent.

"Traveling Discourse"

It is pertinent at this stage to ask how and why the same images of subjugated, hidden, and abused Arab women were offered by Sahrawi officials and students who have lived in countries such as Algeria, Cuba, Libya, and Syria. Following Said's notion of "traveling theory" (1983, 226–247), we could describe these dynamics as embodying a process of "traveling discourse," with the mainstream representation of the camps appearing to have been "inherited" by certain members of the younger generation or at least "transferred" to them by the older elite. We could thus understand the official discourse as having traveled both across time—from the old to the new generations—and across space—from camp-based Sahrawi to those in Cuba and Syria, and simultaneously to non-Sahrawi observers (Fiddian-Qasmiyeh 2012).

Although Cuban-based students' lack of contact with Arab women may partially explain the nature of their assumptions about the female MENA Other, throughout my fieldwork in Damascus it emerged that Sahrawi youth have led relatively secluded lives in close proximity with and dependence on other Sahrawis, while engaging little with Syrian society. By sharing accommodation, meeting in the Polisario office for lunch and/or dinner on a daily basis, and maintaining a strong dependence on the preexisting social group, Sahrawi youth appeared to have had only limited contact with Syrian youth. Part of the reason for this may have been practical in nature, since, unlike in Cuba, students did not receive a scholarship from the host state, only a small allowance from the Polisario/SADR. In this context, going to the Polisario office guaranteed them a hot meal: according to one of my sources, "otherwise we'd just eat once a day" (undergraduate student, Damascus, July 2006).

Such a difficulty in developing connections with their education hosting countries could explain the extent to which Cuban-educated, Syrian-educated, and camp-educated youth and adults reproduced analogous responses to questions about Sahrawi women and their failure to recognize the heterogeneity of Arab women. My conclusions are largely paralleled by Caratini (2003a, 13), who reflects that graduates "could only relay images which were practically caricatures. There was, in reality, some sort of 'closure' in this 'opening' to the world . . . during all of the years spent 'elsewhere' they remained in reality very self-enclosed" (2003a, 13; my translation). More specifically, the proximity to the discourse produced and repeated by Polisario/SADR representatives may be related to the fact that a small group of Polisario/SADR men "monitors" youth's lives while they study abroad (also Caratini 2003a, 13; Gimeno-Martín and Laman 2005, 31).[12] These individuals therefore not only physically separate youth from their host communities but also directly transmit "information"

12. In the case of students in Syria, there is only one Polisario representative in the country.

about the Western Sahara and the refugee camps to Sahrawi youth during their absence from the camps.[13]   •

Having been unable to visit the camps for periods of up to a decade, these students have been exposed to a very particular portrayal of life in the camps[14] via the only sources available to them: official Polisario/SADR accounts. In essence, the international education program in Cuba and Syria emerges as being intimately connected with a perpetuation of both the political cadre and the specific terms of the official rhetoric, because many students are directly encouraged to become involved with the Polisario/SADR system while abroad.[15] The continuity of the official representation can thus be ensured as these students habitually take on significant roles upon their return to the camps, either in ministerial or diplomatic positions or through "accompanying" and interpreting for visitors to the camps (as discussed earlier with reference to female Cuban graduates).

In fact, the university theses that I examined while in Cuba and that had been written by Sahrawi students in the 1980s and 1990s reflected that many humanities and social science students were in many respects being "taught the script" in order to represent the Polisario/SADR cause.[16] Hence, after thanking the SADR Ambassador for his assistance, the very first line of the "historical overview" offered in A. S. Sidi-Zein's international relations thesis reads:

> The traditional Sahrawi society is a society in which women have histor-
> ically occupied a pivotal place in all social arenas, unlike other countries

13. "Purposive transference" often takes place in dormitory settings created for "marginal," and especially nomadic, students, where "cultural supervisors" have habitually kept the official image and understanding of the culture at home alive.

14. On traveling memories of both home camps and the Western Saharan homeland, see Fiddian-Qasmiyeh 2011c.

15. In contrast, Sahrawi youth who have studied in Spain have been individually fostered by Spanish families rather than placed under the direct "responsibility" and control of Polisario/SADR representatives.

16. One student interviewed in Damascus (July 2006) reflected that, through the boarding school system in the camps, "[t]he [SADR] government was a factory, it created all of us the same."

in the region where women's social participation has been undervalued. (1991, 6; my translation)

This thesis parallels other official accounts that prioritize women's position within colonial and precolonial history while dismissing Other Arab women. Such "training" is not unique to Cuba: in 2006 H. A. Musa published his undergraduate political science thesis in Damascus, under the title *The Peace Process in the Western Sahara and Its Horizons* (my translation) and, as he explained in our interview, he was hoping to become a Polisario/SADR official upon graduation (Damascus, August 2006).

In addition to the socioeconomic capital accrued through acting as guides in the camps, while studying abroad youth may decide to join the official system as a result of the advantages that arise from taking part in Polisario-sponsored activities. Hence, two male and two female Cuban-based students whom I interviewed in 2006 had recently traveled to Venezuela to participate in an international Youth Conference. It eventually emerged that they were all direct relatives of key Polisario/SADR/ NUSW members, suggesting the benefits of becoming and remaining closely aligned to the official political and diplomatic structure. This also, of course, suggests the extent to which family connections influence the opportunities offered to refugee youth. In Syria, those young men who indicated that they were either student representatives or claimed they were interested in becoming Polisario diplomats had all reportedly returned to the camps more frequently than those who remained on the margins of politics. Both in Syria and in Cuba, at least two individuals who had agreed to represent their fellow students had reportedly received free tickets to the camps in order to attend Polisario conferences. A combination of material, culinary, and travel-related awards have thus encouraged students both directly and indirectly to stay close to the official stance and terms pertaining to the Sahrawi cause, of which the gendered official discourse is a central part.

"Secularism" and Sahrawi Women

Thus far, I have argued that the official Sahrawi and Spanish Selves are presented as sisters for key political and humanitarian reasons through what we may call "strategic sisterhood" (quoted in Hatem 2006, 27) or even what I would refer to as "sisterhood for survival" in this refugee context. I have also submitted that the Polisario/SADR has discursively strengthened a "bright bond" with the West through distancing the Sahrawi female, and thus national, Self from Other Middle Eastern women. It is important to note that a group's rejection of connections with Arab women (as the most readily identifiable representatives of Other Arab communities)[17] has historically been a clear way of "progressively distancing itself from Islam that thus became its constitutive outside" (Yeğenoğlu 1998, 135). In this section, I propose that gendered claims to "Sahrawi secularism" highlight similarities with the "secular" West precisely by repudiating connections with belief systems associated with the Middle East.

As the Polisario/SADR is acutely aware, the potential to alienate Western solidarity groups is an ever-present possibility. In a context where the negative representation of Islam (and the position of women within Islam) by the media and politicians throughout the West prevails, distancing the Sahrawi Self from Islam appears to be strategic in nature and intimately related to the Polisario/SADR's politics of survival. While historically characterizing many nationalist movements in the past, separating the Sahrawi Self from Islam becomes increasingly urgent given the current geopolitical setting and related rejection of Islam in the West.[18] Indeed, global events such as the First Gulf War (1990), invasions of Afghanistan and Iraq (2001 and 2003, respectively), attacks on/in the United States (2001), and the Madrid and London bombings (2004 and 2005, respectively) have further solidified Western conceptualizations (i.e., "rejection") of Islam. This may explain the particular urgency with which groups such as the Polisario/SADR have attempted to distance themselves from Islamic identity and practice.

17. See Afshar et al. 2005; Bahramitash 2005; Zine 2006.

18. On representations of Islam in the Western media, see Said (1997). "Islamophobia" is a long-standing phenomenon, despite its having been used as a printed term only since 1991 and having been included in the OED since 1997; on Islamophobia before and after September 2001, see Sheridan 2006.

Combined with more localized concerns about an "Islamically dominated North Africa" and "Islamic fundamentalism" in the Saharan desert and Maghreb (Zoubir 2002; Keenan 2004b;), the prospect of creating a secular, modern state is an attractive one actively offered by proponents of Sahrawi self-determination to non-Sahrawi audiences (also see Fiddian-Qasmiyeh 2011a). Public declarations made by and on behalf of the Polisario/SADR must be viewed in relation not only to global shifts in the 1990s and 2000s but also more specifically vis-à-vis high-profile (and thus far unsubstantiated) accusations made by Moroccan officials that the Polisario Front is a terrorist organization tied to Al-Qaeda in the Maghreb (del Pino 2003; Darbouche 2007, 2).[19]

Hence, in 2007 the UN General Assembly was addressed by a Spanish *solidario* who declared that a free Western Sahara "could be an example for the world," "peaceful, respectful of women, freedom-loving, and allied in the struggle against terrorism" (UNGA 2007).[20] Zunes has also suggested that "having such a progressive and democratic model [in the form of an independent SADR] in the Arab-Islamic world may constitute what Noam Chomsky has called 'the threat of a good example'" (Mundy and Zunes 2002, n.p.). In this way, the SADR directly posits itself as an example to be followed by other nations, fulfilling all of the noneconomic priorities associated with contemporary notions of "good governance": "peaceful," "secular," "democratic" and, fundamentally, "respectful of women."

In such a context, the term "secular" and the concepts of "Sahrawi secularism" and "secular Islam" are invoked throughout Polisario/SADR accounts of life in the camps. Such claims may be made indirectly by the Polisario/SADR through distancing Sahrawi women from a range

19. The mid- to long-term impacts of the abduction of Spanish and Italian NGO workers from Rabouni in 2011 remains to be established, as does the identity of the abductors: Al-Qaeda in the Maghreb has been identified by certain observers as being responsible for the abductions, and yet no evidence has yet been presented to substantiate this claim.

20. If the Taliban and al-Qaeda have been associated with "terrorist misogyny" (Ayotte and Husain 2005, 124), the official discourse appears to directly equate the Polisario/SADR with feminism and/or women's empowerment.

of Muslim identities and practices that are considered in the West to be oppressive. Indeed, the "unveiling" of women and officially distancing the national Self from the "Islamic veil" has frequently been interpreted as one of the clearest symbols of secularism (Kandiyoti 1991; Yeğenoğlu 1998, 135; Gökariksel and Mitchell 2005). More explicitly, however, official Polisario/SADR statements projected to the West declare (or "manufacture") the secular, liberal, and modern foundations of the Sahrawi "nation" specifically with reference to Sahrawi women.

One example of an official's declaration of the Sahrawi's "secularism" is embodied in a selection of interviews given by Maima Mahmud Nayem, the director of the Dakhla Women's School and Dakhla's representative of the SADR Secretary of State for Social Affairs and Emancipation of Sahrawi Women. She has re/created a constant connection between the "empowered" position of women in the camps and the Sahrawi's "secularism," both of which are re/produced as unique and exceptional:

> You must remember that the Sahara is a secular country [un país laico] and the position of Sahrawi women is very privileged when compared with other women of the Arab world and Europe. Just to give you an idea, we are the only women who do not suffer physical abuse and our society has imposed a Law [sic] to reject any man who raises his hand to a woman. (quoted in Barrera 2008; my translation)

In this series of accounts, Nayem claims that Sahrawi women are free in "the Sahara" (i.e., the camp-based SADR) specifically because it is a "secular country," a space where the Sahrawi "have" what she labels "islam laico" or "secular Islam": "Here we speak of the rights of women, of the secular Islam which we have" (quoted in Portinari 2007; my translation; see also Zin 2007 and 2008).

A second example derives from an interview held with a member of the Polisario three days before the 2007 NUSW Conference, during which he reiterated the necessity of "stressing Sahrawi women's secularism and modernism" to the non-Sahrawi audience during the Conference (27 February Camp, March 2007). He continued by explaining that this was especially important due to the current situation "globally." Reflecting the official stance of distancing the Sahrawi national Self from Islam, he explicitly indicated that it was vital that the Spanish delegates attending the conference should "recognize" that Sahrawi women are secular and modern. Significantly, no reference was made in either this interview or in any of the documents reviewed to Sahrawi men as "secular," illustrating the symbolic power that is assigned to women, who are the most "visible" demarcators of national and religious boundaries. I shall return to the invisibility of Sahrawi men in the official discourse in Chapter 5.

The remainder of our discussion indicated that Polisario/SADR representatives often officially separate themselves from the range of belief and social systems that are central to "popular discourses" and day-to-day life in the camps. Hence, he bluntly dismissed my observation that camp residents regularly spoke to me about Islam and indicated that their religious belief and practice is central to their identity, social experience in the camps, and hopes for the future. His conclusion was that only a small number of people were "like that" and that it was "just because of their disillusionment or disconnection with reality, it's just a sign of their emptiness."

I do not purport to claim that the Polisario/SADR unequivocally represent the Sahrawi as non-Muslims in their interactions with Western audiences, despite the reality of Sahrawi refugees' commitment to their faith. Rather, this organization has combined a prevalent tendency to "silence" and render invisible the multiple, and at times contested, roles of Islam in the camps[21] with the systematic projection, on those occasions when religion *is* mentioned, of an image of "secular Sahrawi Islam" that is absolutely different from any Other Islam. Hence, the Norwegian Refugee Council indicates that the Sahrawi "distinguish themselves [from their neighbors] by their liberal and relaxed interpretation of Islam" (2008, 6,

---

21. Only two references to Islam are made in the book written by former Polisario/SADR representative Es-Sweiyh (2001, 43; two extracts from the Constitution also include references to Islam: p.125); conversely, there are four references to "secular resistance," including in the second paragraph of the first page (2001, 7, 16, 25, 42).

also 4), while the New Internationalist states that "their form of Sunni Islam is one of the mildest and most tolerant of all" (Brazier 2004, n.p.). Although authors neither justify how they have reached conclusions vis-à-vis the beliefs and practices of "the majority" of the population (some 155,000 people) nor what they are referring to when they define the population's religious outlook as "liberal,"[22] such approaches reveal that religious difference can be understood to demonstrate the separation and uniqueness of the Sahrawi "nation" from Other Muslims, while reinforcing the notion that Other forms of Islam are in essence violent and intolerant.

As noted in the Introduction, processes of secularization may follow social changes (such as bureaucratization, the creation of a state and/or urbanization) that alter the *position* of religious institutions in the social landscape. In the case in question, a range of sociopolitical changes surrounding the creation of these refugee camps have evidently changed individuals' and various groups' relationships both with the SADR "state" and Islam on numerous levels. However, the purpose of this section is not to determine whether "thin," "weak," or "strong" secularism(s) (cf. Modood 2001) factually exist in the camps. Rather, I aim to examine the motivations behind and implications of official proclamations of Sahrawi "secularism" when addressing Western audiences. In this respect I find that the most useful general definition of secularization is that of religion becoming and remaining a *private* matter (e.g., Hann 2000; Asad 2001, 2006, 494).[23]

22. It is important to note that interviewees who are not part of the Polisario/SADR or NUSW also presented this rhetoric at times. For instance, a 14-year-old girl interviewed in the camps by the SARC team, and who lives in Spain, indicated that "[t]heir religion is Islam but it is tolerant." It is possible that having lived in Spain will have influenced the terms with which she describes "their" (rather than "our") religion.

23. Claims regarding European secularism are paralleled by the widespread acceptance—and support—of "Judeo-Christian" and "Christian values" providing "a shared religious heritage" and a "formative cultural influence at the heart of and giving substance to 'European' civilization" (quoted in Asad 2006, 295). The "invisibility" of Christian belief and practice in "secular" Europe must be contrasted with the extreme visibility and rejection of Islam in the name of secularism (Taylor 2002, 15).

Religion in the Sahrawi context can be defined as a private matter in so far as it is separated, not from either the state or the Sahrawi public, but rather from non-Sahrawi observers. The "private" sphere in this sense refers both to Sahrawi individuals' immediate family surroundings and to the broader sociopolitical space of the camps, while "the public" (from whom religion is hidden) are Western observers. The official discourse is thus simultaneously revealed as a mode of "secular gendered public relations," where religious identity and practice are concealed from Western view. The "secular" nature of the Sahrawi nation has thus been "demonstrated" through "its" women: as Sahrawi women have consistently been unveiled by the official discourse, religion has been veiled from "public" view, rendering the Sahrawi camps a "secular" space in Western eyes.

One example of the Polisario/SADR's apparent success in hiding the Sahrawi's religion includes Cazón's reference to a Spanish host family who had been "in solidarity" with the Sahrawi for over a decade before "discovering" that the Sahrawi are Muslim. After the Spanish host mother was reportedly warned by a Sahrawi man to "[r]emember that we, the Sahrawis, are also *moros*" (2004, 59; my translation), she laments: "That man was right. The religion of the Sahrawis *is* the same as that of the *moros*" (ibid., 95; my translation). Her shock that the man was correct that Sahrawis are, after all, Muslims suggests that in her imagination, as in many other Spaniards' minds, the Sahrawi were until then not truly associated with Muslim identity and practice. This element of surprise is also paralleled by the number of questions urgently posed by several Spanish host parents during the interviews conducted by Crivello and myself with Sahrawi children participating in Vacaciones en Paz: Why were the children traveling to Spain with prayer rugs? Why had two girls arrived wearing the hijab? Why wouldn't the children eat pork? (personal observations, Madrid, 2005).

Nonetheless, clearly not all *solidarios* are unaware of the Sahrawis' religion, as reflected by the prevalence of religious terminology used by my Spanish informants as they recalled the colonial period. Indeed, one Spanish *solidario* wrote on his Web page:

> I am disgusted to see that, even among people who help [the Sahrawi] . . .
> there are people who haven't understood a thing. No one seems to have
> realized that the people of the Western Sahara are a Muslim people, who
> pray looking to Mecca and practice the precepts of Islam, even if they
> do it in the flexible way of the people of the desert . . . They are Muslim,
> let us not forget that. To pretend that the children should "learn" to eat
> ham as some Andalusian mamas do because it might seem great to us,
> is to rob them of their traditions, which are theirs, and which they value.
> (Guijarro, 2003: my translation)

However, while Guijarro challenges others to recognize and accept the
Sahrawi's belief system, the benefits of "hiding" the Sahrawi's religious
identity have been recognized not only by the Polisario/SADR but also by
many *solidarios*. This dynamic is reflected upon by Martín-Corrales as he
writes of the ambiguities and "not inconsiderable number of ideological
traps" that characterize "politically correct discourses" in Spain, including that of Spanish civil society "solidarity" with the Sahrawi:

> the sectors of the left and of peripheral nationalisms that trumpet their
> solidarity for certain causes ([. . . including] the *Saharahuis*), make sure
> that they do not mention the religion which these people profess. Thus,
> the fact is silenced that they are all Muslims, that the Constitution of the
> Sahrawi Arab Democratic Republic proclaims that Islam is the official
> religion, etc. (2004, 48–49; my translation)

Martín-Corrales thereby suggests that many *solidarios* are aware of the
reality of the Sahrawi's religious belief and practice but have recognized
that Islam must be publicly sidelined in Spain to ensure the continued
strength of solidarity for "the cause." Such a decision appears to be based
upon an awareness that mainstream references to Islam have the potential to alienate members of Spanish civil societies, a reality to which I
return below.

Although the power dynamic is not as simple as that encompassed
in the terms used by Scott, such mutually reinforcing processes of silencing certain characteristics and priorities while highlighting others con-
firm that the "oppressed" and the "powerful" often "tacitly conspire in

misrepresentation" (1990, 2). Rather than conceptualizing this as a matter of "conspiring," however, I would argue that many *solidarios* have become so committed to "the Sahrawi cause" that they engage in processes of self-censorship vis-à-vis potentially divisive issues. While religious belief and practice is one such issue that is hidden from Spanish view, I return to processes of self-censorship in the following chapter with reference to silences around violence against women in the camps.

Hiding Religious Normality

Mainstream accounts of the Sahrawi refugee camps frequently claim that these are "secular" spaces inhabited by "liberal" individuals for whom religion is "considered a private matter to be practised at home, and has little influence on daily life and politics" (NRC 2008, 6). I agree that religion has become a "private" matter in the camps, and yet I argue that it plays a central role in Sahrawi politics: distancing the Sahrawi Self from Islam during interactions with Western audiences is a highly political process designed by the Polisario/SADR to maximize support for "the cause." Further, Islam has considerable import on daily life in the camps, despite official claims to the contrary.

Hence, although the Polisario/SADR may have created a discourse dominant in the international realm and during interactions with non-Sahrawis visiting the camps, a different set of identifiers, priorities, and dynamics characterize life at the local level and are designed for "internal consumption" alone. Exploring these local priorities enables a discussion of the popular significance of religious identifiers in mediating relations between Sahrawi refugees and Western *solidarios*. This is turn reflects the reality of Sahrawi refugees' resentment toward their aid providers, the reasons for which I will examine further through a case study below.

Reflecting the changing nature of the official discourse in line with shifts in local and international events and priorities, religion has not always been invisible in Western reports on the camps. Non-Sahrawi visitors in the 1980s documented that the construction of mosques was leading, for the first time, to an "institutionalization" of Islamic practices among a formerly nomadic people (Lippert 1987, 160). Early Polisario/SADR materials included photographs of Sahrawis praying and of children studying at Qur'anic schools, and it was reported that "[t]he careful preservation of traditions and Islamic culture is a priority in the camps" (Brittain 1986; on the adaptation of certain Islamic traditions within the camps see Firebrace 1987). The reason for preserving and recognizing the significance of religion for refugees was pinpointed by the headmaster of the 9 June School, who informed a British journalist that "[w]e teach the Koran and Islam as the fundamental cultural values— otherwise the society would simply reject us [the teachers/leaders] and them [the students]" (ibid.).

While recognizing that Sahrawi refugees' personal commitment to Islam could not be denied in/by camp institutions because this would lead to an internal revolt, at a given point the Polisario/SADR appears to have grasped the expediency of making Islam increasingly invisible to Western outsiders. At least from the 1990s onward, coinciding with both the increased number of visitors to Tindouf following the implementation of the ceasefire and increasing tension toward the Middle East and Islam in the West, official Sahrawi guides have consistently presented Western visitors with the aforementioned image of secular, modern, un-veiled and empowered women surrounded by, and working in, an array of "secular" "national" edifices.[24]

One of the clearest examples of this policy's success is that many visitors, including Brazier (1997), Ryan (1999), Bryant (2004), and Thorne (2004) have all erroneously declared that there are "no mosques" in the camps. My own interactions with Spanish *solidarios* in the 27 February Camp indicate that the majority of these were unaware that the yellow-and-green building facing the entrance to the National Women's School was a mosque (see Figure 11). When I informed them of its purpose, many Spaniards were confused by its existence, with one Canary Islander asking me "but . . . why do they have a mosque here?" (27 February Camp, April 2007).

---

24. The presence of SADR jeeps outside of the 27 February Camp mosque during Friday Prayer indicates that some such Polisario/SADR officials attend these same mosques.

Polisario/SADR and Western accounts have also repeatedly failed to document the existence of "modern religious schools" attended by students interested in expanding their knowledge of Islam following, or in parallel to, their "national" education in the camps (Gimeno-Martín and Laman 2005, 23). Despite the SADR Ministry of Justice and Religious Affairs having authorized the creation of two Qur'anic schools in Aaiun, Smara, and Dakhla and one in Ausserd (ibid., 32), these schools are not labeled and heralded as "national" institutions by the Polisario/SADR and are therefore rarely explicitly made visible to Western visitors.

Although such institutions are habitually invisible to Westerners, a critical analysis of social structures in the camps reveals that these are largely based on religiously founded infrastructures. Indeed, the SADR, law, and religion are intimately connected in the camps: even when explicit reference to Shari'a is not made in the SADR Constitution (2003), article 2 indicates that "Islam is the state religion and the fundamental source of law" (my translation),[25] the state legal system is paralleled by the existence of Islamic judges, and the Ministry of Justice and Religious Affairs has joint functions. It must also be recalled that, despite claims to "uniqueness," matters such as family law (including marriage, divorce, and child support issues) have continued to be guided by Shari'a in the camps, as has traditionally been the case throughout the Arab world (Mernissi 2003a, 22; also Sadiqi 2008, 329).

It is not my intention to characterize camp life either solely or primarily in religious terms but rather to briefly note the heterogeneity of religious practice and belief that exists among different groups of Sahrawi refugees. This varies according to multiple factors, including refugees' generation and an exposure to different approaches to Islam through the study abroad program. This is a multiplicity rendered entirely invisible by the official discourse and yet is a highly significant reality in the camps.

25. This corresponds to Art. 3 of the 1976 SADR Constitution.

11. The 27 February Camp's "invisible" mosque, whose existence refutes widespread assertions by European visitors that there are no mosques in the camps (southwest Algeria, March 2007).

The religious schools and mosques established in each camp are admittedly not frequented by the majority of camp inhabitants (as is the case in many if not most MENA countries), and access to institutionalized forms of practicing Islam and learning the Qur'an is mainly limited to those who can afford to pay the relevant fee.[26] Nonetheless, it is common to see Sahrawi refugees praying in their tents or in open spaces, and numerous children attend extracurricular Qur'anic classes.

More broadly, my research and the SARC interviews consistently indicate that religious belief and practice are generally held in esteem and that being a "good Muslim" is considered to be indispensable in the camps (also see Gimeno-Martín and Laman 2005, 34). As discussed earlier, the *milḥafa* that Sahrawi women wear without exception in the camps

26. Although Gimeno-Martín and Laman claim that attending religious schools is "free," since schools are "financed by the population," students' families are clearly expected to ensure their survival (2005, 33).

is conceptualized as enabling women to fulfill their religious obligations. Further, a number of Sahrawi women participating in a preparatory meeting for the NUSW Conference in March 2007 expressed, in Arabic, their desire to perform hajj (the pilgrimage to Mecca that is one of the pillars of Islam; verbatim proceedings, March 2007). In November 2008, and for the first time since the conflict began in the 1970s, fifty Sahrawi refugees traveled to Mecca: this historic event was marked by an official celebration attended by the SADR prime minister, members of the Polisario's National Secretariat and of the Ministry of Justice and Religious Affairs, and SADR President Abdelaziz (SPS 2008). The president asked the pilgrims to "pray for the Sahrawi people" and to "accomplish your religious duty and pray God the Almighty [*sic*] to bring the Moroccan authorities back to reason and cooperate with us" (Bil-Amri and Al-Ashraf 2008; SPS 2008). Abdelaziz concurrently "hailed the steady support of the Algerian authorities," who had reportedly facilitated the pilgrimage (ibid.), again demonstrating the significance of the audience's identity in directing the Polisario/SADR's official statements.

Interviews conducted in Arabic by the SARC team equally reflect the significance given to religion by interviewees, with a 44-year-old woman indicating that "Koranic studies are very important, praying and being a good Muslim is like a capital in life," and a 79-year-old woman recommending that Sahrawi refugee youth

> should not give up their religion, [they should] abide by the beliefs and convictions of the older generations and not surrender. We advise them to follow their Islamic religion, to avoid schisms among themselves, to unite hand in hand

Indeed, ensuring cultural and religious continuity within the refugee camps has in particular been challenged by the study abroad program that has separated thousands of Sahrawi children and children from their families for prolonged periods of time.[27]

---

27. Female and male youth experiences of having studied in, and returned to the camps from a diversity of contexts including Muslim majority countries (Algeria, Libya

Concerns with the transmission of religious belief and practice to the new generation(s) were also expressed by a 40-year-old female SARC interviewee who stated

> I wish that this new generation will keep the good qualities of the Sahrawi people; that they keep their religion and the Sahrawi customs, their generosity, and I hope that the new generation will protect these. Courage, generosity, and justice are good morals, and for protecting our pledge for liberation and the believers if they pledge something, they keep it.

A fear of potentially alienating *solidarios* appears to have led the Polisario/ SADR to sideline refugees' priorities regarding certain religious practices. Hence, Spanish host families are not actively encouraged to refrain from feeding Sahrawi children pork-based products, which are Islamically prohibited (see Crivello, Fiddian, and Chatty 2005). To do so would be to officially recognize the significance of religion to Sahrawi families, in direct contravention of the mainstream representation of "secularism" in the camps.

Indeed, one male Polisario/SADR representative indicated that, although he realized that Sahrawi parents in the camps would be angry with Spaniards if they knew that their child had been fed pork, neither he nor his colleagues had raised this matter directly with Spanish friendship groups, as they "assumed" that the majority of families would respect "the rule" (interview, July 2006). He did not find it significant that my interviews with Sahrawi children and youth in Spain and in Cuba clearly revealed that the majority of these had been given pork to eat while in Spain. In this way, the Polisario/SADR is explicitly failing to enact the requests of its population, who ask the following:

---

and Qatar) or "secular" states (Cuba and Spain) are explored in Fiddian-Qasmiyeh 2013a, 2013d, and unpublished. My interviewees in Syria, Cuba and in the camps all recognized that returning to the camps is a complex process due to the very different forms of socialization which students will have experienced in their different study locations (ibid.; Fiddian-Qasmiyeh 2009, 2010a).

The Sahrawi delegates outside must pay attention to these children [abroad] so that they maintain their links with the Sahrawi culture and its people . . . The westerner [*sic*], for example, does not eat cuscus and does not pray; they have different traditions and customs. Therefore I hope that the guards and representatives are responsible and that they provide the children with proper guidance. (40-year-old female SARC interviewee)

Men, as well as women, highlighted the importance of religion during interviews conducted in Arabic, with a number of male interviewees in the camps actively encouraging me to learn more about Islam. Hence, one Libyan-educated (male) "monitor" who works for the UJSARIO (the National Union of Sahrawi Youth) encouraged me to further improve my Arabic language skills through reading the Qur'an, indicating that I would "learn more than a language" if I did so (27 February Camp, April 2007). A second Libyan-educated male shopkeeper handed me pamphlets about the Revelation and a tape of Qur'anic recitations after we had conversed in Arabic. As a parting gift, he manually copied out sections of the Qur'an for me, reflecting that he had found our conversations important since people "like him" were rarely interviewed or listened to by Western visitors to the camps (27 February Camp, April 2007).

In conclusion, this brief reflection on "religious normality" and the heterogeneity of religious identity and practice in the camps has demonstrated the extent to which the official discourse projected to Western audiences misrepresents the priorities espoused by different groups of Sahrawi refugees. Following Goffman (1971), we could understand this division as characterizing different performances offered by Sahrawis on the "frontstage" (to create an impression among a range of constantly shifting non-Sahrawi audiences) and "backstage" (for or by the Sahrawi "actors" themselves). Scott also presents an analysis of "official transcripts" and "hidden transcripts" used by subjugated populations in their respective interactions "onstage," with those who dominate them, and "offstage," among themselves (1990, 1–4). The official discourse analyzed in this book can thus be conceptualized as the "official transcript" that has been offered during particular stages of the conflict to powerful

Western audiences via the "frontstage," while the "hidden transcript," which reveals the significance of what I have called "religious normality," is offered "backstage," among different groups of Sahrawi refugees alone. It is important to note the ever-changing identity of the audience—including the Swedish feminists, Spanish *solidarios*, or members of Algerian civil society mentioned in this chapter—indicates the extent to which multiple "official transcripts" may be presented by the Polisario/SADR (also see Fiddian-Qasmiyeh 2011a). In the same way a variety of "hidden transcripts" will be enacted, debated, and contested over time by the heterogeneous camp population.

I now discuss the religious terminology used by camp residents "offstage" to refer to Western observers. Such an analysis both confirms the importance of religious identity and difference in the camps and suggests some reasons why certain discursive markers must be concealed from outsiders. This section provides the foundation for a subsequent study of the hidden tension and representational power struggles that characterize the relationship between Sahrawi refugees, the Polisario/SADR, and their Western aid providers.

Naṣārā: Discursive Markers of Religious Difference

The official "sister" projected by the Polisario/SADR to Western audiences is a secular Western sister, while the official Other is a female Muslim Other. Publicly dismissing the importance of religion through these intersecting claims is thus a mechanism designed to "brighten bonds" with Western aid providers. However, my research in the camps and in South Africa reveals the terminology that is habitually used locally, in Arabic, to describe Western visitors to the camps. Hence, although Spaniards are referred to directly (for external use or "exportation") as "sisters," my observations indicate that they are conceptualized and described by Sahrawis on an unofficial level ("offstage") as *Naṣārā*. In this context, *Naṣārā* is specifically a term designed for internal consumption and comprehension. Although this term is not fundamentally a derogatory one, earlier I demonstrated that it intrinsically highlights religious difference and "religious otherness" (Steenbrink 2002, 201). It could therefore be identified as a key marker of "bright boundaries" between Sahrawis and Western observers, with Westerners being conceptualized not as the "official sister" but as the "popular Other" among Sahrawi refugees.

While conducting fieldwork in the camps I rapidly became aware that I was frequently referred to and described by those around me as "*an-Naṣrāniyya*" ("the Christian woman"). Crucially, I was *never* addressed directly in this way. In my daily observations before, during and after the 2007 NUSW Conference, I regularly heard Sahrawi children and adults speak about Spanish visitors in this way, but only "offstage." Significantly, neither I nor other Westerners were referred to as *Naṣārā* "onstage," rather being called by our names or through reference to our role in the camps (i.e., researcher, doctor, etc.). My observations indicate that it was only when Sahrawi speakers assumed that they could not be heard or understood by Western visitors that they used this term.

In addition to my general observations of daily life in the camps, while in South Africa in May 2007 a high-ranking Polisario/SADR representative also asked his Polisario/SADR colleagues "*Wein an-Naṣrāniyya?*" ("Where is the Christian woman?") with reference to a Scandinavian woman participating in the "South African Week of Solidarity with the Sahrawi People." Since I was the only other readily identifiable *Naṣrāniyya* invited to the event, everyone knew exactly who he was referring to.[28]

The widespread usage of this term in "offstage" settings suggests that it was considered to be unproblematic when used "internally" and without "outside" (i.e., Western) knowledge and understanding. However, when I asked speakers in the camps and in South Africa why they described me or other Western women as *Naṣrāniyyāt* (f. pl.), rather than using our names or nationalities, the response was a common one: upon recognizing that the term had been understood, I received profound apologies. Despite having no explicit offensive meaning, when the religious

---

28. Black South Africans, many of whom are Christians, were not described using this term, but rather through other—often racial, rather than religious—descriptors. This highlights the limitations of a definition of *Naṣārā* as "a general term for 'foreigner' (non-Muslim) and especially for tourists," as claimed by Casciarri (2006, 407, footnote 14). The connotations of the term are, rather, more clearly defined through equating *Naṣārā* primarily with white, Western Christians.

identifier entered the public non-Sahrawi realm ("frontstage"), its usage was recognized by Sahrawi speakers to be a potential source of tension with external observers. Indeed, this reflects the scenario envisaged by Ayotte and Husain when they suggest that "[t]he ethnocentrism inherent in the idea of a "Muslim world" can be discerned when one contemplates the likely outcry that would follow the identification of Euro-America as a 'Christian world'" (2005, 120).

In direct contrast with public declarations of Sahrawi secularism designed to blur boundaries with Western observers, I suggest that the "public"·usage of the term *Naṣrāniyya* had the potential to create bright boundaries between aid providers and recipients precisely by demonstrating both the differences between these groups, and the continued importance of religious identity and identifiers in daily interactions in the camps. I shall return below to the dangers that emerge when such religious differences are "brightened" rather than "blurred" in the Spanish eye, demonstrating that silencing or hiding those terms that highlight differences is designed to ensure a broader politics of survival.

Combined with my examination of the term *Naṣārā* during the colonial era, these examples from the camps and South Africa reveal the extent to which Westerners continue to be conceptualized and described as *Naṣārā*, and also the degree to which they often remain, in the popular imagination, as the Other. On the one hand, as stressed by Cole and Kandiyoti,

> [t]he presence of the colonial and postcolonial Other . . . allows actually diverse local populations to sustain an illusion of relative homogeneity over against [*sic*] the hegemonic foreigner, adding to incipient "national" cohesion. (2002, 198)

While the ultimate official and popular Other throughout the late colonial and refugee periods has, of course, been Morocco, the common designation of *Naṣārā* as the popular Other during the colonial and refugee periods could thus be understood as strengthening ties between members of the diverse "Sahrawi" tribes and therefore as solidifying the emerging Sahrawi "national" Self.

Beyond this, however, I conjecture that in this context, as during the colonial era, the term *Naṣārā* encompasses not only religious difference but also provides a means for Sahrawis to reject the unequal power dynamics that have historically characterized their occupation by and dependence upon Westerners, and in particular Spaniards. As indicated earlier, during the colonial period the term *Naṣārā* was closely aligned to the concept of Spaniards as colonizers and occupiers, with the terms being used interchangeably in interviews. Despite the major social, economic, and political shifts that have both affected and been created by Sahrawi refugees since the camps were established in the mid-1970s, my research highlights that this lexical term continues to be prevalent in popular, daily discourses.

A further element of continuity between the colonial and refugee periods is that the two main groups labeled by Sahrawi refugees as *Naṣārā* (colonial Spaniards and Spanish *solidarios*) have consistently conceptualized themselves as attempting to "help the natives." Equally, in both periods the Spaniards' "help" has been accepted by those who have taken jobs with Spanish organizations and have received their pay, while others have continued to be marginalized and separate from these material benefits or have rejected and/or resisted such foreign interventions.

Indeed, dependence on aid providers is often characterized by ambivalence or animosity toward different sectors of the international community, although the discourse officially diffused to Western observers by the Polisario/SADR efficiently eliminates traces of such responses. In this context, I propose that *Naṣārā* could be understood as a term of resistance or a "weapon of the weak" (Scott 1985), reproduced among, by, and for refugees who are in this way able to further reject these unequal power dynamics away from the gaze of their aid providers (Scott 1990, 3; Hyndman 2000, 156). The widespread usage of this term in "offstage" settings points to the reality of historically founded and contemporary resentment toward Spanish civil society that is not expressible in "public."

The tensions underlying the relationship between aid providers and their Sahrawi recipients are vividly present in the following case study of Spanish reactions to the "abduction" of three Sahrawi girls by their camp-based parents. This demonstrates the strain that often typifies Sahrawi-Spanish relations, as well as highlighting what I have referred to as the "conditional" dimension of Spanish public support for "the cause." Having examined a number of ways in which claims of Sahrawi women's equality and secularism have been mobilized to "blur boundaries" and "brighten bonds" with *solidarios*, in the final section of this chapter I demonstrate the dangers that may arise when boundaries are strategically brightened and solidified through reference to gendered and religious difference.

Bright Boundaries: Solidarity under Threat

In Chapter 2 I quoted a prominent member of the Spanish solidarity movement who indicated that his and others' support for the Sahrawi cause is "founded" on the camps being a space for democracy and gender equality.[29] In this section I argue that the solidarity movement also emerges as being dependent upon the same, pinpointing the bases of a "justifiable" or "defendable" solidarity that is threatened if the camps are portrayed as a space of oppression rather than female empowerment and "secularism." The cases of three adolescent Sahrawi girls fostered in Spain in the early 2000s allow us to better understand the ways in which interconnected representations of gender equality and secularism in the refugee camps have been developed as part of the Polisario/SADR's politics of survival. Spanish responses to these girls' situations explicitly demonstrate the power that interconnected ideas/ideals about gender and Islam have to potentially destabilize the solidarity network that is perceived as keeping Sahrawi refugees physically alive and the "cause" on the political agenda in the West. This agenda is heightened when we note that no parallel male-centered high-profile cases have emerged in Spain, despite boys and young men also having been asked to return to the camps. This highlights the extent to which the "abduction" of girls and young women has attracted the Spanish public's imagination and so much media coverage.[30]

29. An earlier analysis of this case appears in abridged form in Fiddian 2006a and Fiddian-Qasmiyeh 2010b.

30. Numerous other female-centered cases have been reported in the Spanish press (see M. P. 2008a/b and 2009; Fiddian-Qasmiyeh 2013).

Aicha, Huria, and Fatimetu

Aicha, Huria, and Fatimetu lived and studied in León, La Rioja, and Asturias for seven, four and three years, respectively, before becoming the center of a chain of Spanish media campaigns between 2001 and 2003. Two of the three girls had arrived in Spain primarily for medical reasons: Huria due to serious dental complications and Fatimetu because of her condition as a person with celiac disease (Fernández 2003). Indeed, hundreds of Saharawi children have moved to Spain for humanitarian and medical reasons, while others, like Aicha, have been invited to live in Spain specifically to allow them to access secondary and tertiary education (see Crivello and Fiddian-Qasmiyeh 2010).

Prior to leaving the refugee camps, the girls' birth and host families signed agreements before a Sahrawi state judge from the SADR Ministry of Justice and Religious Affairs, indicating that the following criteria would be met: (1) the host family would be granted temporary custody and guardianship of the child, (2) that the child would be returned to his/her birth family at the family's request, and (3) the host family would be responsible for maintaining the child's family and cultural ties and facilitating regular communication with the child's parents and family (RASD 2000).[31] These contracts reflect Sahrawi families' concerns that their children might lose their cultural identity and linguistic abilities while abroad (Crivello and Fiddian-Qasmiyeh 2010). Simultaneously, they echo an Islamically based understanding that adoption (and much less so fostering) creates neither legal nor relational ties between individuals (sura 33:4; Mernissi 2003a, 57).

Despite these contracts, Aicha returned only once in seven years to visit her family in the refugee camps and Huria had not seen her biological parents for over 2 years (Díaz 2003). These experiences clearly reinforced the families' anxieties that they might eventually lose their daughters entirely. Shortly after the girls reached puberty, their parents

---

31. See www.elparchedigital.com/pags/huria/Documento_acogimiento.doc for a completed fostering agreement.

separately asked them to return to the camps to help care for their mothers. Aicha's mother was enduring a high-risk pregnancy after having contracted hepatitis; another girl's mother had suffered a miscarriage, while the third had just recently given birth (Castaño-Boullón 2003; Guijarro 2003).All three women therefore required assistance and turned to their eldest daughters accordingly. In each case, the girls' Spanish host families eventually allowed "their daughter" to visit the camps for a short period. However, when their birth families told the girls that they had to stay in the camps rather than return to Spain, the Spanish host families claimed that the girls had been "abducted" and proceeded to vigorously lobby for their "return home," to Spain.

The degree of Spanish public support mobilized cannot be overstated: in Aicha's case, 17,000 Spaniards in the city of León signed a petition for her immediate return (Peregil 2002; Cazón 2004), while 12,000 signatures were collected in Avilés supporting Huria's "liberation" (González 2003a); the relevant debates and legal arguments surrounding Aicha's case reached not only the Spanish public via the media but also through higher political institutions, such as the Spanish Congress, Foreign Ministry, and Senate.[32] Many local-level and several high-ranking politicians offered Aicha and Huria their backing, and the Senate voted in June 2002 in support of Aicha's return to Spain (Cazón 2004, 187). Along with general claims that the girls' rights to health and education were being denied in the camps, the Spanish families and the girls themselves mobilized the Spanish press and political institutions through references to conditions in the camps, in particular claiming that Sahrawi traditions violently oppress women's rights. The extreme representation of the subjugation of Sahrawi refugee women that was repeatedly and purposefully projected by the girls, their host families, and much of the Spanish media was diametrically opposed to the Polisario/SADR discourse vis-à-vis Sahrawi gender relations. Rather, it was directly in line with the monolithic depictions of subjugated,

32. A transcript of the host parents' address to the Senate is available at http://www.senado.es/legis7/publicaciones/html/textos/CS0297.html.

isolated, and violated "third world women" that Mohanty (1988), Spivak (1990, 1993b), and others so vehemently reject. Support was thus explicitly obtained for the girls' "liberation" from the camps via continuously negative references to the Muslim identity of the Sahrawi, pinpointing oppressive veiling and marriage practices and identifying different forms of violence against women. The images mobilized parallel the Orientalist imagery reproduced by the West and indeed by the Polisario/SADR in the official discourse regarding the Muslim Arab Other.

"Saving" Oppressed Sahrawi Women

Undoubtedly the most powerful factor prompting thousands of Spaniards to support the girls' return to Spain was the perception that their rights, as young women, were being denied in the camps.[33] This led to many members of Spanish civil society's advocating the girls' "liberation" from their oppressive birth parents and culture in the refugee camps, thereby directly engaging in "an Orientalist logic that paternalistically seeks to protect women" (Stabile and Kumar 2005, 775). Such a "protection scenario" is dependent on both a "polarization between 'us' and 'them,' but also [upon] caricatures and stereotypes that bear little resemblance to reality" (ibid., 771).

In her letter to the Spanish authorities, Aicha writes:

> Here in the Saharawi Refugee camps [*sic*] I feel I have been kidnapped, forced to adapt myself to so many traditions that I don't know where to start . . . If [X] doesn't manage to speak with [the smuggler], I will spend the rest of my life as a prisoner of my own family, and I will be the crazy one who tried to escape because she didn't agree with her clan's rules (Embarek, n.d.; my translation)

33. The extent to which refugees can be considered to be "voluntarily" living in refugee camps is contestable, since many (if not all) inhabitants would "prefer" to live elsewhere but are unable to do so for a range of reasons. As one *solidaria* wrote "Dear Aicha, whether you like it or not, you're a Sahrawi refugee . . . Whether you like it or not, your family, those who gave you life, live there in regrettable conditions" (Tapias 2003; my translation).

Paralleling claims that Aicha's "clan" had imprisoned her and forced her to adapt to alien "traditions," in a letter to the queen of Spain, Huria denounces the Sahrawi way of life as follows:

> Here the women wear the *burqa*. Their lives are like Afghan women's lives. So, please, help me to leave this place, I beg you. I don't want to live the life that *they* lead, I want *them* to see that it is possible to change all this and to have rights. (Hamoudi 2003; my translation and emphasis[34])

The terms and descriptions offered in these accounts—and especially the explicit references to Afghan women and the burqa—are clearly understood by these young women as epitomizing the "worst" possible conditions for Muslim women (also see Ayotte and Husain 2005, esp. 117). These terms have undoubtedly been strategically exploited by the girls to convince Spanish observers that their plight to flee the refugee camps and their birth families was simultaneously understandable, just, and necessary. As such, they have apparently recognized that a key factor that may pressure Western powers to intervene in a crisis, or may at least be provided as a justification for intervention, is a particular representation of a cultural and religious prison that unjustly oppresses and subjugates women. Summoning the image of forcibly veiled Afghan women is particularly pertinent given that "the plight of Afghan women was invoked as a humanitarian crisis justifying military intervention" (Kandiyoti interviewed by Hammami 2005, 1352).

These images were paralleled and expanded upon by those members of the Spanish media who supported the teenaged refugees' "release,"[35] basing their reports on the specific details delineated in the young women's letters and the Spanish families' statements to the press but

34. Huria's personal (and political) identification rejects the Sahrawi "way of life," speaking of her birth parents and refugee community as *"ellos"* ("them" and "they"). This process of Othering is paralleled by her alignment with Spanish civil society and national institutions (her imagined "we" and "us").

35. A selection of articles and debates surrounding these cases are posted on http://www.entender-sahara.com/articulo.php?sec=documentos&id=11 and at http://elguanche.net/dosopinionesaicha.htm.

simultaneously drawing upon their own, essentially Orientalist, perceptions and beliefs regarding Sahrawi gender relations. Hence, one Internet journalist who has not visited the refugee camps describes Sahrawi society as

> a hell of ancestral customs which stamp on women's most elemental rights; . . . where women never come of age to obtain these [rights] and choose their way of life, not even to choose a husband because their own father chooses one for them when they are still girls, or they sell them or trade them for two camels, two goats, or two donkeys; where men make laws only for themselves, always leaving their women in the margins. (Suárez, 2003; my translation)

Other journalists and commentators stated that Aicha had "won the battle against her parent's ignorance and egoism," parents who expected her to fulfill "the role that is reserved . . . for all of her nation's first-born women: little more than slavery in the *khayma* in the refugee camps" (Alonso 2003; my translation). Alonso concludes that "[s]ome religions and a certain Bedouin atavism keep women tied to the leg of the bed."

In all of these statements, Sahrawi society is "constructed as timelessly misogynistic, barbaric and uncivilized," naturalizing both a "rhetoric of the 'clash of civilizations' and Orientalist constructions of the East upon which such a clash is predicated" (Stabile and Kumar on representations of Afghanistan, 2005, 774). Indeed, one *solidario* recognized that "for [Spanish] trash TV . . . what is useful is to . . . build upon an anti-Muslim prejudice that is sufficiently widespread to guarantee an audience," asking "how many of these signatories [of the petitions] are really informed of the reality of this issue and how many are simply Christian-Castilian-*Leoneses* still enacting the *Reconquista*[36] against the 'moor,' without knowing anything" (Guijarro 2003; my translation). Another *solidaria* rejected the ways in which the popular Spanish press and the host family "have utilized and exploited the overused argument

---

36. Literally meaning "reconquest," this refers to the period in the Middle Ages when Spain attempted to regain control from Muslim rulers.

of the Muslim woman at home, veiled, and with a broken leg" (Tapias 2003; my translation).[37]

It is imperative to note that a large proportion of Spanish solidarity groups denounced the ways in which the "liberation" campaigns had been run, often pointing to the xenophobic nature of the comments made[38] and highlighting that most reporters had not visited the camps and were therefore unfamiliar with the "real" position of women in the camps. Many high-ranking *solidarios*, including Vallina, Medina, and Suárez-Montiel,[39] formally indicated that they shared the Sahrawi parents' concerns about their daughters' prolonged absences from the camps (Díaz 2003; González 2003b) and argued (along with the Polisario) that the Sahrawi families' decisions should be designated "private" matters to be discussed only by Sahrawis rather than by Spanish individuals and organizations. Such a request for "privacy" was directly related to the *solidarios'* recognition that "[the Sahrawi] people's right to self-determination is too serious a matter to be frivolized" and that

> [i]n the end, the least important question is what Aicha will do, whether she will study or not . . . ; what matters is that [this case] causes a lot of damage, not only to the Sahrawi people but to its women who have

37. That the term *Cristianos* should appear more than twenty times in Cazón's text on Aicha's "abduction," and in contexts that directly lead the reader to contrast the Spanish *qua* Christians with the Sahrawi *qua* Muslims, suggests that religious difference is a key player in this account.

38. While denouncing this *form* of xenophobia, however, Martín-Corrales argues that "almost all Spanish society" supports the Sahrawi cause through reinforcing an antagonistic paradigm in which the "noble, loyal, democratic and brave Sahrawi [is] clearly contrasted with the traitorous, fanatic, and despotic Moroccan" (2004, 45; my translation). In his view, the Sahrawi solidarity system is revealed as a key proponent of what he terms Maurophobia (the fear and/or hatred of Muslims in general and Moroccans in particular; ibid., 39).

39. The first two were the president and vice president of the Friends of the Sahara group at the time of Huria's "abduction." Suárez was representing CEAS at the time and was its vice president at the time of writing (see http://elistas.egrupos.net/lista/afaan /archivo/indice/1685/msg/1726/).

created camps from nothing and direct them as no one else could. (Tapias 2003; my translation)

Such responses to these crises demonstrated *solidarios'* commitment both to the Sahrawi's quest for self-determination, and to the central features of the official discourse. Hence, one *solidario* drew readers' attention to "an undeniable reality . . . : that the women of the Sahara have been the authors of this miracle . . . [creating] a survival structure that was first a seed for, and subsequently a real democratic State," asking:

> Who are we to criticize those who have exalted the meaning of the word Woman? [. . .] It's not for nothing that for 25 years they have been a model to be followed by many women who know about [them] . . . by their side, the situation of other women in the West, Spain included, pales in comparison. (Guijarro, 2003; my translation)

Nonetheless, despite many (if not most) *solidarios'* commitment to the Sahrawi cause and the official discourse, the power of the interconnected representations of gender and religion mobilized by the host families and the media was so great that innumerable individuals and groups threatened disengagement from, and even a rejection of, the Sahrawi cause in order to obtain the girls' "liberty." This concurrently indicates the leverage that granting or withdrawing humanitarian and political support may have over recipient populations.

Politicians, journalists, NGOs, and the Spanish host families all utilized their public statements to inform the Polisario/SADR of the serious political and humanitarian damage that the Sahrawi camps could face by losing the Spanish public's support. Hence, a small number of Spanish solidarity groups, including the Riojan Community's Friendship Group, either explicitly or implicitly menaced the Polisario/SADR that, unless each of the girls was allowed to return to "their Spanish family," they would stop campaigning for the cause:

> You must consider, obviously, that these incidents can affect future solidarity relations of a whole Autonomous Community like that of La Rioja with The Sahara. The news about the girls' retention has become a matter of public opinion . . . And, sadly, such disheartening news spreads

quickly and ends up affecting everybody, even their perception of the causes and their desire to collaborate with them.[40]

Such implicit and explicit threats were ultimately highly effective in "resolving" these cases.

Before the extent of Spanish public support for Aicha's "liberation" had become clear, the Polisario's representative in Spain at the time (Brahim Gali) officially indicated that the Polisario would not become involved in Aicha's case, since it was "a very personal problem, between families" (quoted in Peregil 2002; my translation). He argued that, "if more silent methods had been used, this case could have been resolved" (ibid.) and reiterated *solidarios'* claims that these girls' cases were "private" rather than "political" matters. A later communication from the Sahrawi Delegation to Castilla-León indicated that "the Saharawi authorities never become implicated between Saharawi families and the host families given that they do not support temporary adoptions," conceding that "in the case of Aicha . . . the Saharawi authorities are making an effort to convince Aicha's parents, but they do not guarantee anything given the sensitive nature of the case in Saharawi society" (2002; my translation). Despite the Polisario/SADR's initial reluctance to intervene in such "private" and "family" matters, and despite recognizing the "sensitive nature of the case in Sahrawi society," the Polisario/SADR eventually recognized that these Sahrawi families' decisions and acts in reality had the potential to destabilize too important a network. The Polisario/SADR therefore ultimately succumbed to the pressure applied by Spanish civil and political organizations and "negotiated" the girls' "release" from their biological parents and their "return" to Spain (see Fiddian 2006a, 2010b, 2013).

Through this brief case study I have illustrated some of the multiple tensions that exist between certain members of Spanish civil society, dedicated Spanish *solidarios*, different groups of Sahrawi refugees (including the girls and their families), and the Polisario/SADR. A delicate balance is constantly being negotiated between Sahrawis who recognize their

40. Letter to the SADR Ministry of Public Health in April 2001. Accessed at http://es .geocities.com/aichaembarek2/otroscasos/Maribel_Carta1.gif on 01/11/2005; my translation.

dependence upon Spanish humanitarian aid and political support and yet fear that the cohesion and continuity of their families and camps may be at threat due to this dependence. Although Wurud adamantly concludes that "[a]ll of the solidarity offered by all of [the host families in Spain] is not worth the risk of even one of our children being kidnapped [by delinquent *solidarios*],"[41] the Polisario's stance was ultimately directly influenced by Spanish pressure and at odds with local preferences.[42]

These girls' experiences continue to have far-reaching consequences in the camps. Aicha's has by far been the most high-profile case in both Spain and the camps, marking a significant shift in Spanish-Sahrawi relations on multiple levels. During my fieldwork there in 2007, several interviewees made reference to "Aicha," demonstrating the extent to which her name has come to symbolize certain dilemmas and crises in the camps. A Sahrawi man working for an Italian NGO in the 27 February Camp lamented that, "since Aicha," fewer parents are allowing their daughters to study abroad (May 2007). Sahrawi parents' fears that their daughters might stay in Spain rather than return to the camps have been further heightened by an increasing number of Spanish families physically hiding "their" Sahrawi children and refusing to allow them to return to the camps (Europa Press 2008; Jiménez 2008). Simultaneously, fewer Spanish families reportedly offered to host Sahrawi children in 2002 due to "the Aicha effect," with seventy children finding they had no expectant host parents when their plane landed in Castilla-León that year (Rivero 2002).

Crucially, I argue that this case study substantiates that Sahrawi gender relations have become emblematic of the justifiability of "the cause," given that so many Spaniards threatened to withdraw multifaceted and

---

41. Regarding Africa-West relations, Nzenza concludes that "the solidarity we are getting from our sisters in the West may be silencing us, and notwithstanding that it is well-intentioned, it may be a form of cultural imperialism" (1997, 222; also Armstrong and Bennett 2002, esp. 193).

42. In communications with HRW, the SADR indicated that "some Spanish families are profiteering from the tragic situations of Sahrawis to seize some children" (SADR cited in 2008, 184). Although beyond the scope of this chapter, both the NUSW's and UNHCR's silence surrounding these cases is worthy of further examination.

essential support unless the Polisario/SADR demonstrated their "respect for women's rights" by "liberating" these girls. The future of "the cause" therefore depends upon the careful protection, and projection, of idealized notions of Sahrawi women's position in the camps and abroad to ensure the Spanish audience's support. This concurrently exemplifies not only the precarious balance and the power play that may exist between solidarity groups, aid providers, and their recipients but also the fragile nature of the solidarity network currently in place.

Indeed, the public outrage prompted by these crises also clearly demonstrates why the Polisario/SADR has consistently distanced the Sahrawi Self from Other Muslim Arab women. Officials' awareness that many members of their Western audience share an Orientalist outlook both provides the foundation for—and the apparent necessity of—the Polisario/SADR mobilizing images of Sahrawi women to demonstrate that the Sahrawi "nation" is similar to the Spanish Self and wholly separate from the MENA Other. The need to marginalize references to Islam and "oppressive Muslim practices" in the Sahrawi context is particularly significant in the case of a solidarity movement, not only offering solidarity in the abstract but doing so in highly tangible political and material ways.

Conclusion

The mainstream discourse vis-à-vis "free" and "secular" Sahrawi women is a key part of the Polisario/SADR's politics of survival. Given the Sahrawi refugee camps' dependence on externally provided aid, I believe that there is a survival-based apprehension of potentially alienating aid providers. As such, the conditional solidarity that I argue maintains the camps has led to a conditioning of representations of life there.

On one level, this fear of losing Western support is expressed through an official alignment and reproduction of those subject matters that might ensure the continued support of key solidarity networks. The particular terms mobilized to elicit support from Western observers create "bright bonds" with solidarity providers, highlighting similarities through notions of "sisterhood" and a shared dedication to key values such as "secularism" and "gender equality." On another level, this has led the Polisario/SADR to officially distance the Sahrawi "Self" from identifiers, dynamics, practices, and beliefs that could potentially jeopardize the provision of humanitarian and political support. Rather than objecting to and rejecting Orientalist gendered stereotypes, the Polisario/SADR and the NUSW have thus recognized the characteristics that the Western audience negatively associates with Islam and the Arab world and has in effect reversed them in their descriptions of Sahrawi women as freer than Other Muslim Arab women. In the process, the Polisario/SADR has misrepresented the priorities of individuals and families in the camps, as discussed with reference to the continued importance of Islam in the camps, and the tension that characterizes the Sahrawi refugees' dependence upon externally provided aid.

Through different stages of repetition and inscription, the official representation has become an "archive of knowledge" accepted and reproduced by both the Polisario/SADR and the West alike. This core subsequently appears to re/create, rather than challenge, what Abu-Lughod refers to as the West's assumptions of the "incompatibility of Islam with women's rights" (2001, 108). In this manner, the Polisario/SADR's representations not only reproduce images of Arab/Muslim women as perpetual victims (thereby revictimizing them), but simultaneously solidify and recreate Eurocentric systems of knowledge rather than critically engaging with, challenging, and enriching contemporary debates about Islam, gender, and nation.[43]

Without becoming exponents of what Pechey (discussing Bakhtin) describes as "self-sufficient" national cultures that do "not (know) their otherness to others" (1989, 43), the Polisario/SADR has developed this discursive strategy precisely because they *are* aware of the dangers that would arise if "their otherness" were indeed "known" by their own "Others," in this instance the West. A case study of Spanish public and media responses to the "abductions" of Aicha, Fatimetu, and Huria has revealed the dangers that may arise when boundaries are strategically brightened and solidified through reference to gendered and religious difference. Ultimately, the terms and images invoked to mobilize public support for

---

43. See Ahmed 1992; Badran 1995; edited collections by Hadad and Esposito 1998 and Kandiyoti 1991; Abu-Lughod 2001, esp. 108.

these girls' "liberation" demonstrate both the continued power of Orientalist frameworks within certain sections of Spanish civil society and the reasons why the Polisario/SADR has systematically distanced the Sahrawi Self from Other Arab Muslim women.

In the following chapter, I draw together the preceding discussions to examine the impacts and implications of having re/created the camps in the Western imagination as "a twentieth-century democratic nation" characterized by "women's equality" (Harrell-Bond 1999, 156). As explored above, defining the camps via a range of "ideal" characteristics including "gender equality" and "female empowerment" in order to create "bright bonds" with *solidarios* has only been feasible through various processes of silencing and marginalization. While the official discourse concerning Sahrawi women may be part of the Polisario/SADR's politics of survival, I will now focus on the ways in which this discursive strategy has influenced policy development and implementation in the camps, asking whose voices, needs, and rights have been highlighted and whose marginalized and to what effect.

— 5 —

Discursive Silences,
"Ideal Women," and Directing Aid

THE OFFICIAL PRIORITIZATION and centralization of idealized and homogenized "Sahrawi women" has been detrimental to those Sahrawi refugees who are marginalized, silenced, and displaced by the Polisario/ SADR, civil-society solidarity networks, and/or other international actors. In the first part of this chapter, I submit that despite the multiplicity of projects in the camps, most residents' voices and needs have been marginalized through this discursive idealization and homogenization. I then identify three main groups of refugees who have been rendered invisible, or absent(ed) by the official discourse and have in turn been marginalized by Western-sponsored projects. These three groups are "nonideal" Sahrawi women who do not embody the characteristics prioritized by the Polisario/SADR, refugee girls, and young and adult refugee men.[1]

The principal force of my argument is that the official discourse has "created" or "constituted" ideal and idealized "Sahrawi women" by obscuring the existence of social groups that could undermine such a representation. The term *repress-entation* of gender may therefore be apt, since the portrayal of life in the camps to Western audiences is a priori dependent upon the *repression* of differences and discrepancies among

---

1. There are, of course, other groups of Sahrawi who are marginalized and excluded through this representational system, including Sahrawi with diverse disability statuses and gender nonconforming individuals.

and between social groups. The international dynamics of the conditional solidarity network encourage this level of repress-entation through prioritizing and rewarding specific characteristics (democracy and gender equality), while simultaneously threatening to withdraw support if these characteristics are challenged.

Prioritizing "ideal women" is the result of a particular gynocentric international public relations strategy developed as part of the Polisario/SADR's "politics of survival." In addition, however, both the Polisario/SADR and certain non-Sahrawi audiences have designated a number of "issues" as "private" and therefore beyond the scope of Western attention. The policy implications of an emphasis on "Sahrawi women" and what I conceptualize as Western individuals' and agencies' self-censorship regarding cases that unsettle the key foundations of the official discourse will therefore be addressed in the final part of the chapter with particular reference to the silenced reality of violence against women (VAW) in the camps.

As a brief methodological note, it is important to recognize that, just as the majority of my Sahrawi interviewees were ultimately unable (or unwilling) to critique the official discourse vis-à-vis Sahrawi women, so too did they as a whole refrain from openly critiquing the solidarity/NGO system in place in the camps. This reflects a number of the limitations and difficulties faced while conducting research on and in the Sahrawi refugee camps and the strength with which individuals adhere to the official discourse during their interactions with non-Sahrawi observers. Hence, of over 100 interviews conducted in a range of field sites, in the camps only one Cuban-educated teacher, two SADR ministerial aides educated in Algeria and Cuba respectively, and two Cuban-educated technicians working in Rabouni, in addition to two interviewees in Syria and six in Cuba, indicated a number of failures that they identified as underlying the ways in which development and humanitarian projects are currently designed and managed in the camps. I complement these interviews with those conducted by the SARC project across the refugee camps, as well as drawing upon Wurud's blog as a means of further substantiating my research findings. I have evaluated all of these interviews and extracts in light of my field observations of daily life and NGO-Sahrawi interactions in the 27 February Camp. The critiques developed in the following pages therefore primarily reflect my analysis of the situation in the 27 February Camp, and some of my conclusions may not be entirely relevant to the other major camps (Aaiun, Ausserd, Dakhla, and Smara).

The Official Discourse and "Directing Aid"

A main criticism underlying the provision of humanitarian and development aid in refugee and nonrefugee contexts has been that a large proportion of these have tended to be based on (Western) aid providers' understandings and assumptions of beneficiaries' needs (e.g., Escobar 1995; Conyers and Mellors 2005; Lockwood 2005). It has been widely recognized that local-level "representatives may not be representative" (Jacobsen and Landau 2003, 12) and simultaneously that aid agencies habitually prioritize certain groups while others' needs remain "invisible" (El-Bushra and Piza-López 1993, 191; also Escobar 1995, 212). The urgency of developing "a planning framework based on assessment of a broad range of community and individual needs" and enabling "invisible" people to be consulted and actively engaged in the planning process has therefore been promoted (El-Bushra and Piza-López 1993, 191), including by UNHCR in its Age, Gender, and Diversity Mainstreaming framework (also see Fiddian-Qasmiyeh 2014b). The primary purpose of this chapter is not to "find" these "invisible" or marginalized groups. Rather, my research suggests that instead of responding to a variety of problems faced by different social groups in the camps, a core selection of projects are paralleled, mirrored, reproduced, and recycled with the same target groups being the "beneficiaries" of such initiatives. Such beneficiaries, I propose, are rarely "the most vulnerable" inhabitants (to use the UNHCR's terminology) but more exactly the key protagonists of the official discourse: idealized "Sahrawi women."

Harrell-Bond's claim is noteworthy in this respect:

> It is ironical, but the organization which these refugees have developed is so efficient that a casual observer might go away without appreciating the enormous unmet needs which exist. (Harrell-Bond 1981b, 3)

It is arguably not simply the self-sufficient "organization" of the camps lauded by "casual" and professional observers that has led to this failure to identify and address these unfulfilled needs. Rather, the re/creation of the Sahrawi refugee camps *as* the *ideal* refugee camps and the central images of female participation and gender equality presented through the official discourse may have made such a situation possible and perhaps even necessary on certain levels. The official discourse in this way has directly influenced the development and maintenance of such a situation, with the Polisario/SADR "directing aid" in a very specific fashion. Such a connection highlights the tangible effects that this discourse has had on individuals, families, and groups living in the camps and the need for external observers to critically question the legitimacy and potential dangers of such a discourse.

During a camp-based interview, a Cuban-educated teacher expanded on the nature of these needs, indicating that "lots of aid is distributed but it doesn't reach the people who need it the most, to the people who it should reach first" (27 February Camp, April 2007). He concluded:

> The NGOs should go to see the families who hardly have anything, they should look more closely, try to find *the marginalized people,* try to help them *directly* . . . [there are] people *who don't participate, who are marginalized,* who are *in the margins politically* . . . It's important to help them. (my emphasis)

The observations that I draw upon below support this broad claim that many Sahrawi refugees' needs remain unmet despite the myriad of projects in the camps. I argue that this reflects the reality that NGO workers tend to respond to requests presented by the Polisario/SADR and leads us to inquire which residents are marginalized and do not receive aid directly. It is also necessary to engage critically with the mechanisms through which these "nonideal" individuals and groups have been excluded.

Projects for "Ideal/ized Women" in "Ideal/ized Camps"

Sahrawi refugee women are understandably proud of their contribution to the creation and maintenance of the camps, with one 44-year-old female SARC interviewee reflecting:

> We feel that women contributed here a great deal and participated in the
> activities of the camp. They administer the camps and have their own
> organization that promotes their own affairs. They feel free, and no man
> can dictate to her what he wishes.[2]

However, by discursively "creating" the refugee camps as "ideal" feminized, female-centered, and female-oriented spaces, the official discourse
has established the need for specific projects to attend to the camps' "constituted" inhabitants. Through "imagining" the beneficiaries of projects
as static and homogenized "empowered and active women," projects have
often been both poorly designed and implemented. Rather than asking
which social groups are excluded, marginalized, and sidelined, since the
explosion of projects that followed the ceasefire in 1991, initiatives oriented toward "Sahrawi women" predominate in the camps, including
those documented in Chapter 2. While these projects are invaluable for
certain refugees, however, several levels of constitutive marginalization
result from the system that has led to their creation.

In a relatively rare critical reflection on the mechanisms by which
projects are run in the camps, a teacher based in the 27 February Camp
lamented:

> Generally, the projects that arrive come directly to a specific institution
> and it's almost always the same people who run that institution who
> benefit from the project. The people who work to support us here should
> look a bit, and not continue always with the same institution, they should
> approach other people who are more in need, to give them more oppor-
> tunities to work. (May 2007)

Indeed, institutional partnerships and sponsorship abound in the camps,
with the NUSW in particular being seen as an "ideal" partner, that even
the UNHCR EXCOM describes as a role model that the UN agency is

---

2. It is important to note that this interviewee's father works at the SADR Ministry
of Defense and may therefore be directly associated with the camp's political structures.

"learning from" (2001, para. 26).[3] During our interviews in the camps, many Spanish NGO workers informed me that they were "responding to Sahrawi requests" (i.e., Polisario/SADR and/or NUSW) for specific projects through these institutions. They explained that by implementing projects through existing institutions such as the NUSW, not only would "local participation" and "local ownership" characterize these projects but also the institutions themselves would benefit from investments in their administrative structures and buildings, access to local and international transportation, and further funds. In fact, institutional strengthening is an explicit goal behind funds channeled through the NUSW (NUSW document on file with author), and many Spanish NGO workers believed that this should be a priority in any development/humanitarian project.

Although participatory intervention and "local ownership" is promoted by a wide range of institutions and individual researchers (World Bank 1994; Kumar 2001b, 220–224; Chopra and Hohe 2004; Conyers and Mellors 2005), the notion that "local solutions" are favorable has been forcefully critiqued through a recognition that local elites habitually dominate such processes and reproduce, "reinforce[,] and entrench power relations rather than transform them" (Merry 1992, 171; also see Khadiagala 2001, 58ff; and Mosse 2001, 16–35). With specific reference to the difficulties of addressing "local" women's needs, Kandiyoti stresses that:

> [t]he problem everywhere seems to revolve around how donor-led efforts
> and projects relate to local women's groups and movements and whether
> they only select out a narrow range of clients who speak [the donors'
> language] and know how to write proposals and reports. (Hammami
> 2005, 1352)

More broadly, Abu-Lughod indicates that there is a "special difficulty of recuperating the voices of any but middle-class and elite women" (1998b, 24). The following criticisms of the current system were offered by my

---

3. For a critique of the identification of the NUSW as "the ideal partner" for "gender mainstreaming," see Fiddian-Qasmiyeh (2010d), which expands upon a selection of the discussions presented in the following pages, and Fiddian-Qasmiyeh (2014b).

Sahrawi interviewees and are supported by my observations in the 27 February Camp.

First, while recognizing that the NUSW runs many successful projects, a male SADR ministerial aide stressed that "only a section of our society works there . . . they have good intentions, but not all women are involved. That's a major problem" (Rabouni, May 2007). That the NUSW is not representative of most Sahrawi women's priorities was more vehemently denounced by blogger Wurud:

> These women do not bear the truth, they are simply political instruments and emissaries of the power structure [i.e., the Polisario/SADR] that is not on women's side. They are part of that elite which has even monopolized "representing us."

My field observations confirm that even in officially designated "democratic" and "participatory" spaces in the so-called Women's Camp, only a small core of women directly associated with the NUSW tend to participate. Hence, although the pre-Conference *nadwa* held in the 27 February Camp in 2007 was intended to be a space for "all" of the camp's women to debate and elect their representatives for the Fifth NUSW Conference, I calculate that fewer than 100 women attended on the first day and only around sixty voted on Election Day. With the 27 February Camp's total population amounting to approximately 2,000 to 2,500, it is noteworthy that a significant proportion of these attendees were women undertaking courses at the National Women's School, including the CRIC- and NUSW-run computer and driving classes. Another contingent included women working for the SADR in Rabouni, who were eligible to elect a separate representative. Although HRW notes that participants in such events are able to openly criticize those in power and raise concerns about critical politico-administrative issues (2008, 134), a large section of the women present were already directly associated with official organizations at the time of the *nadwa*.

A second criticism offered by the above-quoted ministerial aide is that the members of official organizations such as the NUSW benefit unequally from externally provided investments. For instance, he stated, these officials attend the language or computing courses created, receive access to resources and social capital networks, or have the opportunity to travel abroad.[4] Indeed, upon my arrival to the 27 February Camp in 2007 I proposed offering English lessons for the camp's women and asked the NUSW if I could hold classes in their headquarters. Although I had asked the NUSW to extend the invitation to women from around the camp, only women employed by the NUSW finally attended. An additional example is that after the Fifth NUSW Conference many Spanish delegates left "donation packs" (including toiletries and foodstuff) for distribution among the population: according to my observations at the time of distribution, few of these packs were shared with non-NUSW affiliates.

An additional benefit highlighted by the ministerial aide is that individuals associated with the SADR or NUSW tend to be employed simultaneously by projects funded by external investors. This points to the highly visible camp phenomenon of *pluriempleo* (the term is used in Spanish in the camps), whereby the same individual is concurrently employed by several NGOs and/or SADR agencies, including the NUSW. These individuals accumulate considerable financial and social capital in the process, while socioeconomic differentiation continues to increase and overall unemployment remains high.[5] The system of *pluriempleo* in turn lays, in at least two ways, the foundation for (primarily male) refugees to emigrate to Spain. First, connections with Spanish individuals and organizations enable multiply employed guides and interpreters to obtain invitation letters that thus facilitate their being granted a Spanish visa to leave the camps; at that point they leave not one but two or three jobs behind upon their departure. This is recognized as a key phenomenon affecting the continuity of projects in the camps (interview with Spanish doctor, 27 February Camp, March 2007; document on file with author).

4. Reflecting upon the NUSW representatives' "trips" to Spain, Wurud denounces that "yet again, they have been put up at luxury hotels as 'tradition demands.'"

5. A 41-year-old woman reflected on the difficulties of surviving on rations alone: "we have just enough to keep us alive. We live humbly, we have no source of income except for the international humanitarian organizations, and it is not enough . . . we do not have the ability to build rooms like other people . . . Our tent is ragged and very old. We have no money to buy clothes . . . [the children's shoes] are torn and old" (SARC interviewee).

Second, individuals who are neither employed by official Sahrawi organizations nor by NGO projects find that they are unable to improve their family's living conditions, leading many of them to emigrate in order to send remittances from Spain. I return to this point below.

Related to *pluriempleo* and the tendency for benefits to be made available to the same groups of people through the same "partner" institutions, a parallel between the colonial and refugee periods can be identified: during both of these eras, Spaniards' "help" has been accepted by some, who have taken jobs with NGOs/Spanish institutions and have received their pay, while others have continued to be marginalized and separated from these material benefits. The enduring legacy of the colonial system, which prioritized certain men and women by virtue of their sociopolitical and tribal backgrounds, appears to be clear in the camps in numerous fashions. Hence, female members of elite groups were educated in the Spanish Sahara and many have gone on to become key figures in the camps. At least two of the NUSW's former secretaries general (Guesmula Ebbi and Kheltoum Khayat) in the 1980s and early 1990s fall into this category (Martín 1985; Mardones 1986).[6]

Conversely, while large numbers of refugee girls and women have been educated abroad since the camps were created, and the majority have returned to live and often work in the camps,[7] it has nonetheless continued to be the older elite women who have remained most powerful in the camps by virtue of a combination of their family background, educational background, and generation. My observations indicate that, even though Cuban-educated women are well-trained professionals, their involvement in the 2007 NUSW Conference was as a whole restricted to "accompanying" Spanish and other "visitors" to the camps rather than

6. Both of these women eventually left the camps and "defected" (in the Polisario's eyes) to Morocco in the early 1990s.

7. However, one unemployed 32-year-old women who has a Cuban university degree in educational psychology indicated that "those of us with degrees and diplomas are suffering because there are no jobs, no employment . . . [M]any of our experts, those with specialties, have no jobs, there are no places for them. Only a few people with [degrees] are working" (SARC interviewee).

allowing or actively encouraging them to become involved in the polit-ico-administrative systems in place in the camps. Wurud argues that the relative marginalization of these women has taken root, because "[t]he women who studied in Cuba have been categorized by Sahrawi public opinion as 'weapons of mass destruction' and the leaders have assented. They are blamed for having brought change, the most feared word in Arab societies." While I agree with Wurud that these young women have been categorized as "bad girls" following their return from Cuba, I argue elsewhere that sidelining educated young Sahrawi women from positions of authority could also be perceived as a means of reducing the risk of these younger, educated graduates challenging the NUSW "veterans" and thus the status quo (see Fiddian-Qasmiyeh 2009, 2012a). Indeed, the vis-ibility and audibility of these older women is clear from an examination of the histories of the key members of the NUSW and SADR and was commented upon in passing by a number of Sahrawi interviewees in the camps who were particularly disappointed by the "recycling" (reciclaje) of candidates, representatives and ministers following elections in 2007.

A further major limitation of these NGO projects is that, since their "beneficiaries" usually include women who are already involved in par-ticular institutions, the "image" of Sahrawi women as empowered and socially, politically, and economically active is reproduced, without recog-nizing the existence of other women who are marginalized or feel unable to participate in projects. There are three main issues at hand in this case: (1) by running projects through a particular institution, their members are "always already" prioritized; (2) by failing to have access to "other" women, these marginalized women and their corresponding needs are not identified; and (3) through recognizing that these projects do not pro-vide for their needs, many women decide not to participate.

Two key dynamics support my conclusion that many women are excluded from NGO projects and the spaces where most of these are implemented. My interviews with a selection of refugee women not asso-ciated with the Polisario/SADR or NUSW revealed that not all women frequent what is colloquially known as al-gaws, which is the archway marking the entrance to the National Women's School precinct, where the school's and camp's administration and the majority of NGO projects

12. Photograph of Sahrawi refugee women demonstrating by the *gaws* (gateway) to the confines of the 27 February National Women's School on the occasion of a United Nations visit to the 27 February Camp (southwest Algeria, March 2007).

are based (see Figure 12). These interviewees included two young women whom I had first met (separately) during my trips to the camps in 2002 and 2003 and three women (a mother and two daughters) who were living in a female-headed household on the outskirts of the camp at the time of our interview in 2007.

While three of these women had attended classes in the National Women's School when they were younger, once they had children they were no longer able, or willing, to walk the five- or ten-minute distance to the precinct, preferring (or needing) to stay at home.[8] As indicated by

8. A 40-year-old woman, for instance, indicated that after marrying, she went to the 27 February School and remained there until she became pregnant. At this stage she left the school and moved to live with her mother in Rabouni.

one 41-year-old female SARC interviewee, women often find it "difficult to take care of the children and continue working while [the children are] not yet in school . . . I could not find someone to take care of [my children] in my absence." Despite the existence of a small number of day care centers and kindergartens in the camps, women with small children may still find it impossible to leave home since alternative child-care arrangements cannot be found.

Simultaneously, however, those women who are responsible for their own children, as well as those of their relatives find that their obligations leave them unable to participate in NUSW or NGO projects and events. One of my interviewees was looking after her two children (aged one and six) as well as three of her cousins (aged between five and 16) while her husband worked abroad and her parents and other siblings lived in the *bādiya*:

> After I married, I trained as a secretary and worked in the *idāra*. When I became pregnant, I stopped working, and stayed at home. Now, I am always at home with my children and with my [younger] cousins. My aunt helps me make breakfast sometimes, but normally I am by myself with the children. (27 February Camp, April 2007)

On at least three instances, I saw these women's older female relatives (aunts or mothers) attending political meetings (*mu'tamarāt* and *nadawāt*) held by the NUSW in the *gaws*, while the younger women cared for the family's children. Equally, during the 2002 and 2007 NUSW Conferences, women who hosted non-Sahrawi guests in their *khiyām* were unable to participate in the conference or related activities due to their responsibilities. This reflects the continued reliance of politically active women on other women's and girls' labor, either to care for their children, complete domestic tasks, or host foreign guests and potential donors. As is common among nomadic societies, this in turn reflects the significance of generation and life-cycle in certain forms of female participation outside of the *khayma*. These examples also thus demonstrate that specific groups of refugee women are able to participate in NUSW events and NGO projects, while others are not.

A second related point is the recognition that space is gendered in the camps (as elsewhere), and that access to certain spaces is associated with female activism and participation. In the 27 February Camp, these spaces are primarily the Women's School, the NUSW headquarters, and the sewing/weaving workshop run by the NUSW and CRIC. My fieldwork in the camps between 2002 and 2007 suggests that many individuals and families have decided to minimize their contact with specific spaces and places. In addition to maintaining a distance from the *gaws*, a comparison of the camp's structure and distribution in 2002 and 2007 suggests that new arrivals to the 27 February Camp following the 2006 floods (or those in search of permanent electricity supplies) are pitching their tents away from the politico-administrative core of the camp.

Hence, the female head (in her early 50s) of a family that arrived in 27 February Camp in 2006 reflected:

> Before, we lived our lives and made our decisions. After the rains, we rebuilt our *khayma* here because it is closer to the hospital and there is electricity. My grandchildren walk to school by themselves. The school is good for the children, but I stay at home with my daughters. We do not need to go to the *gaws*. My cousins helped us mend our tent, and we will live our lives here [in this tent] and make our decisions here. (April 2007; my translation from Arabic)

The members of this and another recently arrived female-headed household suggested that their decision to live on the outskirts of the camp reflected their desire for more "independence." Given that houses are more closely located in 27 February Camp than in Dakhla, living away from the core of the camp could be a way of guaranteeing a greater distance from other tents (Figure 13) and hence a greater sense of privacy. Their comments, however, also suggested that they did not feel that they "needed" the projects and services run from the Women's School,[9] with none of these women having participated in any events organized by the NUSW since their arrival. Further, when I asked whether they had

9. Keenan documents an emerging trend for Tuareg women of the Kel Ahaggar (Algeria) to live "independently of men" in a nomadic milieu, in encampments inhabited solely by women and their children (2006, 934).

13. Distribution of tents in the 27 February Camp, with the highest density surrounding the administrative core of the camps (*left*) and new arrivals building their homes at a distance from both this core and other tents (*right*) (southwest Algeria).

sought permission to establish their tent in the 27 February Camp, as is officially required, they clearly stated that they had not and that the official administration could no longer decide where people should or should not live.

In other cases, individuals and families have left the camps permanently or semipermanently, preferring to live in the *bādiya* that, again, allows for greater independence from the core. One overall implication of the physical distance created between certain populations and the projects' physical nucleus is that those individuals who select out of either the NGO projects or the camp's politico-administrative system are thus absent(ed) from the camps. In this way, the camp's population, as perceived by visitors, is reinforced as inhabited by women who are empowered and active in a variety of ways, including through projects run by non-Sahrawis and Sahrawis alike.

"Where Are the Girls?"

As suggested above, one element of the official discourse's repressentation of "women" has been its failure to account for changes and differences in positions, responsibilities, and needs throughout different stages of different women's life cycles. The static and eternalized image of women repress-ented in the Polisario/SADR discourse neither defines the term "Sahrawi women" (thereby eliding the heterogeneity of the term) nor reflects on the processes by which "one becomes" a woman (de Beauvoir 1972, 267).[10] While I have explored some dynamics of girls' transition to womanhood and the importance of puberty in determining their access to particular spaces in preceding chapters, girls are in effect invisible in the official discourse projected to the West and, concurrently, in projects designed for and implemented in the camps.

Nordstrom documents and denounces the tendency for representations of displaced peoples to "focus almost entirely on adults" while failing to ask "where are the girls?" (1999). Indeed, prevailing accounts of, and projects for, conflict-affected "children" systematically fail to ask whether the term *children* really [means] "girls and boys, or just boys?" (Nordstrom 1999, 75), and girls are therefore frequently rendered invisible or muted. As a result of a "gender-blind" approach to childhood in this context, while there are numerous projects "for children" in the camps and beyond, none of those established in 27 February Camp recognize the specific needs and experiences of girls therein.[11] Few academic studies or NGO projects have focused on documenting or addressing girls' experiences of growing up in the camps or in the Vacaciones en Paz hosting program; the major exceptions are Chatty, Fiddian-Qasmiyeh, and Crivello (2010), Crivello and Fiddian-Qasmiyeh (2010) and Fiddian-Qasmiyeh (2009).

One result is that, although a number of "women's" spaces exist in the camp, and boys and young men have access to "public areas," including a space immediately outside of the *gaws* where they regularly play football, there is a distinct absence of facilities, services, or spaces for girls outside of their *khiyām*. My observations are supported by the comments

10. Regarding the distinction between a "girl-child" and a "woman," Elmadmad stresses that "there is no internationally agreed upon definition of a child, and no international consensus on the age of majority or on when maturity is reached" (1999, 262).

11. UNICEF has remained largely invisible in the camps, running its operations from Algiers and Tindouf.

of a 17-year-old girl from 27 February Camp, who stressed in her SARC interview:

> Life is very difficult in the camps, and girls have very limited places to meet or play. We meet with each other in our homes, in my room for example, and discuss school, the future, and politics.

Further, a 54-year-old woman indicated that the international humanitarian system in the camps has failed to address the specific needs of girls, stating that "we need programs that provide skills for girls and enable them to remain near their families" (SARC interview).

Girls' overarching invisibility in the Polisario/SADR discourse, combined with a more general academic and NGO tendency to focus on Sahrawi refugees as active adults there, has impacted upon the development and implementation of projects in the camps. It has led, for instance, to a distinct failure to document and examine the reasons behind girls' early withdrawal from school, despite this being a broader trend throughout refugee and nonrefugee contexts (Glick and Sahn, 1999). Given UNHCR's broader recognition that refugee girls tend to be withdrawn from school earlier than boys, this organization does document the number of schools having "structured girl retention initiatives" and the number requiring such programs. By the end of 2003, UNHCR recognized that no schools in Aaiun camp had such initiatives, and that between 79% and 82% of schools in Ausserd, Smara, and Dakhla *required* these (2004a, 12). No information was provided regarding 27 February Camp or secondary level institutions. With an increasing population and a dramatic decrease in the number of secondary level school places following recent floods, female enrolment rates across the camps will inevitably have suffered.[12]

---

12. Many teenaged boys are also withdrawn from school before completing their studies: their absence from school is particularly noticeable due to their greater visibility in public places than girls. If eldest daughters complete domestic tasks, boys primarily leave school in order to work in the emerging camp economy, either out of choice or as a family livelihood strategy. In one case, the parents of a 12-year-old boy informed me that their son was not attending school in 2007 due to a lack of places in the 12 October School and in Algerian schools. Since his father was a member of the Polisario and his mother was

My research suggests that Sahrawi girls are withdrawn from school at a considerably earlier age than are boys (also see Fiddian 2002). Eldest daughters appear to be the most readily identifiable group of children and youth who have been withdrawn to help their mothers with younger siblings, household tasks, and looking after infirm relatives (on eldest daughters' responsibilities, see Crivello, Fiddian, and Chatty 2005, 13). Interviews conducted by the SARC team highlight that this occurred throughout the 1980s and mirror my own findings regarding the relative frequency with which this continues to occur in the camps today. Hence, two mothers reported that they had asked their eldest daughters to "drop out of school" to help them at home, and six eldest daughters explicitly indicated that they had left school either to care for infirm parents or to help with their younger siblings. One young woman based in the 27 February Camp and interviewed by the SARC project reflected:

> I did grade five and six in 9 June School, and the seventh in 12 October School. I then went to Algeria where I studied until grade nine and passed. However, I dropped out because my mother needed me. She has [young] children and there is no one to help her. Since I returned to the house, I have taken on my mother's work, whether she is here or not. I help the children to bathe, I take care of the sheep, I fold the blankets, clean the house, go to the administration, and bring things that are needed for the house, such as gas, and other household items.

Girls' and women's approaches to this practice vary, with one eldest daughter in her early 20s informing me in May 2007 that she had voluntarily decided to leave school during her mother's last pregnancy and that she had eventually been able to pursue further education classes at the 27

---

working with an NGO in 27 February Camp, there was no pressure for this boy to find a job, and he was expecting to attend an Algerian school in the new school year. Although further research is required, it may be conjectured that boys from poorer, non-elite families will be permanently withdrawn from school earlier than elite boys. This will in turn influence these non-elite boys' opportunities for further education abroad and their subsequent employment possibilities, just as girls' possibilities have long been limited in this way.

February National Women's School. However, the eldest daughter who had been unable to participate in the *riḥla* (activity trip) in Easter 2007 was resentful that she had been withdrawn from school at age 11 to help her mother with her younger siblings[13] and wanted desperately to return to her studies in Algeria.[14] Further research is therefore required to establish how many girls of different ages and backgrounds are not attending school both inside and outside of the camps and how they and their families perceive the motivations for and longer-term implications of the early withdrawal of girls.[15]

In addition to the early withdrawal of girls from school, a brief examination of the way in which the aforementioned activity trip was designed and how children were "recruited" in the camp reveals not only the difficulties that girls may face in accessing projects but also the ways in that Spanish NGO leaders conceptualize the population they are attempting to "help" and whose priorities and needs are addressed in camp-based projects.

As documented earlier, having arranged to take a group of boys and girls to the nearby sand dunes for a number of days, the members of a Spanish NGO expressed surprise and anger when the children's mothers refused to allow their daughters to participate. As I suggested to the Spanish organizers that they ask female, rather than male, Sahrawi "instructors" (*monitores*) to speak with the mothers about the project, the former replied that the mothers were simply "ignorant" (*"son unas ignorantes"*) not to allow their daughters to "have fun" in the dunes. They indicated that

13. This girl's withdrawal became particularly urgent when her father moved to Spain for medical treatment.

14. This was also a concern expressed by a 17-year-old SARC interviewee.

15. Furthermore, a 14-year-old girl from 27 February Camp noted: "Girls also have problems pursuing their education. This depends on the family. Some of the families do not like to see their girls go abroad. Some prefer that the boys study more than the girls" (SARC interview). Wurud more specifically claims that "women's situation since the ceasefire is going backward in all respects. The tiny number of female university students, for example, who have been trained since then is a representative indicator of this fact." On the reduction of girls and women studying in Cuba, see Fiddian-Qasmiyeh (2009).

they were particularly disappointed to encounter such resistance in the 27 February Camp, since it is the home of the National Women's School and the NUSW Headquarters. One of the organizers angrily stated:

> I can't believe this is happening here. We've been running projects around the camps for five years and we've never encountered such ignorance. And this is meant to be the Women's Camp? They are just ignorant.

The NGO stringently declared that, unless the girls were allowed to participate, they would never run a project in that camp again. They demanded that a group of girls be ready for collection in the morning outside of the *gaws* and sent home all the children who were ready. This is another clear example of the conditional nature of the provision of aid and implementation of projects in the camps.

The designation of the mothers as "ignorant," contrasted with the NGO workers' emphasis on the 27 February Camp as a supposedly female-centered and female-powered camp is notable and also reflects their preference and identification with the latter and rejection of the former. "Sahrawi women," in these Spaniards' imagination, should have unequivocally accepted the project without questioning its organizers and should have encouraged their daughters to participate in the outing. Any understanding of Sahrawi mothers' concerns regarding their daughters' contact with unrelated Sahrawi boys and men without proper supervision,[16] especially when their daughters were approaching puberty, was absent.[17]

---

16. If Sahrawi women's "spaces" in the camps are directly associated with their visibility in certain locations, the *riḥla* had the potential to make these girls temporarily "disappear" from the spaces that their parents considered to be appropriate and acceptable.

17. When girls and boys travel to Spain as part of hosting programs they habitually leave with the prospect of obtaining money and social capital for themselves and their families. While in the vicinity of the camps, however, parents may consider this separation from their children to be a futile investment with more threats than possible returns. In this approach to the situation, children can be perceived to be tokens vested with the potential for investment, while women are symbols of the modern nation and both individual and group political capacity.

Such a lack of awareness was evident when one mother allowed one of her younger daughters (aged eight) to participate once a responsible female guardian had been identified, while resolutely prohibiting her eldest daughter (aged 13) from doing so. With the author having accepted the mother's request to act as an intermediary with the Spanish NGO representative, the mother noted:

> I am alone with the children and I need to take my baby to the hospital. She [pointing to her eldest daughter] has to help me with the other children. Ask *her* [the Spanish NGO woman] where the girls will sleep . . . Will she be in the *khayma* with the girls? She will? *Tayeb*. Tell her that I will let my [younger] daughter go with her. Tell her that. [Pointing at the Spanish woman emphatically] *With her.* (my translation and emphasis)

The NGO representative was so happy to have increased her quota of girls that she failed to engage with any of the reasons why the eldest daughter was unable to participate in the project. The possibility of this, or future, projects addressing Sahrawi girls' and women's preferences and needs was also curtailed early on.

The discussions offered above and my observations of other project leaders in the 27 February Camp[18] prompt me to suggest that this NGO's priority was to implement its predesigned plan in the camps and for the Sahrawi to comply with their requirements with unequivocal gratitude. Indeed, returning to Harrell-Bond's designation of the Sahrawi as "good"

---

18. For instance, a group of artists based in a Spanish university arrived in the camps in April 2007 to undertake an "art project" there. Rather than designing a piece of artwork in collaboration with camp residents, this group arrived in the camps with the primary materials, a precise draft version of the final piece designed in Spain, and preexisting internal tensions that led to the Spanish "volunteers" fighting over which one of the original "team" members was in charge. Refugees were invited to collect scrap metal from the outskirts of the camp for the piece and to view the final products, but were not able to play a part in designing or making the final piece. It is not uncommon to find projects that have been designed in Spain being directly implemented in the camps without local involvement. On the three occasions that I visited the exhibition in the Cultural Center, foreign visitors to the camps appeared to be more interested in the postmodern artwork than local residents were.

refugees *because* of their reluctance to "complain" (as quoted in the Intro-duction), we must ask under what circumstances Western observers, including NGOs, *allow* Sahrawis to complain and reject certain interventions. This could thereby lead us to suggest that refugees' responses to the provision of aid may be "conditioned" by the recognition that resisting NGOs' priorities may lead to the withdrawal of projects.

However, just as the Polisario/SADR has developed an alternative to the script through "demonstrating" its self-sufficiency and independence to non-Sahrawi observers, these mothers were also determined to negoti-ate the terms of engagement with the NGO on the basis of their own norms and priorities regarding gendered roles and responsibilities. Their refusal to allow the Spanish women to simply "take" their daughters threatened to precipitate the vulnerability of the Spanish-Sahrawi cultural equation, just as the case of Aicha Embarek explored in the previous chapter chal-lenged both the veracity of the official discourse and the power dynamics underlying Spanish-Sahrawi solidary relations. While an official Sahrawi Self has been presented in the Polisario/SADR discourse, it is clear that many if not most of those who are still living in their *khiyām* have been excluded from a number of discursive, political, and policy realms. Their needs and rights are thus not being addressed by either the Polisario/ SADR or their solidary providers.

Displaced/Absented Men and Male Youth

Matsuoka and Sorensen stress that "[w]omen do not live in gender isolation, and their situations cannot be adequately analysed as if they were" (1999, 226). Nonetheless, this is precisely the way in that the Sah-rawi refugee camps have been habitually examined and imagined in mainstream analyses, reinforcing notions of female isolation within the camps. By focusing so intently on "demonstrating" to the Western audi-ence that Sahrawi women are "free" and "active" within the camps, the official discourse simultaneously re/produces and therefore constitutes the camps as inherently feminized spaces, or as Mundy sees it (2007, 290), as "de-masculinised" ones. While Mundy uses the latter term to refer to the physical absence of men and patriarchal hierarchies in the camps, the Polisario/SADR sponsored official discourse has in effect *absented* adult and youth males from common conceptualizations of the camp population. Where Sahrawi women are presented as having a "special place" in Sahrawi society—and indeed, as living in feminized and female-oriented camps—there is no space or place for most men in the individual camps themselves.[19]

A common understanding of the camps as "feminized space" is largely based on a continued acceptance of wartime demographics, during which time the majority of the population were indeed "womenandchildren."[20] Men's absence from the camps as discursive and geopolitical spaces has continued to be solidified by their frequent marginalization from the UN's and WFP's calculations of the number of refugees deserving food aid, who are broadly classified as vulnerable women, children, and the elderly (i.e., UNHCR 1999, 117, and 2000a, 135; WFP 2002). Since the end of armed conflict in the early 1990s, however, increasing numbers of Sahrawi men have "returned" to the camps, coinciding with the arrival of the first generation of graduates educated abroad; indeed, in 2000 and 2002 the WFP estimated that 40% of the camp population was male (WFP 2000 and 2002). Despite these demographic shifts, however, the official discourse and mainstream understandings of the camps continue to portray women as dominating the camps' sociopolitical structures.

Contrary to the mainstream image of female dominance in the camps, the Polisario/SADR is ultimately an androcentric and male-run institution, and most "local" positions are held by a relatively small group of men engaged in *pluriempleo*. A number of projects employ some young men in the 27 February Camp (including a recycling center, an electrics workshop, and a bakery), some have opened small shops, and others attend technical courses in Gazwane.[21] However, by representing camp inhabitants as ideal women, the males who are absented from and/or by

19. However, there are clear "male" spaces outside of the residential camps, including Rabouni and Gazwane.

20. See Enloe (1990 and 1991) on the usage of this term as a patriarchal "propaganda tool."

21. It is notable that all interviewees listed considerably more "male jobs" than "female jobs" in the camps, finding it particularly difficult to "remember" jobs for women.

the official discourse equally emerge as a primary group sidelined by NGOs and aid providers.

> There are some projects [for men] but they are scarce. But there are other types of jobs that men can do here and that women can't. And men make the most of those jobs . . . for example, opening a shop, selling things, going to Mauritania and doing business like that, things that women here can't do. (Cuban-educated teacher, 27 February Camp, April 2007)

While multiple NGO-sponsored projects have long been available for specific groups of women and children in the 27 February Camp, young men have had little access to the camp's structured social or economic activities, including income-generating or social projects which are primarily oriented toward women;[22] this has led to major frustration.[23] Contrasted with the NUSW's success in securing external funding and developing projects in collaboration with non-Sahrawi organizations, several interviewees indicated that the Sahrawi Youth Union (UJSARIO) has overall failed to "mobilize" the solidarity movement to develop projects for youth in the 27 February Camp.[24] This criticism was offered primarily during my interviews with youth but was also echoed by an older man who is active in the Polisario/SADR (27 February Camp, April 2007).

When I systematically asked my camp-based interviewees which projects they felt were lacking yet necessary in 27 February Camp, most interviewees shared a number of precise suggestions which they felt enthusiastic about and believed would improve conditions in the camps. A key issue emerging among youth who had returned to the camps following a long period abroad was the need for workshops or programs to improve intergenerational communication. Other proposals included more widely accessible cultural events, language training, and the creation of a "space

22. This is often the case in refugee camps and conflict situations (Kumar 2001a, 11).

23. See Turner (1999) on Burundi male perceptions that UNHCR has substituted men's economic and social roles and responsibilities in the refugee camps, leading to claims that women find that "the UNHCR is a better husband."

24. A number of NGO workers and three male interviewees suggested that this might be because youth are seen as threatening.

to speak." Despite pinpointing these needs, interviewees indicated that their priorities and opinions had never been sought either by NGOs, the Polisario/SADR, the NUSW, or UJSARIO. The vast majority agreed that it would be both feasible and desirable for a small group of researchers to visit each household in the small 27 February Camp to identify families' (including youth's) needs and priorities.[25]

Expecting the camps to be full of women, when men and youth are "found" by observers in the camps, their presence is often either ignored as an anomaly or negatively evaluated as a threat to women's "authority" and "power" in the camps,[26] or they are identified as potential "delinquents" and criminals (for instance, see UNHCR 2006b, 4, and below). Hence, ECHO reports increasing rates of school absenteeism and "vandalism" in the camps (2005, 3), while the "youth clubs" that have recently been created by UNHCR in Dakhla and Smara[27] are officially described as being designed to tackle "juvenile delinquency" (ibid.), thereby directly associating (male) youth with dangerous or disruptive behavior in the camps.[28] Rather than being perceived as offering youth an opportunity to participate in the camps' cultural, economic, or political life, a number of my interviewees indicated that the justification underlying the creation of these centers has often reinforced young men's feelings of displacement and marginalization from the camps.

A brief note addressing the term that is used in the camps to refer to "youth" is insightful in this context. Reflecting the socially constructed

25. These and other findings were shared with and broadly welcomed by UNHCR through the launch of a policy briefing (Fiddian-Qasmiyeh, 2011d) in Geneva in June 2011. A podcast of the launch is available from http://www.forcedmigration.org/podcasts/audio /64-protracted-sahrawi-displacement.mp3/view.

26. See Fiddian (2002) regarding the perception of men's return as a "threat" to women's "freedom" in the camps.

27. As documented by the UN's Mission for the Western Sahara, MINURSO (www .minurso.org).

28. When I asked a Cuban-based SADR Embassy employee about the UNHCR's claims vis-à-vis "juvenile delinquency," he adamantly proclaimed that this is not a problem in the camps and that UNHCR was a misleading and inconsistent organization (interview, Havana, December 2006).

nature of social categories pertaining to different life stages (Côté and Levine 2002, 49–51), "youth" as a concept in the camps encompasses individuals from their early teens to their mid-30s, being designated *tirka* (m. pl. youth) in Arabic Hassaniya and *jóvenes* or *juventud* in Spanish. Derived from the Arabic root *taraka* (to leave), *tirka* literally refers to *male* youth as a "legacy," in particular in this context as the legacy of the lineage or extended family to which they belong. However, despite carrying this "legacy" in linguistic terms, young men in the camps appear to have been marginalized from, rather than assigned a role in ensuring the continuation of, the political situation monopolized by some of their fathers and uncles. This sense of political disempowerment was also expressed by a selection of my most "critical" interviewees in Cuba, Syria, and the 27 February Camp.

As argued by a Cuban-educated pharmacist in his early 30s,

> there's one generation which leads the whole country, but this generation no longer has, as it were, continuity. For example, there are some politicians who are trained but didn't make the most of [the] time [available], and they haven't trained others to continue on from them. It's just them. As for us . . . (Rabouni, May 2007)

In this respect, the majority of young men appear to have been left behind (*turikū*), displaced, and absented from the camps.

Despite claims of the camps' "uniqueness," one key concern which is common to many refugee contexts is the reality of unemployment in the camps:

> There is no work; very little. That's one of the reasons why the qualified youth sometimes feel marginalized. And that's why they turn to emigration, to be able to work. (technician, Rabouni, May 2007)

A number of camp-based interviewees indicated that economic inactivity in particular is highly damaging, since "a man's role is to bring money for the family" (18-year-old unemployed man, 27 February Camp, April 2007). Being unemployed "as married men, presents us with problems, especially material problems, because we have no source of income, which places us in difficult and embarrassing situations" (SARC interviewee).

Without employment possibilities in the camps to sustain their families or to afford a reasonable *mahr*, increasing numbers of camp-based young men decide to emigrate and send remittances: "I am like the rest of the youth, I intend to leave the camps to work in my area [of expertise]" (Cuban-educated pharmacist, Rabouni, May 2007).[29] The majority of male Cuban-based interviewees also indicated that they aimed to move to Spain as soon as they graduate, rather than returning to the camps, because "my priority is to work and help my family . . . living in the camps is impossible" (economics student, Havana, December 2006). Another student explained: "The main problem is that when you return to the camps, there's nothing for you to do. That's why it's preferable to go to Spain, where you can continue to offer your support for the cause while you support your family" (dentistry student, Havana, December 2007).[30]

Emigration is described by the NUSW as "a cancer devouring the Sahrawi body, in an era when we cannot allow such a thing to happen" (Arabic-language document on file with author [n.d.], Qasmiyeh's translation) and yet this trend reproduces the camps as "female spaces"[31] and there-

29. However, although he feels it is viable and acceptable for young unemployed men to leave the camps in order to send remittances for their families, "someone who has a job, a politician who we really need, a teacher who is really necessary, if he emigrates, that's painful for us. We need them; we need them to lead the society."

30. My Syrian-based interviewees, in contrast, prioritized returning to the camps. This difference appears to be related to Cuban-educated students' language skills and the fact that Spain recognizes and welcomes Cuban medical- and science-related degrees, while Syrian-educated students' Spanish is limited, and they tend to complete humanities or social science degrees. Only one student revealed his plans to emigrate since his family in the camps are "desperate . . . they only eat once a day" (politics student, Damascus, August 2006). See Fiddian-Qasmiyeh (2011e) for an examination of the short- and long-term implications of the study-abroad programs for Sahrawi refugees and an evaluation of whether the Cuban education system has enhanced self-sufficiency or renewed dependence upon Western humanitarian actors (also see Pacitto and Fiddian-Qasmiyeh, 2013).

31. Keenan also notes that an increase in foreign tourism to the recently sedentarized Kel Ahaggar has "not only provided considerable employment for many of the men in these villages but also ensured their absence from the village for several months of the year, thus partly replicating the labor pattern of the [nomadic] camps" (2006, 927). While men are

fore solidifies the image presented through the official discourse. No projects have been developed to encourage male youth to play an active role in the 27 February Camp, and equally important, no effort has been made to address the impacts and outcomes of these feelings of marginalization and frustration among those male youth who remain in the camps, despite a widespread recognition based on studies in other refugee and nonrefugee contexts, that this can have potentially violent effects.

It is essential that analyses of the camps do not further represent Sahrawi young men either solely or primarily as "delinquents." And yet in the context of the present study that aims to explore the motivations behind, and impacts of, mainstream representations of Sahrawi gender relations, it is indispensable that we briefly examine whether the official discourse may have influenced the way in which VAW is addressed in the Sahrawi camps. In the remainder of this chapter, I suggest that a tendency of marginalizing "problematic" cases, ostensibly to "protect" the cause and ensure the continuation of the official discourse, has led to the Polisario/SADR and non-Sahrawis alike failing to address the urgent needs of certain groups in the camps.

Self-Censorship

Existing research on the camps has typically been categorized by Sahrawi refugees, the Polisario/SADR, and much of Spanish civil society as work produced by either "good" or "bad" researchers. In this schema, "good" researchers may be identified as those solidary individuals and organizations highly "aware" of the potential threats and vulnerabilities that can arise if "critical" research is produced. Below I argue that it is precisely the categorization of certain issues as "private" in order to protect the solidarity system that has led to systematic silence and silencing around a number of potentially controversial matters in the camps, with serious effects.

---

highly mobile, "womenandchildren" could be described as being "internally stuck," a term widely applied in Afghanistan (WHO 2001), and subsequently by organizations including the Badil Resource Centre (2006).

This conclusion is supported by two examples discussed in Chapter 4. First, I have argued that the Polisario/SADR and many *solidarios* have strategically rendered Sahrawi refugees' Islamic belief, practice, and institutions invisible in "public" accounts of the camps. An examination of Spanish responses to the "abductions" of Aicha, Fatimetu, and Huria in turn highlighted the extent to which drawing "public" attention to the Sahrawi's religious identity and practice has the potential to destabilize support for "the cause." This therefore reinforces the assumption that "hiding" Islam from public view is an indispensable means of ensuring the continuation of the solidarity network. Second, the same case study also indicated the extent to which many *solidarios*, along with the Polisario/SADR, argued that these cases were family matters, and should be dealt with "privately" by the girls' respective biological parents. These high-profile cases therefore prompted debates within Spain and the camps about whether such discussions should have arisen in Spain, where they could potentially threaten the stability of the solidarity system, or privately, between the relevant families and the Polisario/SADR.

In the following pages I argue that a third example of this tendency to hide potentially divisive realities from public view is embodied in the strategic "silencing" of VAW in the camps.[32]

Silencing Violence against Women

One of the component parts of the official discourse revealed in Chapter 3 is the claim that Sahrawi women are free from violence in the camps, while all other women (both European and "Arab") are eternal victims of VAW.[33] The interview extracts included earlier reflect not only an awareness of the existence of VAW in a variety of contexts but also

32. At the time of writing, only one NGO report documents cases of VAW in the camps. This is a Human Rights Watch report published in December 2008. Otherwise, it is notable that members of the Spanish group Platform of Women Artists Against Gendered Violence regularly visit the camps and work with the NUSW to promote the Sahrawi cause and that of Sahrawi women and yet have not addressed the matter of VAW while there.

33. An earlier version of certain parts of the following discussion of violence against women appears in Fiddian-Qasmiyeh (2010c).

proffer a clear public condemnation of these practices to Western observers, who are actively reassured that such things do not happen in the camps and that VAW is taken seriously by the Polisario/SADR. In this way, the Sahrawi camps are presented as an ideal and unique violence-free space, unlike other generic MENA contexts and refugee camps but also unlike the West.

Denials of the existence of VAW are not specific to the Sahrawi refugee camps, as this is a particularly sensitive topic to discuss in any context, and its prevalence is frequently denied in both refugee and nonrefugee situations (Kerr 1994; Gill 2004; Rees and Pease 2007). However, by claiming that VAW does not exist in the Sahrawi refugee context and by creating this factor as a significant part of the national identity as projected to an international audience via the official discourse, it becomes increasingly difficult for cases of VAW to be dealt with effectively and holistically in the camps. Indeed, this problem is also recognized by Wurud:

> The topic of physical violence is another issue which our leaders congratulate themselves for every day. It's true that it's not at all normal for a man to hit a woman in our culture. However, no-one intervenes when he does. Our society is not exempt from other manifestations of violence against women . . . These are situations which seriously affect the lives of many women and which, nonetheless, are neither stopped nor treated from a legal point of view.

Before turning to the Polisario/SADR and certain *solidarios'* failure to address VAW through a case study of a gang rape that took place in 27 February Camp in 2007, it is important to briefly indicate that my research validates the existence of different forms of abuse and violence against women in the camps (also see Fiddian-Qasmiyeh 2010c).

I understand VAW to refer to "any act of gender-based violence that results in, or is likely to result in, physical, sexual or psychological harm or suffering to women, including threats of such acts, coercion or arbitrary deprivations of liberty, whether occurring in public or private life" (Art. 1, UN Declaration of Violence Against Women). With this definition in mind, in Chapter 3 I documented the emotional and psychological abuse that may characterize unilateral divorce in the camps, with Wurud also denouncing "the violence and psychological abuse that characterizes our famous repudiations." Outside of the home, another form of violence has been revealed by a Sahrawi woman who reports that "an absence of public transport forces us to [hitch a] ride with any unknown man that means that we are at risk of any kind of violence" (quoted in Gimeno-Martín and Laman 2005, 53; my translation).[34]

A third form of VAW was reported by three of my interviewees and relates to the enforced imprisonment of women who have become pregnant outside of marriage. According to the SADR, between three and five women a year are held without their consent in a secure facility referred to as the Centre for Maternity Assistance. The official rationale, according to the SADR Minister of Justice, for holding these women there is to "protect" them from being victims of "possible revenge attacks" (in HRW 2008, 198) or what Human Rights Watch (HRW) denominate as "honour crimes."[35] In a meeting with HRW, this minister recalled the case of a camp resident who "had killed her out-of-wedlock child to fend off social pressure" and indicated that a woman could be released from the center only if "she resolved her problem with her family, got married, or relocated to a different camp" (ibid., 139). My own interviewees, along with those referred to by Tortajada Orriols (2004) and Caratini (2000, 448), all stressed that unwed mothers were primarily allowed to leave the Centre once they agreed to marry, suggesting that such betrothals are far from voluntary acts. Hence, while the SADR representative to the Middle East publicized the peaceful nature of the camps while/by stating that in Jordan honor crimes prevail and VAW is common, HRW is

concerned that the treatment of women at this facility may resemble the practices followed by other governments in the region that detain

34. While not justified in the following terms, the establishment of a female-run taxi service in the camps may provide a means of protecting women from such situations.

35. In an undetermined number of cases these women have been charged with adultery which is punishable under Article 170 of the SADR's Penal Code to between one and five years in prison (HRW 2008, 198).

women without a trial and against their will, ostensibly for their own protection, because they are suspected of having committed "moral offenses." (2008, 142)

This human rights organization recommended that,

rather than detaining potential victims of "honor crimes," Polisario authorities should protect women and girls from violence, treat victims of violence, and ensure that those who perpetrate or threaten violence are punished. (ibid.)

This critical approach to the Polisario/SADR's failure to protect women from violence perpetrated by family or community members directly challenges the official image projected of the camps as spaces that are free of violence and of Sahrawi women as "free" and "unique."

I shall now address the connection between the official discourse, self-censorship and silences surrounding VAW with specific reference to official responses to rape.

"Public" versus "Private" Rapes

On the one hand, certain high-profile cases of Sahrawi women who have reportedly been raped by members of the Moroccan forces in the Western Sahara have been openly scrutinized and abhorred by Sahrawis and non-Sahrawis alike. These include the experiences of the wife of a high-profile Sahrawi human rights activist, and a member of the Western Sahara-based CODESA association, who respectively presented their cases at the 2007 NUSW Congress[36] and to a range of South African audi-

---

36. This woman spoke before an audience of over 800 people, relaying her account of having been raped by five men in front of her small daughter, whom, she claimed, "the Moroccans" had also threatened to rape. The power of her testimony led to agitated discussions among Sahrawi and non-Sahrawi delegates alike vis-à-vis the "satanic" (her term) methods used by the Moroccans in the Western Sahara and to Spanish delegates in particular applauding the way in which this woman had refused to be silent about such acts of violence and aggression (verbatim proceedings).

ences in May 2007.[37] Their presentations in essence suggest that survivors of Moroccan rapists can be situated as "ideal" representatives of and for the Sahrawi "cause."

On the other hand, camp-based incidents where both the victim and the rapists are Sahrawi have received no international coverage, perhaps reflecting that publicly known incidents of sexual violence in the camps could damage "the cause."[38] One such episode includes a gang rape perpetrated by a group of young Sahrawi men in the 27 February Camp shortly before my arrival in March 2007. This case deserves brief attention.

While initially reticent to discuss such issues with me, four of my interviewees in the 27 February Camp (one man and three women) eventually admitted to me that "there have recently been some rape cases," immediately qualifying this revelation by stressing that "these are very rare and, of course, very problematic" (ministerial aide, Rabouni, April 2007). One of the cases referred to by my interviewees had taken place a few months before the 2007 NUSW Conference, with a hearing held in March in the State Court located within the confines of the 27 February National Women's School. When I indicated that I already knew about the occurrence of this rape, the three female interviewees gradually spoke to me more freely about the incident,[39] progressively explaining the circumstances of the rape itself. They indicated that a young woman had been abducted at night by three or four men who had driven her outside the camp, raped her in turn, and then abandoned her close to her family's *khayma*. Having reported the crime to the police, two of the perpetrators had eventually been arrested: one man, I later heard, had been convicted

37. The CODESA member recounted her experience of being imprisoned and abused by Moroccan forces in the late 1990s during a "week of solidarity" with the Sahrawi people in South Africa (verbatim proceedings and documents on file with the author).

38. On (unsubstantiated) Moroccan claims of sexual abuse as a means of discrediting the Polisario/SADR, see Fiddian-Qasmiyeh (2009).

39. This was clearly a sensitive topic of conversation, and during the interview I drew upon skills developed while I was a legal advisor and gender focal point at the Cairo-based NGO Africa and Middle Eastern Refugee Assistance (AMERA) to mitigate the impact of discussing VAW in this context (see Fiddian 2006b).

of rape in the 27 February Camp State Court and the other had been identified as the driver. They were sentenced respectively to five and two years in prison, and were ordered to pay large fines to compensate the young woman and her family.[40] Although my interviewees provided no further information regarding the woman herself, they indicated that she had not been blamed for the violence that had been inflicted upon her (as is so often the case in rape cases).

It eventually emerged that this was not the only gang rape involving abduction to have occurred in the camps. Particularly disturbingly, "the recent cases" referred to by my interviewees have all reportedly followed the same pattern, although the three young women reassured me that "it" (gang rape) was "more common in the other camps, since they are larger, there is no electricity, they are darker and more dangerous."[41] They continued, telling me that they thought that it had become more hazardous for women over the previous four or five years but repeatedly informing me that it was safe in their own camp. Although the precise number of such rape cases (either reported or unreported) is unknown, these events have evidently affected not only the young women who have been raped and their families but also the broader community. When I asked how this problem was being addressed, they responded that "women are being told to be more careful. We aren't meant to go out when it's dark. We should walk with our friends, not alone. We have to be careful. We all know about this."[42]

40. While compensation can be paid for numerous reasons (including to cover medical expenses), the payment of compensation has commonly been conceptualized as covering both the *mahr* that a woman would have received had she married as a virgin and compensation for the crime itself (Sonbol 1997, 218).

41. I was unable to corroborate the claim of higher incidences of rape in other camps. Understating the risk in their own camp will certainly have been connected to these young women's desire to present their home camp as "better" than the other camps, just as the young woman from Dakhla (quoted in Chapter 3 regarding movement, *mahr*, and marriage) may have done the same.

42. This is also a frequent response in the West. With reference to Iraq, Kandiyoti stresses that imposing stringent limitations on female family members often takes place out of fear rather than social conservatism (2007b, 513).

Official Responses in Context

That some of the perpetrators should have been caught, tried, and sentenced could be taken to indicate that rape cases are taken seriously by both the local authorities and the community as a whole, with the prison sentences sending out a message to Sahrawi men and women alike that such acts of sexual violence are unacceptable and that rapists will be found and prosecuted accordingly. It is, however, unclear whether the sentences will be carried through, and indeed the length of the sentences is arguably short in light of the extent and nature of the crime (involving abduction and gang rape).[43] By means of comparison with other MENA contexts,[44] in Egypt rapists can be sentenced to between three years and life imprisonment, while execution is the punishment for rape following abduction;[45] in Lebanon, rape results in a minimum of five years' forced labor (before considering aggravating factors such as the number of rapists or rape following abduction);[46] convicted rapists in Syria face 15 years in prison; while in Tunisia legislation is "vigorously enforced" to ensure that rapists are sentenced to life imprisonment, and, in the case of rape following abduction, the death penalty applies.[47]

This incident is particularly relevant to the current analysis due to the way in which Sahrawis and non-Sahrawis have dealt with the international implications of this and other cases. Hence, while stressing the frequency of acts of aggression against Sahrawi women by Moroccans, or against European women in general, the NUSW Conference proceedings failed to address the incidence and nature of rape in the camps. Neither Sahrawi nor Spanish delegates referred to violence inside of the

43. These are considered to be aggravating factors by the United Kingdom's Sentencing Advisory Panel, which recommends a minimum of eight years' imprisonment to be augmented in light of these factors. The average sentence for rapists in custody in the country (in 2000) was seven years and one month (available at www.sentencing-guidelines .gov.uk/docs/rape.pdf).

44. The following details pertain to the situation as it existed prior to the Arab Spring.

45. Mohsen (1990); Nazir and Tomppert (2005, 72).

46. Art. 503 of the Lebanese Penal Code: Nazir and Tomppert (2005, 150); USDOS (2006).

47. On Syria see US DOS (2008a); on Tunisia see US DOS (2008b).

camps, rather focusing on highlighting external acts of aggression and abuse. While many Spanish delegates will not have been aware of the gang rape(s), several Spanish NGO workers revealed during our informal interviews after the conference that they were aware of at least one gang rape having taken place in the camps, and yet did not raise concerns about VAW either during the Conference or during their post-Conference meeting with the NUSW. We must therefore ask why, given the vast number of NGOs and solidarity groups that are active in the camps, no projects have been developed in the camps either to identify and address the underlying causes for such acts of violence,[48] or to support survivors of sexual and gender-based violence.

Given the prevalence of sexual and gender-based violence (SGBV) in refugee camps around the world,[49] clear guidelines and operational standards have been developed by the UNHCR (including 1991, 1995, 2002b) to protect refugee women through "remedial action and *preventive* measures" (UNHCR 2002b; my emphasis). Nonetheless, since the 1970s there has been a distinct failure, by internal actors and external observers alike, to adequately address the reality of VAW in the Sahrawi refugee camps.[50] My preliminary explanation for this long-standing failure is that a preference for "privacy" and local solutions may have encouraged non-Sahrawis to remain silent on certain potentially divisive issues via processes of self-censorship. Such a process may be interpreted as a means of "protecting"

48. Vogelman and Lewis argue that "rape is used as a means of thwarting marginalisation, as it is a powerful and effective way of reasserting one's centrality and importance, at least in relation to the victim, and to those in the community who feel threatened by this violence" (1993, n.p.). They identify gang rapes as "primarily a *youth* phenomenon" (my emphasis) and argue that "[w]ithin the subculture of gangs, rape provides a rationale for solidarity and an interaction based on male bonding and masculine validation." Rapes in such a context could potentially be understood as a means through which young men may collectively physically mark out a place and a space for themselves in the camps.

49. See Callamard (1999), Dugan et al. (2000), Scharffscher (2002) and Ganeshpanchan (2005).

50. The UNHCR's commitment to institutionalize a permanent UNHCR presence in the refugee camps, including the presence of protection officers, is to be welcomed in this regard (UNHCR 2011).

the cause, as argued earlier with reference to many *solidarios'* complicity with the Polisario/SADR's misrepresentation of the camps as secular spaces. Indeed, the absence of relevant projects instigated by Polisario/SADR, the NUSW or external observers can in part be explained by the Polisario/SADR camp administration's desire to maintain the official representation of the camps being a VAW-free zone as a means of ensuring the continued support of the Spanish solidarity movement. It is also worth recalling that the Polisario/SADR and NUSW have explicitly contrasted the high prevalence (and high profile) of VAW against women in Spain with the solidarity-friendly notion of the camps as female-centered and VAW-free spaces. To develop campaigns addressing the root causes of VAW in the camps would thus entail the recognition that VAW exists, thereby dismantling a representational system developed and maintained by the Polisario/SADR over several decades.

An alternative reason for Spanish NGOs' failure to address this issue may be related to the metonymic relationship that has in effect been created by the Polisario/SADR between Spanish society and VAW (cf. Yeğenoğlu 1998, 161, footnote 36). By defining Spain *as* a location of VAW, the official discourse could be understood as preemptively undermining these international observers' potential claims to authority were they to attempt to address VAW in the camps. An additional and final reason behind an absence of projects in the camps is that the very possibility of rapes occurring has a priori been dismissed: one of the constitutive implications of the official discourse is thus that rape in the camps can "occur because people do not believe that the rape that is about to occur is at all possible" (Olsen and Scharffscher 2004, 383).[51]

---

51. The UN Declaration on VAW asks that states should "develop, in a comprehensive way, *preventive approaches*" (my emphasis) against any form of violence. Olsen and Scharffscher examine rape in refugee camps as organizational failures; as such, the Polisario/SADR, Western agencies and institutions working in the camps could all be seen as having failed to recognize potential "danger signs," to identify the "latent conditions" that increase the likelihood of rapes taking place, or to act either before or after the so-called incubation period that Olsen and Scharffscher claim precedes a rape or attempted rape (2004, 383).

Conclusion

In this chapter I have argued that the official discourse has directly influenced, and simultaneously been reinforced by policies developed and implemented by solidarity networks in the Sahrawi refugee camps. By constituting the camps as gender-equal spaces that are free from violence, the multiplicity of projects run in the camps have repeatedly targeted the same group of beneficiaries (the key protagonists of the official discourse), while failing to identify or address the needs and rights of social groups that have been marginalized from view. Such a system, however, cannot unequivocally be labeled an overarching "failure," since these projects ultimately respond to and fulfill specific official and solidary needs. Rather, they reflect the extent to which the Polisario/SADR has successfully directed aid in the protracted Sahrawi refugee camps.

By channeling aid through organizations such as the National Union of Sahrawi Women, a core group of members have benefited unequally in the camps, just as elite families had done so during the colonial era. Throughout this book I have contrasted the hypervisibility of these active and employed women with the invisibility of those men and women who are either excluded from or "select out" of such projects, and of those who physically disengage from the politico-administrative center of the camps by moving to Spain or *al-bādiya*. These mutually reinforcing processes of highlighting and sidelining thus solidify the view that the camps are inhabited by empowered women and indeed lead to shifts in the demographic makeup of the camps.

The official discourse's focus on "ideal women" has rendered both women and girls invisible. Although numerous projects are designed for "children" in the camps, few if any provide opportunities and spaces specifically for girls. Through discussing the absence of projects tackling girls' early withdrawal from school, along with mothers' reluctance to allow their daughters to participate in an activity trip organized by a Spanish NGO, I have demonstrated both the difficulties that girls encounter in accessing projects and the limitations of NGOs' conceptualizations of the population they are purportedly attempting to "help." Spaniards' anger at these mothers' "ignorance," and their threat to never return to the camps unless Sahrawi girls were allowed to "have fun," has confirmed the unbalanced power dynamic that characterizes the development of projects in the camps. Rather than attempting to identify the reasons behind these women's reluctance to allow their daughters to participate, the NGO workers' priority was to implement a predesigned project for a predetermined set of "good" beneficiaries who should have unequivocally (and gratefully) accepted the activity program. Any possibility of addressing either the mothers' or daughters' needs in the future was therefore ultimately obstructed, suggesting the extent to which many residents' priorities and voices are silenced by Sahrawi and Spanish authority figures alike.

Through constituting the camps as an ideal female space, the majority of adult and young men have been absented from common understandings of the camps. Although 40% of the camp population is estimated to be male, there are few spaces, places, or NGO programs for men in the refugee camps. When implemented, such projects are often justified as tackling "juvenile delinquency," rather than offering young men an opportunity to participate in cultural, economic or political life in the camps. Male youth may be referred to as *tirka*, or their family's legacy, in the camps, but it is apparent that these young men have been "left behind" in a multiplicity of ways by the Polisario/SADR and non-Sahrawis alike. With increasing numbers of men physically leaving the camps to find work in Spain, the camps are in turn reinforced as "female spaces," leading to increasing feelings of marginalization among those young men who stay behind.

While it is essential not to equate young men with delinquency, in the final part of this chapter I have explored the connection between the official discourse and systematic silencing in the camps surrounding VAW. Since documenting cases that undermine the mainstream representation of the camps as an "ideal space" is ultimately equated with being pro-Moroccan and therefore unacceptable, or "bad" research, I have argued throughout this study that many solidary observers have engaged in practices of self-censorship, ostensibly to protect "the cause." Although rapes committed by "Moroccans" are publicly (and internationally) invoked by the Polisario/SADR, categorizing rapes committed by Sahrawis as "private" reveals the power that such incidents may have to disrupt common understandings of the camps as uniquely "peaceful" and violence free. Through briefly exploring Sahrawi and Spanish failures to respond to and analyze the reasons underlying an emerging "trend" of gang rapes in the camps, I have presented an additional impact of the solidarity system on social life there, undermining the security and safety of many of its so-called beneficiaries.

The nature of projects that are, and are not, developed in the camps simultaneously reflect donors' assumptions about worthy beneficiaries and reveal the dynamics that underlie the Polisario/SADR's relationship with donors. One of the main roles assigned to the SADR Ministry of Cooperation is, in theory, to "coordinate" visits and thereby ensure that projects are equally distributed around the camps (rather than the same group of children and/or women and/or health projects receiving duplicated or triplicated funding). However, my research suggests that the Polisario/SADR's main priority is to accept assistance from NGOs, even if this aid is largely unessential in practical terms. In this way, any visit and intervention emerges as being welcomed precisely because it is interpreted as an embodiment of, or form of tangible solidarity. The arrival of visitors to the camps, it is assumed, is better than the absence of these, since their very presence demonstrates their support for the cause, and it is assumed that they will return to Spain and "spread the word."

In such a situation, the significance of NGO involvement transcends the financial investment, or the material benefits of a project, and rather reemerges as being firmly embedded in the political dimension. Non-Sahrawis' visits provide the Polisario/SADR with legitimacy; their presence confirms to the refugee inhabitants that they have not been "forgotten;"[52] and their media and political statements upon return to Spain ensure that the camps and the cause are reinscribed in the Spanish imagination, guaranteeing the continuation of humanitarian and political support for the

52. One of the most frequently made requests during my visits to the camps was that I should "tell the world" about their existence and their cause.

camps.[53] And yet it is precisely this dependence on observers as political and solidary agents, and the need to secure and maintain their interest and attention, which has led to a situation where the needs and rights of the majority of the population are frequently subjugated to the political aims of the leadership and elite.[54]

Furthermore, this dynamic of dependence and the essential claims to secularity, modernity, and gender equality that underpin what I refer to as the *conditional* solidarity system, has, I believe, led to the Polisario/SADR failing to ask "its" *solidarios* to enact basic steps to maximize *mutual* respect, tolerance, and understanding between Sahrawis and non-Sahrawi visitors. A fear that *solidarios* could potentially be alienated if visitors were asked to adhere to certain Sahrawi customs, or bear in mind local dynamics, may have led the Polisario/SADR to embody a laissez-faire approach to *solidarios*,[55] in turn reflecting a major schism between official and "popular" Sahrawi priorities (also see Fiddian-Qasmiyeh 2011a).

53. Personal observations; interview with Cuban-educated science graduate, Rabouni, May 2007.

54. Blogger Wurud recognizes that "[t]o manipulate reality in this way [i.e., to hide the camps' "deficiencies"] does not favor change; this should be a clear message, especially for the leaders of the NUSW who are the first protagonists in the false discourse when facing the West." She passionately avows that "[o]ur deficiencies will be seen clearly, then, the day that we stop with our 'blah, blah, blah' and with the false messages transmitted to the microphones of journalists and researchers who visit us and swallow everything. We have to regain our courage and valour and say enough, we want a change now, and act accordingly."

55. In addition to the matter of pork discussed in Chapter 4, and Spanish designations of Sahrawi mothers as "ignorant," non-Sahrawi visitors are not asked to dress "modestly" while in the refugee camps. Indeed, information provided to visitors prior to travel often indicates that, while they should be "tolerant of difference," they "do not need to change anything" about themselves (e.g., http://www.sadicum.org/documentos/Recomendaciones _viaje.pdf). Before and during my first visit to the camps in 2002, I was told by Spanish "camp veterans" that Sahrawi refugees "don't mind at all" if visitors wear shorts and t-shirts while in the camps. Although the majority of visitors do wear such items, my fieldwork has confirmed many Sahrawis' preference that Spanish women dress modestly during their visits.

Rather than creating and maintaining a dialogic process between *solidarios* and the recipients of their "solidarity," such a system is largely based on ignoring (or hiding) specific cultural and religious factors that are centrally important to a large proportion of the refugee camps' inhabitants. This official distancing from religious identity and practice, paralleled with a laissez-faire approach to *solidarios'* interactions and behavior in the camps and with Sahrawi children in Spain, is in direct contrast with solidarity projects and internship programs run in other refugee contexts, such as the *Universities' Trust for Educational Exchange with Palestinians* (UNIPAL) and the legal aid NGO AMERA-Cairo, which demand that visitors, academics, *solidarios*, and NGO workers dress, speak, and behave "modestly."[56] These alternative modes of engagement, although limited in their own ways, indicate that the solidarity system that underpins the Sahrawi refugee context is not inevitable and may be redeveloped through a process of mutual reflection. This system is also not viable in the longer term, since maintaining the ideal façade becomes increasingly difficult as larger numbers of visitors spend longer periods of time in the camps and conduct research with a broader base of the population. Challenging these various systems of repress-entation, which I have argued reflect the nature of engagement between Sahrawis and their solidary aid providers, therefore becomes an urgent ethical question for all parties involved.

56. Interviews conducted with former UNIPAL volunteers; my own experience of working with AMERA-Cairo; multiple conversations with Harrell-Bond in Egypt and the UK between 2004 and 2008. See also Armstrong and Bennett on proposals to ethically mediate contact between San communities and academics/journalists (2002, 194).

Conclusion

SINCE THE ESTABLISHMENT of the Sahrawi refugee camps in late 1975, the Polisario/SADR and NUSW have strategically mobilized idealized and homogenized claims vis-à-vis "Sahrawi women" to secure humanitarian and political support from Western nonstate audiences. In this book, I have examined the mechanisms through which Sahrawi women's reported "position of equality" has become "the dominant motif of Saharawi [sic] social organization" (Voutira and Harrell-Bond 2000, 66), and, indeed, the prominent focus of externally projected representations of the camps. A critical and nuanced analysis of the gynocentric discursive strategy that has come to be taken-for-granted by the Polisario/SADR and Western observers alike thus reveals the unequal power dynamics upon which these refugee camps are based, demonstrating that intersecting ideas about gender and Islam mediate international networks that are essential for the Sahrawi's politics of survival. These networks are not only founded, but are ultimately conditional upon, the representation of the camps as democratic, secular, and gender-equal spaces. While this representational mechanism may have been designed and implemented to ensure the continuation of Western solidarity for "the Sahrawi cause," this study exemplifies multiple ways in which the Polisario/SADR and Western NGOs alike have failed to recognize or respond to the needs and priorities of the camps' inhabitants. This book therefore underscores the unequal terms of engagement that exist between Sahrawi refugees, the Polisario/SADR, and their Western observers and the implications of such imbalances.

Contributing to studies into colonial, postcolonial, and neocolonial contexts, this book has examined a selection of discursive, material, and political relationships between members of Spanish civil society and the Sahrawi refugees who were once Spain's colonial subjects. Throughout, a range of parallels has become apparent between the colonial and refugee eras, demonstrating the continued significance of hierarchical frameworks that have historically positioned certain women and men over others. Illustrating the nature of unequal positions both "internally" (i.e., between different groups of Sahrawis) and "internationally" (i.e., between Sahrawis and Spaniards), the preceding chapters have explored and contextualized contemporary modes of interaction between different groups of Sahrawi refugees, their political representatives and their Western aid providers.

As former colonizers and contemporary *solidarios*, numerous Spanish individuals and collectivities have positioned themselves as "helping" the Sahrawi, prompting a range of responses from the latter. Throughout the colonial and refugee eras, Spaniards provided opportunities while creating dependencies and diverse forms of oppression,[1] leading to ambivalent responses among Sahrawi individuals, families, and communities. Over time, Sahrawi communities have negotiated complex sociopolitical and material realities by variously engaging in processes of adaptation, complicity, complacency, resistance, and disengagement from Spanish and Sahrawi authority structures. While exploring the social, organizational, and representational impacts of material and political dependence upon non-Sahrawis, I maintain that power imbalances and relations of dependency cannot be directly equated with powerlessness but can rather lead to the development of innovative ways of maximizing resources and sociopolitical capital. However, I would argue that such innovation should not be uncritically heralded, given the numerous dangers that have accompanied specific mechanisms of repress-entation.

1. One avenue for future research would be to collate and examine Spanish views about the camps and Polisario/SADR, bearing in mind the diversity of and divisions within Spanish civil society. Particular attention may be paid to the Polisario/SADR and NUSW's close relationship with organizations in/from the Basque Country, and the influence that connections with the Basque nationalist movement may have on the Polisario/SADR's ties with Spain's national and regional institutions.

In order to enhance our understanding of the sociopolitical dynamics that have typified both the colonial period and the protracted refugee context, this analysis has built upon, and in turn contributed to, two ever-expanding bodies of literature that document the gendered impacts and experiences of forced migration and refugeedom, on the one hand, and studies of gender and nationalism in the MENA region, on the other. By exploring the complexities of Sahrawi women's, men's, children's, and youth's lives across a range of geopolitical contexts, I have simultaneously demonstrated the extent to which Sahrawi gender relations (both real and imagined) are constructed in relation to and directly implicated in internal and international networks and power structures. While geographically isolated, the Sahrawi refugee camps—and the "national" cause that they house—are thus intrinsically and intimately connected with the West through highly gendered material, political, and discursive ties.[2]

A third major theme emerging in this study is that of the multifarious and far-reaching influence of particular forms of noneconomic conditionalities underlying certain North-South relations. A wealth of studies have examined the ways in which international financial institutions (such as the World Bank and IMF), Western states, and inter/national NGOs have rewarded recipients who have adjusted their institutions, constitutions, and policies in line with what Kandiyoti refers to as "the trinity of democratisation, good governance and women's rights" (2004, 134). In the context under consideration, I have expanded the notion of conditionalities to encompass the provision of "solidarity" by members of Spanish civil society, revealing the ways in which solidarity with the Sahrawi is contingent upon the camps being perceived as "ideal," democratic, secular, and female-empowering spaces. By proposing a distinction between "anonymous" and "official" aid and the "intimate aid" that is distributed personally, and very visibly, to refugees in the camps by Spanish individuals,

2. The range of transnational connections discussed in this book include networks revolving around and providing solidarity, humanitarian aid, education, and fostering opportunities to Sahrawi refugees in different locations.

families, and NGOs, I have highlighted the extent to which protecting these solidary ties is ultimately a matter of political and physical survival in/for the camps. This system of "conditional solidarity" has in turn ultimately conditioned representations of life in the camps by the (androcentric) Polisario/SADR.

This book therefore demonstrates the impacts that Western donor agendas surrounding "women's rights" may have on recipient bodies, precisely by recognizing

> [the] growing gap between the discourses circulating in transnational feminist [and donor] networks, politics at the national [sic] level and the way gender relations, which are embedded in complex layers of historical and cultural determination, are actually played out in everyday livelihood contexts. (Kandiyoti 2004, 135)

Although other actors have often directly challenged Western donor agendas in the name of defending local traditions and cultural authenticity (for instance, on Afghanistan, see Kandiyoti 2007b), the Polisario/SADR and its associated NUSW have effectively mirrored the predominant discourses circulating outside of the camps, recognizing the political advantages of officially embracing, rather than critiquing, the preferences espoused by donors. However, as mainstream accounts of the camps have discursively "mainstreamed" gender equality and have rhetorically centralized "ideal" (i.e., free, active and secular) "Sahrawi women," in reality the Polisario/SADR and NUSW have marginalized the needs and priorities of "nonideal" "ordinary" women with grave effects.[3] Further, combining these processes of discursive idealization with a failure to recognize the relational nature of gender has led to the Polisario/SADR, NUSW, and many Western NGOs alike constructing "ideal" Sahrawi women in isolation from Sahrawi girls, boys, youth, and men, directly influencing the development of projects in the camps. In-depth analysis is therefore

---

3. See Kandiyoti on the discrepancies between normative expectations apropos Western donor agendas and "material realities" (2007b, esp. 512)

urgently needed to identify alternative modes of policy development and implementation in the camps (and indeed in other protracted refugee contexts) in order to transcend existing limitations.

The Polisario/SADR has thus mobilized specific images of Sahrawi women in the international arena to secure aid as a specific response to Western priorities, thereby demonstrating the extent to which Western feminist (and Orientalist) discourses have been politicized by sections of the Sahrawi male-dominated elite. In turn, this study has also elucidated the role played by a range of Western observers in ensuring the reproduction (or recycling) of certain discourses in the international and "local" arenas, and in accepting and reinforcing the designation of specific groups of refugees and women as "ideal" and "good" to the detriment of others. Evaluating refugee (and indeed nonrefugee) situations through comparative frameworks and notions of "positional superiority" (Nader 1989, 324) by necessity constitutes "other" refugee groups and women as "bad," thereby revictimizing these individuals and groups, inducing antagonisms and solidifying hierarchies rather than encouraging observers (and the observed themselves) to contest such processes. This analysis has equally highlighted the "difficulties of developing a principled feminist response (and an appropriate politics of solidarity)"[4] in highly politicized situations characterized by dependence upon external observers and aid providers. As such, it echoes calls made by analysts such as Mohanty (1988) and Spivak (1990 and 1993b) that feminist scholarship should reject and deconstruct monolithic images of "Other" women, wherever they may be located.

Moreover, this book has stressed that discursive idealizations potentially hide conflicts within and between groups, as discussed in the preceding chapters with reference to multiple levels of hidden tensions between Sahrawi refugees, the Polisario/SADR, and Western *solidarios*. Indeed, having demonstrated the disguised tensions that exemplify the Sahrawi-Spanish relationship, Qasmiyeh and I conceptualize this connection as one of "covalent solidarity," in which both parties are ultimately

4. Kandiyoti on Afghanistan and Iraq (2004, 134).

ambivalent toward each other, and yet there is, as a whole, a form of what we refer to as "attraction-to-repulsion stability." I have explored the divergence between what is said to and about Westerners, examining the realities and bases for certain Sahrawis' concerns regarding their dependence upon the West. A related issue that remains to be investigated in greater detail is the Polisario/SADR's complex role as the Sahrawi's "representatives." While the Polisario/SADR has as a whole successfully demonstrated its capacity to externally project the camps as "ideal" spaces, this book reveals a number of existing and potential ruptures between the Polisario/SADR and individuals both within the camps and in the international arena. By habitually disregarding the expectations and tensions felt by members of the camp population, the Polisario/SADR's authority over its refugee-citizens is called into question, leading to an increasingly visible trend of disengagement from the camps' administrative core.

It is thus important to ask in which geopolitical and historical contexts the Polisario/SADR has been accepted and invoked as the Sahrawis' "legitimate representatives" and under which circumstances other *de facto* or *de jure* powers have been called upon by Sahrawis and Spaniards to ensure specific politico-legal outcomes. Hence, Spanish attempts to secure the "liberation" of Sahrawi girls from the Sahrawi refugee camps have ranged from Spanish institutions explicitly lobbying the Polisario/SADR to enact their responsibilities as a *de facto* state, to more recent demands (2008–9) that the Algerian government intervene to "liberate" Mimouna Bachir Mokhtar from the refugee camps as the *de jure* authority (Fiddian-Qasmiyeh, 2013).[5] Exploring such shifts will provide a more nuanced understanding of the Polisario/SADR's spheres of influence and institutional capacity and authority, delineating internal and external challenges to the Polisario/SADR's claims to authority over the camps.

Intimately related to a number of the abovementioned points, a further main contribution of this study revolves around the Polisario/SADR's intersecting repress-entations of gender and Islam to the West. Although religious identity and practice remain key priorities within the refugee

---

5. The latter approach is supported by HRW, as discussed in Chapter 5.

camps, "Islam" emerges as an essentially "private" issue in the Sahrawi context in so far as its significance is not "publicly" declared by the Polisario/SADR to the West. Indeed, through analyzing the essentially Orientalist nature of Spanish responses to the "abductions" of three Sahrawi girls by their camp-based families, I have argued that the Polisario/SADR and many of its *solidarios* have recognized the dangers that may arise if Western observers explicitly associate the Sahrawi with Islam. While ultimately misrepresenting a large proportion of Sahrawi refugees, "demonstrating" the "secularism" and "modernity" of the Sahrawi "nation" through "its" women has thus become an essential feature of the Polisario/SADR's politics of survival.

Although the Polisario/SADR's official discourse hides the heterogeneity of religious belief and practice both within the camps and across Muslim majority contexts in the MENA region and beyond,[6] this book establishes the multilayered significance of Islam by distinguishing between "official" and "popular," and "public" and "private" approaches to religion in the camps. Given the correlation between the discourse projected and the identity of the audience being addressed, future research could critically analyze the concepts invoked by the Polisario/SADR during their interactions with Muslim and Arab counterparts, as well as MENA state and nonstate actors' views of the Sahrawi "cause." Another relevant proposal would be to establish the similarities and differences between the discursive strategies invoked by the Polisario/SADR with those developed by other political representatives of protracted refugee groups, such as the Palestine Liberation Organisation.

Although the Polisario/SADR has been widely heralded by Western NGO workers and academics alike for promoting self-sufficiency and local participation in the camps, and therefore as challenging assumptions

6. See the 2008 special edition of the *British Journal of Middle Eastern Studies*, which explores "Gender and Diversity in the Middle East and North Africa" and aims "to highlight the element of diversity which characterises the lives of these women and the regions they belong to" (Salhi 2008, 295). Also see Fiddian-Qasmiyeh 2013c on the dynamics of intergenerational negotiations of Muslim identity and practice amongst MENA refugees and migrants in Cuba, Algeria and the UK.

regarding "dependency syndrome" among refugee groups, this book has interrogated the bases and implications of such repress-entations, with significant implications for refugee studies more broadly. While "the celebration . . . [and the] enunciation of the margin as the site of creative thinking at first sight appears a salutary corrective, and an empowering one" (Darby 1997, 22), processes of "writing- or speaking-back"[7] require careful examination to determine the precise power dynamics at play when producing knowledge for the West (Abu-Lughod 2001, 105). By exploring "the processes of entanglement" (Abu-Lughod 1998b, 16) between the Polisario/SADR and their Western solidary aid providers, this study therefore complements existing scholarship on "the complex ways that the West and things associated with the West, embraced, repudiated, and translated, are implicated in contemporary gender politics" (ibid., 3). As a whole, the gendered discursive and solidarity systems currently in place are neither inevitable nor sustainable, requiring the critical engagement of all parties involved: Sahrawi refugees, their representatives, and those who purport to "support" or document the complex realities of the Sahrawi refugee camps and their inhabitants.

7. Here I refer to Ashcroft et al.'s *The Empire Writes Back* (1989).

Glossary

—

References

—

Index

Glossary of Key Arabic and Spanish Terms

Ahl al-Kitāb: People of the Book

Ait Arbein: Hassaniya term commonly referred to in English as the "Council of Forty." This supratribal confederation existed prior to and during the colonial era and drew together leaders from the forty tribes to take decisions affecting all of the forty "families." *Ait* is a Berber word meaning "family" or "tribe."

Ajnabī (m. sing.) or *ajnabiyya* (fem. sing): Foreigner.

Arabañol: Neologism used by Cuban-educated Sahrawi youth to refer to the hybridized language formed by combining Arabic and Spanish (*Árabe* + *Español* = *Arabañol*).

Bādiya: Literally meaning "desert" in standard Arabic, this term is usually used to refer to the territories of the Western Sahara that are not under Moroccan control, also referred to as the Liberated Territories. *Al-bādiya* is described as being a cooler and healthier place to live than the refugee camps, with many refugee families moving there in the summer months or sporadically throughout the year. It is estimated that several thousand Sahrawi nomads may live there permanently, herding their camels and goats in the area. It is a densely land-mined territory, leading to frequent, and often fatal, landmine accidents.

Bulūgh: Foodstuff given to young women during the precolonial and colonial periods to "fatten them up." According to Cheikh, in Hassaniya Arabic this refers to "dates that are cut and exposed to the sun to make them mature more quickly" (quoted in Popenoe 2004). The root of the word, however, is *balagha*, meaning "to attain puberty," or "to become marriageable, pubescent." It is, therefore, a foodstuff specifically given to girls to expedite their puberty.

Dā'ira, pl. *dawā'ir*: District. The Sahrawi refugee camps are divided into four *wilayāt* (provinces), which are in turn subdivided into *dawā'ir* (districts). The

273

dawā'ir are at present the units of administration for the refugee camps and are intended to become the SADR's regional and local administrative units when/if an independent Western Sahara is achieved.

Eid: A seasonal Islamic festival, such as *Eid al-Fitr* (also known as *Eid al-Ṣaghīr*) and *Eid al-Aḍḥa* (commonly referred to *Eid al-Kabīr*).

Fitna: Temptation or its related chaos.

Frīg, pl. *firgān*: This Hassaniya Arabic term literally means "group" or "team" and generally refers to a group of people or gathering and is not limited to nomadic contexts. In this case, however, the term refers to the nomadic groups that lived in the territory during the precolonial and colonial times. Each *frīg* was composed of a number of *khiyām* (tents), which in turn were normally each run by a married couple and their children and sometimes included members of their extended family. The *firgān* would undertake seasonal movements along predetermined routes, stopping in small settlements throughout their movements, as well as staying in the *bādiya* (the more remote desert areas) for extended periods of time. In Modern Standard Arabic, the singular term would be transliterated as *farīq* and the plural as *afriqā'* or *furūq*. An alternative singular is *firqa* and its respective plural is *firaq*.

Fuṣḥā: Modern Standard Arabic.

Al-gaws: "The arch" (Modern Standard Arabic: *al-qaws*). This is the colloquial Hassaniya Arabic term used to refer to the archway marking the entrance to the precinct of the National Women's School, where both the school's and camp's *idāra* (administration) but also the majority of NGO projects are based.

Gueton: Nomadic family tent traditionally made of camel hair. Those currently in use in the refugee camps are usually provided by the UNHCR/ECHO and are made of plastic sheeting. Unlike the term *khayma*, the word *gueton* is not used to refer to adobe or cement structures, only tents. This is the spelling commonly used in Spanish.

Ḥay, pl. *aḥyā'*: Each "district" in the refugee camps is subdivided into subdistricts or, according to the Spanish term used in the camps (*barrios*), neighborhoods.

Hassaniya: Arabic dialect spoken by the Sahrawi and the Maure/Moorish peoples of Northern Mauritania.

Idāra: Administration

Al-'idda: The obligatory time (three menstrual periods) that must pass according to the Qur'an from the declaration of the divorce until a woman may remarry (sura 2:228). From the Arabic verb *'adda*, "to count."

Al-iḥtifāl wa it'arqība (الاحتفال و اتعرقيبه): A Hassaniya Arabic term that means "the divorce party." The translation of *al-iḥtifāl* is "the celebration." The meaning of the second part of the term is open to debate given that there are separate roots for the words *t'arqība* or *t'arkība*. The Arabic verb *raqaba* means "to watch over," "to honor," or "to take care of." Alternatively, the verb *rakaba* can be translated as "to ride," "to mount," "to seat oneself," or "to embark" (in the latter case, on a journey/means of transport, for instance). The "divorce party" could therefore arguably refer to either a celebration characterized by (1) members of the community watching over the divorcée and/or supporting her (as is often claimed by Sahrawis) or (2) characterized by a woman sitting (high) on the "special platform" referred to by interviewees and written sources and/or embarking on a new stage of her life.

Khayma, pl. *khiyām*: Nomadic family tent traditionally made of camel hair. Those currently in use in the refugee camps are usually provided by the UNHCR/ECHO and are made of plastic sheeting. This term is now also habitually used to refer to a family's "house," be it a tent or an adobe structure.

Al-khayma al-kabīra: "The big tent," i.e., the parents' tent.

Al-khayma al-ṣaghīra: "The small tent," i.e., the tent of a newly married couple that will, with time, become a *khayma kabīra* as children are born.

Jamā'a: A confederation of tribal representatives created by the Spanish during the colonial era. From the Arabic meaning "congregation," it is often called *La Asamblea* or *Yemaa* in Spanish.

Jarca: Spanish term derived from the Arabic *ḥaraka* meaning "a movement" (as in a political or military movement). The *Spanish Dictionary of the Royal Academy* offers two definitions of the word as used by Spaniards: first, a *Jarca* is a group of Moroccan rebels or a group of native troops organized in an irregular fashion; a second, derogatory meaning is that of "uncouth and unruly people."

Madhhab, pl. *Madhāhib*: Legal school of interpretation of Islam.

Maḥaḍra, pl. *Maḥāḍir*: A sedentary or nomadic educational institution dedicated primarily to Islamic instruction. The word has an Arabic root, deriving from the verb *ḥaḍara* ("to attend") but does not exist in its present form as a noun in Modern Standard Arabic itself. *Maḥāḍir* are widely found in Mauritania (Hamel 1999) as well as in the Western Sahara.

Mahr: "Bridal money given by the husband to his wife at the time of marriage," sura 2:237.

Maurophobia: Term used by Martín-Corrales (2004) to refer to the fear and/or hatred of Muslims in general and Moroccans in particular.

Mesīhī (m. sing.) or *mesīhiyya* (fem. sing.): Modern Standard Arabic term referring to Christians.

Milhafa, pl. *malāhif*: A long piece of cloth worn by women over their clothes and that is loosely wrapped around their bodies and head. The term is derived from the verb *lahafa*, meaning "to cover." A *milhafa* is a dress/layer that is worn over another dress/layer.

Moro, pl. *moros*: A Spanish term with strong derogatory connotations primarily used to refer to Muslims from North Africa. Translated as "moors" in English.

Mrābet: Hassaniya Arabic term referring to a teacher of the Qur'an and religious scholar who often fulfilled the role of *mufti* (Islamic scholar authorized to pronounce legal opinions) or of Imam, commanding Islamic law and acting as a mediator within and between groups (El-Hamel 1999, 79, 81; Kuttab, 2002:62). This Hassaniya term derives from the Modern Standard Arabic word *murābit*. According to El-Hamel, "after the Almoravid movement, the term was used in the Moorish literature to mean a teacher of the *mahadra* or a learned Islamic man in general" (1999, 85). While female religious scholars existed in the region (Rasmussen 1998, 263), they were not referred to in either the SARC or my own interviews.

Mufti, m. sing.: Official interpreter or expounder of Islamic law; deliverer of (formal) legal opinions; deliverer of advisory opinions.

Muhajjaba, pl. *muhajjabāt*: A woman who has taken up the veil. From the Arabic verb *hajaba*, meaning "to conceal" or "to veil."

Mujannada (f. sing.): "Mobilized," "recruited," "enlisted," "drafted," "conscripted," "employed," or "used."

Munaqqaba, pl. *munaqqabāt*: The term used to refer to women who wear the niqab or burqa (El Guindi 1999:144).

Mu'tamar, pl. *mu'tamarāt*: Conference (in Spanish, translated as *Congreso* or Congress).

Nadwa, pl. *nadawāt*: Colloquium or symposium.

Nasrāni, masc. pl. *Nasārā*; fem. sing. *Nasrāniyya*, fem. pl. *Nasraniyyāt*: A Qur'anic term used to refer to Christians, as People of the Book. The term is commonly used in the Sahrawi refugee camps to refer, in particular, to Western women (most frequently those from Spain, given their greater number of visits to the camps).

Pluriempleo: A Spanish term that refers to working for more than one employer.

Reconquista: Spanish term literally meaning "reconquest;" refers to the period in the Middle Ages when Spain attempted to regain control from Muslim rulers.

Riḥla, pl. *riḥalāt*: Trip or journey.

Rūm: Collective term referring to Westerners or members of a Christian denomination.

Shari'a: Islamic religious law, based on the Qur'an.

Shaykh, pl. *shuyūkh*: An old, knowledgeable and respected man in the tribe. The term *shaykh* is not, strictly speaking, an Islamic title but is rather used commonly to refer to "a teacher, a scholar, or an elder in a tribe, or he who has a great status in the eyes of his people regarding his knowledge, virtue, or status" (Al-Munjid 2003, Qasmiyeh's translation).

Solidario, pl. *solidarios*: Spanish term that refers to individuals who support and "care" for others in need. Also an adjective.

Solidaridad: Spanish term meaning "solidarity;" most commonly means the "humanitarian" act of offering moral, political, and/or material support to individuals and collectivities that are conceptualized as being "in need" of and deserving such support.

Tirka: Derived from the Modern Standard Arabic root *taraka* ("to leave"), in the Sahrawi context *tirka* literally refers to male youth as a "legacy," in particular in this context as the legacy of the lineage or family to which they belong.

Vacaciones en Paz: "Holidays in Peace" is an annual Spanish hosting program through which approximately 10,000 Sahrawi children leave the refugee camps and spend the summer with Spanish families.

Wālī, f. sing. *wāliya*: Governor (in this context, of an individual refugee camp).

Wilāya, pl. *wilayāt*: Arabic word meaning "province" and that in the Sahrawi refugee camp setting coincides with the administrative division of the population into self-contained refugee camps. Aaiun, Ausserd, Dakhla, and Smara are hence both "provinces" and "camps." This term is sometimes translated as "town" in the English language literature.

References

Abjean, Annaïg. 2003. "Histoire d'Exils: Les Jeunes Sahraouis." In *Sahraouis: Exils—Identité*, edited by A. Abjean and Z. Julien, 19–129. Paris: Harmattan.

Abjean, Annaïg, and Zahra Julien, eds. 2003. *Sahraouis Exils—Identité*. Paris: Harmattan.

Abu-Lughod, Lila, ed. 1998a. *Remaking Women: Feminism and Modernity in the Middle East*. Princeton: Princeton Univ. Press.

Abu-Lughod, Lila. 1998b. "Introduction: Feminist Longings and Postcolonial Conditions." In *Remaking Women: Feminism and Modernity in the Middle East*, edited by L. Abu-Lughod, 3–31. Princeton: Princeton Univ. Press.

Abu-Lughod, Lila. 2001. "Orientalism and Middle East Feminist Studies." *Feminist Studies*, no. 27: 1, 101–113.

Abu-Lughod, Lila. 2002. "Do Muslim Women Really Need Saving? Anthropological Reflections on Cultural Relativism and Its Others." *American Anthropologist*, no. 104: 2, 783–790.

Abun-Nasr, Jamil M. 1987. *A History of the Maghrib in the Islamic Period*. Cambridge: Cambridge Univ. Press.

Abu-Rabia, Aref. 2006. "The Veil and Muslim Women in France: Religious and Political Aspects." *Anthropology of the Middle East*, no. 1: 2, 89–107.

Agence France Presse (AFP). 2004. "Women of Western Sahara refuse to cede equality in name of Islam." *Agence France Presse*, Oct. 10, 2004.

Africa Confidential. 1977. "Women's Lib in the Sahara." *Africa Confidential*, no. 18: 20.

Afshar, Haleh. 1990. "Review." *British Society for Middle Eastern Studies*, no. 17: 1, 77–80.

Afshar, Haleh, Rob Aitken, and Myfanwy Franks. 2005. "Feminisms, Islamophobia and Identities." *Political Studies*, no. 53, 262–283.

Ager, Alastair, Wendy Ager, and Lynellyn Long. 1995. "The Differential Experience of Mozambican Refugee Women and Men." *Journal of Refugee Studies*, no. 9: 3, 265–287.

Ahmed, Akbar S., and David M. Hart. 1984. *Islam in Tribal Societies: from the Atlas to the Indus*. London: Routledge.

Ahmed, Leila. 1992. *Women and Gender in Islam: Historical Roots of a Modern Debate*. New Haven: Yale Univ. Press.

Alba, Richard. 2005. "Bright vs. Blurred Boundaries: Second-generation Assimilation and Exclusion in France, Germany, and the United States." *Ethnic and Racial Studies*, no. 28: 1, 20–49.

Alberola, Miquel. 2003. "El hombre se lo debe todo a la mujer." *El País*, Aug. 11, 2003.

Alexander, M. Jacqui, and Chandra Talpade Mohanty, eds. 1997. *Feminist Genealogies, Colonial Legacies, Democratic Futures*. New York: Routledge.

Algueró-Cuervo, José Ignacio. 2003. *El conflicto del Sáhara Occidental desde una perspectiva canaria*. Tenerife, Spain: Gobierno de Canarias.

Algueró-Cuervo, José Ignacio. 2006. *El Sáhara y España: Claves de una descolonización pendiente*. Santa Cruz de Tenerife, Spain: Idea.

Ali, Ahmed. 2001. *Al-Qur'an. A Contemporary Translation by Ahmed Ali*. Princeton, N.J.: Princeton Univ. Press.

Al-Jaberi, Mohamed Abed. 2006. *Madhal ila al-Qur'an al-Karim—al juz' al-awal fi tarif al-Qur'an*. Beirut: Markez Dirasat.

Al-Jazeera. 2008. "Fat or Fiction," *Africa Uncovered: Mauritania*. Al-Jazeera, Aug. 11, 2008.

Allen, Tim, and David Turton. 1996. "Introduction: In Search of Cool Ground." In *In Search of Cool Ground: War, Flight and Homecoming in Northeast Africa*, edited by T. Allen, 1–22. Geneva: UNRISD in association with James Currey.

Almeida-Bosque, Juan. 1997. *Algo nuevo en el desierto*. Havana, Cuba: Editora Política.

Almond, Ian. 2007. *The New Orientalists: Postmodern Representations of Islam from Foucault to Baudrillard*. London: I. B. Tauris.

Al-Munjid. 2003. *Al-Munjid fi al-lugha wa-l-a'lam*. Beirut: Dar El-Mashriq.

Alonso, Francisco, and Manuel G. Vicente. 1998. *Territorio ocupado*. Vigo, Spain: Ediçións Xerais de Galicia.

Alonso, Luis. M. 2003. "Esperanza." *El Faro de Vigo*. Accessed at http://www.entender-sahara.com/articulo.php?sec=documentosandid=11.

Amnesty International. 1996. *Morocco: Human Rights Violations in Western Sahara.* London: Amnesty International, International Secretariat.

Amoretti, Biancamaria Scarcia. 1987. "Women in the Western Sahara." In *War and Refugees: The Western Sahara Conflict*, edited by R. Lawless and L. Monahan, 186–193. London: Pinter.

Amuchastegui-Álvarez, Domingo. 1988. *Historia Contemporánea de Asia y África.* Havana, Cuba: Editorial Pueblo y Educación.

Anderson, Benedict. 1991. *Imagined Communities: Reflections on the Origin and Spread of Nationalism*, 2nd ed. London: Verso.

Andrade. 2003. *El Territorio del Silencio: Un viaje por el Sáhara Occidental.* Tegueste, Tenerife, Spain: Ediciones Baile del Sol.

AOE. 1967. "En el Sáhara español no hay esclavitud." *A.O.E. Semanario Gráfico de África Occidental Española*, 9.

Appadurai, Arjun. 2003. "Sovereignty without Territoriality: Notes for a Postnational Geography." In *The Anthropology of Space and Place. Locating Culture*, edited by S. M. Low and D. Lawrence-Zuniga, 337–350. Oxford: Blackwell Publishing.

Armstrong, Sue, and Olivia Bennett. 2002. "Representing the Resettled: The Ethical Issues Raised by Research and Representation of the San." In *Conservation and Mobile Indigenous Peoples: Displacement, Forced Settlement, and Sustainable Development*, edited by D. Chatty and M. Colchester, 188–201. Oxford: Berghahn Books.

ARSO. 2004. "Western Sahara—News. Weeks 43–44: 17.10-30.10.2004." Accessed at http://www.arso.org/01-e04-4344.htm.

ARSO. 2006. "Western Sahara—News. Weeks 07-08: 12–25/02/2006." Accessed at http://www.arso.org/01-e06-0708.htm.

Asad, Talal, ed. 1973. *Anthropology and the Colonial Encounter.* London: Ithaca Press.

Asad, Talal. 2001. *Thinking about Secularism and Law in Egypt.* Leiden, the Netherlands: ISIM, Leiden University.

Asad, Talal. 2006. "Trying to Understand French Secularism." In *Political Theologies: Public Religions in a Post-secular World*, edited by H. de Vries and L. E. Sullivan, 494–526. New York: Fordham Univ. Press.

Ashcroft, Bill, Gareth Griffiths, and Helen Tiffin. 1989. *The Empire Writes Back: Theory and Practice in Post-colonial Literatures.* London: Routledge.

Ayat, G'nah Allah. 1993. "Sahrawi Women, Between Ambition and Suffering." In *Today's Refugees, Tomorrow's Leaders: Report of the Saharawi Women Refugee Conference*, edited by One World Action. London: One World Action.

Ayotte, Kevin J., and Mary E. Husain. 2005. "Securing Afghan Women: Neocolonialism, Epistemic Violence, and the Rhetoric of the Veil." *National Women's Studies Association Journal*, no. 17: 3, 112–133.

Baalbaki, Rohi. 2005. *Al-Mawrid: A Modern Arabic-English Dictionary* 19th ed. Beirut: Dar el-Ilm Lilmalayin.

Badía-Martí, Anna, Xavier Fernández-Pons, Sergio Roman, and Carranza Förster. 1999. *La Cuestión del Sáhara Occidental Ante La Organización de las Naciones Unidas*. Madrid: Instituto de Estudios Internacionales y Europeos "Francisco de Vitoria."

Badil Resource Centre. 2006. *Displaced by the Wall: Pilot Study on Forced Displacement Caused by the Construction of the West Bank Wall and Its Associated Regime in the Occupied Palestinian Territories*. Bethlehem and Geneva: Badil Resource Centre for Palestinian and Refugee Rights and the Norwegian Refugee Council/Internal Displacement Monitoring Centre.

Badran, Margot. 1995. *Feminists, Islam, and Nation: Gender and the Making of Modern Egypt*. Princeton: Princeton Univ. Press.

Bahramitash, Roksana. 2005. "The War on Terror, Feminist Orientalism and Orientalist Feminism: Case Studies of Two North American Bestsellers." *Critique: Critical Middle Eastern Studies*, no. 14: 2, 221–235.

Balac, Ana. 1993. "From Confidence in the Present to Concern for the Future." In *Today's Refugees, Tomorrow's Leaders: Report of the Saharawi Women Refugee Conference*, edited by One World Action, 12–14. London: One World Action.

Barbier, Maurice. 1982. *Le Conflit du Sahara Occidental*. Paris: L'Harmattan.

Bárbulo, Tomas. 2002. *La Historia Prohibida del Sáhara Español*, 1st ed. Barcelona, Spain: Ediciones Destino.

Barnes, Terri. 1999. *"We women worked so hard": Gender, Urbanization, and Social Reproduction in Colonial Harare, Zimbabwe, 1930–1956*. Oxford: James Currey.

Barona-Castañeda, Claudia. 2004. *Los hijos de la nube: Estructura y vicisitudes del Sáhara Español desde 1958 hasta la debacle*. Madrid: Langre.

Barrera, Mora. 2008. "'Están esperando que vayamos a la guerra para incluirnos en su lista de organizaciones terroristas.' Entrevista a Maima Mahamud Nayem. Secretaria de Estado de Asuntos Sociales y Promoción de la Mujer del Frente Polisario." Accessed at http://www.bottup.com/index.php?option=com_con tentandtask=viewandid=2904andItemid=114.

Bartkowski, John P., and Jen'nan Ghazal Read. 2003. "Veiled Submission: Gender, Power, and Identity among Evangelical and Muslim Women in the United States." *Qualitative Sociology*, no. 26: 1, 71–92.

Bashir, Dahi. 1996. "The Case of Western Sahara and the Failure of the United Nations." In *Unrepresented Nations and Peoples Organization Yearbook 1996*, edited by C. A. Mullen and J. Ryan, 221–226. The Hague, the Netherlands: Kluwer Law International.

Belaza, Monica. 2008. "74 mujeres no llegaron a fin de año." *El País*, Jan. 5, 2008.

Bellil, Rachid. 2000. *Les oasis du Gourara (Sahara algérien)*. Paris: Editions Peeters.

Benson, Janet. 1994. "Reinterpreting Gender: Southeast Asian Refugees and American Society." In *Reconstructing Lives, Recapturing Meaning: Refugee Identity, Gender and Culture Change*, edited by L. A. Camino and R. M. Krulfeld, 75–96. Basel, Switzerland: Gordon and Breach.

Bernard, H. Russell. 1995. *Research Methods in Anthropology: Qualitative and Quantitative Approaches*, 2nd ed. Walnut Creek, Calif.: AltaMira Press.

Bernard, H. Russell. 2000. *Social Research Methods: Qualitative and Quantitative Approaches*. London: SAGE.

Bernard, H. Russell. 2006. *Research Methods in Anthropology: Qualitative and Quantitative Approaches*, 4th ed. Lanham, Md.: AltaMira Press.

Betteridge, Anne H. 1985. "Gift Exchange in Iran: The Locus of Self-Identity in Social Interaction." *Anthropological Quarterly*, no. 58: 4, 190–202.

Bhatia, Michael. 2001. "The Western Sahara under Polisario Control." *Review of African Political Economy*, no. 28: 88, 291–298.

Bhatia, Michael. 2003. "Repatriation under a Peace Process: Mandated Return in the Western Sahara." *International Journal of Refugee Law*, no. 15: 4, 786–822.

Bil-Amri, Ramadan, and Hassan Ashraf. 2008. "*Kharajat bi-tamwil Jazairi wa raisuha daa' li-'adam al-ihtikak bi-l-hujjaj al-Maghariba*." *Al-Arabiya*, Nov. 27, 2008. http://www.alarabiya.net/save_print.php?save=1andcont_id=60934.

Black, Richard. 1984. *Helping Refugees to Help Themselves*. Unpublished Work, Refugee Studies Centre Grey Literature Collection, Univ. of Oxford.

Blank, Diana. 1999. "A Veil of Controversy." *Interventions: International Journal of Postcolonial Studies*, no. 1: 4, 536–554.

Bob, Clifford. 2005. *The Marketing of Rebellion: Insurgents, Media and International Activism*. Cambridge: Cambridge Univ. Press.

Bonner, Frances, and Lizbeth Goodman. 1992. "Introduction: On Imagining Women." In *Imagining Women: Cultural Representations and Gender*, edited by F. Bonner, L. Goodman, R. Allen, L. Janes and C. King, 1–12. Cambridge: Polity.

Bonte, Pierre. 2006. "Individuals, Factions and Tribes among Moorish Societies." In *Nomadic Societies in the Middle East and North Africa: Entering the 21st Century*, edited by D. Chatty, 98–122. Leiden, the Netherlands: Brill.

Bontems, Claude. 1984. *La Guerre du Sahara Occidental*, 1st ed. Paris: Presses Universitaires de France.

Bourdieu, Pierre. 1985. "The Social Space and the Genesis of Groups." *Theory and Society*, no. 14: 6, 723–744.

Bowen, Wayne H. 2006. *Spain during World War II*. Columbia: Univ. of Missouri Press.

Brazier, Chris. 1997. "Special Edition: War and Peace in Western Sahara." *The New Internationalist*, no. 297.

Brazier, Chris. 2004. "Country Profile: Western Sahara." *New Internationalist*, no. 374.

Brittain, Victoria. 1986. "Polisario's Battle for the Wall." *The Guardian*, Feb. 2, 1986.

Brown, Lesley. 1993. *The New Shorter Oxford English Dictionary on Historical Principles*. Oxford: Clarendon.

Bryant, Elizabeth. 2004. "Refugees Build a Desert Democracy in Saharan Africa." *United Press International*, May 12, 2004.

Bulbeck, Chilla. 1998. *Re-orienting Western Feminisms: Women's Diversity in a Postcolonial World*. Cambridge: Cambridge Univ. Press.

Butler, Judith. 1988. "Performative Acts and Gender Constitution: An Essay in Phenomenology and Feminist Theory." *Theatre Journal*, no. 40: 4, 519–531.

Butler, Judith. 1990. *Gender Trouble: Feminism and the Subversion of Identity*. New York: Routledge.

Butler, Judith. 1993. *Bodies That Matter: On the Discursive Limits of "Sex."* New York: Routledge.

Butterfield, Jeremy. 2003. *Collins Spanish Dictionary; Collins diccionario inglés*, 7th ed. Glasgow: HarperCollins.

Buzan, Barry, and Ole Weaver. 1997. "Slippery? Contradictory? Sociologically Untenable? The Copenhagen School Replies." *Review of International Studies*, no. 23, 241–250.

Byrne, Bridget. 1996. *Gender, Conflict and Development. Volume 1, Overview*. Brighton, United Kingdom: Univ. of Sussex.

Callamard, Agnes. 1999. "Refugee Women: A Gendered and Political Analysis of the Refugee Experience." In *Refugees: Perspectives on the Experience of Forced Migration*, edited by A. Ager, 196–214. London: Continuum.

Callaway, Helen. 1986. "Survival and Support: Women's Forms of Political Action." In *Caught Up in Conflict: Women's Responses to Political Strife*, edited by R. Ridd and H. Callaway, 214–230. Basingstoke, United Kingdom: Macmillan Education in association with the Oxford Univ. Women's Studies Committee.

Campbell, John R. 2004. "Ethnic Minorities and Development: A Prospective Look at the Situation of African Pastoralists and Hunter-Gatherers." *Ethnicities*, no. 4: 1, 5–26.

Cannon, Garland, and Beatrice Méndez Egle. 1979. "New Borrowings in English." *American Speech*, no. 54: 1, 22–37.

Caratini, Sophie. 1989a. "A Propos des Rgaybat du Sahara Occidental l'Organisation 'Tribal' en Question. (Contribution to Round Table: Le Nomade, L'Oasis et la Ville)." *Villes du monde arabe*, no. 20, 237–245.

Caratini, Sophie. 1989b. *Les Rgaybat (1610–1934)*. Paris: Harmattan.

Caratini, Sophie. 1989c. "A propos du mariage 'arabe': Discours endogame et pratiques exogames-L'Exemple des Rgaybat du nord-ouest saharien." *L'Homme*, no. 29: 2, 30–49.

Caratini, Sophie. 2000. "Système de parenté sahraoui: L'impact de la révolution." *L'Homme*, no. 154–155, 431–456.

Caratini, Sophie. 2003a. *La république des sables: Anthropologie d'une révolution*. Paris: Harmattan.

Caratini, Sophie. 2003b. "Preface." In *Sahraouis: Exils—identité*, edited by A. Abjean and Z. Julien, 9–17. Paris: Harmattan.

Caratini, Sophie. 2006. *La prisión del tiempo: Los cambios sociales en los campamentos de refugiados saharauis*. Bilbao, Spain: Cuadernos Bakeaz.

Casciarri, Barbara. 2006. "Coping with Shrinking Spaces: The Ait Unzar Pastoralists of South-eastern Morocco." In *Nomadic Societies in the Middle East and North Africa: Entering the 21st Century*, edited by D. Chatty, 393–430. Leiden, the Netherlands: Brill.

Castaño-Boullón, Mary Carmen. 2003. "Sr. Director." Accessed at http://www.entender-sahara.com/articulo.php?sec=documentosandid=11.

Cazón, Patricia. 2004. *Lágrimas de arena: La historia de Aicha Embarek*, 1st ed. Barcelona: El Aleph.

Cembrero, Ignacio. 2008. "El Sáhara lastra a Marruecos." *El País*, March 11, 2008.

Chamberlain, Robert. 2005. *Stories of a Nation: Historical Narratives and Visions of the Future in Saharawi Refugee Camps*. Refugee Studies Centre Working Paper 29, Oxford: Refugee Studies Centre.

Chassey, Francis de. 1977. *L'Etrier, La Houe et le Livre*. Paris: Anthropos.

Chatterjee, Partha. 1986. *Nationalist Thought and the Colonial World: A Derivative Discourse?* London: Zed for the United Nations University.

Chatterjee, Partha. 1993. *The Nation and Its Fragments: Colonial and Postcolonial Histories*. Princeton, N.J.: Princeton Univ. Press.

Chatty, Dawn. 2000. "Women Working in Oman: Individual Choice and Cultural Constraints." *International Journal of Middle East Studies*, no. 32, 241–254.

Chatty, Dawn. 2010. "Introduction." In *Deterritorialised Afghan and Sahrawi Youth: Refugees from the Margins of the Middle East*, edited by D. Chatty, 1–36. Oxford: Berghahn Books.

Chatty, Dawn and Colchester, Marcus, eds. 2002. *Conservation and Mobile Indigenous Peoples: Displacement, Forced Settlement, and Sustainable Development*. Oxford: Berghahn Books.

Chatty, Dawn, Elena Fiddian-Qasmiyeh, and Gina Crivello. 2010. "Identity With/out Territory: Sahrawi Refugee Youth in Transnational Space." In *Deterritorialised Afghan and Sahrawi Youth: Refugees from the Margins of the Middle East*, edited by D. Chatty, 37–84. Oxford: Berghahn Books.

Chinkin, Christine, ed. 1993. *Saharawi Women and International Law*. London: One World Action.

Chopra, Jarat. 1994. *United Nations Determination of the Western Saharan Self*. Oslo: Norwegian Institute of International Affairs.

Chopra, Jarat. 1997. "A Chance for Peace in Western Sahara." *Survival*, no. 39: 3, 51–65.

Chopra, Jarat. 1999. *Peace-maintenance: The Evolution of International Political Authority*. London: Routledge.

Chopra, Jarat, and Tanja Hohe. 2004. "Participatory Intervention." *Global Governance*, no. 10, 289–305.

Cisse, M. A. 1985. *El Derecho de Autodeterminación del Pueblo Saharaui*. Trabajo de Diploma de la Facultad de Derecho. Universidad de La Habana, Havana, Cuba.

Coggan, Felicity. 2003. "Sahrawi Leader Tours New Zealand." *The Militant*, June 23, 2003.

Cola Alberich, Julio. 1962. *La etnografía de Ifni y del Sáhara Español*. Madrid: Organización para el Fomento de la Enseñanza.

Cole, Juan R. I., and Deniz Kandiyoti. 2002. "Nationalism and the Colonial Legacy in the Middle East and Central Asia: Introduction." *International Journal of Middle East Studies*, no. 34, 189–203.

Conquergood, Dwight. 1992. "Ethnography, Rhetoric, and Performance." *Quarterly Journal of Speech*, no. 78: 1, 80–97.

Conklin, Beth. 1997. "Body Paint, Feathers, and VCRs: Aesthetics and Authenticity in Amazonian Activism." *American Ethnologist*, no. 24: 4, 711–737.

Conyers, Diana, and Rob Mellors. 2005. "Aid Ineffectiveness in Sub-Saharan Africa: The Problem of Donor Capacity." *Institute of Development Studies Bulletin*, no. 36: 3, 83–89.

Cooke, Bill, and Uma Kothari, eds. 2001. *Participation, the New Tyranny?* London: Zed.

Coomaraswamy, Radhika. 1994. "To Bellow Like a Cow: Women, Ethnicity and the Discourse of Rights." In *Human Rights of Women: National and International Perspectives*, edited by R. Cook, 39–57. Philadelphia: Univ. of Pennsylvania Press.

Côté, James E. and Charles Levine. 2002. *Identity Formation, Agency, and Culture: A Social Psychological Synthesis*. London: Erlbaum.

Cozza, Nicola. 2004. *Singing Like Wood-birds: Refugee Camps and Exile in the Construction of the Saharawi Nation*. Unpublished Dissertation in Development Studies, Univ. of Oxford.

Cozza, Nicola. 2010. "Food and Identity among Sahrawi Refugee Children and Young People." In *Deterritorialised Afghan and Sahrawi Youth: Refugees from the Margins of the Middle East*, edited by D. Chatty, 119–144. Oxford: Berghahn Books.

Criado, Ramón. 1977. *Sáhara: Pasión y muerte de un sueño colonial*. Paris: Ruedo Ibérico.

Crisp, Jeff. 1999. "'Who has counted the refugees?' UNHCR and the Politics of Numbers." *New Issues in Refugee Research*, Working Paper No. 12. Geneva: UNHCR.

Crisp, Jeff. 2003. *No Solution in Sight: The Problem of Protracted Refugee Situations in Africa*. San Diego: Univ. of California.

Crivello, Gina, Elena Fiddian, and Dawn Chatty. 2005. *Lessons Learned Report: The Transnationalisation of Care: Sahrawi Refugee Children in a Spanish Host Programme*. Oxford: Refugee Studies Centre.

Crivello, Gina, and Elena Fiddian-Qasmiyeh. 2010. "The Ties That Bind: Sahrawi Children and the Mediation of Aid in Exile." In *Deterritorialized Youth: Sahrawi and Afghan Refugees at the Margins of the Middle East*, edited by D. Chatty, 85–118. Oxford: Berghahn Books.

Daha, Lehdia. 2004. "¿Donde estan nuestras mujeres?," Nov. 15, 2005. Accessed at http://sahara_opinions.site.voila.fr/.

Damis, John J. 1983. *Conflict in Northwest Africa: the Western Sahara dispute*. Stanford, Calif.: Hoover Institution Press.

Darbouche, Hakim. 2007. *What Will It Take to Resolve the Dispute in Western Sahara?* Centre for European Policy Studies Policy Brief, no. 133.

Darby, Phillip. 1997. "Postcolonialism." In *At the Edge of International Relations: Postcolonialism, Gender, and Dependency*, edited by P. Darby, 12–31. London: Pinter.

de Beauvoir, Simone. 1972. *The Second Sex*. (Translated by H. M. Parshley). Harmondsworth, United Kingdom: Penguin.

Delegación Saharaui Castilla y León. 2002. "Memorando." Accessed at http://es.geocities.com/aichaembarek2/constitucion/carta_ayunta_2.JPG.

del Pino, Domingo. 2003. "España y Marruecos: reencuentro con soluciones a medias." *Real Instituto El Cano*, ARI N° 147–2003.

Déniz-Ramírez, Francisco Antonio. 1991. *R.A.S.D.: Educación y proceso de liberación nacional*. Federación Canaria de Ayuntamientos y Cabildos Hermanados con el Pueblo Saharaui.

Department of Foreign Affairs of the Republic of South Africa. 2007. *Notes from Media Briefing on UNGA 62 and UNSC,* Sept. 13, 2007. Accessed at http://www.dfa.gov.za/docs/2007/un0914.htm.

Department of Foreign Affairs of the Republic of South Africa. 2008. *Transcript of Media Briefing on the United Nations Security Council*, Union Buildings, Pretoria, South Africa. Accessed at http://www.info.gov.za/speeches/2008/080 42510151001.htm.

Díaz del Ribero, Francisco-Lorenzo. 1975. *El Sáhara Occidental: Pasado y presente*. Madrid: Gisa Ediciones.

Díaz, Lorena. 2003. "La Asociación Critica a la Familia Asturiana: Amigos del Sáhara rechaza la vuelta de Huria." *La Voz de Asturias*, July 16, 2003. Accessed at http://www.lavozdeasturias.es/noticias/noticia.asp?pkid=71799.

Diego-Aguirre, José Ramón. 1988. *Historia del Sáhara Español*. Madrid: Kaydeda.

Diego-Aguirre, José Ramón. 1991. *Guerra en el Sáhara*. Madrid: Ediciones Istmo.

Diego-Aguirre, José Ramón. 1993. *La última guerra colonial de España: Ifni-Sáhara (1957–1958)*, 1st ed. Málaga, Spain: Editorial Algazara.

Draper, Patricia. 1975. "!Kung Women: Contrasts in Sexual Egalitarianism in Foraging and Sedentary Contexts." In *Toward an Anthropology of Women*, edited by R. Reiter, 77–109. New York: Monthly Review Press.

Dugan, Julie, Carolyn J. Fowler, and Paul A. Bolton. 2000. "Assessing the Opportunity for Sexual Violence against Women and Children in Refugee Camps." *The Journal of Humanitarian Assistance*, Aug. 2000. Accessed at http://www.jha.ac/articles/a060.htm.

Eagleton, Terry. 1983. *Literary Theory: An Introduction*. Oxford: Basil Blackwell.

ECHO. 2001. *Évaluation des plans globaux humanitaires de echo en faveur des réfugiés sahraouis. Rapport final. Secteurs: Réhabilitation / produits non-alimentaires.* Accessed at http://ec.europa.eu/echo/evaluation/country_en.htm#sah and http://ec.europa.eu/echo/pdf_files/evaluation/2001/sahara3_annex.pdf.

ECHO. 2005. *Decision to Grant Humanitarian Aid.* ECHO/DZA/BUD/2005/01000.

Edward, Jane Kani. 2001. "South Sudanese Refugee Women: Questioning the Past, Imagining the Future." In *Women's Rights and Human Rights: International Historical Perspectives*, edited by K. H. Grimshaw and M. Lake, 272–289. Hampshire, United Kingdom: Palgrave.

Edwards, Catherine. 1999. "Saharawi Republic Waits to Be Born." *Insight on the News*, Oct. 4, 1999. Accessed at http://findarticles.com/p/articles/mi_m1571 /is_37_15/ai_56184193/pg_3.

EFE. 2007. "Las niñas de Ceuta vuelven al colegio con el velo tras el requerimiento del Ministerio," Oct. 10, 2007. Accessed at http://www.publico.es/espana /005429/ninas/ceuta/velo.

El-Bushra, Judy. 2000. "Transforming Conflict: Some Thoughts on a Gendered Understanding of Conflict Processes." In *States of Conflict: Gender, Violence and Resistance*, edited by S. Jacobs, R. Jacobson and J. Marchbank, 66–86. London: Zed Books.

El-Bushra, Judy, and Cécile Mukarubuga. 1995. "Women, War and Transition." *Gender and Development*, no. 3: 3, 16–22.

El-Bushra, Judy, and Eugenia Piza-López. 1993. *Development in Conflict: The Gender Dimension.* Oxford: Oxfam/ACORD.

El-Fethi, Khadija. 2007. "*Lil-zafr bi-zawj wa sawnan lil-ard.*" ("To win a groom and to preserve honor"). *Al-Arabiya*, Dec. 17, 2007.

El-Guindi, Fadwa. 1999. *Veil: Modesty, Privacy and Resistance.* Oxford: Berg.

El-Guindi, Fadwa. 2003. "Veiling Resistance." In *Feminist Postcolonial Theory: A Reader*, edited by R. Lewis and S. Mills, 586–609. Edinburgh: Edinburgh Univ. Press.

El-Hamel, Chouki. 1999. "The Transmission of Islamic Knowledge in Moorish Society from the Rise of the Almoravids to the 19th Century." *Journal of Religion in Africa*, no. 29: 1, 62–87.

Elizondo, Luis, Chejna Mohamed Mehdi, and Marisa Sanz. 2008. *Micro-créditos en el Sahara: Manual para la solicitud de credito en los campamentos Saharauis.* Bilbao, Spain: HEGOA.

Elmadmad, Khadija. 1999. "The Human Rights of Refugees with Special Reference to Muslim Refugee Women." In *Engendering Forced Migration: Theory and Practice*, edited by D. Indra, 261–271. New York: Berghahn Books.

Embarek, Aicha. n.d. "Para las autoridades españolas." Accessed at http://es .geocities.com/aichaembarek2/primeracarta/cartaautoridades.

Engels, Friedrich. 1902/1884. *The Origin of the Family, Private Property and the State*, (Translated by E. Untermann.) Chicago: Charles H. Kerr.

Enloe, Cynthia H. 1989. *Bananas, Beaches and Bases: Making Feminist Sense of International Politics*. London: Pandora.

Enloe, Cynthia H. 1990. "Womenandchildren: Making Feminist Sense of the Persian Gulf Crisis." *The Village Voice*, Sept. 25, 1990.

Enloe, Cynthia H. 1991. "'Womenandchildren': Propaganda Tools of Patriarchy." In *Mobilising Democracy: Changing the US Role in the Middle East*, edited by G. Bates, 89ff. Monroe, Me.: Common Courage Press.

Enloe, Cynthia H. 2000a. *Bananas, Beaches and Bases: Making Feminist Sense of International Politics*. Berkeley: Univ. of California Press.

Enloe, Cynthia H. 2000b. *Maneuvers: The International Politics of Militarizing Women's Lives*. Berkeley: Univ. of California Press.

Ennaji, Moha. 2008. "Steps to the Integration of Moroccan Women in Development." *British Journal of Middle Eastern Studies*, no. 35: 3, 339–348.

Escobar, Arturo. 1995. *Encountering Development: The Making and Unmaking of the Third World*. Princeton, N.J.: Princeton Univ. Press.

Esposito, John L. with Natana J. DeLong-Bas. 2001. *Women in Muslim Family Law*. Syracuse: Syracuse Univ. Press.

Es-Sweyih, Mohamed-Fadel. 2001. *El Primer Estado del Sáhara Occidental* (Translated by N. Raballand and C. Astiaso). Available at http://www.cemoc.com .ar/estadosaharaui.pdf.

Esteso, Maria José. 2006. "Entrevista: Fatma el Mehdi, Secretaria General de la Union Nacional de Mujeres Saharauis." *Diagonal*, March 16–29, 2006. Accessed at http://diagonalperiodico.net/spip.php?article423.

EU. 2004. *EU Humanitarian Aid to Sahrawi Refugees in Algeria. Summary: July 22, 2004: Commission Allocates €8 Million in Humanitarian Aid to Sahrawi Refugees in Algeria (Brussels)*. EU.

Europa Press. 2008. "La Policía encuentra en el País Vasco a una niña saharaui desaparecida hace un año." *El País*, June 28, 2008.

Fanon, Frantz. 1963. *The Wretched of the Earth*. London: MacGibbon and Kee.

Fanon, Frantz. 1965. *Studies in a Dying Colonialism*. New York: Monthly Review Press.

Farah, Randa. 2006. "Oral History in the Palestinian and Sahrawi Contexts: A Comparative Approach." *Al-Majdal*, no. 32, 25–30.

Fenster, Tovi. 1999. "Gender, Planning and Human Rights: Practical Lessons." In *Gender, Planning and Human Rights*, edited by T. Fenster, 3–24. London and New York: Routledge.

Feo, Pilar. 2003. "Hijas de la Arena." *Diario de Avisos*, Feb. 2, 2003. Accessed at http://www.elguanche.net/hijasdelaarena.htm.

Fernández, E. 2003. "Movilización por la niña mariposa." *El Mundo*, Sept. 7, 2003.

Fernández-Puertas, Antonio. 1994. "Sobre los relieves en la predela de los retablos de la Capilla Real de Granada." *Anales de la Historia del Arte*, no. 4.

Fernández-Aceytuno Gavarrón, Mariano. 1996. *Siroco: Recuerdos de un oficial de grupos nómadas: La verdadera historia del pueblo saharaui*, 2nd ed. Valladolid, Spain: Simancas.

Ferrer, Isabel. 2008. "Holanda inaugura el primer Salón del Divorcio." *El País*, Feb. 11, 2008.

Ferrer-Lloret, Jaume. 2002. *La aplicación del principio de autodeterminación de los pueblos: Sáhara Occidental y Timor Oriental*. Alicante, Spain: Universidad de Alicante.

Fiddian, Elena. 2002. *Promoting Sustainable Gender Roles during Exile: A Critical Analysis with Reference to the Sahrawi Refugee Camps*. Unpublished MSc Thesis, London School of Economics and Political Science, Univ. of London.

Fiddian, Elena. 2006a. "Education in Exile: Gendered Dilemmas," Unpublished paper presented at the Theory and Methodology Seminar Series, Gender Studies Centre, Univ. of Cambridge, Feb. 9, 2006.

Fiddian, Elena. 2006b. "Relocating: The Asylum Experience in Cairo." *Interventions: International Journal of Postcolonial Studies*, no. 28: 2, 295–318.

Fiddian-Qasmiyeh, Elena. 2009. "Representing Sahrawi Refugee's 'Educational Displacement' to Cuba: Self-sufficient Agents or Manipulated Victims in Conflict?" *Journal of Refugee Studies*, no. 22: 3, 323–350.

Fiddian-Qasmiyeh, Elena. 2010a. "Education, Migration and Internationalism: Situating Muslim Middle Eastern and North African Students in Cuba." *The Journal of North African Studies*, no. 14: 3, 137–155.

Fiddian-Qasmiyeh, Elena. 2010b. "When the Self Becomes Other: Representations of Gender, Islam and the Politics of Survival in the Sahrawi refugee camps." In *Dispossession and Displacement: Forced Migration in the Middle East and North Africa*, edited by D. Chatty and B. Finlayson, 171–196. Oxford: Oxford Univ. Press.

Fiddian-Qasmiyeh, Elena. 2010c. "Concealing Violence against Women in the Sahrawi Refugee Camps: The Politicization of Victimhood." In *Global Perspectives on War, Gender and Health: The Sociology and Anthropology of Suffering*, edited by H. Bradby and G. Hundt, 99–110. Farnham, United Kingdom: Ashgate.

Fiddian-Qasmiyeh, Elena. 2010d. "'Ideal' Refugee Women and Gender Equality Mainstreaming: 'Good Practice' For Whom?" *Refugee Survey Quarterly*, no. 29: 2, 64–84.

Fiddian-Qasmiyeh, Elena. 2011a. "The Pragmatics of Performance: Putting 'Faith' in Aid," *Journal of Refugee Studies* (Special Issue on "Faith-Based Humanitarianism in Contexts of Forced Displacement"), no. 24: 3, 533–547.

Fiddian-Qasmiyeh, Elena. 2011b. "Histories of Displacement: Intersections between Ethnicity, Gender and Class." *Journal of North African Studies*, no. 16: 1, 31–48.

Fiddian-Qasmiyeh, Elena. 2011c. *Sahrawi Refugees' Protracted Displacement: Challenges and Opportunities beyond Encampment*, Refugee Studies Centre Policy Briefing, no. 7. Oxford: Refugee Studies Centre.

Fiddian-Qasmiyeh, Elena. 2011d. "Paradoxes of Sahrawi Refugees' Educational Migration: Promoting Self-sufficiency or Renewing Dependency?" *Comparative Education*, no. 47: 4, 433–447.

Fiddian-Qasmiyeh, Elena. 2012a. "Invisible Refugees and/or Overlapping Refugeedom? Protecting Sahrawis and Palestinians Displaced by the 2011 Libyan Uprising," *International Journal of Refugee Law*, no. 24: 2, 263–293.

Fiddian-Qasmiyeh, Elena. 2012b. "Conflicting Missions? The Politics of Evangelical Humanitarianism in the Sahrawi and Palestinian Protracted Refugee Situations," Max Planck Institute for the Study of Religious and Ethnic Diversity Working Paper, no. 12: 6.

Fiddian-Qasmiyeh, Elena. 2013a. "Transnational Childhood and Adolescence: Mobilising Sahrawi Identity and Politics across Time and Space," *Journal of Ethnic and Racial Studies*, no. 36: 5, 875–895.

Fiddian-Qasmiyeh, Elena. 2013b. "Transnational 'Abductions' and Transnational Interventions? Coercive, Discursive and Legal Battles over Sahrawi Girls and Women," *Gender, Place, and Culture*, iFirst article 2013. DOI: 10.1080/0966369X.2013.769427.

Fiddian-Qasmiyeh, Elena. 2013c. "Inter-Generational Negotiations of Religious Identity, Belief and Practice: Child, Youth and Adult Perspectives from Three Cities." In *Rescripting Religion in the City: Migration and Religious Identity in the Modern Metropolis*, edited by J. Garnett and A. Harris, 163–76. Farnham, United Kingdom: Ashgate.

Fiddian-Qasmiyeh, Elena. 2013d. "The Intergenerational Politics of 'Travelling Memories': Sahrawi Refugee Youth Remembering Home-Land and Home-Camp," Journal of Intercultural Studies, 34(6). DOI: 10.1080/07256868.2012.746170.

Fiddian-Qasmiyeh, Elena. forthcoming/2014a. "Embracing Transculturalism and Footnoting Islam in Accounts of Arab Migration to Cuba," *Interventions: the International Journal of Postcolonial Studies.*

Fiddian-Qasmiyeh, Elena. forthcoming/2014b. "Gender and Forced Migration," in *The Oxford Handbook of Refugee and Forced Migration Studies,* edited by E. Fiddian-Qasmiyeh, G. Loescher, K. Long and N. Sigona. Oxford: Oxford University Press.

Fiddian-Qasmiyeh, Elena. unpublished. "Sahrawi-Libyan Exchanges (1976–2011): Reflections and Expectations." Unpublished manuscript on file with author.

Fiddian-Qasmiyeh, Elena, and Yousif M. Qasmiyeh. 2010. "Muslim Asylum-Seekers and Refugees: Negotiating Identity, Politics and Religion in the UK," *Journal of Refugee Studies,* no. 23: 3, 294–314.

Fiddian-Qasmiyeh, Elena, and Yousif M. Qasmiyeh. unpublished. "Citation and Recitation: Post/colonial Linguistic Legacies." Unpublished manuscript on file with authors.

Finlay, Linda, and Brendan Gough. 2003. *Reflexivity: A Practical Guide for Researchers in Health and Social Sciences.* Oxford: Blackwell Science.

Firebrace, James. 1985. *Summary Report on the Sahrawi Refugee Camps, Southern Algeria—A Visit by James Firebrace, War on Want Programme Officer 9–17 April 1985.* London: War on Want.

Firebrace, James. 1987. "The Sahrawi Refugees: Lessons and Prospects." In *War and Refugees: The Western Sahara Conflict,* edited by R. Lawless and L. Monahan, 167–185. London: Pinter.

Firebrace, James, and Jeremy Harding. 1987. *Exiles of the Sahara: The Sahrawi Refugees Shape Their Future.* London: War on Want.

Flores-Morales, Angel. 1946. *El Sáhara Español: Ensayo de geografía física, humana y económica.* Madrid: Alta Comisaría de España.

Forsythe, Diana E. 1999. "'It's Just a Matter of Common Sense': Ethnography as Invisible Work." *Computer Supported Cooperative Work,* no. 8: 1–2, 127–145.

Foucault, Michel. 1979. *Discipline and Punish: The Birth of the Prison.* Harmondsworth, United Kingdom: Penguin Books.

Foucault, Michel. 1989. *Foucault Live: Interviews 1966–84.* New York: Semiotext.

Foucault, Michel. 2006. *The Archaeology of Knowledge.* (Translated by A. M. S. Smith.) Oxford: Routledge. Originally published 1972.

Gandolfi, Nicoletta. 1989. "A propósito del Sáhara Occidental: Testimonios de los Canarios que allí residieron durante el periodo colonial." Accessed at http://www.arso.org/canariosita.htm.

Ganeshpanchan, Zinthiya. 2005. "Domestic and Gender Based Violence among Refugees and Internally Displaced Women." *Humiliation Studies*. Accessed at http://www.humiliationstudies.org/documents/GaneshpanchanDomestic ViolenceIDPS.pdf.

García, Alejandro. 2001. *Historias del Sahara: El mejor y el peor de los mundos*. Madrid: Catarata.

Gaudio, Attilio. 1975. *Sahara espagnol, Fin d'un mythe colonial?* Rabat, Morocco: Arrissala.

Gaudio, Attilio. 1978. *Le dossier du Sahara occidental*. Paris: Nouvelles Éditions Latines.

Gaudio, Attilio. 1993. *Les populations du Sahara occidental: Histoire, vie et culture*. Paris: Karthala.

Geertz, Clifford. 1973. *The Interpretation of Cultures: Selected Essays*. New York: Basic Books.

Gill, Aisha. 2004. "Voicing the Silent Fear: South Asian Women's Experiences of Domestic Violence." *The Howard Journal of Criminal Justice*, no. 43: 5, 465ff.

Gimeno-Martín, Juan Carlos, and Mohamed Ali Laman. 2005. *La Juventud Saharaui: Una Realidad. Preocupaciones y Expectativas*. Rabuni, Sahrawi Arab Democratic Republic: UJSARIO-CJE-UAM.

Glick, Peter and David E. Sahn. 2000. "Schooling of Girls and Boys in a West African Country: The Effects of Parental Education, Income, and Household Structure." *Economics of Education Review*, no. 19, 63–87.

Goffman, Erving. 1971. *The Presentation of Self in Everyday Life*. Harmondsworth, United Kingdom: Penguin. Originally published 1959.

Gökariksel, Banu, and Katharyne Mitchelli. 2005. "Veiling, Secularism and the Neoliberal Subject: National Narratives and Supranational Desires in Turkey and France." *Global Networks*, no. 5: 2, 147–165.

González, Jesus. 2003a. "Denuncian la 'retención' de una joven saharaui por su familia. La pareja con la que vivió una adolescente en Avilés reúne 12.000 firmas de apoyo." *La Voz de Asturias*, July 13, 2003.

González, Jesus. 2003b. "Servicios Sociales no cree que la niña saharaui vuelva a Avilés." *La Voz de Asturias*, Aug. 5, 2003.

Gonzálvez-Pérez, Vincente. 1994. "Descolonización y Migraciones Desde el África Española (1956–1975)." *Investigaciones Geográficas*, no. 12, 65–84.

Gould, Carol C. 2007. "Transnational Solidarities." *Journal of Social Philosophy*, no. 38: 1, 148–164.

Goytisolo, Juan. 1979. *El problema del Sáhara*. Barcelona: Editorial Anagrama.

Graham-Brown, Sarah. 2003. "The Seen, the Unseen and the Imagined: Private and Public Lives." In *Feminist Postcolonial Theory: A Reader*, edited by R. Lewis and S. Mills, 502–519. Edinburgh: Edinburgh Univ. Press.

Grami, Amel. 2008. "Gender Equality in Tunisia." *British Journal of Middle Eastern Studies*, no. 35: 3, 349–362.

Guijarro, M. 2003. "La mujer saharaui sigue." Accessed at http://www.entender sahara.com/articulo.php?sec=comentarioandid=23.

Hacene-Djaballah, Belkacem. 1985. *Conflict in Western Sahara: A Study of Polisario as an Insurgency Movement*. Miami: Univ. Microfilms International.

Hadad, Yevonna Yazbecj, and John L. Esposito, eds. 1998. *Islam, Gender and Social Change*. Oxford: Oxford Univ. Press.

Hale, Sondra. 1996. *Gender Politics in Sudan: Islamism, Socialism, and the State*. Boulder: Westview.

Hamdan, Amani. 2007. "The Issue of Hijab in France: Reflections and Analysis." *Muslim World Journal of Human Rights*, no. 4: 2, Article 4.

Hamdi, Khadija. 1993. "Saharawi Women, Looking to the Future." In *Today's Refugees, Tomorrow's Leaders: Report of the Saharawi Women Refugee Conference*, edited by One World Action, 25–28. London: One World Action.

Hammami, Rema. 2005. "Deniz Kandiyoti." *Development and Change*, no. 37: 6, 1347–1354.

Hamoudi, Huria. 2003. "Letter to the Queen of Spain." Accessed at http://www .elparchedigital.com/pags/huria/ruedadeprensa_20Dic2003.htm.

Hamudi, Embarca. (n.d.). "El matrimonio y el divorcio en la sociedad musulmana en particular la saharaui." Accessed at http://www.nodo50.org/mujeresred /sahara-matrimonio.htm.

Hann, Chris. 2000. "Problems with the (De)Privatization of Religion." *Anthropology Today*, no. 16: 6, 14–20.

Hansen, Lene. 2000. "The Little Mermaid's Silent Security Dilemma and the Absence of Gender in the Copenhagen School." *Millennium: Journal of International Studies*, no. 29: 2, 285–306.

Hansen, Ronny. 2007. "Generations in Exile from Africa's Last Colony." *Forced Migration Review*, no. 27, 76.

Hardy, Cynthia, Bill Harley, and Nelson Phillips. 2004. "Discourse Analysis and Content Analysis: Two Solitudes?" *Qualitative Methods: Newsletter of the*

American Political Science Association Organized Section on Qualitative Methods, no. 2: 1, 19–21.

Harrell-Bond, Barbara E. 1981a. *The Struggle for the Western Sahara*. Hanover, N.H.: American Universities Field Staff.

Harrell-Bond, Barbara E. 1981b. *A Visit to the Sahrawi Refugee Camps*. Unpublished work, Refugee Studies Centre Grey Literature Collection, Univ. of Oxford.

Harrell-Bond, Barbara E. 1986. *Imposing Aid: Emergency Assistance to Refugees*. Oxford: Oxford Univ. Press.

Harrell-Bond, Barbara E. 1999. "The Experience of Refugees as Recipients of Aid." In *Refugees: Perspectives on the Experience of Forced Migration*, edited by A. Ager, 136–168. London: Pinter.

Harrell-Bond, Barbara E. 2000. "Are Refugee Camps Good for Children?" *Journal of Humanitarian Assistance*, Working Paper No. 29.

Hart, David M. 1998. "The Rgaybat: Camel Nomads of the Western Sahara." *The Journal of North African Studies*, no. 3: 4, 28–54.

Hart, David M. 2000. *Tribe and Society in Rural Morocco*. London: Frank Cass.

Hart, David M. 2001. *Qabile: Tribal Profiles and Tribe-State Relations in Morocco and on the Afghanistan-Pakistan Frontier*. Amsterdam: Het Spinhuis.

Harter, Pascale. 2003. "Sahara Women Relish Their Rights." *BBC News Online*, Oct. 10, 2003. Accessed at http://news.bbc.co.uk/go/pr/fr/-/2/hi/africa/3227997.stm.

Harter, Pascale. 2004. "Divorce Divides Morocco and W Sahara." *BBC News Online*, Aug. 4, 2004. Accessed at http://news.bbc.co.uk/go/pr/fr/-/2/hi/africa/3532612.stm.

Harter, Pascale. 2007. "Mauritania, Fatness and Beauty," *BBC World Assignment*. Accessed at http://www.bbc.co.uk/worldservice/specials/1327_assignment_2007/page9.shtml.

Harvey, Leonard Patrick. 2005. *Muslims in Spain, 1500 to 1614*. Chicago: Univ. of Chicago Press.

Hatem, Mertav Fayez. 2006. "In the Eye of the Storm: Islamic Societies and Muslim Women in Globalization Discourses." *Comparative Studies of South Asia, Africa, and the Middle East*, no. 26, 22–35.

Heng, Geraldine. 1997. "'A Great Way to Fly': Nationalism, the State, and the Varieties of Third-World Feminism." In *Feminist Genealogies, Colonial Legacies, Democratic Futures*, edited by M. J. Alexander and C. T. Mohanty, 30–45. New York: Routledge.

Heyneman, Stephen P. 2004. *Islam and Social Policy,* 1st ed. Nashville: Vanderbilt Univ. Press.

Hirschkind, Charles, and Saba Mahmood. 2002. "Feminism, the Taliban, and Politics of Counter-insurgency." *Anthropology Quarterly,* no. 75: 2, 339–354.

Hodges, Tony. 1983. *Western Sahara: The Roots of a Desert War.* Westport, Conn.: Lawrence Hill.

Hodges, Tony. 1984. *The Western Saharans.* London: Minority Rights Group.

Hodges, Tony. 1987. "The Origins of Saharawi Nationalism." In *War and Refugees: The Western Sahara Conflict,* edited by R. I. Lawless and L. Monahan, 31–65. London: Pinter.

Hodges, Tony. 1991. *The Western Saharans: A Minority Rights Group Update.* London: Minority Rights Group International.

Holt, Maria. 1996. "Palestinian Women and the Intifada: An Exploration of Images and Realities." In *Women and Politics in the Third World,* edited by H. Afshar, 189–206. London: Routledge.

Hoodfar, Homa. 1991. "Return to the Veil: Personal Strategy and Public Participation in Egypt." In *Working Women: International Perspectives on Labour,* edited by N. Edclift and T. Sinclair, 104–124. New York: Routledge.

Horst, Cindy. 2006a. *Transnational Nomads: How Somalis Cope with Refugee Life in the Dadaab Camps of Kenya.* Oxford: Berghahn.

Horst, Cindy. 2006b. "Introduction. Refugee Livelihoods: Continuity and Transformations." *Refugee Survey Quarterly,* no. 25: 2, 6–22.

Human Rights Watch. 2008. *Human Rights in Western Sahara and in the Tindouf Refugee Camps: Morocco/Western Sahara/Algeria.* New York: Human Rights Watch.

Hyndman, Jennifer. 2000. *Managing Displacement: Refugees and the Politics of Humanitarianism.* Minneapolis: Univ. of Minnesota Press.

Hyndman, Jennifer, and Margaret Walton-Roberts. 2000. "Interrogating Borders: A Transnational Approach to Refugee Research in Vancouver." *The Canadian Geographer,* no. 44: 3, 244–258.

Ibn Manzur, M. 1997. *Lisan al-Arab.* Beirut: Dar Sadir.

Ibn-Khaldun, Abdel Rahman. 1967. *Al-Muqaddimah: An Introduction to History.* (Translated by F. Rosenthal.) Abridged and edited by N. J. Dawood. London: Routledge.

Indra, Doreen. 1996. "Some Feminist Contributions to Refugee Studies." In *Development and Diaspora: Gender and the Refugee Experience,* edited by W. Giles, W. M. Giles, P. Van Esterik and H. Moussa, 30–43. Ontario: Artemis Enterprises.

Indra, Doreen M. 1999a. "Interview with Barbara Harrell-Bond." In *Engendering Forced Migration: Theory and Practice,* edited by D. M. Indra, 40–62. New York: Berghahn.

Indra, Doreen M. 1999b. "Not a "Room of One's Own": Engendering Forced Migration and Practice." In *Engendering Forced Migration: Theory and Practice,* edited by D. M. Indra, 1–22. New York: Berghahn.

Íñiguez, Fernando. 2000. "Entrevista: Mariam Salek—Ministra de Cultura y Deporte de la RASD." *El País,* March 27, 2000.

Instituto Geográfico, Catastral y de Estadística. 1932. *Censo de la población de España según el empadronamiento hecho en la península e islas adyacentes y posesiones del norte y costa occidental de África el 31 de diciembre de 1930.* Madrid: Talleres del Instituto Geográfico y Catastral.

International Court of Justice. 1975. *Sahara occidental: Avis consultatif du 16 octobre 1975. Western Sahara: Advisory Opinion of 16 October 1975.* The Hague, the Netherlands: International Court of Justice.

Jacob, M. Francis, et al., eds. 2001. *Colloque des juristes sur le Sahara occidental.* Paris: Harmattan.

Jacobsen, Karen. 2002. "Livelihoods in Conflict: The Pursuit of Livelihoods by Refugees and the Impact on the Human Security of Host Communities." *International Migration,* no. 40: 5, 95–123.

Jacobsen, Karen. 2005. *The Economic Life of Refugees.* Boulder, Colo.: Kumarian.

Jacobsen, Karen and Loren B. Landau. 2003. "Researching Refugees: Some Methodological and Ethical Considerations in Social Science and Forced Migration." *New Issues in Refugee Research,* Working paper no. 90. Geneva: UNHCR.

Jacobson, Ruth, Susie Jacobs, and Jen Marchbank. 2000. "Introduction: States of Conflict." In *States of Conflict: Gender, Violence and Resistance,* edited by Susie Jacobs, R. Jacobson and J. Marchbank, 1–24. London: Zed Books.

James, Paul. 1997. "Postdependency?" In *At the Edge of International Relations: Postcolonialism, Gender, and Dependency,* edited by P. Darby, 61–83. London: Pinter.

Jammal, Laila. 1985. *Contributions by Palestinian Women to the National Struggle for Liberation.* Washington, D.C.: Middle East Public Relations.

Jasper, James M. 1997. *The Art of Moral Protest: Culture, Biography, and Creativity in Social Movements.* Chicago: Univ. of Chicago Press.

Jean-Klein, Iris. 1997. "Palestinian Militancy, Martyrdom and Nationalist Communities in the West Bank during the [First] Intifada." In *Martyrdom and*

Political Resistance: Essays from Asia and Europe, edited by J. Pettigrew, 85–110. Amsterdam: VU Univ. Press.

Jeffrey, Patricia. 1979. *Frogs in a Well: Indian Women in Purdah.* London: Zed Books.

Jiménez, Lidia. 2008. "Una mujer del Sáhara recupera a su hija tras dos años de litigio." *El País,* June 24, 2008.

Joseph, Suad. 2000. "Gendering Citizenship in the Middle East." In *Gender and Citizenship in the Middle East,* edited by S. Joseph, 3–32. Syracuse: Syracuse Univ. Press.

Joseph, Suad, and Afsaneh Najmabadi. 2003. *Encyclopedia of Women and Islamic Cultures.* Leiden, the Netherlands: Brill.

Juliano, Dolores. 1998. *La causa saharaui y las mujeres: "Siempre fuimos tan libres,"* 1st ed. Barcelona: Icaria.

Julien, Zahra. 2003. "L'Identité Sahraouie en Questions." In *Sahraouis : Exils—Identité,* edited by A. Abjean and Z. Julien, 131–237. Paris: Harmattan.

Kagwanja, Peter. M. 2000. "Ethnicity, Gender and Violence in Kenya." *Forced Migration Review,* no. 9, 22–25.

Kandiyoti, Deniz, ed. 1991. *Women, Islam, and the State.* Philadelphia: Temple Univ. Press.

Kandiyoti, Deniz. 1992. "Islam and Patriarchy: A Comparative Perspective." In *Women in Middle Eastern History,* edited by N. Keddie and B. Baron, 23–42. New Haven: Yale.

Kandiyoti, Deniz. 1996. "Contemporary Feminist Scholarship and Middle East Studies." In *Gendering the Middle East: Emerging Perspectives,* edited by D. Kandiyoti, 1–28. Syracuse: Syracuse Univ. Press.

Kandiyoti, Deniz. 1998. "Bargaining with Patriarchy." *Gender and Society,* no. 2: 3, 274–290.

Kandiyoti, Deniz. 2000. "The Awkward Relationship: Gender and Nationalism." *Nations and Nationalism,* no. 6: 4, 491–494.

Kandiyoti, Deniz. 2002. "Post-colonialism Compared: Potentials and Limitations in the Middle East and Central Asia." *International Journal of Middle East Studies,* no. 34, 279–297.

Kandiyoti, Deniz. 2004. "Political Fiction Meets Gender Myth: Post-conflict Reconstruction, 'Democratisation' and Women's Rights." *IDS Bulletin,* no. 35: 4, 134–136.

Kandiyoti, Deniz. 2007a. "Old Dilemmas or New Challenges? The Politics of Gender and Reconstruction in Afghanistan." *Development and Change,* no. 38: 2, 169–199.

Kandiyoti, Deniz. 2007b. "Between the Hammer and the Anvil: Post-conflict Reconstruction, Islam and Women's Rights." *Third World Quarterly*, no. 28: 3, 503–517.

Karam, Azza. 1998. *Women, Islamisms and the State: Contemporary Feminism in Egypt.* New York: St. Martin's Press.

Kawar, Amal. 1996. *Daughters of Palestine: Leading Women of the Palestinian National Movement.* Albany: State Univ. of New York Press.

Kay, Diana. 1988. "The Politics of Gender in Exile." *Sociology*, no. 22: 1, 1–21.

Keddie, Nikki R. 2007. *Women in the Middle East: Past and Present.* Princeton: Princeton Univ. Press.

Keenan, Jeremy. 2004a. *The Lesser Gods of the Sahara: Social Change and Contested Terrain amongst the Tuareg of Algeria.* London: Frank Cass.

Keenan, Jeremy. 2004b. "Waging War on Terror: The Implications of America's 'New Imperialism' for Saharan Peoples," Saharan Studies Programme Conference, Univ. of East Anglia, June 22–24, 2004.

Keenan, Jeremy. 2006. "Sedentarisation and Changing Patterns of Social Organization amongst the Tuareg of Algeria." In *Nomadic Societies in the Middle East and North Africa: Entering the 21st Century,* edited by D. Chatty, 916–939. Leiden, the Netherlands: Brill.

Kerr, Joanna. 1994. *Calling for Change: International Strategies to End Violence against Women.* The Hague, the Netherlands: Development Cooperation Information Department, Ministry of Foreign Affairs.

Khadiagala, Lynn S. 1996. "The Failure of Popular Justice in Uganda: Local Councils and Women's Property Rights." *Development and Change*, no. 32: 1, 55–76.

Khoury, Nabil F., and Valentine M. Moghadam. 1995. *Gender and Development in the Arab world: Women's Economic Participation: Patterns and Policies.* London: Published for the United Nations Univ. World Institute for Development Economics Research (UNI/WIDER) by Zed Books.

Knight, Nicola, and Rita Astuti. 2008. "Some Problems with Property Ascription." *Journal of the Royal Anthropological Institute*, 142–158.

Korteweg, Anna, and Gökçe Yurdakul. 2008. "Islam, Gender, and Immigrant Integration: Boundary Drawing in Discourses on Honour Killing in the Netherlands and Germany." *Ethnic and Racial Studies*, no. 32: 2, 1–21.

Kristeva, Julia. 2000. *The Sense and Non-sense of Revolt.* (Translated by J. Herman.) New York: Columbia Univ. Press.

Krulfeld, Ruth M. 1994. "Changing Concepts of Gender Roles and Identities in Refugee Communities." In *Reconstructing Lives, Recapturing Meaning: Refugee*

Identity, Gender and Culture Change, edited by L. A. Camino and R. M. Krulfeld, 71–74. Basel, Switzerland: Gordon and Breach.

Kumar, Krishna. 2001a. "Civil Wars, Women and Gender Relations: An Overview." In *Women and Civil War: Impact, Organizations, and Action*, edited by K. Kumar, 5–26. London: Lynne Rienner Publishers.

Kumar, Krishna. 2001b. "Lessons and Recommendations for the International Community." In *Women and Civil War: Impact, Organizations, and Action*, edited by K. Kumar, 215–224. London: Lynne Rienner Publishers.

Küng, Hans. 2007. *Islam: Past, Present and Future*. Oxford: Oneworld Publications.

Kuttab, Mustafa. 2002. *Riwaya min as-Sahra' al-Gharbiya: autaad al'arḍ*. (Translated title: The Pegs of the Land: A Novel from Western Sahara). Damascus: Muasasat al-Tibaa al-Taswiria.

La Ventana. 2002. "Las mujeres Saharauis por la paz, el progreso y la libertad." *La Ventana*, no. 9.

Laffey, Mark, and Jutta Weldes. 2004. "Methodological Reflections on Discourse Analysis." *Qualitative Methods: Newsletter of the American Political Science Association Organized Section on Qualitative Methods*, no. 2: 1, 28–30.

Lafuente, Javier. 2008. "Más juezas que jueces." *El País*, April 22, 2008.

Lancaster, William, and Fidelity Lancaster. 1998. "Who Are These Nomads? What Do They Do? Continuous Change or Changing Continuities?" In *Changing Nomads in a Changing World*, edited by J. Ginat and A. M. Khazanov, 24–37. Sussex, United Kingdom: Academic Press.

Lawless, Richard I., and Laila Monahan, eds. 1987. *War and Refugees: The Western Sahara Conflict*. London: Pinter.

Layachi, Azzedine. 1994. "The OAU and Western Sahara: A Case Study." In *The Organization of African Unity after Thirty Years*, edited by Y. El-Ayouty, 27–39. Westport: Praeger Publishers.

Lewis, Reina. 1995. *Gendering Orientalism: Race, Femininity, and Representation*. New York: Routledge.

Lewis, Reina. 2003. "On Veiling, Vision and Voyage: Cross-Cultural Dressing and Narratives of Identity." In *Feminist Postcolonial Theory: A Reader*, edited by R. Lewis and S. Mills, 520–541. Edinburgh: Edinburgh Univ. Press.

Lewis, Reina, and Sara Mills, eds. 2003. *Feminist Postcolonial Theory: A Reader*. Edinburgh: Edinburgh Univ. Press.

Lindisfarne-Tapper, Nancy, and Bruce Ingham. 1997. *Languages of Dress in the Middle East*. Richmond, United Kingdom: Curzon.

Lippert, Anne. 1985. *The Saharawi Refugees: Origins and Organization, 1975–1985.* Saharan Peoples Support Committee Occasional Paper No. 3.

Lippert, Anne. 1987. "The Sahrawi Refugees: Origins and Organization, 1975–1985." In *War and Refugees: The Western Sahara Conflict,* edited by R. Lawless and L. Monahan. London: Pinter.

Lippert, Anne. 1992. "Sahrawi Women in the Liberation Struggle of the Sahrawi People." *Signs,* no. 17: 3, 636–651.

Lockwood, Matthew. 2005. *The State They're In: An Agenda for International Action on Poverty in Africa.* Warwickshire, United Kingdom: ITDG Pub.

Lopez-Zarzosa, Helia. 1998. "Refugee Voices: Internal Exile, Exile and Return: A Gendered View." *Journal of Refugee Studies,* no. 11: 2, 189–198.

Luke, Timothy W. 1989. *Screens of Power: Ideology, Domination, and Resistance in Informational Society.* Urbana: Illinois Univ. Press.

Lynn Price, David. 1981. *The Western Sahara.* Beverley Hills: SAGE Publications.

Maazouzi, Mohamed. 1976. *Tindouf et les frontiers meridionales du Maroc.* Casablanca: Dar el Kitab.

MacCannell, Dean. 1973. "Staged Authenticity: Arrangements of Social Space in Tourist Settings." *The American Journal of Sociology,* no. 79: 3, 589–603.

MacCormack, Carol P., and Marilyn Strathern. 1980. *Nature, Culture and Gender.* Cambridge: Cambridge Univ. Press.

Mahamoud, B. A. 1986. *La lucha del pueblo Saharaui: Desarrollo, evolución y perspectivas.* Trabajo de Diploma de la Facultad de Filosofía e Historia, Universidad de La Habana, Havana, Cuba.

Malkki, Liisa. 1992. "National Geographic: The Rooting of Peoples and the Territorialization of National Identity among Scholars and Refugees." *Cultural Anthropology,* no. 7: 1, 24–44.

Malkki, Liisa. 1995a. *Purity and Exile: Violence, Memory and National Cosmology Among Hutu Refugees in Tanzania.* Chicago: Univ. of Chicago Press.

Malkki, Liisa. 1995b. "Refugees and Exile: From 'Refugee Studies' to the National Order of Things." *Annual Review of Anthropology,* no. 24, 495–523.

Malkki, Liisa. 1996. "Speechless Emissaries: Refugees, Humanitarianism, and Dehistoricization." *Cultural Anthropology,* no. 11: 3, 377–404.

Mälksoo, Maria. 2006. "From Existential Politics towards Normal Politics? The Baltic States in the Enlarged Europe." *Security Dialogue,* no. 37: 3, 275–297.

Mani, Lata. 1986. "The production of an Official Discourse on Sati in Early Nineteenth Century Bengal." *Review of Women's Studies in Economic and Political Weekly,* no. 21: 17, 32–40.

Mani, Lata. 1989. "Contentious Traditions: The Debate on Sati in Colonial India." In *Recasting Women: Essays in Colonial History*, edited by K. Sangari and S. Vaid, 88–126. New Delhi: Kali for Women.

Marcus, George E., and Michael M. J. Fischer. 1986. *Anthropology as Cultural Critique: An Experimental Moment in the Human Sciences.* Chicago: Univ. of Chicago Press.

Mardones, Inmaculada G. 1986. "Keltum Jayat: La mirada profunda del Frente Polisario." *El País.* 20/02/1986.

Marks, Thomas A. 1976. "Spanish Sahara—Background to Conflict." *African Affairs*, no. 75: 298, 3–13.

Martín, Carmelo. 1985. "Guesmula Ebbi." *El País*, July 2, 1985.

Martín-Corrales, Eloy. 2004. "Representaciones e interculturalidad: Maurofobia/islamofobia y maurofilia/islamofilia en la España del siglo XXI." *Revista Cidob d'Afers Internacionals*, no. 66–67, 39–51.

Martínez, Gema. 2003. "Las mujeres saharauis gobiernan el día a día mientras los hombres van a la Guerra." *Ahige*, Oct. 14, 2003. Accessed at http://www.ahige .org/texto_noti.php?wcodigo=12023.

Martín-Márquez, Susan. 2006. "Brothers and Others: Fraternal Rhetoric and the Negotiation of Spanish and Saharawi Identity." *Journal of Spanish Cultural Studies*, no. 7: 3, 241–258.

Mas, R. (2006) 'Compelling the Muslim Subject: Memory as Post-Colonial Violence and the Public Performativity of "Secular and Cultural Islam"'. *The Muslim World*, no. 96, 585–616.

Massad, Joseph. 1995. "Conceiving the Masculine: Gender and Palestinian Nationalism." *Middle East Journal*, no. 49: 3, 467–483.

Matsuoka, Atsuko and John Sorensen. 1999. "Eritrean Canadian Refugee Households as Sites of Gender Renegotiation." In *Engendering Forced Migration: Theory and Practice*, edited by D. Indra, 218–241. New York: Berghahn.

McClintock, Anne. 1995. *Imperial Leather: Race, Gender and Sexuality in the Colonial Contest.* New York: Routledge.

McLennan, Gregor. 2003. "Sociology, Eurocentrism and Postcolonial Theory." *European Journal of Social Theory*, no. 6, 69–86.

Mehdi, Fatma. 2006. "Las Mujeres Saharauis Como Ejemplo de Empoderamiento." *Forum de Política Feminista, Asociación Amigos del Pueblo Saharaui de Madrid, PAZ AHORA, ACSUR—Las Segovias Madrid y el Consejo de la Mujer de la Comunidad de Madrid*, June 9, 2006. Accessed at http://www.mujeresenred .net/news/article.php3?id_article=609.

Meintjes, Sheila. 2000. "The Aftermath: Women in Post-war Reconstruction." *Agenda*, no. 43, 4–10.

Menski, Werner. 2006. *Comparative Law in a Global Context: The Legal Systems of Asia and Africa*, 2nd ed. Cambridge: Cambridge Univ. Press.

Mercer, John. 1976. *Spanish Sahara*. London: Allen and Unwin.

Mercer, John. 1979. *The Sahrawis of Western Sahara*. London: Minority Rights Group.

Mernissi, Fatima. 2003a. *Beyond the Veil: Male-Female Dynamics in Modern Muslim society*. London: Saqi Books.

Mernissi, Fatima. 2003b. "The Meaning of Spatial Boundaries." In *Feminist Postcolonial Theory: A Reader*, edited by R. Lewis and S. Mills, 489–501. Edinburgh: Edinburgh Univ. Press.

Merry, Sally Engle. 1992. "Popular Justice and the Ideology of Social Transformation." *Social and Legal Studies*, no. 1, 161–176.

Miské, Ahmed-Bâba. 1978. *Front Polisario: L'âme d'un peuple*. Paris: Éditions Rupture.

M.O. 2008. "Guipúzcoa ve en decadencia los proyectos de hermanamiento." *El País*, May 21, 2008.

Modood, Tariq. 2001. "Their Liberalism and Our Multiculturalism?" *British Journal of Politics and International Relations*, no. 3: 2, 245–257.

Moghadam, Valentine M., ed. 1994. *Gender and National Identity: Women and Politics in Muslim Societies*. London: Zed Books.

Moghadam, Valentine M. 1997a. *Gendering Economic Reform: Women and Structural Change in the Middle East and North Africa*. Boulder, Colo.: Lynne Rienner Publishers.

Moghadam, Valentine M. 1997b. "Women's NGOs in the Middle East and North Africa: Constraints, Opportunities, and Priorities." In *Organizing Women: Formal and Informal Women's Groups in the Middle East*, edited by D. Chatty and A. Rabo, 23–55. Oxford: Berg.

Moghadam, Valentine M. 2003. *Modernizing Women: Gender and Social Change in the Middle East*, 2nd ed. Boulder, Colo.: Lynne Rienner.

Moha, Edourd. 1990. *Le Sahara occidental, ou, La sale guerre de Boumédiene*. Paris: J. Picollec.

Mohamed, Boughadadi. 2001. *Le conflit Saharien. Une nouvelle lecture. Dans un nouveau contexte international*. Rabat: Arrisala.

Mohanty, Chandra Talpade. 1988. "Under Western Eyes: Feminist Scholarship and Colonial Discourses." *Feminist Review*, no. 30, 61–88.

Mohanty, Chandra Talpade. 1991. "Under Western Eyes: Feminist Scholarship and Colonial Discourses." In *Third World Women and the Politics of Feminism*, edited by C. T. Mohanty, A. Russo, and L. Torres, 51–80. Bloomington: Indiana Univ. Press.

Mohanty, Chandra Talpade, Anne Russo, and Lourdes Torres, eds. 1991. *Third World Women and the Politics of Feminism*, Bloomington: Indiana Univ. Press.

Mohsen, Safia K. 1990. "Women and Criminal Justice in Egypt." In *Law and Islam in the Middle East*, edited by D. Dwyer, 15–54. New York: Bergin and Garvey.

Montero, Rosa. 2007. "Injusticias." *El País*, Jan. 16, 2007.

Moore, Henrietta L. 1988. *Feminism and Anthropology*. Minneapolis: Univ. of Minnesota Press.

Morán, Carmen. 2008. "Aído no prevé reformas en la ley contra la violencia." *El País*, July 12, 2008.

Mortimer, Robert A. 1993. "The Greater Maghreb and the Western Sahara." In *International Dimensions of the Western Sahara Conflict*, edited by Y. H. Zoubir and D. Volman, 169–185. New York: Praeger Publishers.

Moser, Caroline, and Fiona Clark. 2001. "Introduction." In *Victims, Perpetrators or Actors? Gender, Armed Conflict and Political Violence*, edited by C. Moser and F. Clark, 3–12. London: Zed Books.

Mosse, David. 2001. "'People's Knowledge,' Participation and Patronage: Operations and Representations in Rural Development." In *Participation: The New Tyranny?* edited by B. Cooke and U. Kothari, 16–35. London: Zed.

Mowles, Chris. 1986. *Desk Officer's Report on Trip to the Sahrawi Refugee Camps near Tindouf, Southern Algeria, June 16–21, 1986*. Oxfam. Refugee Studies Centre Grey Literature Collection, Univ. of Oxford.

M.P. 2008a. "El juez investiga una denuncia de secuestro de una saharaui." *El País*, Aug. 20, 2008.

M.P. 2008b. "El padre de la supuestamente secuestrada dice que está a salvo en Tinduf." *El País*, Aug. 20, 2008.

M.P. 2009. "Una juez culpa a una familia saharaui de raptar a su hija y llevarla a Argelia." *El País*, Feb. 13, 2009.

Muhibbu-Din, Murtalal A. 2000. "Ahl Al-Kitab and Religious Minorities in the Islamic State: Historical Context and Contemporary Challenges." *Journal of Muslim Minority Affairs*, no. 20: 1, 111–127.

Mulero-Clemente, Manuel. 1945. *Los territorios españoles del Sáhara y sus grupos nómadas*. Sáhara y Las Palmas de Gran Canaria: El Siglo.

Mundos de Mujeres. 2008. "Senia Ahmed." Accessed at http://www.mmww08 .org/index.cfm?nav_id=63.

Mundy, Jacob A. 2007. "Performing the Nation, Pre-figuring the State: the Western Saharan Refugees, Thirty Years Later." *Journal of Modern African Studies*, no. 45: 2, 275–297.

Mundy, Jacob A., and Stephen Zunes. 2002. "Western Sahara." *Z Magazine*. October 2002. Available at http://www.zcommunications.org/western-sahara-by -jacob-mundy-1.

Musa, H. A. 2006. *Amaliyat as-salam fi as-Sahra al-Gharbiya wa afaaqaha.* ("The Peace Process in the Western Sahara and Its Horizons"). Undergraduate thesis in Political Sciences, Univ. of Damascus, Damascus.

Nader, Laura. 1989. "Orientalism, Occidentalism and the Control of Women." *Cultural Dynamics*, no. 2: 3, 323–355.

Naldi, Gino J. 1994. "UN Buries Its Head in the Desert Sands: The Saga of the Western Sahara." *African Journal of International and Comparative Law*, no. 6: 4, 653–660.

Navarrio-Asín, Maria. (n.d.). "La mujer saharaui en los campamentos." Accessed at www.radiokcentrale.it/news171.htm.

Nayouf, H. 2008. *"Al-da`iya Houda Habash: Al-muftiyaat tuwafir `ala an-nissa' al-haraj. Suriyya tashhad "muftiyaat lil-nisaa' " fi khutwa naadira min naw`aiha"* ("The Preacher Houda Habash: The *Muftiya* Saves Women 'embarrassment.' Syria Witnesses '*Muftiyat* for Women' in an Unprecedented Step"). *Al Arabiya*, June 10, 2008.

Nazir, Sameena, and Leigh Tomppert. 2005. *Women's Rights in the Middle East and North Africa: Citizenship and Justice.* Lanham. Md.: Rowman and Littlefield.

Nesiah, Vasuki. 2003. "Placing International Law: White Spaces on a Map." *Leiden Journal of International Law*, no. 16, 1–35.

Ng, Edgar. 1997. "When Ordinary People Gather: The Concept of Partnership in Development." In *At the Edge of International Relations: Postcolonialism, Gender, and Dependency,* edited by P. Darby, 148–166. London: Pinter.

Nordstrom, Carolyn. 1999. "Girls and War Zones: Troubling Questions." In *Engendering Forced Migration: Theory and Practice,* edited by D. Indra, 63–82. New York: Berghahn.

Norris, H. T. 1962. "Yemenis in the Western Sahara." *The Journal of African History*, no. 3: 2, 317–322.

Norris, H. T. 1964. "The Wind of Change in the Western Sahara." *Geographical Journal*, no. 130: 1, 2–14.

Norwegian Refugee Council. 2008. *NRC Reports: Western Sahara. Occupied Country, Displaced People.* Norwegian Refugee Council.

Nzenza, Sekai. 1997. "Women in Postcolonial Africa: Between African Men and Western Feminists." In *At the Edge of International Relations: Postcolonialism, Gender, and Dependency,* edited by P. Darby, 197–213. London: Pinter.

O'Barr, Jean. 1985. "Introductory Essay." In *Passbook Number F.47927: Women and Mau Mau in Kenya,* edited by M. Likimani, 23–35. Basingstoke: Macmillan.

Ochoa de Olza, Daniel. 2008. "Polisario Rebels Celebrate 35th Anniversary." *Associated Press,* May 20, 2008.

Olsen, Odd Einar, and Kristin S. Scharffscher. 2004. "Rape in Refugee Camps as Organisational Failures." *The International Journal of Human Rights,* no. 8: 4, 377–397.

Ong, Aihwa. 2003. "State Versus Islam: Malay Families, Women's Bodies and the Body Politic in Malaysia." In *Feminist Postcolonial Theory: A Reader,* edited by R. Lewis and S. Mills, 381–412. Edinburgh: Edinburgh Univ. Press.

Pacitto, Julia, and Elena Fiddian-Qasmiyeh. 2013. "Writing the 'Other' into humanitarian discourse: Framing theory and practice in South-South humanitarian responses to forced displacement." Refugee Studies Centre Working Paper, No. 93, Oxford: Refugee Studies Centre.

Pain, Rachel. H. 1997. "Social Geographies of Women's Fear of Crime." *Transactions of the Institute of British Geographers,* no. 22: 2, 231–244.

Pazzanita, Anthony G. 1994. "Morocco versus Polisario: A Political Interpretation." *The Journal of Modern African Studies,* no. 32: 2, 265–278.

Pazzanita, Anthony G., and Tony Hodges. 1994. *Historical Dictionary of Western Sahara,* 2nd ed. Metuchen, N.J.: Scarecrow Press.

Pechey, Graham. 1989. "On the Borders of Bakhtin: Dialogisation and Decolonisation," in *Bakhtin and Cultural Theory,* 39–67. Manchester: Manchester Univ. Press.

Pensky, Max. 2007. "Two Cheers for Cosmopolitanism: Cosmopolitan Solidarity as Second-Order Inclusion." *Journal of Social Philosophy,* no. 38: 1, 148–164.

Peralta, Vicky. 2007. "Información: Nota de Prensa Grupo Apoyo U.N.M.S." 23/05/2007. Accessed at http://www.saharalibre.es/modules.php?name=Newsandfile=articleandsid=1065.

Peregil, Francisco. 2002. "El tormento de Aicha." *El País,* May 26, 2002.

Pérez, E. C. 2004. "Cuba es el más grande ejemplo de cooperación con otros pueblos." *Granma,* April 2, 2004. Accessed at http://www.granma.cubaweb.cu/2004/03/04/nacional/articulo07.html.

Pérez-Embid, Florentino. 1962. *Enciclopedia de la cultura española*. Madrid: Editora Nacional.

Perregaux, Christiane. 1987. *L'école sahraouie: De la caravane à la guerre de libération*. Paris: Harmattan.

Perregaux, Christiane. 1990a. *Femmes sahraouies, femmes du désert*. Paris: Harmattan.

Perregaux, Christiane. 1990b. "Dans les Camps de Réfugiés Sahraouis: Education Scolaire entre Present et Avenir." *Genève Afrique*, no. 28: 2, 39–51.

Peteet, Julie M. 1991. *Gender in Crisis: Women and the Palestinian Resistance Movement*. New York: Columbia Univ. Press.

Peteet, Julie M. 1997. "Icons and Militants: Mothering in the Danger Zone." *Signs*, no. 23: 1, 103–129.

Petrich, Blanche. 2005. "Los avances de las saharahuíes ejemplo para el mundo árabe." *La Jornada*. Accessed at http://www.jornada.unam.mx/reportajes/2005/sahara/61/index.php.

Pettman, Jan J. 1996. *Worlding Women: A Feminist International Politics*. New York: Routledge.

Pineda, Francisco. 1991. *La Mujer en la Revolución Saharaui*. Córdoba, Spain: Excma. Diputación Provincial.

Planelles, Manuel. 2008a. "Un juez quiere anular a saharauis la nacionalidad española." *El País*, May 29, 2008.

Planelles, Manuel. 2008b. "Una 'marcha verde' a la inversa: Cientos de saharauis acuden al Registro Civil de Córdoba para nacionalizarse." *El País*, May 12, 2008.

Popenoe, Rebecca. 2004. *Feeding Desire: Fatness, Beauty, and Sexuality among a Saharan People*. London: Routledge.

Portinari, Beatriz. 2007. "Entrevista: Maima Mahmud Secretaria de Estado de Asuntos Sociales y Promoción de la Mujer del Sáhara: 'Quiero que cuando una mujer abra las piernas sepa por qué lo hace.'" *El País*, May 12, 2007.

Punch, Maurice. 1994. "Politics and Ethics in Qualitative Research." In *Handbook of Qualitative Research*, edited by N. K. Denzin and Y. S. Lincoln, 83–97. Thousand Oaks, Calif.: Sage.

Ramcharan, Bertrand G. 1998. "Recourse to the Law in the Settlement of International Disputes: Western Sahara." In *African Yearbook of International Law*, edited by A. A. Yusuf, 205–224. The Hague, the Netherlands: Martinus Nijhoff Publishers.

RASD. 2000. "Acogimiento Provisional." Accessed at http://www.elparchedigital.com/pags/huria/Documento-acogimiento.doc.

Rasmussen, Susan J. 1998. "Reflections on Myth and History: Tuareg Concepts of Truth, 'Lies,' and 'Children's Tales.'" *Oral Tradition*, no. 13: 2, 247–284.

Rees, Susan and Bob Pease. 2007. "Domestic Violence in Refugee Families in Australia: Rethinking Settlement Policy and Practice." *Journal of Immigrant and Refugee Studies*, no. 5: 2, 1–19.

Reiter, Rayna R. ed. 1975. *Toward an Anthropology of Women*. New York: Monthly Review Press.

Reporters Without Borders. 2007. "Polisario Front Briefly Detains Two Australian Filmmakers at Refugee Camp." *Reporters Without Borders*, June 9, 2007.

Republic of South Africa. 2008. *Government's Programme of Action 2007: International Relations, Peace and Security Cluster*. Accessed at http://www.info.gov .za/aboutgovt/poa/report2007/july2007/irps07.htm.

Rguibi, Mohamed, and Rekia Belahsen. 2006. "Fattening Practices among Moroccan Saharawi Women." *Eastern Mediterranean Health Journal*, no. 1: 5, 619–624.

Ricœur, Paul. 1976. *Interpretation Theory: Discourse and the Surplus of Meaning*. Fort Worth: Texas Christian Univ. Press.

Rivero, Virginia. 2002. "La falta de familias de acogida deja por primera vez en tierra a 70 niños saharauis," *ABC*, July 15, 2002.

Rosaldo, Michelle Zimbalist, Louise Lamphere, and Joan Bamberger, eds. 1974. *Woman, Culture, and Society*. Stanford: Stanford Univ. Press.

Rosaldo, Renato. 1993. *Culture and Truth: Remaking of Social Analysis*. Boston: Beacon Press.

Rouse, Carolyn M. 2004. *Engaged Surrender: African American Women and Islam*. Berkeley: Univ. of California Press.

Roussellier, Jacques Eric. 2007. "Elusive Sovereignty: People, Land and Frontiers of the Desert: The Case of the Western Sahara and the International Court of Justice." *The Journal of North African Studies*, no. 12: 1, 55–78.

Rucz, Claude. 1994. "Un Referéndum au Sahara Occidental?" *Annuaire Français de Droit Internacional*, no. 40, 243–259.

Ruiz-Miguel, Carlos. (n.d.). "Una documentación esencial para conocer el Sahara Occidental." Accessed at http://www.umdraiga.com/documentos/RASD /RECONOCIMIENTOS_DE_LA_RASD.htm.

Ruíz-Miguel, Carlos. 2001. "Recientes Desarrollos del Conflicto del Sáhara Occidental: Autodeterminación y Estatalidad." *Anuario Mexicano de Derecho Internacional*, no. 1, 343–362.

Rutter, Jessica. 2004. "'Saving' Women in Algeria and Afghanistan: (Neo)Colonialism, Liberation and the Veil." *Eruditio Online*, no. 24 (Spring 2004).

Ryan, Nick. 1999. "North Africa's Forgotten War." *Mother Jones*, March 2, 1999.

Sadiqi, Fatima. 2008. "The Central Role of the Family Law in the Moroccan Feminist Movement." *British Journal of Middle Eastern Studies*, no. 35: 3, 325–338.

SADR/RASD. 1980. *La Republica Árabe Saharaui Democrática*. Ministerio de Información de la Republica Árabe Saharaui Democrática.

SADR/RASD. 1999. *Constitution de la RASD: Adoptée par le dixième Congrès national, 26.08–04.09.99*. Accessed at http://www.arso.org/03-const.99.htm.

SADR/RASD. 2003. *Constitución de la RASD, 2003*. Republica Árabe Saharaui Democrática.

Said, Edward W. 1979. *Orientalism*, 1st ed. New York: Vintage Books.

Said, Edward W. 1983. *The World, the Text, and the Critic*. London: Vintage.

Said, Edward W. 1997. *Covering Islam: How the Media and the Experts Determine How We See the Rest of the World*. London: Vintage.

Salhi, Zahia Smail. 2008. "Introduction: Gender and Diversity in the Middle East and North Africa." *British Journal of Middle Eastern Studies*, no. 35: 3, 295–304.

Salzman, Philip Carl. 1980. "Introduction: Processes of Sedentarization as Adaptation and Response." In *When Nomads Settle: Processes of Sedentarization as Adaptation and Response*, edited by P. C. Salzman, 1–19. New York: Praeger.

San-Martín, Pablo. 2005. "Nationalism, Identity and Citizenship in the Western Sahara." *Journal of North African Studies*, no. 10: 3, 565–592.

San-Martín, Pablo. 2010. *Western Sahara: The Refugee Nation*. Cardiff: Univ. of Wales Press.

Sanz, Juan Carlos. 1997. "Los saharauis seguirán en el desierto si no hay independencia." *El País*, Aug. 18, 1997.

Saxena, Suresh Chandra. 1995. *Western Sahara: No Alternative to Armed Struggle*. Delhi: Kalinga Publications.

Sayeh, Ismaèl. 1998. *Les Sahraouis*. Paris: Harmattan.

Sayigh, Rosemary. 1998. "Palestinian Camp Women as Tellers of History." *Journal of Palestine Studies*, no. 27: 2, 42–58.

Scharffscher, Kristin S. 2002. *A Time for Gender? Protection against Rape in Refugee Camps*. Stavanger, Norway: Stavanger Univ. College.

Scheper-Hughes, Nancy. 1998. "Maternal Thinking and the Politics of War." In *The Women and War Reader*, edited by L. A. Lorentzen and J. Turpin, 227–233. New York: New York Univ. Press.

Scott, James C. 1985. *Weapons of the Weak: Everyday Forms of Peasant Resistance*. New Haven: Yale Univ. Press.

Scott, James C. 1990. *Domination and the Arts of Resistance: Hidden Transcripts.* New Haven: Yale Univ. Press.

Scott, James W. 2007. *The Politics of the Veil.* Princeton, N.J.: Princeton Univ. Press.

Scott, Shirley. 1996. "The Australian High Court's Use of the Western Sahara Case in Mabo." *International and Comparative Law Quarterly,* no. 45, 923–927.

Seddon, David. 2000a. "Britain and Western Sahara: Examining the Debate." *Review of African Political Economy,* no. 27: 85, 459–462.

Seddon, David. 2000b. "Western Sahara: Point of no Return?" *Review of African Political Economy,* no. 27: 84, 338–340.

Serrano-Borrull, Nina. 1999. "La Mujer Saharaui en los Campos de Refugiados." Accessed at http://www.ub.es/solidaritat/observatori/sahara/transver/mujer.htm.

Shaaban, Bouthaina. 1988. *Both Right and Left Handed: Arab Women Talk about Their Lives.* London: Women's Press.

Shami, Seteney. 1996. "Transnationalism and Refugee Studies: Rethinking Forced Migration and Identity in the Middle East." *Journal of Refugee Studies,* no. 9: 1, 3–26.

Shelley, Toby. 2004. *Endgame in the Western Sahara: What Future for Africa's Last Colony.* London: Zed Books in association with War on Want.

Sheridan, Lorraine P. 2006. "Islamophobia Pre-and Post-September 11th, 2001." *Journal of Interpersonal Violence,* no. 21: 3, 317 ff.

Sidi-Zein, A. S. S. 1991. *El Conflicto del Sáhara: estado actual y perspectivas.* Trabajo de Diploma en Relaciones Internacionales, Universidad de La Habana, Havana, Cuba.

Simons, Margaret A. 1979. "Racism and Feminism: A Schism in the Sisterhood." *Feminist Studies,* no. 5: 2, 384–401.

Sonbol, Amira, ed. 1996. *Women, the Family, and Divorce Laws in Islamic History.* Syracuse: Syracuse Univ. Press.

Sonbol, Amira. 1997. "Rape and Law in Ottoman and Modern Egypt." In *Women in the Ottoman Empire: Middle Eastern Women in the Early Modern Era,* edited by M. C. Zilfi, 214–231. Leiden, the Netherlands: Brill.

Sorensen, Birgitte. 1998. *Women and Post-Conflict Reconstruction: Issues and Sources.* UNRISD.

Soroeta-Liceras, Juan. 2001. *El conflicto del Sáhara Occidental: Reflejo de las contradicciones y carencias del derecho internacional.* Bilbao, Spain: Universidad del País Vasco.

Spivak, Gayatri C., ed. 1990. *The Post-Colonial Critic: Interviews, Strategies, Dialogues.* London: Routledge.

Spivak, Gayatri C. 1993a. "Can the Subaltern Speak?" In *Colonial Discourse and Post-colonial theory,* edited by P. W. L. Chrisman, 66–111. New York: Harvester Wheatsheaf.

Spivak, Gayatri C. 1993b. *Outside in the Teaching Machine.* New York: Routledge.

SPS. 2004. "Participación feminista sueca en la conferencia sobre derechos de la mujer y de la infancia en los campamentos de refugiados." Oct. 20, 2004. Accessed at http://www.spsrasd.info/sps-s201004.html.

SPS. 2005. "Polisario Front/Anniversary: The President of the Republic put the First Brick in the New Building of the Saharawi Parliament," May 22, 2005. Accessed at http://www.spsrasd.info/sps-e220505.html.

SPS. 2008. "50 Saharawi Refugees Travel for the First Time to the Pilgrimage in Mecca." Accessed at http://www.spsrasd.info/en/detail.php?id=3359.

Stabile, Carol A., and Deepa Kumar. 2005. "Unveiling Imperialism: Media, Gender and the War on Afghanistan." *Media Culture Society,* no. 27, 765–782.

Steans, Jill. 2006. *Gender and International Relations: Issues, Debates and Future Directions,* 2nd ed. Cambridge: Polity.

Steenbrink, Karel. 2002. "Muslims and the Christian Other: Nasara in Qur'anic Readings." In *Mission Is a Must: Intercultural Theology and the Mission of the Church,* edited by F. Wijsen and P. Nissen, 200–222. Amsterdam: Rodopi.

Stepputat, Finn. 1999. "Dead Horses?" *Journal of Refugee Studies,* no. 12: 4, 416–419.

Stillman, Yedida Kalfon. 2003. *Arab Dress, A Short History: From the Dawn of Islam to Modern Times,* 2nd ed. Leiden, the Netherlands: Brill.

Sturcke, James. 2006. "Straw: I'd Rather No One Wore Veils." *Guardian Unlimited,* Oct. 6, 2006. Accessed at http://politics.guardian.co.uk/homeaffairs/story/0,,1889173,00.html.

Suárez, I. 2003. "Aicha Embarek, La Hurí de ojos negros y piel canela." Accessed at www.elparchedigital.com/pags.huria/ruedaprensa_20Dic2003.htm.

Sunder Rajan, Rajeswari. 1993. *Real and Imagined Women: Gender, Culture, and Postcolonialism.* London: Routledge.

Sunderland, Jane, and Lisa Litosseliti. 2002. "Gender Identity and Discourse Analysis: Theoretical and Empirical Considerations." In *Gender Identity and Discourse Analysis: Discourse Approaches to Politics, Society, and Culture,* edited by L. Litosseliti and J. Sunderland, 3–42. Amsterdam: Benjamins.

Talhami, Ghada Hashem. 2001. "Women and Philanthropy in Palestinian and Egyptian Societies: The Contributions of Islamic Thought and the Strategy of

National Survival." In *Women, Philanthropy, and Civil Society*, edited by K. D. McCarthy, 245–270. Bloomington: Indiana Univ. Press.

Tapias, Alicia. 2003. "Querida familia acogedora." Accessed at http://www .entender-sahara.com/articulo.php?sec=documentosandid=11.

Taylor, Charles. 2002. "Democratic Exclusion (and Its Remedies?)." Available from www.eurozine.com.

Taylor, Jeffrey. 2005. *Angry Wind: Through Muslim Black Africa by Truck, Bus, Boat, and Camel.* New York: Houghton Mifflin Harcourt Books.

Tempest, Matthew. 2006. "Blair Backs School in Veil Row." *Guardian Unlimited*, Oct. 17, 2006. Accessed at http://education.guardian.co.uk/schools/story/0,,1924 479,00.html.

Temple, Bogusia, and Rosalind Edwards. 2002. "Interpreters/ Translators and Cross-language Research: Reflexivity and Border Crossings." *International Journal of Qualitative Methods*, no. 1: 2. Accessed at http://www.ualberta.ca/~ijqm.

Tendeiro-Parrilla, Nuria. 2007. "Khadidja Hamdi: 'Los jóvenes saharauis no deben ser condenados como pueblo prohibido.'" Accessed at http://www.levante -emv.com/secciones/noticia.jsp?pNumEjemplar=3397andpIdSeccion=16and pIdNoticia=261626andrand=1168633955310.

Thorne, John. 2004. "Sahara Refugees Form a Progressive Society." *The Christian Science Monitor*, March 26, 2004.

Tillion, Germaine. 2007. *My Cousin, My Husband: Clans and Kinship in Mediterranean Societies.* (Foreword by Deniz Kandiyoti, translated by Q. Hoare.) London: Saqi Books.

Tortajada Orriols, Ana. 2004. *Hijas de la Arena*, 2nd ed. Barcelona: Debolsillo.

Tortella, Gabriel. 1996. "A Latecomer: The Modernization of the Spanish Economy, 1800–1990." In *The Industrial Revolution in National Context: Europe and the USA*, edited by M. Teich and R. Porter, 184–200. Cambridge: Cambridge Univ. Press.

Tucker, Judith E. 1985. *Women in Nineteenth-Century Egypt.* Cambridge: Cambridge Univ. Press.

Turner, Stephen. 1999. "Angry Young Men in Camps: Gender, Age and Class Relations among Burundian Refugees in Tanzania." *New Issues in Refugee Research*, Working Paper No. 9. Geneva: UNHCR.

Turner, Stephen. 2001. "What Is the Problem with Experts?" *Social Studies of Science*, no. 31: 1, 123–149.

Turton, David. 1999. "Response to Kibreab." *Journal of Refugee Studies*, no. 12: 4, 419–422.

Umar, Muhammad Suhail. 2006. *Islam and Colonialism: Intellectual Responses of Muslims of Northern Nigeria to British Colonial Rule.* Leiden, the Netherlands: Brill.

UNDP. 2011. *Human Development Report 2011.* UNDP.

UNGA (1975) Report of the United Nations Visiting Mission to Spanish Sahara, 1975, in *The Report of the Special Committee on the Situation With Regard to the Implementation of the Declaration on the Granting of Independence to Colonial Countries and Peoples,* U.N. Doc. A/100023/Add.5

UNGA. 1993. *Declaration on the Elimination of Violence against Women.* A/RES/48/104: UNGA, 85th Plenary Meeting, Dec. 20, 1993.

UNGA. 2004. *World Survey on the Role of Women in Development. Report of the Secretary-General, Addendum Women and International Migration.* New York: United Nations.

UNGA. 2007. *Fourth Committee Urges Decolonisation Progress for 16 Remaining Non-self-governing Territories, Hears Additional Petitioners on Western Sahara Dispute.* New York: United Nations General Assembly, Department of Public Information.

UNHCR. 1991. *Guidelines on the Protection of Refugee Women.* Geneva: UNHCR.

UNHCR. 1995. *United Nations High Commissioner for Refugees, Guidelines on the Protection of Refugee Women (1995).* Geneva: UNHCR.

UNHCR. 1996. *Populations of Concern to UNHCR: A Statistical Overview (1995).* Geneva: UNHCR.

UNHCR. 1998. *Refugees and Others of Concern to UNHCR: A Statistical Overview (1997).* Geneva: UNHCR.

UNHCR. 1999. *Global Appeal 2000.* Geneva: UNHCR.

UNHCR. 2000a. *Global Appeal 2001.* Geneva: UNHCR.

UNHCR. 2000b. *Global Report 1999.* Geneva: UNHCR.

UNHCR. 2001. *Refugee Women and Mainstreaming a Gender Equality Perspective.* Geneva: UNHCR.

UNHCR. 2002a. *Statistical Yearbook.* Geneva, Switzerland: UNHCR.

UNHCR. 2002b. *UNHCR Remedial Actions and Preventive Measures against Sexual Exploitation and Abuse of Refugees.* UNHCR Press Releases.

UNHCR. 2002c. *UNHCR Cuba-Country Report (1 January to 31 December 2001).* Geneva: UNHCR.

UNHCR. 2003a. *Summary Update of Machel Study: Follow-up Activities in 2001–2002, Refugee Children Coordination Unit.* Geneva: UNHCR.

UNHCR. 2003b. *UNHCR Cuba-Country Report (1 January to 31 December 2002).* Geneva: UNHCR.

UNHCR. 2004a. *Refugee Education Indicators 2003: Education Indicators and Gap Analysis Covering 118 Refugee Camps in 23 Asylum Countries Based on Initial Data from the Camp Indicator Report*. Geneva: UNHCR Population Data Unit/PGDS and Education Unit/WCCDS Division of Operational Support.

UNHCR. 2004b. *Statistical Yearbook*. Geneva: UNHCR.

UNHCR. 2004c. *Protracted Refugee Situations*. UNHCR EXCOM Standing Committee, 30th Meeting.

UNHCR. 2005. *Information Note: Western Saharan Refugee Students in Cuba*. Geneva: UNHCR.

UNHCR. 2006a. *Global Report 2006*. Geneva: UNHCR.

UNHCR. 2006b. *Country Operations Plan. Executive Committee Summary. Country: Algeria. Planning Year: 2007*. Geneva: UNHCR.

UNHCR. 2008. *Handbook for the Protection of Women and Girls, First Edition*. Geneva: UNHCR.

UNHCR. 2010. *UNHCR Algeria Factsheet (August 2010)*. Geneva: UNHCR.

UNHCR. 2011. *UNHCR Global Report Update 2011*. Geneva: UNHCR.

UNHCR EXCOM. 2001. *Refugee Women and Mainstreaming a Gender Equality Perspective*. UNHCR Doc. No. EC/51/SC/CRP.17. 30/05/2001.

UNHCR EXCOM. 2008. *41st Meeting of the Standing Committee (4–6 March 2008). Agenda Item 6(b). Outline for the Oral Update on Protracted Situations which Would Benefit from International Support Presented by the Assistant High Commissioner (Operations) and the Assistant High Commissioner (Protection)*. Geneva: UNHCR EXCOM.

UNHCR/WFP/INRAN. 2005. *Nutrition Information in Crisis Situations—Algeria*. United Nations System Standing Committee on Nutrition.

US Committee for Refugees and Immigrants. 1998. *Cuba Report*. USCRI.

US Committee for Refugees and Immigrants. 1999. *Cuba Report*. USCRI.

USDOS. 2006. *Lebanon: Country Reports on Human Rights Practices—2005*. U.S. Bureau of Democracy, Human Rights, and Labor.

USDOS. 2007. *Country Report on Human Rights Practices: Algeria 2006*. U.S. Bureau of Democracy, Human Rights, and Labor.

USDOS. 2008a. *Syria: Country Reports on Human Rights Practices—2007*. U.S. Bureau of Democracy, Human Rights, and Labor.

USDOS. 2008b. *Tunisia: Country Reports on Human Rights Practices—2007*. U.S. Bureau of Democracy, Human Rights, and Labor.

Vallbé Bach, Fermí. 2002. "Cartas al Director: Aicha." *El País*, May 29, 2002.

Vargas-Llosa, Mario. 2007. "El velo no es el velo." *El País*, Oct. 7, 2007.

Velázquez-Gaztelu, Juan Pedro. 2001. "Solos en el desierto." *El País*, March 9, 2001.

Velloso de Santisteban, Agustín. 1992. *Education and War in the Western Sahara.* Refugee Studies Centre Grey Literature Collection, Univ. of Oxford.

Velloso de Santisteban, Agustín. 1993. *La educación en el Sáhara Occidental.* Madrid: UNED.

Vidal, D. (1986). "Apre, doux, suave." *Révolution,* March 22, 1986.

Vilar-Ramírez, Juan Bautista. 1969. *El Sáhara y el hamitismo norteafricano: Estudios antropo-históricos sahárico-magrebíes.* Madrid: Instituto de Estudios Africanos, Consejo Superior de Investigaciones Científicas.

Vilar-Ramírez, Juan Bautista. 1970. *España en Argelia, Túnez, Ifni y Sahara, durante el siglo XIX.* Madrid: Instituto de Estudios Africanos, Consejo Superior de Investigaciones Científicas.

Vilar-Ramírez, Jaun Bautista. 1977. *El Sáhara español: Historia de una aventura colonial.* Madrid: Sedmay

Viñes-Taberna, Rafael. 2003. *Notas históricas sobre el Sáhara occidental,* 1st ed. Las Palmas de Gran Canaria, Spain: Ediciones del Cabildo Insular de Gran Canaria.

Vogelman, Lloyd, and Sharon Lewis. 1993. "Gang Rape and the Culture of Violence in South Africa." *Centre for the Study of Violence and Reconciliation.* Accessed at http://www.csvr.org.za/wits/papers/paplvsl.htm.

Volman, Daniel. 1993. "The Role of Foreign Military Assistance in the Western Saharan War." In *International Dimensions of the Western Sahara Conflict,* edited by Y. H. Zoubir and D. Volman, 151–168. New York: Praeger.

Von Hippel, Karen. 1996. "Sunk in the Sahara: The Applicability of the Sunk Cost Effect to Irredentist Disputes." *The Journal of North African Studies,* no. 1: 1, 95–116.

Voutira, Eftihia, and Barbara E. Harrell-Bond. 2000. "'Successful' Refugee Settlement: Are Past Examples Relevant?" In *Risks and Reconstruction: Experiences of Resettlers and Refugees,* edited by M. M. Cernea and C. McDowell, 56–76. Washington, D.C.: World Bank.

Warner, Daniel. 1999. "Deterritorialization and the Meaning of Space." *Journal of Refugee Studies,* no. 12: 4, 411–416.

Warner, Michael. 2007. "Secularism." In *Keywords for American Cultural Studies,* edited by B. Burgett and G. Hendler, 209–213. New York: New York Univ. Press.

Welchman, Lynn. 1988. "The Development of Islamic Family Law in the Legal System of Jordan." *International and Comparative Law Quarterly,* no. 37, 868–886.

Welchman, Lynn. 2004. "Egypt: New Deal on Divorce." *The International Survey of Family Law*, no. 123–142.

WFP. 1997. *Project Algeria 4155 (Exp. 6) (WIS No. ALG 0415506): Food Assistance to Vulnerable Groups among Western Sahara Refugees*. World Food Programme.

WFP. 1998a. *Protracted Relief and Recovery Operation Approved by the Executive Director (1 July–31 December 1998)–Algeria 4155.08: Assistance to Sahraoui Refugees in Algeria*. World Food Programme.

WFP. 1998b. *Protracted Refugee and Displaced Person Project Algeria 4155.07: Food Assistance to the Most Vulnerable Groups among Western Sahara Refugees*. World Food Programme.

WFP. 1999. *Protracted Relief and Recovery Operation Approved by the Executive Director (1 January–30 June 1999)–Algeria 6099.00: Assistance to Western Sahara Refugees*. World Food Programme.

WFP. 2000. *Protracted Relief and Recovery Operation—Algeria 6234.00: Assistance to Saharawi Refugees*. World Food Programme.

WFP. 2002. *Protracted Relief and Recovery Operation—Algeria 10172.0: Assistance to Western Sahara Refugees*. World Food Programme.

WFP. 2004. *Protracted Relief and Recovery Operation—Algeria 10172.1: Assistance to Western Saharan Refugees*. World Food Programme.

WFP. 2006. *WFP Assists Sahrawi Refugees Hit by Torrential Rains*. World Food Programme.

WFP. 2008. *Protracted Relief and Recovery Operation Algeria 10172.2: Assistance to the Western Saharan Refugees*. World Food Programme.

White, Hayden V. 1987. *The Content of the Form: Narrative Discourse and Historical Representation*. Baltimore: Johns Hopkins Univ. Press.

WHO. 2001. *Brief Report of WHO Afghanistan Activities since 11 September, as of 9 October 2001*. World Health Organization.

Wilde, Lawrence. 2007. "The Concept of Solidarity: Emerging from the Theoretical Shadows?" *British Journal of Politics and International Relations*, no. 9, 171–181.

Williams, Harriette. 2005. "Protecting the Vulnerable: The Case of Displaced Women in Africa." *Conflict Trends*, no. 3, 17–22.

Williams, Michael C. 2003. "Words, Images, Enemies: Securitization and International Politics." *International Studies Quarterly*, no. 47: 4, 511–531.

Wilson, Alice. 2010. "Democratizing Elections without Parties: Reflections on the Case of the Saharawi Arab Democratic Republic." *Journal of North African Studies*, no. 14: 4, 423–438.

Wirth, Rafael and Balaguer, Soledad. 1976. *Frente Polisario la última guerrilla*. Barcelona: Laia.

Woodhull, Winifred. 2003. "Unveiling Algeria." In *Feminist Postcolonial Theory: A Reader*, edited by R. Lewis and S. Mills, 567–597. Edinburgh: Edinburgh Univ. Press.

World Bank. 1994. *The World Bank and Participation*. Washington D.C.: World Bank.

Yanguas-Miravete, José and M. Guijarro y Ajero. 1964. *Sáhara: Ifni*. Madrid: Publ. Españolas.

Yara, Ali Omar. 2001. *Genèse politique de la société sahraouie*. Paris: Harmattan.

Yara, Ali Omar. 2003. *L'insurrection sahraouie: De la guerre à l'Etat, 1973–2003*. Paris: Harmattan.

Yeğenoğlu, Meyda. 1998. *Colonial Fantasies: Towards a Feminist Reading of Orientalism*. Cambridge: Cambridge Univ. Press.

Young, Robert J. 2001. *Postcolonialism: An Historical Introduction*. Oxford: Blackwell.

Yusuf, Hajiya Bilkisu. 2005. *Sexuality and the Marriage Institution in Islam: An Appraisal*. Lagos: ARSC.

Yuval-Davis, Nira. 1997. *Gender and Nation*. London: SAGE.

Zin, Hernán. 2007. "Mujeres saharauis, lucha y ejemplo." *Viaje a la Guerra*. Accessed at http://blogs.20minutos.es/enguerra/post/2007/04/16/mujeres-saharauis-lucha-y-ejemplo.

Zin, Hernán. 2008. "Mujeres que cambian el mundo: Mamia Mahamud." *Mujeres Saharauis: La voz de las hijas del Sáhara Occidental*. Accessed at http://mujeresaharauis.blogspot.com/2008_02_01_archive.html.

Zine, Jasmin. 2006. "Between Orientalism and Fundamentalism: The Politics of Muslim Women's Feminist Engagement." *Muslim World Journal of Human Rights*, no. 3: 1.

Zoubir, Yahia H. 1996. "The Western Sahara Conflict: A Case Study in Failure of Prenegotiation and Prolongation of Conflict." *California Western International Law Journal*, no. 26: 2, 173–213.

Zoubir, Yahia H. 1998. "International Relations of the Western Sahara Conflict." In *L'Ouest saharien: Etat des lieux et matériaux de recherche; The Western Sahara: Status of Studies and Research Materials*, edited by P. Boilley, E. Martinoli and A.O. Yara, 127–140. Paris: Harmattan.

Zoubir, Yahia H. 2002. "Algeria and U.S. Interests: Containing Radical Islamism and Promoting Democracy." *Middle East Policy*, no. 9: 1, 64–81.

Zoubir, Yahia H. and Volman, Daniel, eds. 1993. *International Dimensions of the Western Sahara Conflict*. Westport: Praeger.

Zuhur, Sherifa. 1992. *Revealing Reveiling: Islamist Gender Ideology in Contemporary Egypt*. Albany: State Univ. of New York Press.

Zunes, Stephen. 1988. "Participatory Democracy in the Sahara: A Study of Polisario Self-Governance." *Scandinavian Journal of Development Alternatives*, no. 7, 141–156.

Zunes, Stephen. 1999. "Unarmed Resistance in the Middle East and North Africa." In *Nonviolent Social Movements: A Geographical Perspective*, edited by S. Zunes, L. R. Kurtz and S. B. Asher, 41–51. Oxford: Blackwell Publishing.

Zunes, Stephen and Jacob Mundy. 2010. *Western Sahara: War, Nationalism, and Conflict Irresolution*. Syracuse: Syracuse Univ. Press.

Index

Islam (*cont.*)

    mrābeṭ (Qur'anic teacher), 50–52,
77; praying, 51, 53, 137, 196, 197–98,
201; "progressive" ("liberal"), 6, 194;
Prophetic sayings (Hadith) 85n8,
161; Qur'an, 20–21, 203; Shari'a (law),
160–61, 199; sisters, 180–81; Sunna,
85n8. *See also* education; food; "good";
Orientalism; religion; schools; secu-
larism/secularization; veiling

Kel Ahaggar, 246n31

Khayat, Kheltoum, 229

khayma (tent), 50, 52, 54, 103, 142, 233, *234*,
235

kinship, 17, 50, 64, 142, 144–45, 189, 211n33,
245. *See also* tribes/tribal identity

knowledge, 10–11, 52, 205, 219; archive
of, 15, 42, 219; of Islam, 161; monopoly
of religious, 52; production of, 10, 79,
124, 269

language: Hassaniya, 18, 90, 156, 165–66,
245; onstage and offstage, 165, 173, 201,
204–8; and religion, 203; and research,
36–37, 75, 203; and resistance, 207;
translation and mistranslation, 74–77,
116. *See also* discourse

law, 141, 199; court proceedings, 252–54;
personal status law, 85n8, 156, 157n28,
161, 165n38; proposed Sahrawi Family
Law, 168–69; refugee legal system, 161,
199, 252–53; SADR Penal Code, 250n35.
See also divorce; Islam; marriage

livelihood, 18, 49–50, 56, 58, 236n12;
remittances, 80, 90, 124, 151–52, 246.
See also employment

machismo, 66, 77

Marhba, Senia Ahmed, 98, 117

marriage, 126, 150–52; age, 53n11, 151;
celibacy or, 163; fattening practices
and, 54, 55n15, 151; *la'alāqa* (not in a
relationship), 167; *mahr* (bridal money),
44n36, 55n15, 126, 150, 151–52, 246;
polygamy, 6, 127, 128, 162, 166–67;
reputation and, 127, 144–45, 154. *See
also* age; child care; divorce; law

Mauritania/Mauritanians, 17, 18, 21, 26,
130–31, 141, 159n32, 165, 243; migrants
in camps, 89–91; Tripartite Interim
Administration, 26; and Western
Sahara conflict, 26, 29, 69–70; women,
89n10

media, 16, 36n29, 70, 127, 190, 209–10,
259; *BBC World*, 157; blogger, 159–60,
175, 222, 227; campaigns, 209–11,
213, 215; *El País*, 119, 136, 137. *See also*
representation

Mehdi, Fatma, 128, 146–47, 148, 178–79

MENA (Middle East and North Africa),
249, 258, 261, 262, 264, 267; generic
image of, 181; relationship with Polisario, 22–31, 117, 182n7. *See also* "Other";
Pan–Arabism; study-abroad programs

men and masculinity, 8, 22–24, 50, 52,
60–61, 63, 71, 86, 90, 94, 97, 99, 100–103,
144, 152, 155, 158, 162n37, 166, 168, 187,
208, 235, 241–47, 255n48, 258

migration: to camps, 90; commuting
(between camps), 143–44, 145, 149; to
Spain, 90, 148, 228–9, 243, 245–46, 257.
See also livelihood; nomadism; space;
study-abroad programs

military: action, 29, 31, 49, 107; Algerian,
27, 29, 34, 84, 86, 107; landmines,

representation: idealization, 3, 7, 46, 83,
125, 149, 163, 170, 176–77, 218, 221;
façade, 81, 82, 105, 175, 261; misrepresentation, 197, 268; of (refugee) women
as victims, 4, 7, 9, 104, 132, 181, 266.
See also discourse; performances;
repress–entation
repress–entation, 13, 221–22, 234–35, 261,
263, 267
research methods and ethics, 34–42
resistance: anticolonial, 22, 49, 69, 71, 77;
discursive, 13–14, 207; Palestinian,
23; refugee, 171, 207, 239, 241, 263;
secular, 193n21, veiling as, 134. *See also*
discourse
rūm (Westerners, Christians), 76

SADR (Sahrawi Arab Democratic Republic), *19*, 30–31, 39, 43, 48, 58, 83, 84, 120,
122–23; independence, 108n7, 191, 196;
ministries, 83, 94, 116–18, 199, 201, 209,
259; Western Sahara conflict, 16–34.
See also national institutions; Polisario;
politics; referendum for self-determination; refugee camps
Sahrawi/SADR Constitution, 9, 112, 117,
199
Salek, Mariem, 108n24, 117, 127
Sayed, El-Ouali Mustafa (Luali), 21, 23, 28
schools, 99; boarding, 68, 94, 95, 96n17,
142, 188n16; enrollment, 62–64, 94–97,
236; girls' withdrawal from, 96–97,
236–38; *maḥāḍir* (Qur'anic schools), 51;
mobile, 51–52, 59, 63; *mrābeṭ* (Qur'anic
teacher), 50–51; national (and other)
women's, 40, 84, 86, 96, 142, 145, 192,
227, 230, 231, 233; primary and pre-
schools, 62, 63, 64, 86, 89, 94; religious
(camp-based), 198, 199–200; secondary,

63, 94, 95, 236; Spanish colonial, 50–52,
58–59, 62–67. *See also* education
secularism/secularization, 2–3, 45, 133,
262–63, 267–68; and "gendered public
relations," 195; Islam, 192; Sahrawi, 6,
15, 190–204. *See also* feminism/femi-
nists; religion; space
SGBV (sexual and gender-based violence): public and private, 259; sedentarization and, 68; silencing of, 255–57.
See also violence against women
shaykh, 50, 61–62
slavery, 20, 24, 69
socioeconomic status: conditions, 97–98,
150–51; differentiation, 98, 124, 151,
153, 228
solidaridad (solidarity), 32–33; in Cuba,
120–22; Amigos del Pueblo Saharawi
(Friends of the Sahrawi People),
32, 110; Coordinadora Estatal de
Asociaciones Solidarias con el Sahara
(State Coordinator of Associations
of Solidarity with the Sahara), 110;
Federación Estatal de Instituciones
Solidarias con el Pueblo Saharawi
(Federation of the Friends of the
Sahrawi People, FEDISSAH), 110;
fostering programs, 108, 151; Friends
of the Sahara Associations, 108, 119;
Riojan Community's Friendship
Group, 215; *solidarios* (Spain), 263–64;
in South Africa, 120–21, 122–23;
Spanish friends, 110; Vacaciones en
Paz (Holidays in Peace), 109, 146, 235;
volunteers, 35n27, 110, 240n18. *See also*
NUSW; NUSW conferences; parades
for visitors
space: access to by age, 95, 147, 235, 244–46;
"de-masculinized," 241, 242–44;
female-dominated, 102, 103n20, 225;